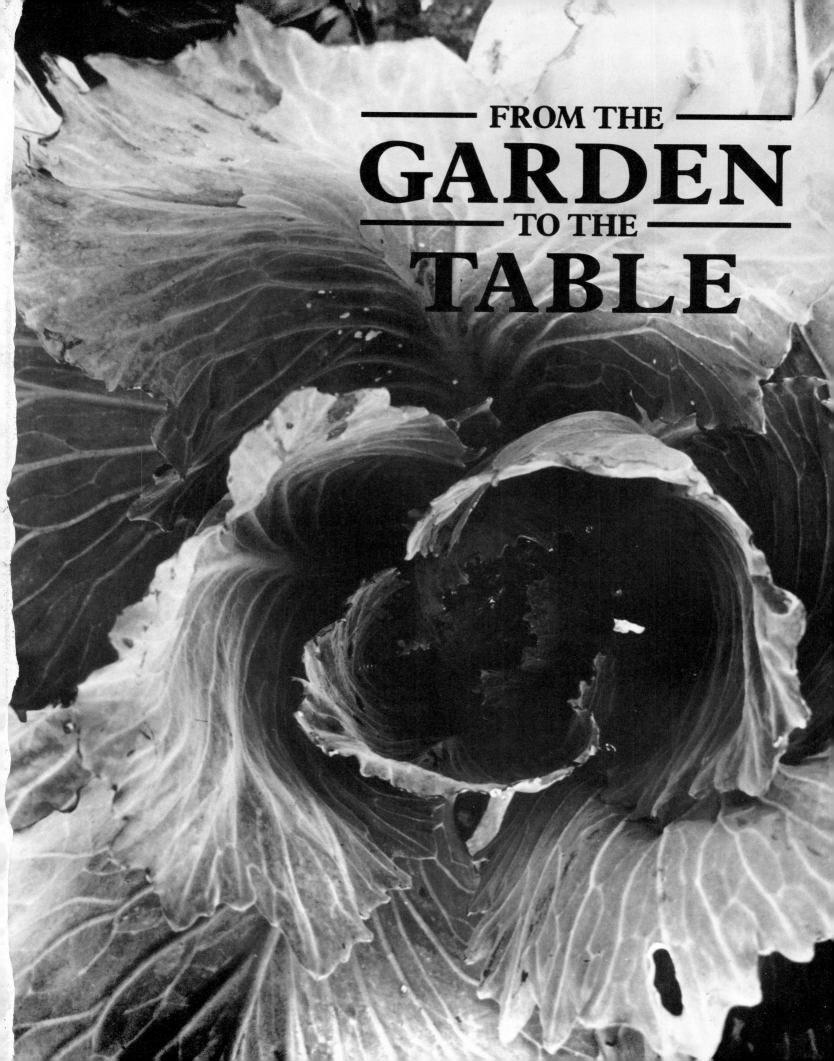

FROM THE
GARDEN
TO THE
TABLE

FROM THE
GARDEN
TO THE
TABLE

*An illustrated guide to growing and
cooking your own food*

Crescent Books
New York

FROM THE GARDEN TO THE TABLE
was edited and designed by
Mitchell Beazley Publishers Ltd.,
Artists House 14-15 Manette Street
London W1V 5LB
under the title
Your Kitchen Garden
© 1975 Mitchell Beazley Publishers

This 1989 edition published by Crescent Books
distributed by Crown Publishers, Inc.,
225 Park Avenue South,
New York, New York 10003

Editor
Rachel Grenfell

Art Editor
Barry Moscrop

Assistant Editors
Gillian Abrahams
Gail Howell-Jones

Designers
Len Roberts
Mike Rose

Editorial Assistant
Margaret Little

Executive Editor
Glorya Hale

ISBN 0-517-68376-8

h g f e f d c b a

Printed in Portugal by Printer Portuguesa Ltda.

Contents

The History of the Kitchen Garden

The Garden of Eden was, first and foremost, a kitchen garden. It was not entirely typical, having arrived ready made and apparently needing no human to tend it. But in other ways it was the prototype of the epicurean kitchen garden, which has flourished in times of affluence throughout civilized history. Such a garden is designed more to gratify the tastes of its owner than to fill his stomach.

The ancient Greeks had epicurean gardens and so had the Romans, who introduced them to much of Europe including Britain. The Normans revived them in England after the Dark Ages, and they thrived again under the late Tudors and Stuarts. The last flowering of the epicurean kitchen garden was in the nineteenth century in the châteaux of France and the stately homes of England.

Adam's other kitchen garden—that to which he was banished among thistles and thorns outside Eden—was a different kind altogether. This was the garden of adversity, tilled at a time when man struggled to keep alive. It was the garden of the Dark Ages, of the Wars of the Roses, of the Civil War, of the dispossessed agricultural laborers of the nineteenth century and of the two world wars of the twentieth century.

Our kitchen garden of today, created out of the times in which we live, is developing a character of its own between these two extremes. In the last two decades, through more extensive traveling and trading abroad, we have become aware of a whole new range of fruits and vegetables. And science has provided us with varieties of many of these newly appreciated vegetables which will grow even in the Northern states. In that sense we have become epicurean gardeners; our cabbage patch has become a veritable garden.

In the past few years, on the other hand, we have, in our hundreds of thousands, become gardeners of necessity. We have grown weary of the tastelessness and tiredness of the fresh fruits and vegetables on sale. Increasingly, we have become worried about the use of poisons in the growing of our food. Many of us have felt that the only solution is to grow our own.

The final spur in what has now become a dramatic rush back to the kitchen garden has been the soaring cost of living. While the fruits of our own bit of earth may not be free, the cost is largely that of our own labor. And as Thomas Jefferson, the third President of the United States, wrote when he was sixty-eight years old, "No occupation is so delightful to me as the culture of the earth, and no culture is comparable to that of a garden. . . . Under a total want of demand except for our family table, I am still devoted to the garden."

An old north-country gardener had a favorite saying: "There are two things you should always keep out of a garden—a woman and a scratching hen." But history is against him; women were the first vegetable gardeners, or so it would seem from the sparse evidence before recorded history. The historians' theory is that while the men spent their time and energies hunting, the women collected wild roots, leaves and fungi, and by slow degrees became not just collectors but cultivators. There is support for this theory in historical times, and contemporary attitudes in many societies make it credible. Even today, some farmers regard the care of the kitchen garden as something beneath them, although, at times, they may be willing to help with the digging.

Whoever the first gardeners were, the first gardens arrived late in the world's history—not much more than a mere ten thousand years ago. Compare this with the half million years that man has known how to use fire—although not for cooking; that came much later.

When mankind finally did light on the idea of growing food instead of just foraging for it, the advance occurred independently in several parts of the world—the Near East, Central America and Southeast Asia—over a period of several thousand years. Between them the peoples of these areas were then cultivating what are still the world's major food crops.

It was from the Near East—the fertile valleys of the Euphrates and Tigris—that the knowledge of agriculture and horticulture spread southward to Egypt, westward along the Mediterranean, northward into Europe and to Britain. In about 2400 B.C., Mediterranean settlers, a short, dark people, arrived in England. They brought with them domesticated animals and seeds, which they cultivated on the chalk hills of southern England. The women tilled the soil as best they could with sticks and stone hoes. When these early people vanished so did this primitive horticulture. The Celts, pushing into Britain from France and Germany in the first century B.C., revived it; they were skilled farmers, working first with bronze and later with iron hoes.

But their skill was rudimentary, whereas around the Mediterranean throughout this time agricultural methods were far more sophisticated. Although the staple diet of ordinary Egyptians was onions, washed down with beer, the rich lived in fine style on the varied produce of their large, slave-tended gardens and vineyards. The ancient Egyptians were particularly attached to their vineyards. Wine had been made since at least 4000 B.C. and was first used for temple rituals and only later for drinking. The influence of Egyptian horticulture on other civilizations was immense, as was their use of herbs and vegetables in medicine. Homer acknowledged their superiority when he wrote, "In Egypt the men are more skilled in medicine than any of the human kind." Almost all their remedies were of vegetable origin and their medical writings are a great storehouse of plant lore. For two thousand years and more this knowledge was passed on through classical and medieval writers and the compilers of the famous herbals of the fifteenth and sixteenth centuries.

Toward the end of the pre-Christian era, Greece was becoming an increasingly barren land. And, although their after-dinner conversation was excellent, the Greeks had no great reputation as gourmets. But at the beginning of the first century B.C., in Homer's time, men of substance had elaborate gardens to supply the needs of their tables. The garden, however, was the responsibility of the mistress and not the master.

Homer described a large walled garden, in the town of Scheria, which belonged to Alcinous. It included a variety of vegetables set out in beds, and an orchard with apples, pears and figs. There were also olive trees and a vineyard. The Greeks knew the importance of maintaining the fertility of the soil and if there was a shortage of other manures they would resort to green manuring. Beans were one of the crops they grew for plowing in—the leaves added humus to the light Grecian soil and the bean roots provided nitrogen.

To the Romans, blessed with a good climate and a fertile soil, vegetables were of vital importance to both rich and poor. On their little patches of land the poor cultivated a wide range of vegetables. The rich not only ate well, but drew much of their wealth from the sale of fruit and vegetables raised by their slaves in market gardens on the outskirts of the city. They were gentlemen market gardeners. The kitchen garden of the Roman villa was the woman's responsibility and a woman was judged by how well it was run. Pliny wrote, "It was the sign of a woman being a bad and careless manager of her family when the kitchen garden was negligently cultivated; as in such case her only recourse was, of course, to the shambles or the herb market."

Salads—or what the Romans called "vinegar diets"—were an important part of these gardens, and for the interesting reason, as given by Pliny, that they did not need cooking, so the family economized on fuel. They were also "found to be easy of digestion, by no means apt to overload the senses, and to create but little craving for bread as an accompaniment." The saving of bread must have been an important consideration, for wheat had to be imported in vast quantities from North Africa and was expensive. To bring down the cost of living, bread was heavily subsidized, but at times these subsidies got completely out of hand, as when under the Emperor Augustus one-third of the population of Rome was receiving free bread.

What were the vegetables on which the Romans so largely lived? Cato mentioned turnips, radishes, beans, basil, garlic, asparagus and cabbages. Later writers added carrots, parsnips, beets, onions, peas, lettuces, chicory, parsley, sorrel, fennel, skirret, mustard, melons, gourds and fungi gathered in the fields and woods—a formidable list. People in many parts of Europe owed their first taste of some of these vegetables to the Romans, who came as conquerors.

Many vegetables were widely distributed throughout the world long before that, either cultivated or growing wild. The oldest uncultivated vegetables in the world appear to have been such roots as turnips and radishes, members of the cabbage family and onions. (While many vegetables exist today in both wild and cultivated states, the onion is one of the exceptions; no wild form of the onion as we know it now survives.) Scarcely any place in the Old World can claim any vegetable as exclusively native to that area. The radish, for example, could have been found from earliest times in the mountains of central China and in central Asia. Onions were common to the Near East and to central Asia.

It took several thousand years for the cultivation of vegetables to develop, but by 3500 B.C. it was firmly established among the Sumerians in the valley of the Euphrates. The Sumerians were largely vegetarians, and their staple foods were barley, onions and beans. But they also grew leeks and garlic, turnips, lettuces, cress and cucumbers. By 2000 B.C. the Egyptians were cultivating onions and garlic (the amounts they consumed of these were stupendous) as well as peas, cabbages, celery, lettuces, asparagus, chards, radishes (another great favorite) and such exotic fruits as melons, pomegranates, lemons, dates and figs. In Solomon's time the Jews were also growing onions and garlic, cucumbers and melons and herbs. Indeed, the vegetables grown in all countries around the eastern Mediterranean were much the same, for many of them were indigenous to the area. Different peoples, however, had different favorite vegetables. The Egyptians, for example, had an obsession with onions, while the Romans had a penchant for cabbages. Cato, the Roman poet and farmer, thought cabbage the best vegetable of all.

Such then were the culinary riches of the Mediterranean world which the Romans bestowed on Europe as they advanced northward, finally to reach the unsuspecting Britons. After two abortive attempts by Julius Caesar, the tribes of Britain were first reduced by the Roman armies and then seduced by the Roman life-style. The change was dramatic, not least in the food they ate. The only thing the victors and vanquished had in common when the Romans invaded Britain in A.D. 43 was an attachment to cabbage. Over the next three centuries the Britons were to learn the pleasures of the good life—their first experience of *la dolce vita*.

The Romans set out to make inhospitable Britain a home away from Rome, for they had no intention either of leaving the island or of living as the Britons did. Even when they had subdued the tribes they still had the climate to contend with. And as bad luck would have it, two and a half of the four centuries they were in Britain were notably wet. In spite of this the Romans worked near miracles. Elegant cities were built, and as the forts and villas spread throughout the country, the Romans established gardens of fruits, vegetables and the inevitable herbs, both medicinal and culinary. In the south they planted vineyards.

Among the native Britons, now citizens of the Roman Empire, the upper classes began to enjoy themselves in a thoroughly Roman way, while slaves and serfs looked after the prosperous farms of their masters. The Roman-British day, the eating and the social life,

followed the Roman pattern. An early light breakfast would include fruit. Vegetables were served at the midday meal, which also was not substantial. The main meal of the day —"the elegant banquets" of which Tacitus wrote—began in the late afternoon and, with all the paraphernalia of silver dishes and goblets, finger bowls and dancing girls, continued in a leisurely way through several courses.

Suddenly the bottom fell out of this society. Late in the fourth century, the Picts and Scots and Saxon pirates started being troublesome. Nevertheless, the Romans hung on for another fifty years until the rottenness at the center of the empire forced them to pull out of Britain and make for home. Invaded by the Angles and the Saxons, the Vikings and the Danes, Britain had to wait five centuries before Norman invaders introduced a standard of living that at all approached that of the Roman

occupation. On the other hand, for the better part of three centuries the weather improved.

These were the Dark Ages of all Europe. Roman culture died out, and the agriculture and horticulture the Romans had brought with them all but vanished. The Roman influence and habits faded astonishingly quickly in Britain. The epicurean kitchen gardens disappeared and with them the "artificial dainties" of the table which Queen Boadicea had ranted against when first the Romans arrived. Many varieties of vegetables which the Romans introduced were no longer cultivated; it was several centuries before they were reintroduced. Until then the great stand-bys were leeks, cabbages, and dried peas and beans.

There is little information from the end of the Roman Empire until the Norman Conquest, six centuries later, about the state of gardening in Britain or in Europe generally. In Britain the leek was in the ascendancy; it could almost be regarded as the national emblem of the Saxons. It gave a new name to the kitchen garden—"leac tun"—and the names of several towns are derived from it. Basic gardening was, of course, continued by the peasantry, and a more refined form was developed by the church.

In the sixth century, St. Benedict decreed that Benedictine monasteries must be self-supporting, a rule which almost makes him the patron saint of horticulture through those dead centuries. Not only were monasteries called on to create vegetable and herb gardens within their walls, but the Benedictine monks had to work in them, although there might have been a professional gardener to help.

The most celebrated plan for a monastery garden, which never became a reality, dates from the ninth century. Drawn up for Switzerland's abbot of St. Gall, it shows the ideal garden in great detail. The cloister garden would have flower beds. Sixteen raised rectangular beds, each labeled on the plan with the names of the herbs to be grown, comprised the herb garden. The vegetable garden was planned as a large square containing eighteen raised beds. Fruit trees were to be planted between the rows of graves in the cemetery.

Plans also exist, from the early twelfth century, of the monastery gardens at Canterbury —an herbarium, orchards and vineyards, all to be watered by elaborate means of irrigation.

Roman traditions of gastronomy and gardening probably remained stronger in the monasteries of Italy, Spain and France than in those of England. But all monks, by the nature of their monastic life, had an interest in the cultivation of vegetables. They were allowed to eat meat only on prescribed days, so fish, fruit and vegetables became of greater importance than they were outside the monastery walls. Inside the monastery walls, too, life was somewhat sheltered from the turbulent times outside and was more conducive to the cultivation of gardens.

Although war when waged at a distance is an incentive to grow food, gardening becomes impossible if the fighting is actually taking place on your land. The nobles learned this lesson during the next few centuries. They had managed to maintain a certain style of living in the post-Roman period: but later, to defend themselves, they were forced to build castles, which were mountain or moated fortresses and had no room for great gardens. It was then that women came into their own again, growing medicinal herbs and vegetables in their small plots. English history of that period can be best described as chaos punctuated by uneasy or unpleasant calm. One such calm period covers much of the tenth century, which was as settled politically as it was climatically—the first of two centuries of warm, dry weather during which wine production in England reached its peak.

The Norman Conquest ended another period of turmoil and brought in a spell of efficient despotism. The Norman nobles, who took over the estates of the English nobility, laid a Norman veneer on English society in much the same way as there had been a Roman veneer. Life at the top must have been both pleasant and well fed. But for the serfs, who had no choice but to grow food for their masters—and a little for themselves as a reward —life was both oppressive and squalid.

The Normans, by the rigidity of their feudal system, affected British agriculture for centuries after their rule ended. In this way, as in others, including their magnificent architecture, their influence was greater than that of the Romans. But the veneer of good living vanished after them as quickly as it had after the Roman departure eight centuries earlier.

In the twelfth century the Crusaders went warring against the Muslims in the Holy Land, and among the treasures they brought home were shallots. The thirteenth century opened stormy, and throughout northern Europe the fourteenth century was cold and snowy. This may have been the reason, or it may have been coincidence, that the cultivation of vegetables was neglected. But whatever the climate, the warm wind of the Renaissance was beginning to blow, a prelude to one of the most dramatic changes in history that occurred in the sixteenth century, opening up vast new experiences, not least in our food. Nothing like it had been seen since the Roman invasion. This time Europe and Britain benefited not from invasion but from exploration, and the booty came not from the Old but from the New World.

The cultivation of food began in the New World several thousand years later than it did in the Old World, but in many ways it was more advanced by the time the Europeans, begin-

The History of the Kitchen Garden

ning with Cortés and Columbus, arrived. Caves in the Tehuacán Valley, south of Mexico City, have in the last two decades yielded up the secrets of man's development in the New World, which he may have reached more than thirty thousand years ago. The first nomads who used the caves merely collected wild plants to supplement their meat diet. But eight thousand years ago the cultivation of plants began, and slowly, over the next seven thousand years, a highly civilized society based

Raised beds enclosed by boards were a feature of sixteenth-century gardens, as shown in this woodcut of 1542.

on agriculture emerged. It was from such centers of established civilizations in America that European explorers—and pirates—of the sixteenth and seventeenth centuries brought home fruits, vegetables and grains they had never encountered before. Only a handful of plants out of the thousands growing in the New World already existed in the Old World.

The two American plants destined to become the most important in Europe were the potato (especially in the north) and corn (in the south). But the others include bush and kidney beans, gourds, sweet peppers, Jerusalem artichokes, tomatoes (although it was a long time before they were accepted) and the cultivated strawberry. As William Harrison, Dean of Windsor in the late sixteenth century, wrote, "Strange herbs, plants and annual fruits are daily brought to us from the Indies, Americas . . . and all parts of the world."

As though this influx were not enough, Elizabethan England was finding in Europe a host of vegetables which were either new to Britain or had gone out of cultivation since Roman times. These included asparagus from France, globe artichokes and improved celery from Italy, cauliflowers from Spain, rutabagas from Bohemia and garden carrots brought by Flemish refugees. (They and other refugees brought many gardening skills with them.)

Paradoxically, one of the greatest periods of gardening, which lasted from the start of the fifteenth century until the English Civil War, coincided with the beginning of the "Little Ice Age," which continued for three centuries until the 1850s. There were upheavals at home and wars abroad, but gardening flourished. The day of the epicurean kitchen garden had returned. In fact, one major upheaval, the Dissolution of the Monasteries, helped to establish the grand gardens of Tudor times. The monasteries, which had done much to keep alive the growing of vegetables since Roman times, lost their lands. The nobles, into whose hands the land fell, created beautiful gardens on their ill-gotten estates. Such were Beaulieu, Audley End and Woburn. A list of the vegetables grown at Woburn includes asparagus, cucumbers, celery, peas, beans, onions, leeks, lettuces, chicory and radishes, and among the fruits were strawberries, raspberries, peaches, nectarines, cherries and pears.

Even so, in many gardens the vegetable and herb gardens were beginning to take second place to the flower gardens. In 1629, Parkinson, in his *Earthly Paradise*, advocated putting the flower gardens at the front of the house "in sight and full prospect of all the chief and choicest rooms of the house, so contrariwise, your herb garden should be on the one or other side of the house for the many different scents that arise from the herbs, as cabbage, onions, etc., are scarce well pleasing to perfume the lodgings of any house." On the other hand, the gardens of the small manor houses and farms as well as the cottage gardens of the poor were still used strictly for practical purposes.

The revival of vegetable gardening was general throughout Europe. The Dutchman Erasmus, in *Convivium Religiosum*, described a kitchen garden which consisted of a vegetable garden—"the women's kingdom"—a

Monasteries were often self-supporting, as was the monastery near Turin, above, where hermit monks occupied separate buildings, each of which had its own garden attached. The engraving, right, shows the work for April in progress in a sixteenth-century castle garden.

medicinal garden and orchard. In France, the great agricultural writer Olivier de Serres stressed the importance of the vegetable and herb gardens and the orchards and vineyards rather than of the flower gardens.

It was a great time not only for gardening, but for writing about it. Herbals started pouring off the newly invented presses in Germany, the Low Countries, Italy and England. They were largely concerned, in a scientific or pseudoscientific way, with the medicinal qualities of plants, but are particularly enjoyable, even today, for anyone interested in the history of vegetables as well as for the often brilliant woodcuts and engravings which adorn them. John Gerard is undeservedly the best-known name among the English herbalists, for his *Herbal* of 1597 was merely a translation from a Belgian work to which Gerard's major contribution appears to have been the mistakes. Thirty-six years later, however, Thomas Johnson corrected, enlarged and improved the *Herbal*, and it is on this edition that Gerard's reputation rests. John Parkinson, apothecary to James I and botanist to Charles I, was much less concerned with the kitchen garden than he was with flowers. The last of the well-known English herbalists was Nicholas Culpeper (1616–54), whose obsession was botany "explained in terms of astrology." One little volume published in 1603 is worth mentioning.

Its title is *Profitable Instructions for the Manuring, Sowing and Planting of Kitchen Gardens.* It is said to be the first book dealing only with vegetables, and it was written by a linen draper in Shrewsbury who also sold seeds and vegetables.

Pleasure gardens, which flourished under the late Tudors and early Stuarts, were not to the taste of Oliver Cromwell, who approved of only utilitarian kitchen and fruit gardens. But the lavish epicurean tradition had not had time to die out before it was given new life under the restored Charles II. It continued among the aristocracy during the eighteenth and nineteenth centuries, but has diminished almost to the point of vanishing under the economic pressures of the mid-twentieth century. These families could no longer afford the upkeep of great flower and vegetable gardens and greenhouses for exotic plants with scores of ill-paid gardeners.

Early settlers in the American colonies brought British gardening traditions with them. In the founding years of the United States, major emphasis was on food-producing plants imported as seed from the Old World. The original settlers from England created kitchen gardens which combined native American plants with imported European staples.

Horticulturists began to hybridize species discovered in the New World while also striving to improve the yield and adaptability of European vegetable strains. Many prominent statesmen were also practical farmers, including George Washington and Thomas Jefferson. The first nationally known seedsmen were the eighteenth-century Shakers, all members of a religious group. The Shakers distributed seeds imported from Europe but also grew their own strains on American soil. Gradually purely American seed houses developed. Some of the nineteenth-century firms are still doing business today, but offer greatly improved varieties bred especially for disease resistance, taste and adaptability. Sweet corn, the first home vegetable to be widely available as an improved hybrid, was soon followed by tomatoes and cucumbers when, in 1945, the W. Atlee Burpee Seed Company released the first of many hybrid vegetable creations.

Vegetable improvement continues now on an international scale. So far the results have been dramatic. The Netherlands, the United States and Japan have developed hybrids of vegetables which in their original form would never have survived the winters nor matured and ripened in the shorter summers of northern climates. But not all the changes have been for the good; improving the profit of a crop has often been a greater consideration than improving its taste. Unfortunately, too, many old, popular varieties have been lost. But on balance the kitchen garden, even the humblest, has never been better than it is now.

The History of the Greenhouse

Who loves a garden, loves a greenhouse too,
Unconscious of a less propitious clime
There blooms exotic beauty, warm and snug,
While the winds whistle and the snows descend.

It may seem odd to write even a bad poem in praise of a greenhouse, but many will agree with the sentiments of the eighteenth-century English poet William Cowper. Gardeners find it a great challenge to grow fruit, flowers and vegetables at times of the year and in places that Nature never intended.

The Greeks and Romans appear to have been the first to practice the art of forcing plants, and the Emperor Tiberius (42 B.C.–A.D. 37) gets most of the credit, or at least the publicity for it. He insisted on having his favorite cucumbers all the year round, and, Pliny records, "he had raised beds made in frames upon wheels, by means of which the cucumbers were moved and exposed to the full heat of the sun; while in winter they were withdrawn and placed under the protection of frames glazed with Lapis secularia." (The simple but unwieldy system of beds on wheels was also tried out in England in the early seventeenth century. The boxes of rich soil in which the plants were growing were hauled under cover every night.)

Although there is no supporting evidence,

the Romans may have brought their forcing methods with them when they invaded Britain. It was much later, in the thirteenth century, that the practice of forcing was developed in Europe. According to one story, the famous theologian and herbalist Albertus Magnus (1193–1280) was suspected of witchcraft because of his skill in growing fruit and flowers out of season. But the real pioneers were the Dutch and the French, and even when the use of hotbeds and frames spread to England the results were for a long time not as good as those in Holland and France.

At first, at the end of the sixteenth century, hotbeds were used only to raise the seedlings of cauliflowers, cucumbers and melons. But by the seventeenth century, forced plants were spending all their growing lives on hotbeds. The beds were made with several feet of fresh horse manure, which generated great heat when the bacteria got to work on it. The manure was covered with 12 inches (30 cm) of earth in which the plants grew. As well as being pampered by the warmth from below, the vegetables were given protection against the cold from above. This was usually a covering of straw mats or painted cloth, supported by poles at the corners, or, as a refinement, an arch of poles over the bed. This somewhat rudimentary protection persisted in Britain

for a long time and was still being used fifty years after glass frames and cloches had been introduced from France, where they were used with great success at Versailles.

By the middle of the eighteenth century, things were changing in London: the great enclaves of market gardens stretching westward from Westminster to Chelsea and Fulham had caught up with Continental ideas. In February 1748, a visiting Swedish horticulturist was greatly impressed. In one garden, in beds covered by glass frames, matting and straw, he saw cauliflowers 4 inches (10 cm) high and asparagus 1 inch (2 cm) high "and considerably thick." He also records the use of bell cloches with a few cauliflowers growing under each.

Lettuces, radishes, turnips and spinach, as well as the more exotic cucumbers and melons, were widely grown in systems of intensive intercropping, which made the operation exceedingly profitable. But in the middle of the nineteenth century, the expansion of London forced these market gardeners out into the country. Vegetable growing became less intensive, frames and cloches fell into disuse and France began supplying many of the early vegetables for the London market.

Historically, the heated greenhouse developed alongside the hotbed and the frame. The ruins of a kind of greenhouse were found at

Pompeii, but it was not until the late-sixteenth and early-seventeenth centuries that greenhouses were built in Europe. Greenhouses were then orangeries. There was an extraordinary one at Heidelberg, where in autumn each year a large wood-and-glass structure was erected to cover the Elector Palatine's four hundred orange trees. It was heated all winter and taken down in spring.

In England, many orangeries were in the grand style—substantial buildings of stone with large windows in the south wall and a stove or open fire to keep the plants warm. Others were more modest; indeed, some are described as little more than sheds.

When Cowper wrote his lines to a greenhouse it had already changed its character. The orangery had been adapted to accommodate the exotic plants which were all the rage at the end of the seventeenth century. It was not until late in the next century that vegetables—lettuces, cucumbers and bush beans among them—were being forced in greenhouses.

During the period of greenhouse building which began after the Restoration, there was little understanding of the problems involved. Greenhouses were inadequately lit; there was little glass in the walls and none in the roofs until the early-eighteenth century. Moreover, they were often sited so that they missed rather than caught the precious winter sun. The crudeness and inefficiency of early attempts at heating were almost laughable, but methods improved after the introduction of hot-water systems in 1816—forty years after the French first used them.

There was a great technical leap forward in greenhouse construction in the 1830s with the production of sheet glass, which could be made in large sizes. Its use became general after the tax was taken off glass in 1845. Sir Joseph

Sir Joseph Paxton's great conservatory at Chatsworth, above, which was followed by the Crystal Palace, marked the zenith of greenhouse construction in the nineteenth century. These greenhouses were preceded by many less successful endeavors such as the one at left.

Paxton, a pioneer in the use of sheet glass, used it to build a large conservatory in 1837 at Chatsworth, when he was head gardener there. It covered more than 34,000 square feet (3,160 sq m)—although that was a mere nothing compared with the 19 acres (8 ha) covered by his vast glasshouse at the Great Exhibition of 1851—the greenhouse's greatest triumph and memorial.

But the day of the grand conservatory on private estates is over, for the costs of upkeep and heating are astronomical. The twentieth century is the century of the small greenhouse in small gardens. Over the past few years thousands of such greenhouses have been sold annually. "Who loves a garden, loves a greenhouse too." Cowper was right.

Growing Under Lights

Of course not everyone has the room or the money for a greenhouse, but there are other ways to grow sturdy vegetables under cover. Using artificial light is a practical way to provide enough illumination for seedlings and even raise a crop. Because fluorescent lamps are relatively cool, and use less electricity for the intensity they give than do incandescent lamps, the fluorescent tubes are preferred over incandescent bulbs for plant growing.

Fluorescent fixtures for growing vegetables do not have to be anything special. A simple reflector and tube are sufficient. However, some have advantages. Most of the portable plant light fixtures have adjustable legs so you can keep the lamps just a few inches above the foliage, to provide maximum light intensity.

Other more sophisticated arrangements have a cart of two to four tiers with shelves. A fluorescent fixture hangs over each shelf. These are ideal light stands for growing a number of vegetables in the basement, heated garage or spare room. Since the shelves are one above the other, you gain in growing space. The upper shelves receive some heat from the lamps below and so are well suited to germinating seed of warm-growing crops such as tomatoes and eggplants.

Most efficient are fixtures that hold four 40-watt lamps. Fixtures with two-way switches permit you to use two lamps or all four lamps. To start a few tomatoes or squashes several weeks before outdoor planting, you can get by with using only two lamps if seedlings are kept directly below the tubes. However, to grow vegetables in the winter, or for earlier starts in the spring, the four-lamp fixtures are much preferred.

The 40-watt fixtures are 48 to 50 inches (120 to 124 cm) long and have an effective spread of light 18 inches (45 cm) wide.

For starting seeds a few weeks before outdoor planting, a standard industrial fluorescent fixture with two 40-watt lamps is adequate. Here assorted vegetables, including some tomatoes in Jiffy-7 pots, are growing well under fluorescent light. Other seedlings are in plastic compartmentalized flats which give each root system a separate growing area. Having each seedling in its own pot or compartment makes transplanting to the garden easier and safer for the plants.

Trays and lamps

Under each fixture arrange a waterproof tray filled with moist gravel. This will provide extra humidity around the vegetables. If the relative humidity is always at least 40 to 50 percent, you will not have to use trays filled with moist gravel or perlite, but few homes are so humid.

Also, the fluorescent ballasts create some heat and this reduces the relative humidity somewhat. An alternative to trays filled with wet material are water-filled trays covered by a plastic grid, wire mesh or wood slats. The seed flats or pots are placed on the tray covering. Water draining from the pots goes into the trays and additional water is poured directly into the trays. By keeping the plants above these mini-ponds you will provide added humidity from water evaporation.

To start a few seedlings indoors the common inexpensive cool-white or warm-white fluorescent tubes are satisfactory. However, for the best growth, especially with vegetables that need full sun outdoors, horticultural fluorescent lamps are best. Gro-Lux is an excellent rosy-toned tube for starting garden vegetables. The seedlings grow compact, then transplant outdoors with minimum shock. To grow a complete crop under lights, as with vegetables in the winter, use broad-spectrum fluorescent

lamps. Nationally available broad-spectrum fluorescent tubes suitable for growing vegetables indoors include Agro-Lite, Vita-Lite and Wide Spectrum Gro-Lux. These lamps have been formulated to provide a sunlike spectrum which helps plants make sturdy mature growth.

Attach the fluorescent fixtures to an automatic timer which will control the length of daylight for your seedlings. If you are using a cart with tiers or several fixtures near one another, obtain fixtures that have an electrical input. With an input you can plug one fixture into the other, then plug the final fixture into the automatic timer. The timer will then control several fixtures at once. Set the timer to provide 14 to 16 hours of light per 24-hour period. If the plants are growing where they get some sunlight, arrange the timer to turn on the lights at sunrise or slightly before, otherwise the vegetables will be receiving a longer light period than required.

Keep seedling foliage 3 to 4 inches (8 to 10 cm) below the lamps. When seedlings first sprout you can get them close to the lamps by putting the seed flats on top of inverted pots or on upside-down plastic flats. With portable fixtures that have adjustable legs you need only raise the legs as plants grow.

Unless you are growing seedlings in a mix with soil or added nutrients you will have to fertilize your plants once they have a second set of leaves. Starting vegetable seeds in a peat-lite mix such as Jiffy or Terralite seed starting soil is best because you avoid soil diseases and pests.

Milled sphagnum moss is another excellent seed sowing medium but it lacks available nutrients. Once seedlings have germinated and grown leaves, they will require a dilute water-soluble fertilizer. Use a balanced formula such as Hyponex or Miracle-Gro at one-third strength in warm water. Apply this fertilizer solution every second watering. This will be sufficient for seedlings to be transplanted outdoors.

For vegetables you are going to grow inside, transplant the seedlings into larger containers, using one of the commercially prepared growing formulas, then add slow-release vegetable fertilizer if it is not already contained in the potting mix you choose (see the directions on the bag).

Hardening-off

Starting at least a week before you will transplant the seedlings outdoors, begin taking the seed flats outside on mild days. Expose the seedlings to morning and late-afternoon sunlight the first 7 or 8 days, then gradually let them receive the stronger midday sun, using care that the growing medium never dries out. After 10 to 14 days of this treatment, leave the seedlings outdoors at night if temperatures stay above 60°F (15°C). This process will gradually harden the tiny vegetables to outdoor conditions and you can then transplant them with maximum success. If there is a chance that a cold spell may occur, protect the transplants with Hotkaps or A-frames of glass or plastic.

All-America Selections

Since 1932 the All-America Selections organization has been testing new plants from breeders around the world. The organization is a nonprofit educational group formed to evaluate new seed-grown flowers and vegetables from plant breeders in any country.

The organization is called All-America Selections because the tests are done in the United States and in Canada. Seeds are planted in test gardens throughout the states and Canada, thus providing a complete example of how a new variety does under widely differing conditions. Growing side by side with the new selections are older varieties that are considered the best currently available. During the growing season and at harvest, the trial plants are evaluated by some of the world's most experienced authorities in horticulture. The judges serve as volunteers but are required to devote many hours each season in order to decide whether the trial plants are truly superior to the most comparable variety of the same type plant already in commerce. Some years the judges give several awards to outstanding new vegetables while other years they find no new variety sufficiently superior to merit one of the awards.

Entries come into the All-America Selections from plant breeders in Europe, Asia, Africa, South America, the United States and Canada. All of these entries must be carefully grown in the more than fifty trial garden locations, then studied by the judges. The vegetables are evaluated for value to the home gardener, and thus any new vegetable that wins one of the All-America awards is superior in many ways to older selections. For example, the judges evaluate vegetables on the basis of continuing productivity, vigor, improved flavor, convenient fruit size, and resistance to

Four famous All-America vegetables are representative of the carefully selected modern varieties tested nationwide. At the top is Spirit pumpkin, an early-maturing, compact, sure-fruiting bright-orange type useful for cooking or decoration, at center right is Savoy Ace cabbage, an F_1 hybrid selected for tasty, dark-green crinkled foliage and adaptability. At left is Melody spinach, chosen for hybrid vigor, disease resistance and leaf quality. At bottom center is Scallopini summer squash, an F_1 hybrid which is part zucchini and part scallop, or patty pan, squash. Scallopini is useful raw in salads or cooked like zucchini.

pests and adverse weather. Once a variety is judged worthy of an award, the judges confer to decide whether the plant gets a bronze medal, silver medal, or the very top gold medal. After awards are made they are announced to the press with photos, press releases and related publicity. The public can learn about new winners each year after October 1, although media in the Northern states often delay publicizing new vegetables until midwinter, when gardeners are starting to look through seed catalogs. The All-America vegetable winners are usually available from many different mail-order sources and often as started plants in local garden centers.

Test of time

The main reason for having an All-America

Selections group is to identify and publicize the very best new plants. Because plant breeders are continuously striving to create better selections, it is natural that older vegetables be gradually replaced by improved types. However, as an indication of how well the judges do their job, you can still find more than eighty All-America vegetable winners from past years in present catalogs. Some of the most popular home garden vegetables are past winners of the All-America award; for example, Buttercrunch lettuce, generally agreed to be the best all-round lettuce for home gardens, Small Fry cherry tomato, Waltham butternut squash, Fordhook 242 lima bean and many other favorite currently grown vegetables. The new All-America selections shown above in the painting by Marcy Kier-Hawthorne will become the favorites in future gardens. Savoy Ace cabbage won a gold medal award in 1977. The first heads of the season can be harvested at 1-pound (.4 kg) size while plants that grow all summer will reach 4- to 5-pound (2 to 2.4 kg) size. Melody spinach won a silver award for its excellent taste, vigor and disease resistance. The unique Scallopini summer squash won a bronze medal. Spirit pumpkin, another bronze medal winner, produces excellent fruit in an average-sized garden. The All-America vegetable selections are well worth trying in your garden, so look for them in catalogs and at garden centers.

Your Kitchen Garden

Everyone can have some kind of kitchen garden, even if it is only a few pots in the kitchen. The darkest basement kitchen could provide the perfect conditions for producing a constant supply of mushrooms and bean shoots, with herbs in a window box outside. In a well-lit kitchen, mustard and cress, chives and many herbs could be grown inside, and dwarf tomatoes outside in a window box.

On patios and balconies

A surprisingly large range of vegetables, fruits and herbs can be grown in containers on patios. Among them are such salad vegetables as lettuces, scallions, and tomatoes and cucumbers grown in peat bags. (See page 96.) Other vegetables and herbs include runner beans and squashes grown in tubs and trained up wigwams, bush beans and zucchini in containers, a bay tree in a tub, and many other herbs in boxes and troughs. Strawberries can be grown in large strawberry pots, and cordon gooseberries, red currants and vines can be grown against a sunny wall by taking up some of the paving to provide pockets of soil.

The choice is somewhat more restricted for balconies, which tend to be windy and scorchingly hot in the sun. Also they might not bear the weight of soil in large containers.

There is no lack of choice of containers for growing vegetables and herbs. Those made of plastic are the lightest. Hardwood containers are expensive but beautiful, and those made in such heavy materials as concrete and asbestos cement come in bold, simple shapes. Whatever type of containers you choose, always fill them with a suitable mix, such as one of the peat-lite types. Use care to provide water and fertilizer as required since container plants are fully dependent on you.

In the flower garden

There are vegetable plants which in beauty of form rival conventional flowering plants and can be happily planted with them. Indeed, runner beans, tomatoes and peas were first grown for their appearance and not for eating. The foliage of asparagus, globe artichokes and fennel looks elegant among taller flowers. The leaves of beets, Swiss chard, carrots and dwarf lettuce form varied, attractive ground cover. Chives, parsley and thyme make striking edging plants.

In the vegetable garden

A vegetable garden is, of course, the only way to grow vegetables in any quantity. An area of 100 square yards (84 sq m) should provide a family of four with adequate lettuces, runner beans, peas, carrots and turnips in summer, and with leeks, cabbages and sprouts in winter. To be self-supporting in most vegetables, given a family with hearty appetites, four times as much ground, 400 square yards (335 sq m), would be needed. Further land would be required for main crop potatoes—100 square yards (84 sq m) or more, depending on the family's fondness for them. To estimate how much land you would need to give over to potatoes, you can reckon to get 12 pounds (6 kg) of main crop potatoes for every 10 feet (300 cm) of row cultivated.

In the Kitchen

On the Patio

In the Flower Garden

In the Vegetable Garden

The Layout of Your Garden

The ideal kitchen garden does not exist; we have to compromise with reality. But, compared with the problems of weather and soil, the layout of a vegetable garden is a comparatively simple matter.

The gardens of most houses are rectangular. This is a good shape for the formal layout in which vegetables are most efficiently grown. Beds of regular shape are easier to dig, and it is more convenient to stake, and hoe between, plants in rows. A garden left as one large rectangle, however, looks intolerably dull. It is better split into several squares and rectangles, creating a pattern that gives character to the garden.

The most beautiful garden in which I have ever worked was surrounded by a twelve-foot-high wall covered with trained fruit trees. Between gravel paths, there were square and rectangular beds edged with box. Pheasants laid eggs among the rhubarb, and if you were lucky, for this was wartime, abandoned them to you. This was not a typical modern garden, but if you scale down the essentials of it, as in the illustration opposite, the result is both practical and attractive.

The hypothetical garden on the opposite page is assumed to be a garden at the back of a house. It has three vegetable beds of roughly equal size, and the three main groups of vegetables—peas and beans, brassicas and roots—occupy each bed in turn over a period of three years. If the garden is large enough to grow main crop potatoes for the household, a fourth bed can be added, making a four-year rotation. (The rotation of crops is explained on pages 20 and 21.) Asparagus and rhubarb, raspberries, currants and other soft fruits are given permanent beds.

Walls, fences and hedges are an important feature of the garden and must be considered carefully. A brick wall is ideal for the boundary on the north side of the garden, for it blocks the cold winds of winter. On the southern boundary an open fence is best. Chain-link fencing, for example, lets in the sun but tempers the wind. A garden entirely surrounded by walls tends to be a frost trap in winter, but if a fairly open hedge is grown at the lowest part of the garden, the cold air can escape.

Walls and fences are put to the fullest use if cordon apples, pears, gooseberries and red currants are trained against them. Sunny south-facing walls give larger and better-flavored fruit, but by planting soft fruits against a north-facing wall the season can be extended.

Paths must be wide enough—36 to 48 inches (90 to 120 cm)—to provide easy access with a wheelbarrow to all parts of the garden. Because kitchen-garden paths get hard wear they must be laid on a solid foundation.

Space has been found in our hypothetical garden for frames and a greenhouse. The essential compost heaps are given a place at the bottom of the garden behind a screen of Oregon Thornless blackberries. If there is room, a shed can also be hidden away behind the blackberry bushes.

There is a lawn edged with runner beans or climbing roses. A few beds have been reserved for flowers; some have been strategically placed at points where the flowers will have most impact. Trees should not be planted in a vegetable garden, but think hard before cutting down any that are already there.

The garden in front of a house is often characterless. It can be turned into a beautiful and useful herb garden, conveniently close to the house. The illustrations below suggest one conversion—a rockery with herbs and scented flowers in pockets of soil among stepping stones, which give easy access for picking the herbs. A hedge of fierce Scotch thistle guards against acquisitive passers-by, although Scotch, or burnet, roses would be a more permanent and bristly alternative, as well as being attractive.

The illustration opposite shows a well-planned back garden designed to include all the major features of a typical kitchen garden, as well as flower beds and a lawn.

1. This is the first of the vegetable beds in a three-year rotation. Planted with peas, beans and lettuces as a catch crop, it is intercropped with onions, leeks, celery and spinach. The bed has been given manure or compost. Herbs can be grown in the space nearest the house.

2. Cordon fruit trees (apples and pears) and fruit bushes (gooseberries and red currants) are growing against a south-facing wall.

3. Because it can be seen from the house, this slightly raised flower bed is planted with spring bulbs, followed by summer bedding plants.

4. The second vegetable bed is currently occupied by roots which have been given only fertilizer.

5. The greenhouse is sited in an open position.

6. Raspberries.

7. Currant bushes.

8. A row of thornless blackberry canes.

9. Two compost heaps; one contains maturing compost while the other is being filled with fresh garden and kitchen vegetable waste.

10. Rhubarb, horseradish and Jerusalem artichokes.

11. A shapely, compact evergreen bush.

12. Globe artichokes.

13. Asparagus bed.

14. An open fence to admit as much sunshine as possible and provide protection against wind.

15. Strawberries, cloched in spring.

16. Sweet corn.

17. Frames of Dutch lights for raising and hardening off plants in spring, growing cucumbers in summer and overwintering lettuce.

18. The third vegetable bed, planted with brassicas which have been limed and fertilized.

19. This slightly raised bed is filled with flowering perennials.

20. Lawn.

21. A trellis with runner beans growing against it.

22. Annuals in summer.

W

S ——|—— N

E

Rotation & Intensive Cropping

The vegetable garden is usually divided into three parts. Each part is devoted for one year to one of the three main groups of vegetables—peas and beans, brassicas and roots—in turn. After one year, the brassicas are moved to the ground where the peas and beans were growing, the peas and beans are moved to where the roots had been and the roots are moved to the bed previously occupied by the brassicas. Also, each of the three parts of the garden is manured according to the needs of the crop it carries that year. This process, known as the rotation of crops, is repeated year after year.

The reasons for not growing the same vegetables in the same part of the garden every year are twofold: to make the best use of the fertility of the garden, and to lessen the danger of disease.

Such vegetables as peas and beans, onions, leeks, celery, spinach and tomatoes need a rich soil and whatever manure the gardener can obtain. They also have first claim on the compost he makes.

Peas and beans, in league with microorganisms in the soil, are able to fix nitrogen from the air and leave the soil richer in nitrogen through having grown in it. To supplement this nitrogen, a general fertilizer (nitrogen, phosphoric acid and potash) is given to the brassica crop which follows the peas and beans.

The general practice is to lime one-third of the garden each year, if a soil test shows that lime is needed. The lime is applied to that part of the garden where brassicas are growing because they appear to be more prone to club root, their most destructive disease, if the soil is short of lime.

Root vegetables often grow misshapen if they are given manure, so the ground they occupy in the rotation receives only a general fertilizer, there being adequate lime left from the previous brassica crop. Potatoes grown alongside the roots can be manured, but they must not have lime because it may encourage scab.

If many potatoes are grown, the vegetable garden can well be divided into four, one part being given over entirely to potatoes. The vegetable cycle would then spread over four years instead of three, the peas and beans following the potatoes.

Besides being effective and economical in the use of manure and fertilizers, such a rotation helps to keep the plants healthy. Different vegetables attract different pests and diseases. The cabbages, for example, might suffer heavily one year from cabbage root fly, but the root crops which followed would not be affected. And the cabbages would not be attacked by the maggots of the pea moth. So the rotation, while it certainly does not guarantee a disease-free garden, does help toward it.

Not all vegetables are included in the three- or four-year rotation. More permanent beds must be found for the perennial vegetables—asparagus, for example—and for soft fruits. Even with these it is good practice to change the site of the beds when the useful life of the occupants is over and they have to be replaced.

Crop rotation is a concept to be adapted to each individual garden. What is grown in a garden will, in the first place, be decided by the likes and dislikes of the gardener within the limits imposed by space and weather.

More than eighty vegetables are described in this book; it is unlikely that anyone will want to grow all of them. Concentrate on those that you really enjoy eating—the rest are a waste of your time. So, too, are surplus vegetables. It is impossible to ensure that you will never suffer from gluts, but to have far more vegetables than you can eat fresh, freeze, preserve or even give away, is bad planning. It is equally pointless to grow a crop which you know will be wasted because it will be ready when you are away on vacation. These points must be taken into consideration when you are turning the rotation plan into reality.

The smaller the garden the more impractical it becomes to follow a rotation plan rigidly, but the basic aims remain—to satisfy the nutritional needs of each vegetable and to help it to resist pests and diseases.

Rotation of crops (opposite)
Bed A. Peas, beans, onions, leeks, shallots, lettuces, chicory, celery, radishes.
Bed B. Cabbages, Brussels sprouts, cauliflowers, broccoli, kale, spinach.
Bed C. Beets, carrots, turnips, rutabagas, parsnips, celeriac, salsify, scorzonera, potatoes.
Bed D (semipermanent). Asparagus, rhubarb, herbs, raspberries, red and white currants, gooseberries.

Intensive cropping
There are several ways of using a limited area to the full. You can, for example, sow and plant vegetables closer together in the rows, especially if you choose the smaller-growing, but still heavy-cropping, varieties. Conventional sowing and planting distances usually assume a fertile garden in a warm part of the country. In such a garden, growth can be exceedingly lush, and cutting down on the spacing of vigorous-growing varieties can lead to overcrowding, diminished crops and increased threat of disease. But where luxuriant growth is unlikely, planting distances can be reduced without danger of overcrowding.

Reducing the space between rows, instead of between plants in the row, might rule out intercropping, which means sowing or planting smaller, quick-growing vegetables between the widely spaced rows of taller vegetables.

Different times of planting and rates of maturing are the basis of catch cropping, which involves sneaking in a quick-maturing crop before the ground is occupied by another crop.

Some quick-maturing vegetables which may be used for intercropping and catch cropping are: radish (ready from 6 weeks); kohlrabi and globe beet (8 weeks); lettuce and Chinese cabbage (9 weeks); carrots (10 weeks); spinach (11 weeks); and Swiss chard (4 weeks).

Crops which follow other crops are usually called succession crops. Some are, in fact, quick-maturing catch crops which will be harvested before winter begins. Others, for example cabbages, will stay in the ground over the winter. Succession crops are not to be confused with successional sowings—sowings of the same vegetables at intervals in order to avoid a glut.

Always be ready in spring, summer and early autumn to fill any ground which becomes vacant unexpectedly. This may happen if a crop has been harvested early or if a sowing has failed. It is wise to jettison a row where germination has been very poor and to start again with the same vegetable or with another one.

In the Northern states only limited catch cropping is possible because of the shorter summer.

A. Manure or Compost

B. Fertilizer-Lime

C. Fertilizer only

B. Fertilizer-Lime

C. Fertilizer only

A. Manure or Compost

C. Fertilizer only

A. Manure or Compost

B. Fertilizer-Lime

D. Fruit

D. Fruit

D. Fruit

The Soil

Soil is formed over many millions of years by the gradual breaking up of the rocks of the Earth's crust. Different rocks produce soils with different characteristics, which are of vital importance to the gardener when he comes to cultivating them.

The texture of a soil depends on the size of the particles of which it is made. Sand particles vary from 2 millimeters to 0.02 millimeters; silt ranges from 0.02 to 0.002 millimeters and clay particles are less than 0.002 millimeters.

Sandy soil

Sandy soils are those in which more than 75 percent of the soil is sand particles. They are fast-draining because these comparatively large particles are irregular and there is plenty of space between them. Although sandy soils are easy to work and quick to warm up in spring, nutrients in the soil are soon washed out and deficiencies of calcium, nitrogen, phosphorus and potassium may develop. (For information about correcting these deficiencies, see pages 28 and 29.) Also, in sandy soils there is little reserve of moisture for plants in dry weather.

To overcome the drawbacks of sandy soil without destroying its virtues, add—and keep on adding—organic matter to the soil. This will be broken down by microorganisms in the soil to form humus. Humus is the complicated substance that gives the soil its true fertility. It is present in the soil as minute, black, amorphous particles, or as a jellylike coating of the sand, silt and clay particles.

In sandy soil the breakdown of organic matter into humus is fairly rapid, so even crude cow, pig or deep-litter poultry manure can be applied in quantity if it is dug in during the autumn or winter. Compost, spent mushroom compost and peat can be used as mulches to build up a fertile topsoil. Green manuring helps: sow lupins or mustard and, before it flowers, dig it in to rot in the ground.

On a sandy soil thus improved, soft fruits, apples and pears, peas and beans, cauliflowers and potatoes will crop well.

Clay soil

Clay soils, which consist of at least 75 percent clay and silt particles, are at the opposite extreme from sandy soils. The particles are minute and tightly packed together, so that even in hot weather the water is held in the soil instead of draining away. As a result the soil is cold and warms up only slowly in spring. When a clay soil is wet, it is sticky; when it is dry, it is like rock. Also, plant nutrients are not easily washed out of clay soils.

To make the most of its fertility, clay soil needs massive additions of humus in the form of farmyard manure, compost or peat. Combined with the clay particles, the humus will form a loamy texture, making the soil warmer, more aerated and less waterlogged.

Soil conditioners can be used to create an open crumb structure in clay soil; calcium sulphate (horticultural gypsum) is widely used. Lime will also improve the soil's texture, and it makes the nutrients in the soil more available for the plants, as well as reducing its acidity. Improved in this way, clay soils will grow good crops of most fruits and vegetables, apart from roots.

Loamy soil

Loamy soils, consisting of more sand than clay particles and a lot of organic matter, are regarded as ideal for vegetables. They are reasonably warm and easy to work; they hold moisture well, and the plant nutrients are not rapidly washed out. The balance between sand and clay in a loamy soil is geological chance, but man can greatly change the other component parts, for better or worse.

Highly alkaline soil

Some areas of the Southwest and dry semi-desert regions often have soil which is very alkaline. Moreover, the water supply in these areas may also be full of minerals which further contribute to the alkalinity of garden soil. Digging in coarse peat moss is the first step in making a too-alkaline soil suitable for vegetables. Humus from compost, especially evergreen needles and oak leaves, is another helpful ingredient. Remember that some vegetables actually prefer a rather high pH, so in alkaline regions you often obtain excellent crops of fruits, peas, beans and brassicas.

Very acid soil

If your garden is in a region populated by many oak trees, evergreen conifers, wild blueberries and similar acid-loving native plants, you will have to provide lime in order to grow most vegetables. The slowly released long-lasting dolomite limestone is excellent. Some vegetables, such as onions, potatoes and celery, will do especially well on a slightly acid soil. Blueberries are very successful in acid soil, but apples and pears prefer an almost neutral pH. Your local county Extension Agent can usually arrange to have a soil sample tested, then recommend any required modifications for the crops you wish to grow.

Elements in the soil

The elements which provide the plants with the nutrients they need to grow are present in all these soils in varying degrees. Some are present in large quantities, although not in their pure state, but as compounds. The three most important are nitrogen, phosphorus and potassium.

Nitrogen is made available to plants by the action of soil bacteria, which convert ammonia and nitrite into nitrate. It is particularly important for the growth of leaves and stems. A deficiency is indicated by yellowing leaves and stunted growth. An excess produces very dark green, sappy leaves, which look healthy but have little resistance to pests and diseases. The production of fruit and seeds also suffers.

Although phosphorus is present in considerable quantities in the soil, only a little of it is in a form available to plants. It is vital for the development of a good root system and for the plant's seed production. A deficiency is evident in stunted growth.

Potassium improves the quality and flavor of fruit, counteracts some of the effects of excess nitrogen and makes plants more resistant to disease. A deficiency is most likely to arise on sandy soils.

Other elements are vital for balanced plant growth, although they may be needed in smaller, or even minute, quantities. These include magnesium and sulfur and the "trace elements" iron, boron, copper, manganese, molybdenum and zinc.

Finally, it should be pointed out that much of "the soil" is not soil at all. As the great agricultural scientist Sir John Russell summed it up: "It seems incredible, but nevertheless it is true, that in an apparently solid clod of earth only about half is usually solid matter, the other half is simply empty except for the air and water it contains."

Life in the soil

Unceasing warfare is carried on in those air spaces between the solids in the soil. For, contrary to appearance and preconceptions, a garden is not a peaceful and idyllic place: it is a minute sector of a battlefield that covers most of the Earth and life on the Earth depends on the outcome of the battle. Before the gardener starts taking a hand in the fighting, it is as well for him to know who are his enemies and who are his allies.

His greatest allies are the bacteria in the soil. They are inconceivably small and are present in the soil in inconceivably large quantities. They multiply furiously; in theory, in a day one bacterium could turn into a colony of 1,300 square yards (1,000 sq m). In practice, however, long before that stage is reached, the bacteria would have starved themselves to death or been killed by the pollution of their own excreta.

The soil bacteria have two virtues. Some of them play a vital part in breaking down organic matter into humus, and a few of them are responsible for making nitrogen available to plants—perilously few, it seems at times, especially when you realize that without nitrogen the plant life we know, and therefore animal and human life, would not exist.

Some of these microorganisms, for example clostridia and azotobacters, fix nitrogen from the air. Some groups fix nitrogen in the soil in association with such plants as peas, beans and clover. Even fewer bacteria can change the ammonia released from decomposing organic matter into nitrate, and fewer still can change nitrite into nitrate, without which not many of our crops would grow. These beneficial bacteria have their enemies in the soil. Fortunately, the beneficial bacteria normally have the upper hand.

Some soil fungi are good, others are bad. The good fungi live on dead plants or animal remains, build up humus and when dead provide plant food. The bad ones are the parasitic fungi, which destroy plant tissues. A particularly unpleasant one is the fungus which causes club root in brassicas.

Actinomycetes, which are a bit like fungi and a bit like bacteria, also attack beneficial bacteria. Some are parasites on plants; the best-known one causes scab on potatoes. (And the reason why you do not lime potato beds is because actinomycetes do not thrive in acid soil.)

How a plant grows

In daylight hours, plants manufacture food (carbohydrates) in their leaves. The process is called photosynthesis. Chlorophyll, the green pigment in plant cells, absorbs light energy from the sun, and this energy is used to split water into hydrogen and oxygen molecules. The hydrogen combines with the carbon dioxide, which is absorbed by the plant through pores, or stomata, on the leaves, to form a sugar compound. This compound can either be stored in the leaves in the form of insoluble starch or transported to other parts of the plant. The spare oxygen diffuses into the atmosphere through the stomata.

Energy required for the growth of the plant is derived from the food stores when they are broken down in the presence of oxygen absorbed from the atmosphere. This process is known as respiration. In many ways it is the reverse of photosynthesis. It happens, however, not just part of the time, but all the time.

Water and the mineral salts of the soil dissolved in it are drawn up into the plant through fine root hairs. The mineral salt solution is carried through the thick white roots to the stem, and through channels, the xylem vessels, to the leaves. Water evaporates from the stomata. This process causes water to be drawn up through the roots and is called transpiration.

Nitrogen absorbed through the roots can combine with some carbohydrates to form proteins, which are an important part of the plant structure and are needed for growth.

Cross section of stem showing mineral salt solution traveling along the xylem vessels.

Magnification of section of a leaf showing stomata.

There are six major elements taken up in solution via the xylem.

Nitrogen (N) is vital in protein-building and photosynthesis. It promotes leaf growth, and deficiency leads to stunted, possibly yellow, leaves.

Phosphorus (P) is particularly important for development of the root system and the ripening of the crop. Poor growth results from deficiency.

Potassium (K) assists in photosynthesis and the production of carbohydrate. It protects plants against diseases, and is important in the growth of root vegetables and fruits. Deficiency leads to soft growth.

Calcium (Ca) is essential to allow the young plant growth to develop sturdily. Deficiency results in general lack of vigor.

Magnesium (Mg) is part of the chlorophyll molecule. Deficiency affects photosynthesis and shows as yellowing of the leaves.

Iron (Fe) helps in formation of chlorophyll. Deficiency causes yellowing.

Magnification of roots showing mineral salt solution being drawn up by fine root hairs.

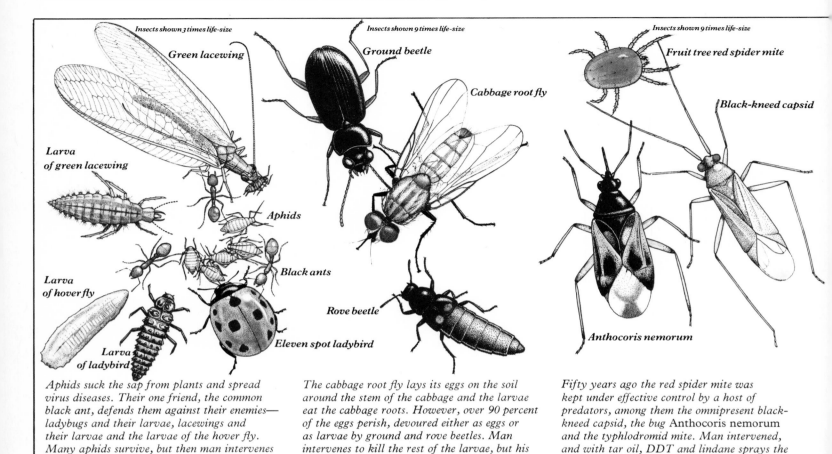

Insects shown 3 times life-size

Green lacewing

Larva
of green lacewing

Larva
of hover fly

Larva
of ladybird

Aphids

Black ants

Rove beetle

Eleven spot ladybird

Ground beetle

Cabbage root fly

Insects shown 9 times life-size

Fruit tree red spider mite

Black-kneed capsid

Anthocoris nemorum

Insects shown 9 times life-size

Aphids suck the sap from plants and spread virus diseases. Their one friend, the common black ant, defends them against their enemies—ladybugs and their larvae, lacewings and their larvae and the larvae of the hover fly. Many aphids survive, but then man intervenes with insecticides. These, however, also kill his allies—the ladybug, hover fly and lacewing.

The cabbage root fly lays its eggs on the soil around the stem of the cabbage and the larvae eat the cabbage roots. However, over 90 percent of the eggs perish, devoured either as eggs or as larvae by ground and rove beetles. Man intervenes to kill the rest of the larvae, but his insecticides have proved more effective against the predatory beetles than against the pest.

Fifty years ago the red spider mite was kept under effective control by a host of predators, among them the omnipresent black-kneed capsid, the bug Anthocoris nemorum *and the typhlodromid mite. Man intervened, and with tar oil, DDT and lindane sprays the predators have been effectively killed, while the red spider mite flourishes.*

The virus enemies of the bacteria are bacteriophages; the name simply means "bacteria devourers." Not all phages attack all bacteria, but for every group of bacteria there is a corresponding enemy phage. The mode of attack is curious. The phage forces the contents of its head through its own tail into the bacterium, and then completely disappears from view. Eventually, the cell of the bacterium dissolves and out of it emerges a host of phages.

Moving up in the size scale—although some can scarcely be seen—are innumerable small animals and insects inhabiting the air spaces in the soil. Mites are minute animals living on the remains of plants, or such other small soil animals as eelworms (nematodes) and small worms. One such mite, the chigger, has a fondness for human legs. Numerous in the soil are springtails, insects which feed on dead vegetable and animal matter, and are preyed on by mites, beetles and spiders. These can reasonably be classed as goodies.

Not so the eelworms, of which there may be up to two million in the soil beneath 1 square yard (1 sq m) of garden. Some feed on bacteria, other small soil animals and, occasionally, on the plant juices in the roots. But the evil ones are the parasitic eelworms which attack potatoes, tomatoes, beans and strawberries. Eelworms sometimes devour each other and are destroyed by some fungi, but there are not enough predators to prevent them from being a menace. The problem is that man has found no way of killing the egg-containing cysts, which can stay dormant but alive in the soil for many years.

Every gardener should feel the same affection for worms as did Gilbert White three hundred years ago when he wrote: "Worms seem to be the great promoters of vegetation, which would proceed but lamely without them, by boring, perforating and loosening the soil . . . and most of all by throwing up worm casts, which being their excrement is a fine manure. . . ." Charles Darwin, who was also an enthusiast for worms, pointed out in the book he devoted to them that all the soil in the country had passed through the bodies of worms many times and would continue to do so over and over again. There are more than two hundred species of worms. Only two of these species make casts, and because of this they are misguidedly poisoned. Man by his digging is also continually upsetting the good work worms do; far fewer worms are to be found in gardens than in undisturbed pastureland. Applying manure and compost helps to increase the worm population.

Of the thirteen hundred species of beetles whose main home is the soil, only one or two are the gardener's foes (one eats his strawberries). Indeed, many ground beetles and rove beetles are his firm allies. They have a great appetite for cabbage root fly, lettuce-root aphids and slugs.

Some beetles must be classed as enemies because of their destructive habits. Click beetles produce wireworms, which stay in the soil for several years, playing havoc with potatoes, before turning into beetles. Japanese beetles produce white grubs, which remain in the soil for two years getting fatter and lazier on the roots they eat. Fortunately, many birds find both these larvae very tasty.

Centipedes are good, whereas millipedes are bad, so it is important to distinguish between them. Their coloring is often similar, but the carnivorous centipedes have a faster turn of speed and wriggle more, and the vegetarian millipedes are fatter and slower.

At the surface of the soil, some damage may be done by earwigs, which eat tender leaves, and by woodlice in greenhouses and frames, but it is not usually excessive. Slugs and snails often become a plague. Some eat such plants as lettuces, which grow near the ground. Some climb up the plant for a feed. Some eat underground and especially enjoy the tubers of potatoes. Thus, although they are effective scavengers, on balance they are enemies. Bran and porridge oats are their undoing, for man panders to the slugs' weakness for them, but adds poison.

These are but some of the inhabitants of the soil, the devourers of dead plant life and of one another. All of them end up by providing food for a plant to grow. The seed that comes to life in the soil among this warfare emerges as a plant above ground to find itself in the middle of another battlefield. On it are engaged more bacteria and fungi, a whole range of predatory animals, birds, rival plants—and man.

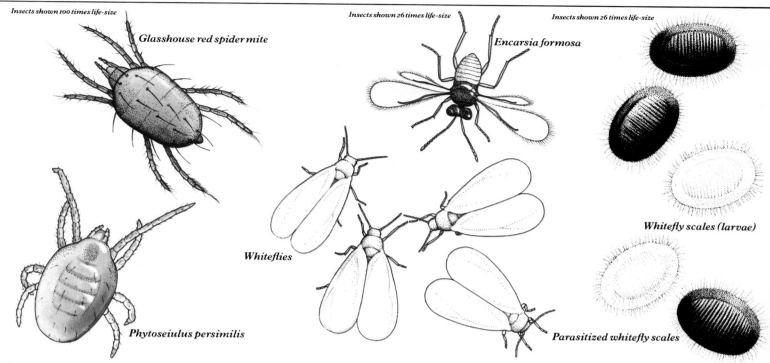

Insects shown 100 times life-size

Glasshouse red spider mite

Insects shown 26 times life-size

Encarsia formosa

Insects shown 26 times life-size

Whiteflies

Phytoseiulus persimilis

Whitefly scales (larvae)

Parasitized whitefly scales

Not all of man's interventions are harmful. Phytoseiulus persimilis, *for example, has been used to kill the greenhouse red spider mite, which is a menace to greenhouse crops. The predatory mite breeds faster than its prey, which it devours so voraciously that it can eventually starve itself to extinction.*

Greenhouse whiteflies are among the most persistent pests in the greenhouse. They resemble tiny white moths and are usually to be found clustering on the underside of leaves, where they lay their eggs. The larvae which emerge are minute, flat and transparent and are hard to see with the naked eye. These immature whiteflies are destructive, feeding on the sap

of plants and causing them to wilt. They also excrete a sticky substance on the leaves which encourages the growth of sooty molds. The introduction of the parasitic wasp Encarsia formosa *may efficiently eradicate this pest. The wasp lays an egg in a whitefly scale, the egg hatches and the scale turns black.*

Pest control

Although there may seem to be a formidable number of pests, fungi and viruses, the gardener is unlikely to come across all of them. Certainly through the years he can expect to encounter some pests and diseases among his plants, but not enough to justify indiscriminate chemical warfare.

There is no "safe" pesticide, fungicide or herbicide. If they were "safe" they could not do their job, which is to kill. The "safest" are the least effective. Each gardener must decide for himself which he is prepared to use.

Insecticides

The "safest" insecticides are derived from plants. Those which are more effective—and more harmful—are made from synthetic chemicals.

Rotenone is manufactured from the roots of derris. It can be applied as a spray or powder. Rotenone is safe only because it is not persistent. If plants are sprayed in the evening, after the bees are back in the hive, the rotenone will have lost its toxicity by the time the bees are foraging again in the morning. It is not injurious to man or animals, but it is fatal to fish. It is harmful also in varying degrees to a number of beneficial insects.

When mixed with pyrethrum, rotenone can be used to kill aphids, caterpillars, red spider mites, flea beetles, sawflies and pea thrips.

For use against aphids, a safe alternative to rotenone is quassia, which is used as a spray. It

is harmless to bees and ladybugs.

Pyrethrum is made from the flower heads of several species of pyrethrum and is also not persistent. Used as a dusting powder, pyrethrum kills aphids, whiteflies, beetles, sawflies and weevils. It is particularly useful against two mushroom pests, sciarid and phorid flies.

Bacillus thuringiensis, sold as Thuricide, is a natural control for foliage-feeding caterpillars. This bacteria harms only leaf-chewing pests and is thus safe to beneficial predators and parasites. Diazinon, found in several commercial vegetable sprays and dusts, is a modern control for maggots that attack roots. Sevin (carbaryl) and malathion are quick-acting useful insecticides but they do kill helpful insects too. Use them only when really required. Apply all preparations strictly according to package directions and observe all precautions.

Molluscicides

Metaldehyde—or preferably methiocarb—mixed with bait in pelleted form is a chemical which kills slugs. Always prop a tile or slate over the bait so that animals and birds cannot eat it and be poisoned.

Fungicides

Maneb or Zineb is used on lettuce to prevent botrytis, and on lettuce and onions to prevent downy mildew.

Bordeaux mixture is a copper fungicide once widely used as a spray. It is harmless to

most beneficial insects. Most often used to prevent blight on potatoes and outdoor tomatoes, it will also control mildew on peas, turnips and spinach; rust on asparagus foliage; artichoke, celery and broad bean leaf spot; and halo blight on beans. A more effective modern fungicide is Maneb, now used instead of Bordeaux mixture.

A well-nourished soil does not prevent the appearance of pests and diseases, but it does make plants more able to resist them. Regrettably, the longer and more extensively that any vegetable has been grown, the more firmly established are its particular pests and diseases.

Many of the newer and less popular vegetables, on the other hand, are fairly pest and disease free.

Herbicides

There is little reason why herbicides should be used to kill weeds in the vegetable garden. Mulches would be far better; they not only smother the weeds, but also improve the quality of the soil.

Alternatively, constant hoeing, although tedious, will keep annual weeds under control at no cost at all. The roots of perennial weeds should be pulled out of the soil during digging.

If total weed killers are used on paths, take great care that they do not come in contact with any plants, or those will be totally killed as well.

Cultivation

Always keep a spade straight. If you dig at an angle you will have to push the spade as far into the soil, but you will not dig as deep.

Spread manure or compost with a spade or a fork along the length of the trench. The soil from the next row of digging will cover it.

A motor cultivator speeds up the laborious process of digging a large garden or preparing new ground.

Left to its own devices the last thing that soil would do would be to grow bumper crops of vegetables in neat rows with the aim of feeding a family of four. To do that the soil has to be tamed.

Gardeners usually set about the taming by digging. First buy a really good spade. (For tools, see pages 36 and 37.) Then tackle the digging slowly, turning over small spadefuls at a time and stopping for the day before exhaustion sets in.

Generally speaking, there is no need to dig deeper than one spade's depth (a spit deep, as it is called). There are exceptions, for example when you need to enrich deeper pockets of soil for permanent plants or to improve the drainage of heavy soils.

Dig a shallow trench at one end of the plot, but instead of laboriously wheeling the soil to the other end of the plot, as is usually recommended, merely throw spadefuls of soil well behind you. Loosen the soil at the bottom of the trench with a fork (although you can omit this). If you are to dig in manure or compost, spread it along the shallow depression, which will now be all that is left of your original trench, and working back along the plot turn another row of soil onto the top of the manure. Loosen the soil in the trench thus made, and so on. The less soil you try to turn over at once, the deeper the trench will be.

Try to keep the trench straight, and if it goes askew, dig along only part of it until the whole length is straight again.

When you get to the end of the plot, you will have a shallow trench left. Next year, therefore, start digging at that end.

The reasons for digging are to bury the weeds, to incorporate manure or compost into the soil and to aerate the soil. Whenever possible, it is done in the autumn or early winter. The surface is left rough to expose as much soil as possible to the frosts of winter; this lightens its texture. In spring, all that it should be necessary to do is to rake or lightly fork the soil to prepare it for sowing or planting.

If the ground you are digging needs lime, whatever form of lime you use can be scattered over the soil and not dug in. The rains will wash it down. But never lime ground into which you have just dug manure—lime and manure interact chemically.

It is perfectly possible to grow good crops of vegetables without digging at all. No-diggers sow and plant in compost which is merely spread on the surface of the soil. Behind the practice is the theory of the "primeval forest floor," where year after year, layers of decaying vegetable and animal refuse are built up and converted into humus by bacteria. The no-diggers also point out that while digging does bury weeds, at the same time weed seeds which have been lying dormant in the soil are brought to the surface, where they spring to life. They contend, too, that worms are more efficient than man at taking organic matter down into the soil and aerating it.

The no-digging method certainly works; over the years great fertility builds up and vegetables grow exuberantly. But the labor saved by not digging must be set against the labor spent on making large quantities of compost or buying it. Coarse peat moss and dried manure are a fair substitute for compost.

Digging is usually a once-a-year task, but weeding is a continuous chore. If the weeds are allowed to get out of hand, they may have to be skimmed off the surface with a spade. It is easier to tackle them with a hoe when they are small. If hoeing is done when the soil is dry, the weeds can be left to die on the surface.

Hoeing not only destroys weeds but also creates a layer of loose soil, which helps to conserve the moisture in the soil below.

Mulching has two advantages over hoeing. First, there is no danger of damaging the roots of plants near the surface of the soil and, secondly, when the mulch is eventually dug into the soil, or taken down by worms, it is converted into humus. Compost, peat and leaves all make excellent mulches. They need to be applied to a depth of at least 2 inches (5 cm) to be effective. A mulch should always be applied when the soil is moist; it will then keep the moisture in. Similarly, never lay a mulch down before the soil has warmed up in the spring, or it will hold the coldness in and block out the sun.

Straw is an effective mulch to keep down weeds in areas that are particularly difficult to get at, such as around currant and gooseberry bushes. The straw should be about 6 inches (15 cm) deep, and is best put down in spring rather than autumn. Only a thin layer of lawn mowings should be put down at a time, or the mulch will turn into a steaming, slimy mess. Sawdust can also be used in moderation.

The modern mulch is strips of black plastic film placed between rows of vegetables. It is certainly effective in holding in moisture and smothering weeds, but it adds nothing to the fertility of the garden.

Spades and hoes are for cutting into the soil; forks and rakes are for scratching it. A fork is usually used for surface cultivation. You would, for example, use it for forking in fertilizer that has been scattered over the surface. In sticky or very stony soil, however, a fork can be a very useful substitute for a spade.

The rake is used to break the soil down to a fine tilth after digging.

When the gardener has carried out all these steps of cultivation, he has formed a thoroughly domesticated soil, eminently satisfactory for his needs.

A fork, rather than a spade, should be used to turn over heavy or stony soil, for shallow surface cultivation and for lifting root crops.

A Dutch hoe is used to kill young weeds by slicing them just below the surface of the soil and exposing the roots.

A rake, although not used as much as a hoe, is invaluable for breaking down the soil to the fineness needed for a seedbed.

Hydroponics

Although the gardener spends the major part of his time cultivating, feeding and watering the soil and fighting the pests and diseases that inhabit it, soil is not an essential part of a garden. It is perfectly possible and simple to grow vegetables while dispensing with the use of soil altogether.

The soilless culture of plants is called hydroponics. By this method the minerals which the plant normally obtains via the soil are fed directly to the roots in a solution of mineral salts in water.

The first experiments in soilless culture go back nearly two hundred years, but the breakthrough came about a century ago. It was not until the 1920s, when Americans took it up, however, that hydroponics came to be exploited. During the Second World War, it was used on a large scale to grow fresh vegetables for troops stationed in isolated places. Many of the carnations and roses sold by florists are grown hydroponically, and so are many tomato, cucumber and lettuce crops.

Hydroponic enthusiasts get as excited about their methods as dedicated organic gardeners or no-diggers do about theirs. They point out that soilless culture involves no digging or weeding. There is no manuring, and hence no smell. There is no soil and therefore no dirt. Germination is faster and the plants grow to maturity more quickly. They also insist that hydroponically grown plants taste better than plants grown in soil. What is certain is that the plants are less disease prone.

On a commercial scale, crops are often raised hydroponically in large tanks filled with a nutrient solution in which the roots of the plant are always immersed. This method (true hydroponics) is both tricky and expensive. The amateur can use the simple method of growing plants in containers filled with an inert aggregate which is kept moist with a mineral solution to provide the plants, essential needs of nitrogen, potassium, phosphorus, calcium, sulfur, magnesium and iron. Container cultivation makes it possible to grow at least some vegetables without a garden—either indoors, or on a patio, or on a flat roof (an excellent place).

All kinds of containers can be used—pots, window boxes, tubs, old kitchen sinks, wooden and plastic boxes (galvanized containers should be painted inside). Whatever the container it must have a drainage hole, or holes.

A box should be 6 to 8 inches (15 to 20 cm) deep and not too large to handle, say 24 to 30 inches (60 to 75 cm) long and 18 inches (45 cm) wide. Make a few drainage holes in the bottom. If it is a wooden box line it with polyethylene in which a few drainage holes have been cut. Place the box on a tray to catch the solution as it drains through. There is no need to empty the tray. The solution will be drawn up again.

Fill the box almost to the top with the aggregate which has been soaked in water. The aggregate can be coarse sand—fine sand becomes waterlogged; gravel or pebbles, perhaps mixed with some sand; broken bricks—the pieces $\frac{1}{2}$ inch (1 cm) or smaller; or possibly vermiculite. The box is then ready for sowing, which you do as though you were sowing in soil.

To feed the plants, the aggregate is watered with a solution made by mixing mineral preparations with water. These have been specially formulated to take the guesswork out of the process; just follow the instructions. Nationally available brands of water-soluble fertilizer include Hyponex, Miracle-Gro and various Peters formulas, including one (Hydro-Sol) developed for hydroponics. It is much easier to use professionally prepared fertilizers, but if you wish to make your own formula mix, use 20 ounces (560 g) of ammonium sulfate, 10 ounces (280 g) of superphosphate, 7 ounces (210 g) of potassium sulfate, 3 ounces (90 g) of magnesium sulfate and a tiny pinch of iron sulfate. Dissolve $\frac{1}{3}$ ounce in a gallon of water (10 g in $4\frac{1}{2}$ liters) for feeding plants.

In hot weather the aggregate must be watered daily, and every other day in cooler weather. Once a week, spray the plants with plain water.

After the crop has been picked, pour boiling water over the aggregate (to help keep it disease free) and make the next sowing. Among the plants which do well when grown hydroponically are lettuce and chicory (take care that the lower leaves do not droop onto the wet aggregate and rot), bush beans, tomatoes and strawberries.

Cross-section of a hydroponic bed.

Drainage holes

Aggregate

Container

Solution

Tray

Feeding the Soil

Farmyard manure and compost are the two great, bulky organic manures which both feed the soil and improve its texture. If you are able to obtain as much farmyard manure as you want you belong to a privileged minority. But any gardener can make compost, because the raw material of the compost heap is all the vegetable waste (if it is not diseased) from the garden and kitchen. If you do not recycle it in this way, you will be throwing away next year's food.

An enclosed compost heap works better than a heap in the open, which is liable to cool down and dry out before it has totally decomposed. In a properly made heap, spring rubbish should be compost by summer, summer rubbish compost by autumn, while autumn rubbish, taking longer to decompose through the winter, will be ready for use in spring. If the heap goes cold or dry before it has decomposed, turn it over with a fork so that the top of the heap ends up on the inside. Water the compost as you turn it.

Sphagnum peat moss, especially the rough type that comes in bales from Europe or Canada, is useful to dig into soil where more organic matter is required, such as for heavy clay or light sandy soils. Peat moss is acid so apply a dusting of dolomite limestone when you use peat for vegetables, unless you are trying to obtain a more acid balance.

Testing for lime
Most vegetables grow best in a slightly acid soil, but if the soil becomes too acid other essential elements become unavailable to the plants. The acidity or alkalinity of the soil is expressed in what is called the pH value. This is reckoned from a base of pH 7; any higher pH number indicates the soil is alkaline and any lower pH number indicates the soil is acid. Because the scale is logarithmic, a change of one unit represents a tenfold increase or decrease in the soil's acidity; pH 5.5 soil, for example, is ten times more acid than pH 6.5 soil, which suits most vegetables.

There are cheap and simple soil-testing kits available to determine the pH value of the soil. It is then possible to work out how much lime, if any, should be added.

Testing for other deficiencies
There are other kits on the market for testing the levels in the soil of such important elements as nitrogen, phosphorus and potassium. Any deficiency can be made good by the use of organic or inorganic fertilizers.

Organic fertilizers
Organic fertilizers cost more than inorganic fertilizers. In general they act more slowly, but their effects last longer.

There are several types of organic fertilizers available. One made from ground hooves and horns of animals contains 12 percent nitrogen and acts slowly over two years. Allow 2 ounces to every square yard (60 g to 1 sq m). Another, made from ground, dried animal bones, acts slowly over three years. It contains at least 20

A common way of making compost is in two wooden boxes built side by side. While one is full of maturing compost the other is being filled with fresh vegetable waste. Gaps in the framework admit the air the bacteria need to break down the material.

Soil
Vegetable waste
Sulfate of ammonia or farmyard manure
Vegetable waste
Lime
Vegetable waste
Sulfate of ammonia or farmyard manure
Vegetable waste
Lime
Vegetable waste

Build up the heap with 6- to 8-inch (15 to 20 cm) layers of vegetable waste. If you are short of vegetable material, buy straw, wet it thoroughly and incorporate it in the layers. Spread some farmyard manure or sulfate of ammonia—½ ounce to the square yard (15 g to 1 sq m)—over alternate layers, and a sprinkling of lime over intervening layers. Alternatively, spread one of the proprietary activators over each layer. Water each layer as you build the heap. When the box is full, cover the top of the heap with a 1-inch (2 cm) layer of soil.

Compost bins of various designs can be bought ready for use. Those with a capacity of about 15 cubic feet (½ cu m) are suitable for a small garden with limited vegetable waste.

percent phosphate, and is low in nitrogen. Fish-meal fertilizer, made from dried, ground fish waste, acts slowly over two years. It contains about 10 percent nitrogen and 12 percent phosphate, although these percentages vary. Fertilizer made from powdered seaweed acts fairly quickly. It contains about 5 percent potash and trace elements. Dried blood is a fast-acting fertilizer, especially when it is applied as a liquid feed—use 1 ounce to 1 gallon (30 g to 4½ liters) of water. It contains at least 10 percent nitrogen.

Inorganic fertilizers

On the whole, inorganic fertilizers, which are made from chemicals, act quickly in providing the plant with vital elements, but they are soon washed out of the soil and leave no lasting improvement.

The formula for balanced fertilizers appears on the bag, with nitrogen listed first, then phosphorus, followed by potassium (potash). Slow-release fertilizers, such as Osmocote, are coated with compounds to provide a gradual release of nutrients with each watering over a period of months.

A straight fertilizer is used to remedy a marked deficiency of one element in the soil or to give a plant a boost. Nitrogen can be cheaply provided by using sulfate of ammonia, which is 20 percent nitrogen and which acts within a few weeks. Use ½ ounce to the square yard (15 g to 1 sq m). Sodium nitrate, which is 16 percent nitrogen, acts instantly. Use not more than 1 ounce to a square yard (30 g to 1 sq m).

Phosphorus is usually supplied by super-phosphates, which are 20 percent phosphoric acid. Use 2 ounces to the square yard (60 g to 1 sq m) in spring or summer. On acid soil, however, it is better to use basic slag, which acts much more slowly. It contains 17 percent phosphoric acid. Apply ½ pound to the square yard (¼ kg to 1 sq m) in autumn or winter.

Potassium is generally provided by sulfate of potash, which is 50 percent potash. Apply 1 ounce to the square yard (30 g to 1 sq m).

Watering the soil

However well fed a plant may be it will still not grow without plenty of water. Soils vary in how much water they can hold. The limit for sand is about 10 percent; the limit for loam is up to 30 percent, and the limit for clay is even higher. (When the soil can hold no more water it is at "field capacity.") As the soil dries out, the plant finds it harder to draw up water, even though there may be up to 20 percent of water still left in clay. When the plant can no longer draw up any water, "wilting point" has been reached. The gardener should try to ensure that this never happens.

Absolutely no good is done by merely damping the surface of the soil. During a hot, rainless week in summer, the gardener may have to provide the equivalent of 1 inch (2 cm) of rain, and that means 4½ gallons of water for every square yard (20 liters to 1 sq m). This is a formidable task for a man with only a water-ing can. Using a hose or sprinkler increases the chances that the plants will get enough water.

In autumn, apply lime—as ground dolomite limestone—to the surface of the soil. Do not apply manure or artificial fertilizers at the same time.

At the end of winter, a dressing of sulfate of ammonia will put new life into spring cabbages by giving them a nitrogen boost.

A watering can with a fine rose is essential for watering seedlings and newly transplanted plants.

The fastest way to feed a plant is through the leaves. The foliar sprays, although not cheap, can be used to help to revive plants after a setback.

The best type of sprinkler for the vegetable garden is one with a spray that covers a square or a rectangular area.

A perforated plastic pipe running along the rows is a labor-saving method of watering plants.

Growing under Glass

Spring comes earlier and the onset of winter is later in a greenhouse, in frames and under cloches. All of them "trap" the sun. The short-wave rays from both direct sunlight and diffused light pass through the glass and warm up the soil. The soil in turn give off this heat as long-wave heat rays, which will not pass through glass, so the heat builds up inside the greenhouse.

In the middle of winter, however, the temperature inside a greenhouse without artificial heating may be only a few degrees above the temperature outside. Even in a heated greenhouse you cannot create perpetual summer, for in winter lack of light inhibits plant growth. There are too few hours of daylight and the light is not strong enough to encourage growth.

Facing the greenhouse east to west makes the most of winter sunlight. The gain is even greater if the roof is angled to reflect the minimum of light, but this is costly, and if the house is angled north to south there is no advantage.

Greenhouses glazed to the ground obviously admit more light than those built on 2 to 3 feet (60 to 90 cm) of brick wall, which are warmer. The framework of an aluminum house obstructs less light than a wooden framework. These are two important facts to consider well when choosing a greenhouse.

A great deal of light is lost because of dirty greenhouse windows. Regular and thorough cleaning of the greenhouse will also help to combat plant diseases.

Obviously a greenhouse should be built where it is not shaded by the house or by trees. But the farther it is from the house, the greater will be the cost of taking water, electricity or gas to it.

In summer the heat trapped in a closed greenhouse can raise the temperature so high that plants are damaged. Adequate ventilation is essential, therefore, and a system of automatic ventilation, although not cheap, avoids the necessity of having to visit the greenhouse several times a day.

Automatic watering devices also save a lot of time and work in the greenhouse. They include simple capillary trays or mats on which plants stand; trickle irrigation lines with drip nozzles at intervals; and full-scale combined trickle and mist watering systems, activated by the strength of the sunlight.

The most convenient—and now most expensive—way of heating the greenhouse is by electricity. Fan heaters and tubular heaters are widely used. If natural gas can be piped to the greenhouse the gardener is lucky, since it is relatively cheap. Artificial gas gives off fumes which kill plants, but the carbon dioxide given off by natural gas is beneficial to green plants, although it can be fatal to mushrooms.

The temperature of the greenhouse can be lowered, and the cost of heating cut, if a propagator is used for seed raising. A propagator is basically a miniature greenhouse which is heated cheaply, even to 70°F (21°C), by soil-warming cables. A large, thermostatically controlled propagator would make early seed raising feasible inside a cold greenhouse.

One piece of equipment that is vital in a greenhouse is a maximum-minimum thermometer; guesswork may kill your plants.

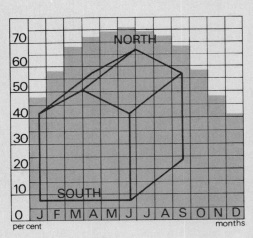

Short-wave rays from the sun pass through the glass of the greenhouse and warm the soil inside. Because long-wave rays given off by the soil do not pass out through the glass, the temperature rises inside the greenhouse.

In winter, the glass of a north-to-south, even-span greenhouse admits less than half the available sunlight; it reflects the rest. When a greenhouse is situated east to west, about a quarter more sunlight penetrates in winter.

To germinate plants, it costs far less to heat a propagator than to heat a whole greenhouse.

Electricity is the most convenient form of heating, but natural gas is cheaper and gives off carbon dioxide, which is beneficial to plants.

Seedlings are cheaply raised in a heated frame in the greenhouse.

In this condensed drawing are many of the modern greenhouse controls that greatly simplify regulation of humidity, temperature, circulation of air, shading and even watering. Automatic heaters, ventilators and humidifiers are standard equipment for most greenhouses in the United States, but the gardener's skill is still required for success with varied crops.

Electric fumigator

Automatic ventilator

Sun visors

Shading blind

Control panel

Air circulator

Soil steriliser

Humidifier

Mist propagator

Ventilator

Fan heater

Thermostat

Propagator

External blinds

Automatic watering by capillary action

Automatic heating

Growing under Glass

A garden frame, especially one which is heated, can be used in conjunction with, or as an alternative to, the greenhouse. It is used for raising seed or growing less-hardy vegetables.

The simplest frames are made of Dutch lights supported on a brick or wooden base. (Dutch lights consist of a grooved wooden framework holding a piece of glass of a standard size—56 × 28¾ inches [140 × 72 cm].) Others, which have metal frameworks and glass sides, admit more light, but are colder at night. Resourceful gardeners can use old storm windows or window frames covered with plastic to do the same job as expensive Dutch lights. Frames can be heated by electric cables in the soil (like underfloor heating) or by air-warming cables fixed to the sides of the frame. Better still, the two methods can be combined. Fixing the cables is a job for a qualified electrician.

A cold frame is used for the toughening-up stage in the life of a greenhouse-raised plant, to prepare it for the rigors of the outside world.

Dutch lights are versatile. Greenhouses, as well as fixed frames, can be built from them, and they can be used to give portable protection to anything in the garden. For example, you may lean a row of lights against a wall to protect newly planted tomatoes. The lights must be firmly secured, otherwise, being large and fairly light, they are liable to be caught by gusts of wind and smashed.

Bell cloches have been used for centuries, mainly in Europe. Continuous cloches are an English idea, and their use, which dates from the beginning of the twentieth century, reached a peak in the 1950s. When interest in vegetable growing declined, cloches went out of fashion and many well-known designs went out of production. Hotkaps are a modern wax-paper version of the glass bell cloche. With care a wax-paper Hotkap will last for two seasons.

Cloches are most useful to the gardener who lives in the colder areas. They enable him to sow crops earlier, especially if the cloches have been placed in position about two weeks before sowing to warm up the soil. The less-hardy vegetables, which would fail in the open, can also be grown under them. Moving cloches can be wearying, but by careful forward planning of where vegetables are to be grown, the cloches can be lifted from one crop to another in an adjoining row.

Glass cloches are still the best, even though they are heavier, more liable to be broken and more expensive than those made of plastic. Gardeners with small, baseball-playing children may prefer plastic for the safety of both cloches and offspring. Because they are so light and liable to be blown away, plastic cloches must be firmly anchored in the soil.

Tent and barn cloches (the names describe the shapes) are made of glass and plastic. There are also small tunnel cloches made of rigid plastic, and long tunnel cloches made of polyethylene stretched over hoops. Polyethylene-covered frames have a fairly short life, but are correspondingly inexpensive.

Antique bell cloche

Glass barn cloche

Rigid plastic cloche

Polythene tunnel

Tent cloche

Frame with under soil and warm-cable air heating

This modern cold frame, called the Vent O'Matic, has a thermostatic device to open the top automatically when inside temperature reaches 72°F, then closes the top when temperature drops to 68°F. Modern prefabricated cold frames are making it much easier for gardeners to start their own vegetable plants or to raise crops during the winter.

All-glass frame

Planting Charts

Imagine a recipe which said "Cream together the butter and sugar when all danger of frost is past." Or, imagine if it were possible to make Yorkshire pudding only when there were more than fourteen hours of daylight. The cook has problems, but they are seldom climatic. The gardener, on the other hand, is the prisoner of the weather and can do nothing to change the overall pattern of the climate of his region.

As well as suffering, or enjoying, the weather of its own region each garden has a microclimate of its own. Although some of the factors in creating this microclimate may be beyond his control—the site of the garden, for example, or the shade or protection from wind of adjoining houses—the gardener can do much to make conditions more favorable for his plants.

Walls, fences and hedges temper the wind But a solid wall may only divert the wind over the top, sometimes causing enough turbulence to damage the plants beyond the lee of the wall. More open fences or hedges are often preferable because they do not merely divert the wind but reduce its force. Plants growing against the sunny side of a wall, on the other hand, benefit from the heat which the wall reflects. Cold air flows downhill; if your garden is on a slope, provide some way out at the bottom for the cold air to escape, or you will have made yourself a frost pocket. Late spring frosts are a particular menace if you are growing apples, peaches, pears, many soft fruits and potatoes.

Heavy clay soils are cold, but will warm up sooner in the spring if their texture is lightened with large quantities of organic matter. Dark, humus-rich soil absorbs more heat than light-colored soil. Mulches, too, help to keep heat in the soil.

The most obvious way of mitigating the cold is to grow crops under glass—greenhouses, frames or cloches. But even in heated greenhouses, the growth of plants in winter will still be inhibited by lack of light.

Nothing can be done about excessive rain, but drought can be overcome, laboriously with watering cans or effortlessly with sprinklers, provided no watering restrictions are in force in the part of the country where you live. In a drought, large quantities of water will be needed (see page 29). Mulches help to prevent evaporation from the soil.

Too high a temperature can stop plants from growing, but in the North it is only in greenhouses that this is likely to be a problem. Outdoors, plants which wilt during the day, because they give off more moisture through the leaves than they can take up through the roots, will revive at night. Tomatoes and potatoes, for example, prefer a cooler temperature at night than in the daytime and strawberries develop their best flavor in temperatures of about 50°F (10°C).

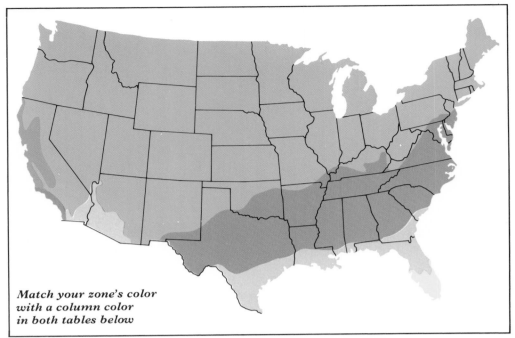

Match your zone's color with a column color in both tables below

Planting charts courtesy O. M. Scott & Sons Co.

The map above is a general guide to regions of the United States according to basic climate. Since the map is general it does not indicate local microclimates or variations in climate due to altitude. To find out more precise information related to planting dates, contact your local agricultural Extension Agent. Local extension agents, and often state agricultural departments, can provide week-by-week recommendations for planting various vegetables. For general planning, these charts, prepared by the O. M. Scott & Sons Company, will be very useful in your vegetable gardening.

Cool-weather crops

CROP	NORTH	SOUTH	GULF & SOUTHWEST	TROPICAL FLORIDA	CALIFORNIA NORTH	CALIFORNIA SOUTH
Beets	Apr-July	Feb-Apr, Aug-Sep	Oct-Feb	Oct-Feb	Feb-Sep	All year
Broccoli*	Apr & Aug	Feb-Apr, Aug	Sep-Jan	Oct-Jan	Mar-Apr, Aug-Sep	Sep-Feb
Cabbage*	Apr-July	Feb-Apr, Aug	Oct-Jan	Oct-Jan	Mar-Apr, Aug-Sep	Sep-Mar
Carrots	Apr-July	Feb-Apr Aug	Oct-Mar	Oct-Feb	Jan-Sep	Sep-June
Collards	Apr-Aug	Feb & Aug	Sep-Dec	Sep-Jan	Mar-Apr, Aug-Sep	Sep-Mar
Lettuce	Apr-May, Jul-Aug	Feb-Apr, Aug-Sep	Sep-Feb	Sep-Jan	Feb-Apr, Aug-Oct	All year
Mustard	Apr-Aug	Feb-Apr, Aug-Sep	Sep-Feb	Sep-Mar	Feb-Apr, Aug-Oct	Oct-Mar
Onions	Mar-May	Feb-Apr, Sep	Oct-Feb	Sep-Mar	Sep-Apr	All year
Parsley	Apr-July	Feb-Apr	Dec-Jan	Sep-Jan	Feb-Apr, Aug-Oct	Oct-Mar
Peas	Mar-Apr, Jul-Aug	Dec-Apr	Sep-Feb	Sep-Feb	Oct-Apr	Oct-Mar
Radishes	Apr-May, Aug-Sep	Feb-May, Aug-Sep	Sep-Feb	Oct-Mar	All year	All year
Spinach	Mar-Apr, Aug-Sep	Feb-Apr	Oct-Jan	Oct-Nov	Oct-Mar	Oct-Feb
Turnips	Mar-Apr, Aug-Sep	Feb-Apr, Aug	Sep-Feb	Oct-Feb	Feb-Mar, Aug-Oct	All year

*Transplant

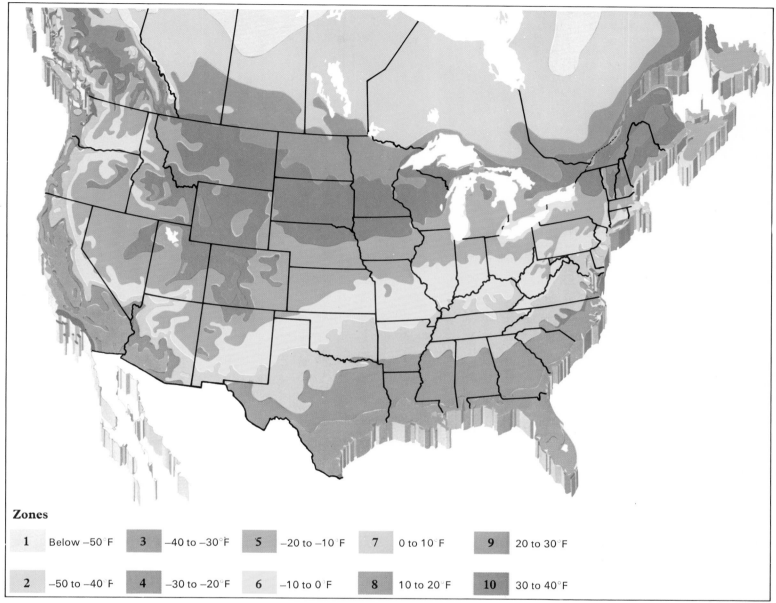

Zones

1 Below −50°F	**3** −40 to −30°F	**5** −20 to −10°F	**7** 0 to 10°F	**9** 20 to 30°F
2 −50 to −40°F	**4** −30 to −20°F	**6** −10 to 0°F	**8** 10 to 20°F	**10** 30 to 40°F

Warm-weather crops

CROP	NORTH	SOUTH	GULF & SOUTHWEST	TROPICAL FLORIDA	CALIFORNIA NORTH	CALIFORNIA SOUTH
Beans, lima	May-June	Apr-Aug	Mar-Apr	Oct-Apr	Apr-June	Apr-July
Beans, pole	May-June	Apr-July	Mar-Apr	Jan-Feb	Apr-June	Apr-July
Beans, snap	May-July	Apr-July	Mar-Apr	Oct-Mar	Apr-June	Mar-July
Corn, sweet	May-June	Mar-July	Mar-Apr	Jan-Feb	Apr-July	Mar-July
Cucumber	May-June	Apr-May	Mar-Apr	Jan-Feb	Apr-June	Apr-June
Eggplant★	May-June	Apr-May	Mar-Apr	Dec-Feb	Apr-June	Apr-June
Okra	May-June	Apr-May	Mar-May	Feb-Mar	May-June	Apr-June
Peas, southern	May-June	Apr-Aug	Mar-May	Feb-Mar	★★	★★
Pepper, sweet★	May-June	Apr-May	Mar-Apr	Jan-Feb	Apr-May	Apr-May
Pumpkin	May	Apr-May	Apr	Mar	May-June	June
Squash, summer	May-June	Apr-May	Mar-Apr	Jan-Feb	Apr-May	Apr-June
Squash, winter	May-June	May-July	Mar-Apr	Jan-Feb	Apr-May	Apr-June
Tomatoes★	May-June	Mar-May	Mar-Apr	Oct-Mar	Apr-June	Mar-June

★Transplant   ★★Not common

The zone map above, prepared by the United States Department of Agriculture, shows the expected minimum temperatures in most of the horticulturally important areas of the United States (excluding Alaska and Hawaii) and Canada. The ten hardiness zones are appropriate for general reference. Most seed and fruit plant catalogs will refer to the various zones by number when describing the hardiness and adaptability of the plants they offer, or proper planting dates for various crops. The minimum winter temperature in your zone will influence how much gardening you can expect to do in the colder months, and how much protection will be required if you expect to have vegetables during the winter. The helpful charts at the left provide basic information about when popular garden vegetables should be planted for the best crops. Locate your general area on the map shown at the top of page 34, then consult the charts to find out general planting dates. Keep your own records from year to year.

Tools & Machinery

It is a false economy to buy cheap gardening tools, so be prepared to spend money on them. Begin with the five basic tools, and add to them only to get better results or to save labor. Avoid gadgets, invariably they are not used.

The five basic tools are spade, fork, hoe, rake and trowel. Add pruners to this list if you are growing fruit. Next on the list of priorities are a watering can and a wheelbarrow. A dibble is useful for making holes to plant a vegetable such as cabbage. It can be made from the handle and about 8 inches (20 cm) of the shaft (sharpened at the end) from a broken spade. But that presupposes the existence of a broken spade; until then the trowel is a perfectly good alternative for transplanting.

A garden line to mark out straight rows for planting is basically only a long piece of strong string tied to two sticks. Curiously, most gardeners either lose a homemade line or get the string in a hopeless tangle, whereas they take great care of the easily wound metal contraption they buy.

Spades
The standard size of blade is $11\frac{1}{2}$ inches (29 cm) long and $7\frac{1}{2}$ inches (19 cm) wide, but the small size, $10\frac{1}{2} \times 6\frac{1}{2}$ inches (26×16 cm), makes digging easier. Stainless-steel blades go through the soil more easily, are easier to clean and do not rust. The price may be double that of an ordinary spade, but it is worth paying. Wooden shafts should be close-grained and smooth. Polypropylene handles are lighter. Handles are either D- or T-shaped; the choice depends on which you find easier to handle.

Forks
The standard size of a digging fork is $12 \times 7\frac{1}{2}$ inches (30×19 cm); the small size is $10\frac{1}{2} \times 6\frac{1}{2}$ inches (26×16 cm). The tines may be of stainless or ordinary steel, and the handles of wood or polypropylene.

Hoes
The most important hoe is the Dutch scuffle hoe, used for weeding. The hoe for making drills for sowing is the garden hoe.

Rakes
Rakes are invaluable in creating the fine tilth needed for a seedbed. Widths range between 12 and 16 inches (30 and 40 cm) and shafts are about 60 inches (150 cm) long. Wooden shafts should be smooth and close-grained, and, therefore, unlikely to splinter.

Hand tools
Stainless steel is worth investing in for a hand trowel, and probably for a hand fork, because both are frequently left out in the garden. Only the best pruners are worth buying; blades which do not cut cleanly cause terrible damage.

Gloves
Many gardeners cannot bear to wear gloves. Others agree with the nineteenth-century gardener Loudon, who wrote in his *Encyclopedia of Gardening*: "Never perform any operation without gloves on your hands that you can do with gloves on. Thus no gardener need have hands like bears' paws."

Dutch scuffle hoe

Garden rake

Garden hoe

Spade

Digging fork

Watering can

Bucket

Hand fork

Garden trowel

Dibble

Basic tools
These basic tools will be sufficient for a small garden. A spade and a fork should be chosen with as much care as a golfer takes in choosing clubs. Balance varies surprisingly according to how tools are held, so handle them in the shop before buying them. For the elderly or handicapped, specially designed spades are available which take much of the labor out of digging.

Additional equipment
Although the tools and equipment illustrated here are not basic necessities, they will save time and cut the amount of work required in the garden. Some, such as the wheelbarrow and the cultivator, are modern adaptations of equipment that has been in use for centuries. Others, including the pressure sprayer and the sprinkler, are comparatively new inventions.

Hose and reel

Rotating sprinkler

Rotary cultivator

Pressure sprayer

Pruners

Pruning knife

Measuring tape

Yardstick

Triangular hoe

Modern scuffle hoe

Potato fork

Gardening gloves

Wheelbarrow

Reel and line

Sowing

A seed is created to grow: that is its purpose. The gardener does not have to cajole it into growing, he merely has to give it the opportunity. For germination he provides a growing medium (not necessarily soil), moisture, warmth, and, for healthy growth, adequate light and space.

Sowing under glass

Most vegetable seeds need a temperature of about 65°F (18°C) for germination. To avoid the heavy cost of heating the whole greenhouse to this temperature, a propagator can be used. If it is large and tall enough, the seedlings can be allowed to grow on in it, but at a lower temperature. This would, however, be a rather wasteful use of a propagator. If the seedlings are moved to the benches of a heated greenhouse, or to a heated frame within a cold greenhouse, the propagator can be used for raising a further batch of seeds.

The choice of a proper mixture is the most important single factor in sowing. Any old soil will not do. There are specially formulated commercial seed and potting composts, which consist of sterilized loam, peat and sand, plus fertilizers. Soilless composts are usually based on peat with vermiculite or perlite, plus fertilizer. Commercial soil composts can be extremely variable in quality, but buying from a reputable source is some safeguard. The soilless composts, called peat-lite mixes, are less variable, but need great care in watering. (Once peat has dried out it is hard to get it to absorb water again.)

Plastic seed trays can be kept cleaner than wooden boxes. Fill the tray or box level to the top with moist, but not sodden, compost and then firm it down with your hand. Scatter the seeds very thinly on the surface of the compost. By using your finger and thumb for sowing you will be able to space the seeds better than you will if you scatter them from the packet. (The

larger pelleted seeds can be spaced as you wish.) Sift a shallow covering of milled sphagnum moss, not soil, over the seeds and firm gently. Label the tray with the name of the seeds and the date of sowing. Cover the tray with a sheet of glass to prevent the compost from drying

out in the propagator. Wipe condensation off the glass every day. At the first sign of the seedlings coming through, remove the glass.

Pots are often used instead of trays for plants which will not tolerate the root disturbance involved in pricking-out from a seed-box. It also makes sense to use pots if only a few plants are being grown. Conventional round pots made of clay or plastic take up more room than trays, however. Space-saving alternatives are square, compressed peat pots (individual or in strips) filled with a seed compost, or peat blocks. These are made of a prepared peat compost, which is compressed into a block in a simple machine. If two seeds are planted in each block (pelleted seed can be used) and the weaker seedling removed, there

is no root disturbance later. Jiffy-7s are peat pellets which expand for use when watered.

If seeds are going to germinate, they usually do it fairly quickly. Many germinate within a week, although the time will depend on the temperature. The bulk of seeds will germinate within one to two weeks. Celery takes up to three weeks and parsley is unpredictable.

Pricking-out

As soon after germination as possible, prick out the seedlings into another box or into pots. This is usually left too late. A seedling pricked out two days after germination suffers far less setback than one pricked out a week after germination. They may be fiddling little things to handle at two days, but the roots are less liable to be damaged then. Lift each seedling gently, hold it by one of the leaves—not by the stem—and replant it, using a plastic or wooden seed label as a dibble.

It is far better at this stage to prick out the seedlings into pots containing potting compost than into other boxes from which they may have to be moved again. Peat blocks made of potting compost can also be used. The old practice was first to prick out the seedlings, then to move the growing plant from a box to a pot (potting-off). When the pot became too small, the plant was moved to a larger pot (potting-on). Every such change is a major setback to the plant. It may, however, be necessary to compromise at the pricking-out

stage because of the demand on space in the greenhouse at the height of the seed-raising

season; pots do take up more space than boxes.

When the pricked-out plants have been watered from a watering can with a fine rose, they can be put in a heated frame in a cold greenhouse or outside. Alternatively, they can be transferred to the benches of a heated greenhouse. The temperature is first reduced by about 5°F (3°C) from what it was in the propagator. Later, it can come down to 50°F (10°C). Do not force the plants; steady, sturdy growth is the aim.

Eventually, when the weather is suitable, the pots are transferred to a cold frame outdoors for hardening-off. To harden-off, raise the frame light a little at first, on mild days, but close the frame at night. The plants can be given a little more air each day until they are ready for planting out in the garden.

Outdoor seedbeds

Some vegetables, notably brassicas (see page 47), are sown out of doors in seedbeds. Level and rake a few square feet of the garden and, for brassicas, cover it with good compost from the compost heap. Make shallow drills with a stick 6 inches (15 cm) apart and sow the seeds thinly. Cover them with a scattering of sifted compost. Use the head of the rake to firm the bed. Do not let the bed dry out as the seedlings grow, but water gently from a watering can with a fine rose.

Planting out

When the time finally comes for planting out, water the plants in the seedbeds or pots the day before the move. If possible, choose the evening of a cloudy day for planting out. However sturdy the plants may appear, treat them gently. Disturb the roots as little as you can by lifting them with as big a ball as possible of the soil or compost in which they have been

growing. Lower them into holes made with a trowel or dibble. Plants grown singly in pots or Jiffy-7s suffer the least disturbance, and they will forge ahead faster than others. Avoid damage to leaves or stems which would make the plants vulnerable to diseases. Firm the soil around the transplanted plants and water.

Sowing outdoors in rows

Some vegetables, especially root crops, cannot be successfully transplanted. Instead, they are sown in rows in that part of the garden where they are to grow and mature. As a general but not rigid rule the rows run north to south, so that each side of the row gets its share of the sun.

Mark where the row is to be with a garden line, and alongside it make a drill in which the seeds will be sown. The phrases "½-inch (1 cm) drills" and "1-inch (2 cm) drills" should not be interpreted too literally; with even the finest tilth such precise measurements are impossible. Therefore regard a "½-inch (1 cm) drill" as shorthand for a very shallow depression in the soil along which very small seeds will be sown and very thinly covered. The simplest way of making such a shallow drill is by pressing the arm of the rake into the soil along the length of the row. The "1-inch (2 cm) drill" is somewhat deeper, but still shallow. This, and deeper drills, can be made with a garden hoe.

Sowing along the drill can be done in two ways—either thinly in a continuous row, if the seeds are small, or in groups of one, two or three seeds, placed at intervals along the row, if the seeds are large. The second is called station sowing, and the distances between the stations are given in the sowing instructions for individual vegetables. Pelleting of seeds makes it possible to sow even minute seeds in stations.

Seeds sown in stations of two or more will need thinning by the careful removal of the weaker seedlings in each station. (The risk involved in planting only one seed is that it may not germinate, or may turn out a weakling.)

Continuous sowing will involve thinning

along the row to leave adequate space for each plant to grow. Sowing thickly should be avoided; the plants will suffer all their lives from overcrowding at the seedling stage, and the thinning of crowded seedlings disturbs the roots of those which are left.

Times of sowing

Times of sowing given on seed packets must be seasonally adjusted—to steal the statistician's phrase—to your own garden. "Early April" may mean daffodils for some and battling through a blizzard for others.

The seed allows gardeners considerable latitude. Sir Alexander Fleming, of penicillin fame, was a gardener who was both unorthodox and successful. André Maurois wrote that Sir Alexander "liked sowing and planting out in those months of the year which were not advised by the experts, just to prove that the experts were wrong." His attitude was that plants "are responsive to kindness, but they can also withstand any amount of hard treatment. In other words, they are like human beings."

Making seed and potting composts with soil

Seed and potting composts can be bought ready-made, but whether they will contain top-grade loam and fertilizers is another matter. If a gardener can obtain a good loam he can make these composts himself. After mixing, the compost should not be stored for more than a few weeks.

The quantities given here may be scaled down or up according to how much is needed, as long as the proportions are the same. Many gardeners still think in terms of the now-discarded bushels rather than cubic yards. For practical purposes a bushel is one-twentieth of a cubic yard.

To make a seed-sowing compost: mix 2 parts (by bulk not weight) of sterilized medium loam to 1 part of granulated peat and 1 part of sharp sand. To 1 cubic yard (1 cu m) add 1 pound (½ kg) of ground limestone and 2 pounds (1 kg) of superphosphate.

To make a potting compost (for slow-growing seedlings): mix 7 parts of sterilized medium loam with 3 parts of granulated peat and 2 parts of sharp sand. To each cubic yard add 1 pound (½ kg) of ground limestone and 5 pounds (2½ kg) of base fertilizer. The base fertilizer is made of 2 parts (by weight) of hoof and horn or dried blood to 2 parts of super-

phosphate and 1 part of potassium sulfate. To make an all-purpose potting compost (which is the one most generally used), add twice as much base fertilizer, and to make a rich potting compost (used for tomatoes) add three times as much base fertilizer.

Composts without soil

To make soilless seed compost according to the formula developed at the University of California, mix equal parts (by bulk) of granulated peat and washed sand. To each cubic yard (1 cu m) add 5 pounds (2½ kg) of ground limestone, 1¼ pounds (600 g) of superphosphate, 15 ounces (450 g) of potassium sulfate and 10 ounces (300 g) of ammonium sulfate.

The University of California potting compost is made by mixing equal parts (by bulk) of granulated peat and washed sand. To each cubic yard (1 cu m) add 5 pounds (2½ kg) of chalk or ground limestone, 2½ pounds (1¼ kg) of magnesium limestone, 3¾ pounds (1¾ kg) of ammonium nitrate, 3¾ pounds (1¾ kg) of hoof and horn, 2½ pounds (1¼ kg) of superphosphate and 1¼ pounds (600 g) of potassium sulfate.

It is easier and just as effective to buy Jiffy-Mix or another commercially prepared peat-lite-type planting compost. The peat-lite mixes, using vermiculite or perlite with coarse peat, are even more popular around the country than the heavier sand formulas.

Pelleted seeds

Pelleted seeds are small seeds that have been given a coating of soil-clay to make them large enough to handle. They can thus be sown in stations, reducing or eliminating the need for thinning.

The soil in which pelleted seeds are planted must be moist enough to soften the coating or the seed will not be able to germinate. But if the soil is overwet, the clay coating will cling to the seed, preventing germination.

If the seeds are sown indoors, cover them with a layer of fine compost no deeper than the diameter of a pellet. If they are sown outdoors, the covering should be to a depth of twice the diameter of a pellet. Germination will take a day or two longer than for ordinary seed. The soil must never be allowed to become dry after sowing; overwatering will also be disastrous.

The life of seeds

The seeds of such vegetables as turnips, parsnips and parsley have to be fresh to germinate properly. Others, including broad, bush and runner bean seeds, pea seeds and spinach seeds will germinate reasonably well after two years. Seeds of such vegetables as leeks, carrots, kohlrabi, cabbages, cauliflowers, Brussels sprouts, broccoli, kale, lettuces and mustard and cress can be left for three years, while onion, radish and beet seeds can be planted when they are four years old.

Any seeds left over after the year's sowing is completed must be kept dry at normal room temperature or they will deteriorate. Remember to write the year of purchase on the packet.

A Gardening Guide

The novice gardener always asks for precise answers to questions to which there are no precise answers.

"How much of the garden will I have to dig up to grow enough vegetables for the family?"

"How many hours a week will I have to spend in the garden?"

"How much money will it save me?"

The answer to these questions—and to many others—is "it depends," which is honest, but irritatingly unsatisfactory. The answers depend on the weather, the fertility of the soil, the absence or prevalence of pests and diseases, on how quickly the novice learns and on luck. It would, however, be cowardly not to attempt some answers to these questions.

Size of the garden
A garden measuring 400 square yards (335 sq m) can meet most of the vegetable requirements of a family of four.

The return from a garden in a novice's first year will be less than in later years. Even the second year will show a considerable increase. By the fourth year the garden will be reaching its peak, but only if you have invested in the fertility of the soil and not robbed it.

Time spent in the garden
A garden of 300 square yards (250 sq m) will take at least one hundred and fifty hours a year to cultivate. A 400-square-yard (335 sq m) plot which included potatoes would add more than fifty hours, for potatoes take up a lot of time. But the work is not spread evenly throughout the year. March, April, May and June are laborious months, needing eight to ten hours a week in the garden. At the other extreme, you need hardly move out of doors in December and January.

There are ways of saving time. Cut out the tedious and lengthy earthing up of potatoes by growing them under black polyethylene sheeting. Grow self-blanching celery, which needs no trenching or earthing up. Reduce weeding by using weed-smothering mulches. A few years' experience will also make the work easier and faster, especially as you will learn when to cut corners.

On the other hand, an enthusiast can extend the time he spends in the garden to fill all the time he has to spare. And that is the reason many non-gardeners often get the discouraging impression that gardening is an endless task.

Saving money
Precisely how much money will be saved by growing your own vegetables is all but impossible to estimate. In the first year it could be nothing, especially if you are a beginner and have to buy all the tools you need. Any economy on tools should be made by buying only those which are essential. Gadgets are a luxury at any time, and most certainly at the start. But do not try to save money by buying shoddy basic tools—spade, fork, hoe, trowel and rake—if only because you will suffer even more than the garden.

After tools, the first spending priority is to buy fertility, especially for an impoverished garden. But avoid throwing money away on highly publicized patent fertilizers, and still

less on pesticides. The money is far better spent on peat, and on straw for making compost. Neither straw nor peat is cheap now, but building up the fertility of the garden is a long-term and profitable investment.

At first, therefore, do not imagine that you will be saving a fortune, although that may come later. Bear in mind, to avoid being discouraged at the start, that the gardening year is longer than twelve months. It would be that only if everything was sown in January and eaten by December. But vegetable sowing can go on over nearly nine months of the year, and harvesting over a period of eighteen months. That makes the first "year" short and not very profitable. Not until the second and third years will expenditure and returns from the garden establish a pattern by which profitability can be judged.

In limited space
Even tiny backyards, city terraces and confined suburban gardens will produce a rewarding crop of fresh vegetables when you select varieties with care. Most practical in limited space are small-growing hybrids bred for maximum production on midget plants. For example, some seed catalogs list more than fifteen midget vegetables well suited to the small home garden or city terrace. Dwarf Morden, a Canadian cabbage, grows 4-inch (10 cm) heads in only 55 days; Tiny Sweet carrot produces 3-inch (8 cm) sweet, crisp roots in 62 days. Even sweet corn has been bred as a dwarf. Golden Harvest grows only 36 inches (90 cm) tall, has 4-inch (10 cm) sweet ears in about 60 days. Tiny Tim and Pixie tomatoes grow a compact 24 inches (60 cm). Small Fry tomato has 1-inch (2 cm) fruit, grows about 36 inches (90 cm) tall and is very resistant to disease. All of the midget selections will thrive in large containers of peat-lite mix when fertilized according to directions with the planting formula you use. The midget vegetables are perfect for winter growing in heated greenhouses, and the smaller sorts, such as lettuce, carrots, tomatoes and cress can even be grown under broad-spectrum fluorescent lights (see pages 14 and 15).

Started plants
Modern mail-order nursery firms now offer started vegetable plants. Garden centers all over the country also sell vegetable seedlings during the spring planting season. If you want to save time, or if you do not have the room or facilities to start your own melons, eggplants, tomatoes, cabbages and other long-season crops, it is wise to purchase the plants you need as started seedlings. Choose compact plants with good root systems. Avoid overgrown, wilted or blooming plants. The young, sturdy seedlings will quickly establish in your garden. To ease transplanting shock, water newly transplanted vegetables with a weak hormone solution made for transplanting, such as Ortho Head Start or Transplantone.

Seeds and supplies
Sources for top-quality seeds and helpful growing supplies are listed on the following page. American gardeners are very fortunate to have available the best varieties of vegetables from all over the world. Seedsmen not only work to breed better plants for American gardens but also import the best selections from other areas of the world. Some seed firms specialize in imported seeds, others in seed of short-season crops for the North and still others offer a wide selection of heat-tolerant vegetables for planting in the Southern states.

Send for the catalogs listed at the right. Most catalogs not only list seed but also provide detailed descriptions of new hybrids, planting suggestions, crop maturation times, garden plans and suggestions for crop succession. A number of seed firms also offer growing supplies that may be difficult to obtain from local garden centers. In all cases, mail-order catalogs make fascinating reading.

Sources of Seeds and Supplies

Bio-Control Co.
10180 Ladybird Dr.
Auburn, CA 95603
Live ladybugs, praying mantis egg cases, other beneficial insects. Free list.

Burgess Seed and Plant Co.
P.O. Box 218
Galesburg, MI 49053
Free catalog features blizzard-belt-hardy strains of seeds and fruits, many unusual tomatoes.

W. Atlee Burpee Co.
Warminster, PA 18974
Free color catalog with best in seeds and supplies. Free leaflets on vegetable growing.

Chevron Chemical Co.
Att.: Mr. L. F. Czufin
P.O. Box 3744
San Francisco, CA 94119
Annual "Ortho Lawn & Garden Book" available from local garden stores.

J. A. Demonchaux Co.
225 Jackson St.
Topeka, KS 66603
Free catalog lists more than 100 types of epicurean vegetables, many from France.

Henry Field Seed Co.
Shenandoah, IA 51602
Seeds, supplies, fruits, free catalog.

Floralite Co.
4124 E. Oakwood Rd.
Oak Creek, WI 53154
Fluorescent light fixtures and light stands. Free list.

Dean Foster Nurseries
Hartford, MI 49057
Free catalog of fruits, herbs, seed potatoes, asparagus.

Gardens for All, Inc.
P.O. Box 371
Shelburne, VT 05482
Free information about local garden projects and community gardens.

The Green House
9515 Flower St.
Bellflower, CA 90706
Gardening light stands.

Gurney Seed & Nursery Co.
Yankton, SD 57078
Free old-time catalog has unusual vegetables.

Joseph Harris Co.
Rochester, NY 14624
Free catalog features modern hybrids.

HHH Horticultural
68 Brooktree Rd.
Hightstown, NJ 08520
Zone maps, plant finder lists, vast selection of books.

J. L. Hudson Seedsman
P.O. Box 1058
Redwood City, CA 94064
Unusual seeds from around the world featured in 50¢ catalog.

Jackson & Perkins Co.
Medford, OR 97501
Free catalog of vegetable seed and some started vegetable plants.

Johnny's Selected Seeds
Albion, ME 04910
Catalog for 50¢ features organically grown seeds, some supplies.

Kelly Bros. Nurseries
115 Maple St.
Dansville, NY 14437
Many fruit trees, grapes.

Le Jardin du Gourmet
Dirt Road
West Danville, VT 05873
Catalog for 25¢ features leeks, shallots, garlic, herbs.

A. M. Leonard & Sons
P.O. Box 816
Piqua, OH 45356
Free catalog of tools, books, growing supplies.

Henry Leuthardt
East Moriches, NY 11940
Handbook/catalog for 50¢ lists unusual espalier fruit trees, all dwarf.

Lord & Burnham Co.
Irvington, NY 10533
Free folder on greenhouses.

Marko Co.
94 Porete Ave.
North Arlington, NJ 07032
Free folder on indoor light units.

Mellinger's
2310 W. South Range Rd.
North Lima, OH 44452
Free comprehensive catalog of growing supplies, fruit plants, seeds, cold frames.

Geo. W. Park Seed Co.
P.O. Box 31
Greenwood, SC 29647
Free catalog of supplies and many modern vegetable seeds.

Peter Reimuller Greenhouses
980 17th Ave.
Santa Cruz, CA 95062
Free catalog of greenhouses with redwood frames.

O. M. Scott & Sons Co.
Marysville, OH 43040
Free booklet on home vegetable gardening.

Shoplite Co.
566 Franklin Ave.
Nutley, NJ 07110
Complete 25¢ catalog features many garden light fixtures and different types of lamps.

Stark Bros. Nursery
Louisiana, MO 63353
Free catalog of fruits, many dwarf fruit trees, some seeds.

Steele Plant Co.
Gleason, TN 38229
Free catalog of sweet-potato plants and onions.

Stern's Nurseries
Geneva, NY 14456
Catalog includes new fruit hybrids.

Stokes Seeds
1017 Stokes Bldg.
Buffalo, NY 14240
Very wide selection of vegetable seed in free catalog. Helpful planting information, supplies.

Texas Greenhouse Co.
2717 St. Louis Ave.
Ft. Worth, TX 76110
Free catalog of greenhouses and growing supplies.

Thompson & Morgan, Inc.
P.O. Box 24
Somerdale, NJ 08083
Free catalog includes many new vegetables from Europe, also seeds for sprouting.

Vegetable Factory Greenhouses
71 Vanderbilt Ave.
New York, NY 10017
Free catalog and guide to greenhouse heating.

List compiled by Charles Marden Fitch.

Salad Plants

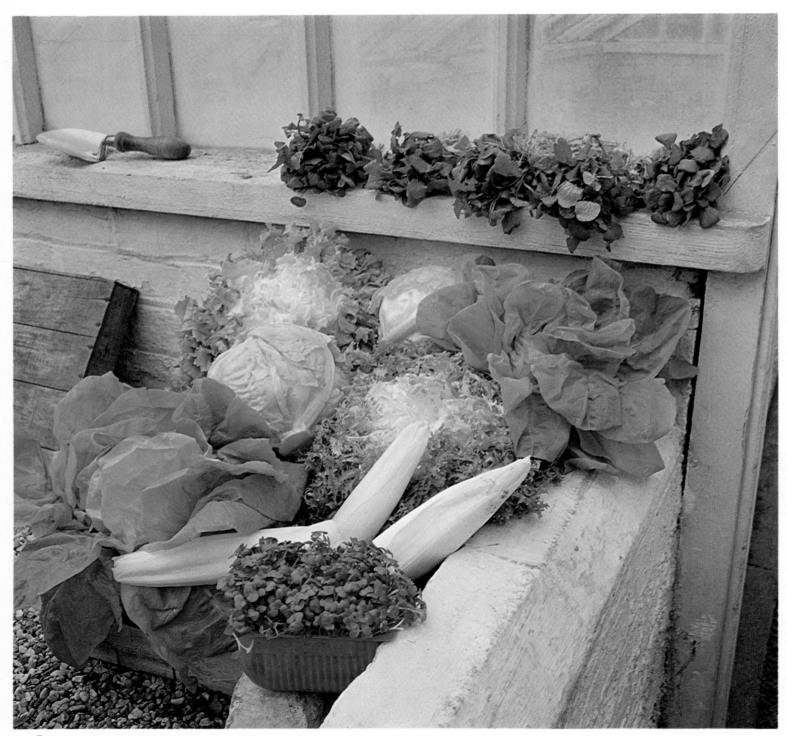

Almost all vegetables may be eaten raw, although most people prefer them cooked. With salad plants, however, the preference is reversed. Lettuce, Brussels chicory (endive) and chicory may indeed be cooked, but they then lose their greatest appeal—their cool, refreshing crispness. To enjoy salad plants at their best they must be home-grown, for they cannot stand up to the disturbances and delays of marketing. When planning your salad beds do not stick to only the ubiquitous lettuce. Grow Brussels chicory (endive) and chicory, too. American cress and corn salad are unusual and worthwhile salad plants, easy to grow and very nutritious.

1 Watercress
2 Chicory
3 Lettuce (crisp-hearted heading type)
4 Lettuce (soft, round heading type)
5 Brussels chicory (endive)
6 Mustard

*L*ettuce

The lettuce (*Lactuca sativa*) is firmly rooted in myth, even from the time of the immortals. Aphrodite laid Adonis, killed by the boar, on a bed of lettuce (not, of course, in the culinary sense). Some writers, from Pliny

in his *Natural History* to Beatrix Potter in *The Tale of the Flopsy Bunnies*, point to the soporific qualities of lettuce and others extol its health-giving properties. Even dragons, according to Aristotle, knew that its milky juice relieved the nausea that assailed them in the spring.

Suggestions about the origin of lettuce range from the Mediterranean to Siberia. It was being cultivated in England in the fourteenth century, but Catherine Parr, Henry VIII's sixth wife, preferred to send to Holland if she wanted a salad—as, in winter, the British still do. Today, it is feasible, however, to grow lettuce, outdoors in summer or under glass, all year around.

Varieties

For summer: Soft, round heading types: Tom Thumb, small, early maturing, for early sowing; unrivaled for sowing through spring and summer. Fordhook is especially good for June and July sowing. Buttercrunch is an All-America favorite for thick, crisp, tender leaves; good sown from April into August for successive crops.

Crisp-hearted type: Webb's Wonderful is very large—allow 18 inches (45 cm) between plants; stands summer heat well.

Cos types: Little Gem, early dwarf, excellent sweet flavor; plant 5 inches (13 cm) apart. Paris White has flavor like Brussels chicory.

Non-heading type: Salad Bowl, a loose-leaved variety; sow April to July and pick a few leaves from each plant as you want them.

For winter: Burpee's Greenhart.

For spring under glass: Grand Rapids Forcing, Washington and Domineer.

For spring in open: Imperial Winter and Arctic King.

GROWING LETTUCE

Preparing the soil

Ideally, lettuce needs a rich, humus-laden soil that will hold moisture in summer. It also needs lime (pH 6.5), so test the soil. Lettuce, however, is often grown between rows of slower-growing vegetables or as a catch crop, using ground before or after another crop.

Sowing and transplanting

Lettuce can be sown in seed boxes or beds and the seedlings transplanted about a month later when they are not more than 1 inch (2 cm) high. Handle them with the utmost tenderness, for a damaged seedling is particularly menaced by gray mold. In spring and summer, you can sow lettuce in

½-inch (1 cm) drills in the open and thin the plants by stages until they are finally 10 to 12 inches (25 to 30 cm) apart, depending on the variety and the soil and weather you are blessed with. To ensure a steady supply of lettuce and to avoid a glut, sow little and often.

Lettuce seed needs a cool temperature to germinate well. In Southern states, home gardeners may have trouble growing lettuce during warm summer months. To minimize difficulties, gardeners in the South should select varieties listed as heat-resistant. To further ensure that seed germinates well during warm weather, give it a cold treatment in the refrigerator. Mix seed with moist peat moss and perlite, keep in refrigerator for five days, then plant in the garden.

New hybrids

Among the best varieties for home gardens are hybrids bred for heat tolerance and slow bolting (seeding). Buttercrunch is an outstanding All-America winner, much better than similar Bibb lettuce. Burpee's Dark

Green Oak Leaf is another heat-resistant salad type that remains succulent and sweet even during summer heat. Indoors under lights or in a sunny window, for wintertime salads, select a dwarf variety. Tom Thumb

produces compact, well-folded heads, medium green on the outside, creamy white inside.

The year's work

Winter lettuce: Sow Burpee's Greenhart or Deci-Minor (Boston type) in a frame from early September. Transplant the seedlings to the greenhouse; the temperature must not fall below 50°F (10°C). Plant the seedlings in rows 6 inches (15 cm) apart, staggering them at 16-inch (40 cm) intervals. Keep the plants moist and well ventilated. The lettuces should be ready to harvest about three months after transplanting.

Summer lettuce: In warmer areas begin sowing in March, elsewhere in April, and continue every two or three weeks until July. Allow about 10 inches (25 cm) between the transplanted or thinned plants in the row. The rows must be 12 inches (30 cm) apart.

Harvesting

Pull the lettuces out with the roots. Never let the plants go to seed in the rows. Remove them as soon as they begin to bolt.

Pests and diseases

Millipedes attack the roots of young plants, which then wilt. The best way to trap millipedes is to punch holes in the bottoms and sides of old tin cans and fit them with wire handles. Fill the cans with potato peelings and bury them upright alongside the lettuces, leaving the handles above the ground. Lift up the cans every few days and destroy the contents. Millipedes, which curl up when they are disturbed, are sluggish vegetarians and are not

to be confused with the livelier carnivorous centipedes, which are good to have around.

Slugs are a menace. Use methiocarb or metaldehyde baits to destroy them.

To prevent gray mold on stems and leaves, which indicates an attack by the fungus botrytis, spray with thiram.

Whitish powder on the underside of the leaves is the downy mildew fungus. Spray with thiram.

Chicory

Chicory (*Cichorium intybus*) is one of the simplest salad plants to grow, as well as one of the most desirable. It is neither the root nor the leaves which are eaten, but the blanched chicons, which are produced by forcing the roots in darkness and warmth.

Varieties

Witloof (Brussels chicory or endive) is the one to grow for the chicons. There is another variety, Sugarhat, which, like lettuce, does not require blanching. Sow Sugarhat from April to July. Thin the plants to 15 inches (38 cm) apart.

Curly Chicory

The origin of chicory (*Cichorium endivia*) is highly disputed. In American markets it is often sold as chicory, yet seed catalogs list it as endive. Full Heart Batavian is a type called escarole! Whatever the name, the greens are delightful in salads.

Varieties

Green Curled has curly, crisp leaves. Florida Deep Heart and Broad Leaved Batavian have thicker heart; large, broad, slightly curled leaves. Salad King tolerates heat.

GROWING BRUSSELS CHICORY (ENDIVE)

Preparing the soil

Choose a part of the garden well manured and cultivated for a previous crop, such as leeks or celery, since newly manured land can cause forking of the roots.

Sowing

Sow the seeds early in May in the North and in mid-April in the South. With earlier sowing, the plants may run to seed in the warm weather. Sow in ½-inch (1 cm) drills 12 inches (30 cm) apart, and thin the seedlings to 10 inches (25 cm) apart.

The year's work

Hoe to kill weeds, and water in dry weather. A mulch will help to keep the soil moist and to suppress weeds.

Harvesting

October/November. To begin, carefully dig up a few roots for forcing. Cut off the tops just above the crown. Plant the roots close together in a box of loamy soil with the

crowns of the roots at soil level. Water and cover with another box. The chicons must

grow in total darkness if they are not to be bitter. Place the box in a greenhouse or even in a kitchen cupboard where the temperature is not less than 50°F (10°C). In four weeks or so the chicons will be about 6 to 8 inches (15 to 20 cm) long and ready for harvesting. If you break the chicons off carefully, instead of cutting them, a second crop of chicons will appear, smaller and looser, but just as tasty.

In November, when the foliage of the remaining plants has died back, dig up the roots and trim and store them in sand in a cool but frostproof room. Remove and force as many as you want every three or four weeks. Never pick the chicons until you need them. After even an hour in the light they will become limp.

Pests and diseases

Fairly trouble free.

GROWING CURLY CHICORY

Preparing the soil

Like most salad vegetables, endive needs a soil rich in humus that will not dry out easily. In a hot summer, chicory soon runs to seed, so plant it in a slightly shaded spot in the garden and do not sow too early.

Sowing

From mid-April. It is best not to transplant endive, so, having got the soil to a fine tilth, sow the seed of the curled varieties thinly in ½-inch (1 cm) drills 14 inches (35 cm) apart. Thin the plants to 12 inches (30 cm) apart. Another sowing can be made three weeks later, and yet another sowing—of the hardier Batavian type—on July 1.

The year's work

Hoe between the rows and keep the soil moist, occasionally using weak liquid manure. In October, put the late-sown plants under cloches so that you will have chicory until the end of the year.

Harvesting

About 90 days after sowing. Curly chicory is bitter if it is not blanched. Begin blanching three to four months after sowing. Put a large flowerpot (with the hole covered) over the plant, or replant the chicory in moist soil in a pot or box and put it in a dark cellar or shed. In three weeks or more it will be creamy-colored and crisp, the bitterness gone. Whichever way you blanch, the leaves must be dry when you begin or they will rot. To blanch Batavian, tie the leaves together lightly. This prevents the light reaching the inner leaves.

Pests and diseases

Fairly trouble free.

Mustard and Cress

Man was eating mustard (*Sinapis alba* and *Brassica nigra*) seeds before 10,000 B.C. Cress (*Lepidium sativum*) has the pepperwort as its ancestor and the Romans among its devotees. Tendergreen mustard (below, left) is good in salads.

GROWING MUSTARD AND CRESS

In winter, sow cress indoors. Fill a small box with moist soil or peat-lite mix and scatter the seeds over the soil. Press the seeds down with your hand. Cover the box with paper until the seeds germinate.

Mustard germinates faster than cress. Sow it in the same way four days later, either over the cress or in a separate box.

Sow about every two weeks and cut with scissors 15 to 20 days later.

From spring to September sow out of doors in exactly the same way.

American Cress

Similar in flavor but easier to grow than watercress, American cress (*Barbarea praecox*) also needs shade and tolerates considerable dampness—a welcome change from most garden plants.

GROWING AMERICAN CRESS

Fork plenty of organic material lightly into the soil. Firm the soil and rake it to a fine tilth. Sow the seeds every three weeks from April to August. Sow thinly in ½-inch (1 cm) drills 10 inches (25 cm) apart. Germination takes about three weeks. When the plants are big enough to handle, thin them to 6 inches (15 cm) apart.

Cut the cress eight to ten weeks after sowing. Cut only the young, tender shoots. To prolong the crop into winter, cover the late-sown rows with cloches.

Corn Salad

Corn salad (*Valerianella locusta*), also known as lamb's-lettuce, is an ideal winter substitute for lettuce. Verte de Cambrai is a frost-resistant type.

GROWING CORN SALAD

Plant corn salad in a sunny, humus-rich plot which has been used for a previous crop. Fork the soil over lightly, firm it and rake it to a fine tilth.

Sow the plants in late spring and mid-September in drills 1 inch (2 cm) deep and 10 inches (25 cm) apart. Thin the seedlings at the three-leaf stage to 6 inches (15 cm) apart. Use cloches or straw to protect the plants in winter.

Harvest a leaf or two from each mature plant as you need them.

Dandelion

The dandelion (*Taraxacum officinale*) is almost universally regarded as an intolerable weed. Not so on the European continent, where excellent strains of dandelion have been cultivated.

GROWING DANDELIONS

Dandelions will grow in any well-drained corner of the garden. For succulence, however, give them rich soil. Sow in April in shallow drills 12 inches (30 cm) apart. Thin the plants to 8 inches (20 cm) apart. Later, when the plants mature, be sure to cut off all the flower heads. Harvest in November. Carefully lift the roots, trim them and blanch a few of them as you would chicory. They will be ready in two weeks if kept in a temperature of about 60°F (16°C). Store the remaining roots in sand until you are ready to blanch them.

Watercress

Although watercress (*Nasturtium officinale*) is an aquatic plant, you can grow it without running water. It is a good way to make use of a dank, shady part of the garden.

GROWING WATERCRESS

Dig a trench 24 inches (60 cm) wide and 12 inches (30 cm) deep. At the bottom put 6 inches (15 cm) of decayed manure covered by 3 inches (8 cm) of soil. Make it firm and wet it well. Plant in early summer. Buy a bunch or two of healthy-looking watercress and plant those cuttings which have small roots on them. Set them 4 inches (10 cm) apart each way. Water assiduously. As they grow, pinch out the leading shoots to make them bushy. Cut them right back if they start to flower. Watercress can also be raised from seed sown in spring.

Celtuce

Celtuce (*Lactuca sativa*, var. *angustana*) is a lettuce on a stem. It comes from America, but now is grown in Asia and Europe too. The leaves and the stem, or heart, may be eaten.

GROWING CELTUCE

Celtuce requires a soil that has had plenty of organic manure forked in. Firm the soil and then rake it. Sow from spring to early July at two-week intervals in shallow drills 18 inches (45 cm) apart. Thin the seedlings, when they are 2 inches (5 cm) high, to 12 inches (30 cm) apart. Water the plants well. They will be tough if kept short of water. Hoe well between the rows to keep them free of weeds. Harvest the leaves as they form. The stems will be ready to eat in less than three months from sowing.

Brassicas

Brassicas are the backbone of many vegetable gardens. Three of them—Brussels sprouts, kale and cabbage—might indeed have been created for the climate of temperate North America, although in fact they are immigrants, not natives. These three need plenty of rain and they can brave Northern winters.

Do not be alarmed by the seemingly fearsome pests and diseases which attack brassicas, for they are most likely to bring disaster to undernourished plants struggling to survive in poor soil. The remedy is in the gardener's hands. Economies should not be made where the fertility of the soil is at stake. All the brassicas, even kale, hardiest of them all, appreciate a rich, fertile soil which has been well manured for a previous crop.

Adaptable F_1 hybrid Brussels sprouts produce abundant crops in 90 to 160 days. In states where winter temperatures stay above 20°F (7°C) mature plants can be protected with Hotkaps or A-frames to keep off frost and sprouts are then harvested through the winter.

The cabbage, the chief of the brassica tribe, is still suffering unfairly from its past reputation. Older generations find it hard to forget the evil smell and unpleasant taste of the winter cabbages, savoys and tough spring greens of their childhoods. But the improvement in cabbage over the past two decades has been even more remarkable than in Brussels sprouts. Newer varieties are more subtle in flavor. It is a pleasant change to be able to turn what is usually a complaint into a compliment by saying that the taste is better because there is less of it. Nevertheless, those who still find cabbage overpowering should grow the milder Chinese cabbage.

The cauliflower did not always have its present appearance. When it was first cultivated in Britain more than two centuries ago, its head, when full grown, was no bigger than a golf ball. The modern, improved cauliflower, the real favorite among brassicas, is the result of much painstaking work over the years. The cauliflower does not, however, take kindly to Northern climates. The alternative is sprouting broccoli: the white and purple varieties are harvested in winter and spring, and the delectable green sprouting broccoli is harvested in late summer and autumn. The real cauliflower enthusiast might like to grow star broccoli. Although perennial, it is best to replace the plants every three years. Cultivated in the same way as other sprouting broccoli, each plant will produce six to twelve cauliflowers a year, if generously fed.

1 *Purple sprouting*
  broccoli
2 *Chinese cabbage*
3 *Red cabbage*
4 *Curly kale*
5 *Cauliflowers*
6 *Winter cabbage*
7 *Brussels sprouts*
8 *Savoy cabbage*

BRASSICAS
Preparing the soil

The normal three-year rotation of crops in the vegetable garden (see pages 20 and 21) ensures that brassicas are planted where peas and beans grew the previous year. If, as the rotation plan provides, the bed was well manured for the peas and beans, no further manure or compost is needed for the brassicas. The peas and beans will, indeed, have left behind in their roots some of the nitrogen they themselves produced. However, a balanced vegetable fertilizer, 2 ounces to the square yard (60 g to 1 sq m), can be hoed in before transplanting.

If the cabbage patch was not manured for a previous crop, manure and compost will have to be provided. Brassicas must be fed well. Brussels sprouts need more feeding than cabbages, and cauliflowers are positively greedy. At the same time, they must not be given too much nitrogen, which makes them flabby.

Brassicas—especially Brussels sprouts and cauliflowers—need a firm soil, so the plot should be dug months in advance, giving the soil time to settle.

Lime is important. An acid soil discourages growth and encourages that scourge of brassicas, club root—aim at pH 6.5 to 6.8. It is also for the same reason—to keep club root at bay—that brassicas are not grown on the same piece of land more than one year in three. Land heavily infected by club root must not be planted with brassicas for seven years. (See page 55.)

Seedbeds for brassicas

Brassicas are usually raised in outdoor seedbeds and transplanted. The only exceptions are certain varieties of kale. A highly fertile soil is required to give the plants a good start in life. The ideal would be to cover the bed, after leveling and raking it, with thoroughly mature, sifted compost. Tread over this to make it firm and rake it lightly. Make shallow drills with a stick, 6 inches (15 cm) apart, and sow the

seeds thinly. Cover them with a scattering of compost and firm the bed with the head of the rake. This is a better method than

tramping over the bed and then having to rake lightly again. Always mark both ends

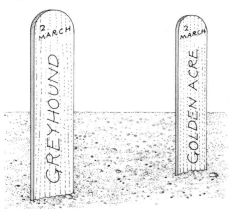

of the rows. Do not use empty seed packets on a piece of stick; they will probably disappear even before the seeds have germinated. Buy wooden labels or collect popsicle sticks and, with an indelible pencil, write on them the name of the variety and the date of sowing. Keep the seedbed moist, using a watering can with a fine rose.

The stage at which cabbage and Brussels sprouts should be transplanted is comparatively flexible. The sooner cauliflowers are in their permanent beds, however, the better. Water the seedbed well the day before you intend to transplant.

Transplanting

If practicable the rows should run north to south to get all possible sun. Mark out the rows with string for a straight line. With a dibble or trowel make holes ready to receive the plants, and if the soil is dry fill the holes with water. If you can arrange it, wait until late in the day to do the transplanting, especially on sunny days, to

minimize the plants' suffering; for them it is a major operation.

Lift the plants from the seedbed with as much soil as you can. Handle only a dozen plants at a time so as not to keep them out

of the ground too long. Lower each plant into its hole. With cabbages, the leaves at the base of the stem go down to soil level. Cauliflowers, however, must not be planted

any deeper than they were in the seedbed. Push the dibble or trowel into the soil alongside the plant—about 1 inch (2 cm) away—and press against it to make the soil firm. Or firm the soil around the plant with your hands, the dibble or the handle of the trowel. Brassicas must be planted firmly. Water seedlings with Transplantone or Ortho Up-Start solution. In a

few days the plants should perk up.

Planting distances and the year's work are dealt with under each type of brassica.

Cabbage

In childhood, cabbage (*Brassica oleracea*, var. *capitata*) was something that one was always being told to eat up. Nothing changes. The Emperor Tiberius reprimanded his son Drusus for not eating his greens.

The Greeks looked upon cabbage both as a means of preventing drunkenness and as a cure for a hangover. The Romans thought highly of it as a medicine, although they did not know that it is, indeed, rich in sulfur and nitrogen. Cabbage seems to go back in prehistory to the eastern Mediterranean and Asia Minor. The Romans brought it northward, and in Britain in the Middle Ages monks were growing it in their kitchen gardens. The earliest cabbages were non-heading. Headed varieties turned up in the thirteenth century, hard, round-headed types in the sixteenth century and pointed heads in the eighteenth century. Although cabbage is too often badly cooked, it is an indispensable vegetable.

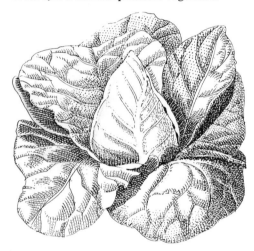

Early varieties

For spring sowing: Golden Acre, early maturing, medium-sized solid heads. Greyhound, firm, pointed hearts with few outside leaves, or the newer Greyhound-type F$_1$ hybrid, Hispi. Savoy Ace is a crumpled-leaf All-America winner, excellent.

Midseason varieties

To sow in early summer: Perfection Drumhead.

Savoys (*Brassica oleracea*, var. *bullata subauda*): Best of All or All-America winner Savoy Ace hybrid.

Late fall to winter varieties

To sow in midsummer: Burpee's Surehead is a large cabbage with a 93-day growing season. Savoy Ace matures in about 75 days and thus will also crop quickly enough. Ruby Ball hybrid is another All-America selection which matures in 68 days, good in salads or cooked.

The year's work

Cabbage is a cool-weather crop, best for winter in the South and for a spring or fall crop in the North. Check the seed catalogs for the best type in your area. Sow seed indoors in early March or outside after frost. Thin the seedlings carefully to 1 inch (2 cm) apart when they are large enough to handle. They are ready to leave the seedbed in May or early June, when the plants are about 4 inches (10 cm) in height. If necessary they could stay longer in the seedbed, but later transplanting sets them back. Plant 18 inches (45 cm) apart in rows also 18 inches (45 cm) apart.

Hoe, but carefully, since cabbages hate disturbance. When they have grown large enough, the plants themselves will smother the weeds. Never let them get dry.

The year's work

Sow the seeds out of doors in shallow drills in late April or May for autumn and winter cabbages. Use a watering can with a fine rose and water the seedbed well. In July, plant out the seedlings 18 inches (45 cm) apart in rows 24 inches (60 cm) apart.

Firm the plants well with your hands or the dibble. Water them thoroughly but gently or, if the weather is very dry, fill the dibble holes with water before planting. Hoe lightly between the rows to keep down the weeds, being careful not to damage the young plants.

Savoys are sown in May and planted out in July or early August, 24 inches (60 cm) apart each way.

The midseason cabbages will be ready for harvesting from August. The winter varieties will be ready for harvesting from late October or November.

The year's work

Because late-season cabbages mature quickly they never grow as large or as coarse as early cabbages. Plant them in a sheltered part of the garden which had been well manured for a previous crop.

Sow the seeds thinly (in cold areas in July, in warm areas early in August) in shallow drills 6 inches (15 cm) apart. Keep the seedbed moist.

Transplant the seedlings into moist soil in September 12 to 16 inches (30 to 40 cm) apart in rows 18 inches (45 cm) apart.

For a month after planting out, hoe shallowly between the rows. When growth begins, hoe in a high-nitrogen fertilizer.

Chinese Cabbage

Chinese cabbage (*Brassica pekinensis*) does not look like cabbage—it suggests rather an aristocratic Cos lettuce—and, praise be, it

does not smell like cabbage when it is cooking. Chinese cabbage has been known in China and parts of Asia since the fifth century. Europe had to wait until the middle of the nineteenth century for it to arrive and only now is it becoming appreciated for its delicate flavor, either cooked or raw in salads. Chinese cabbage is easy to grow as long as it is not sown too early (it will bolt) and is not transplanted.

Confusingly, there is another vegetable claiming the names of "cabbage" and "Chinese"—*Brassica chinensis*—but it is encountered more frequently in Chinese restaurants than in Western gardens. It does not heart, but grows like spinach, for which it can be regarded as a hardy substitute.

Varieties

Michihli, a large, tall head. Nagaoka (F_1), solid and cylindrical. Springtime, good for June sowing, July–August harvest.

GROWING CHINESE CABBAGE

Preparing the soil

Unless it has a humus-laden, moisture-holding soil and a little bit of shade, Chinese cabbage is liable to bolt in high summer.

Sowing

Late June to July. Because it quickly goes to seed after hearting up, sow a little and often. The seeds are quite large and are planted 4 inches (10 cm) apart in ½-inch (1 cm) drills with 12 to 18 inches (30 to 45 cm) between rows. Thin to 8 inches (20 cm) apart.

The year's work

Never let Chinese cabbage go short of water. When they begin hearting, tie the leaves together with raffia.

Harvesting

Chinese cabbages grow quickly and may be ready only nine weeks after sowing. Pick

Red Cabbage

Of all the cabbages the red cabbage is the difficult one. To be at its best it needs a long growing season, which involves overwintering.

Varieties

Red Head is magenta-red, delicious cooked. Meteor is earlier, has good color.

GROWING RED CABBAGE

The year's work

Sow the seeds in August or early September in a well-firmed and lightly raked seedbed or frame in shallow drills 6 inches (15 cm) apart. Thin the seedlings in the seedbed.

A general fertilizer can be hoed in along the row before planting—2 ounces to the square yard (60 g to 1 sq m). When the seedlings are about 4 inches (10 cm) high, plant them out 24 inches (60 cm) apart each way. Plant firmly or they will not grow large, solid heads.

In May, a handful of sulfate of ammonia can be scattered around each plant to encourage it for harvesting in the autumn.

them, either as a salad vegetable or to cook, as soon as they are well hearted. Once they bolt they are useless except, of course, for compost.

Brussels Sprouts

Belgium can lay greater claim to Brussels sprouts (*Brassica oleracea*, var. *bullata gemmifera*) than any other country. The Belgians

seem to think they got them from the Romans, although the sprouts mentioned by Pliny may have been broccoli. It can, however, be reasonably assumed that Brussels sprouts have been growing in Belgium for eight centuries. Properly grown (solid), picked at the right moment (when small) and correctly cooked (not overcooked), Brussels sprouts are one of the great garden vegetables of autumn and winter.

Varieties

Many of the older favorites have been superseded by F_1 hybrids. Since more, and sometimes better, hybrids appear each year it is sensible to try new varieties from time to time.

Current F_1 hybrids include: Jade Cross, early, dark green, of excellent flavor. Peer Gynt, fairly dwarf, with medium-sized buttons. Early Dwarf Danish, offered by Johnny's Selected Seeds, matures before other types in Northern areas. Focus F_1 hybrid, imported by Thompson & Morgan, keeps a long while on the stalk while retaining excellent flavor and small size.

GROWING BRUSSELS SPROUTS
Preparing the soil

While Brussels sprouts must have a fertile soil, it is better if the soil has been well manured for a previous crop. Above all, if

they are to produce the desired solid buttons, Brussels sprouts need a firm soil in which to anchor themselves. A fairly heavy soil works for the gardener here. A light, sandy soil will make it difficult to get the vital firmness.

Dig as far ahead as possible to let the soil settle.

Do not forget that Brussels sprouts have the brassicas' need for lime (pH 6.5 to 6.8).

Sowing

February, March/April. Brussels sprouts have a long growing season and need to be sown earlier than cabbage. Start in February in a frame, or out of doors mid-March to April in the kind of seedbed suggested for brassicas generally. (See page 48.) Sow in drills $\frac{1}{2}$ inch (1 cm) deep and 10 inches (25 cm) apart.

Brussels sprouts are a cool-climate crop and therefore grow poorly in summer for Southern and Midwestern gardens. However, in these sections, seed planted in August will usually produce a satisfactory harvest from late fall into winter.

Planting

May/June. As early as the weather allows, or late summer in Midwest and South.

Choose a wet day and, if possible, plant in the evening to help the seedlings make a quick recovery. Firm the soil around each plant with your hands or with a dibble. Firm planting helps to produce tight, firm sprouts.

Planting distances vary with the size and vigor of the variety—24 to 36 inches (60 to 90 cm) each way. Do not skimp on space —for their sakes and for yours when you come to pick among them on cold, wet fall days. The space is not wasted because, while the sprout plants are still small, quick-growing crops can be planted between the rows.

The year's work

Hoe and water if necessary. Brussels sprouts should not be pushed ahead with nitrogenous fertilizers; they have to grow hard to face the cool weather. In autumn, go

along the rows taking off yellowing leaves, firming the soil around the stem of each plant and drawing more soil around it to give support against the wind. Tall-growing varieties should be staked; it is disheartening to see a row flattened in a strong wind.

When the lower sprouts start to reach harvestable size pinch out the growing top from each plant. This causes all sprouts along the stalk to develop faster, thus as-

suring a crop before killing frosts. Where winters are mild leave the growing tops so that your harvest is spread over many weeks. In country gardens where birds and deer may raid sprouts, erect a simple wire hood over the stalks. Stakes holding the wire will also help to support the stalks.

Harvesting

September to March. Pick the sprouts from the bottom of the stem as they get big enough. They can (lazily) be snapped off, but cutting causes less damage.

Cauliflower

To the gardener, cauliflowers (*Brassica oleracea*, var. *botrytis cauliflora*) and heading broccoli are the same thing, but heading broccoli and sprouting broccoli are two different things altogether. The confusion is less if they are divided into summer cauliflowers, winter cauliflowers (which are heading broccoli) and sprouting broccoli (which is primarily grown for its sprouts and not for any head it may form). The sprouting broccoli is easy to

grow, summer cauliflowers less so, being not only greedy, but often temperamental, and winter cauliflowers are best forgotten in the colder parts of the country. On the other hand, producing a cauliflower with a flawless white curd is one of the really satisfying achievements of amateur vegetable growing.

The cauliflower is another brassica of antiquity, with a history going back thousands of years in Syria, Turkey and Egypt. It was introduced into Spain in the twelfth century, and appeared in England and France around the end of the sixteenth century.

It is an immensely popular vegetable—hence all the trouble taken to have it on sale all year around. There are, however, critics. Mark Twain dubbed it "a cabbage with a college education," and that most respected of English cookery writers Elizabeth David damns it for its "normal coarse flavor and soggy texture" and consigns it to soup.

Cauliflower devotees with a greenhouse and a warm garden can have summer cauliflowers from May to November, followed by winter cauliflowers from January to May. Gardeners laboring in a cold climate can gamble on an unusually mild winter, or grow sprouting broccoli instead.

Varieties

Summer cauliflowers to harvest in June/July: All the Year Round. Snowball. Burpeeana.

GROWING CAULIFLOWER
The year's work

Start in a cold frame or under lights 4 to 6 weeks before last killing frost. Sow the seeds thinly in a moist, firm seedbed. As soon as the first leaves are formed, transplant the

seedlings to a frame. Plant them 1 inch (2 cm) apart. Harden off for planting out mid-April to May.

Cauliflowers, if they are to produce large, compact heads, must be planted in humus-rich soil. Shortly before transplanting, hoe in a general fertilizer, 2 ounces to the square yard (60 g to 1 sq m). Cauliflowers, like all brassicas, require lime (pH 6.5 to 6.8). Lift the seedlings from the seedbed with as much soil as possible and plant them 24 inches (60 cm) apart, with the same distance between rows.

Reject all "blind" seedlings—those which have produced nothing more than the two seed leaves. It is pointless to plant them—they are barren.

Cauliflowers are fussy about being transplanted and if not handled with care produce small, premature buttons in lieu of heads. They should be replanted as quickly as possible and no deeper than they were in the frame. Their roots must be made firm if they are to make firm heads,

and they must be watered. As they grow they must never be short of moisture.

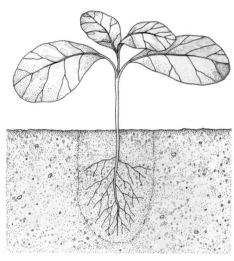

When the curds form, bend or tie a few leaves over them to protect them from the

sun. If too many cauliflowers are ready for harvesting at the same time do not leave them in the garden to bolt. Lift them with their roots, shake off the excess soil and hang them upside down indoors in a cool place and spray them regularly with water.

For direct sowing, Tropical Snow, a quick-maturing type, is useful to plant after harvesting early crops. Snow King is also an excellent quick grower, resistant to summer heat.

Autumn Cauliflower

Autumn cauliflowers to harvest from August to November: All the Year Round (August/September heading). Self-Blanche, developed at Michigan State, needs no tying to blanch heads if plants mature during cool weather. Dominant, a Danish hybrid, tolerant of dry summers, matures in 90 days from spring sowings or in about 70 days from summer sowings.

The year's work

No sowings should be made out of doors until the pleasanter days of April. Sow the seeds in brassica-type seedbeds (see page 48) in shallow drills 6 inches (15 cm) apart. Cover them with a sifting of compost and firm the bed. If the weather is dry, keep the seedbed moist, using a watering can with a fine rose. Transplant the seedlings in late June to July—they must not be planted any deeper than they were in the seedbed—spacing the young plants 24 to 30 inches (60 to 75 cm) apart each way.

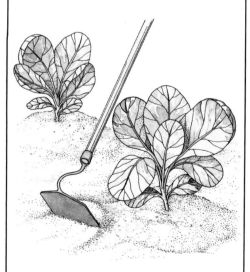

In late summer it is a sensible precaution to draw soil around the stems of the cauliflowers for support; like other brassicas they resent being rocked in the wind.

Winter Cauliflower

In the South and other areas with mild winters, fall to early-spring sowings are useful. Igloo is a compact type with heavy foliage which protects heads from frost. Newton Seale, a British hybrid, is frost tolerant, develops in 90 to 100 days.

The year's work

Sow seeds from mid-April to mid-May, according to package notes. Transplant 24 inches (60 cm) apart each way. Water in dry weather and add a mulch of compost.

To help prevent winter cauliflowers from being killed by severe frost, heel them over before November so that they spend the winter facing north. (It is the sudden thawing of the frozen plant by direct sunlight which does the damage. If it faces north the plant thaws out gradually.)

To heel a plant over, move some soil away from the plant on its north side with a trowel. Push the plant over, carefully, and draw soil against its stem on the opposite side to hold it down, facing north. Firm the soil. As curds develop, break some leaves over them to protect them.

Soil deficiencies and how they affect cauliflowers

The importance of the elements in the soil to the proper growth of a plant cannot be overemphasized, and few vegetables demonstrate more vividly than cauliflowers when they are short of either major or trace elements.

A deficiency of the trace element molybdenum causes an extraordinary malformation of the leaves called whiptail. It is most likely to occur on acid soils in dry weather. The plant may go blind (that is, lose its growing points) and the curds may be nonexistent or minute. A couple of ounces of ammonium molybdate to the acre (60 g to ½ ha) would probably remedy the deficiency if such a small dressing were practicable. Instead, to make the molybdenum in the soil available to the plant, apply lime to bring the soil near to pH 7, which is approaching a neutral—neither acid nor alkaline—soil.

Boron is another vital trace element. Lacking it, cauliflowers grow small curds which are bitter, and both curd and flower stems turn brown. Boron deficiency can be corrected by watering the soil with a borax solution, using the finest of roses on the watering can. Use ½ ounce (15 g) of borax in ½ gallon (2 liters) of water to treat 30 square yards (25 sq m). Too much borax can make the soil toxic. There are other reasons for the browning of cauliflowers, especially winter cauliflowers; they are currently the subject of an extensive research study.

Starved of magnesium, the leaves of cauliflowers turn yellow, red or purple in patches (magnesium, one of the vital elements in the soil, is necessary to produce chlorophyll, the substance which makes plants green). Growth is poor and the plants become more liable to downy mildew. Signs of magnesium deficiency are frequently seen in highly cultivated gardens. It is not that magnesium is missing from the soil, but it has been made unavailable to the plant because other elements have been thrown out of balance. This may be the gardener's fault in applying inorganic fertilizers containing too much potash over a period of years. By using farmyard manure, or compost, or digging in green manure, that particular trouble can be avoided.

A potassium deficiency, causing yellowing of cauliflowers and poor curds, can follow heavy-handed nitrogenous manuring, throwing the nitrogen/potassium ratio in the soil out of balance.

These problems must not be regarded as diseases of cauliflowers, which are subject to enough already. They are mineral deficiencies which will affect many plants, although not always as spectacularly.

Broccoli

It would be an extravagance bordering on the criminal to buy frozen broccoli spears when broccoli (*Brassica oleracea*, var. *italica*) is so easy to grow. Unfortunately, it is not as hardy as purple or white sprouting broccoli; its

season will generally be over by October.

After the main cauliflowerlike head has been cut, numerous side shoots sprout and grow smaller heads. These spears are superior in flavor to the first head.

Varieties

Premium Crop is a fine All-America winner. Green Comet (F_1) matures 55 days after transplanting, concentrates on a larger head and few side shoots. Italian Sprouting has particularly good flavor.

Purple Sprouting Broccoli

The sprouting broccolis (*Brassica oleracea*, var. *botrytis cymosa*) are among the most satisfying vegetables to grow because the home-grown shoots are so much better in flavor than those grown commercially.

The flavor of green or purple sprouting broccoli is similar to cauliflower. The vege-

table turns a light-green color when cooked. White sprouting broccoli is often grown in Europe but is difficult to find in U.S. seed catalogs.

Varieties

These strains are sometimes listed under Cauliflower in catalogs and culture is the same. Christmas Purple Sprouting, planted in midsummer, will furnish sprouts into late winter. Purple Head is like true solid cauliflower. Royal Purple resembles a fine-budded broccoli.

Kale

Kale (*Brassica oleracea*, var. *acephala*) is a cabbage without a solid heart or head. It is either flat-leaved or curly-leaved. Healthy, health-giving and hardy beyond belief, kale would be the ideal winter green if only its

flavor matched its other qualities. In the first millennium A.D. it was the staple of the peasants' diet in northern Europe. In Holland, its name is *boerenkool* (peasants' cabbage). In Scotland, *kail* soup is a traditional Highland dish.

Varieties

Blue Curled Scotch is compact, bluish-green. Vates is an adaptable cold-hardy type with very curled blue-green foliage. Colored-leaf ornamental kale can also be eaten.

GROWING BROCCOLI
Sowing
April. Broccoli needs the same kind of good, firm soil as other brassicas. Sow in the seedbed in early April, thinning the seedlings as soon as possible. Never allow them to get crowded before transplanting.

Planting
May. When the seedlings are 3 inches (8 cm) high they are ready for planting out, 20 inches (50 cm) apart in rows 24 inches (60 cm) apart. Plant firmly. Plant out on a showery day and, if necessary, continue watering until the plants have settled down.

The year's work
In the short growing season keep the plants moist and weed free.

Harvesting
July/September. Cut the center head before it flowers. Afterward spread a handful of general fertilizer around the plant. Side shoots begin to appear a couple of weeks later. Harvest the side shoots with 4 to 6 inches (10 to 15 cm) of stem.

GROWING BROCCOLI
Sowing
April. Sow thinly in April in the previously prepared seedbed. (See page 48.)

Planting
May. When the seedlings are 4 inches (10 cm) high they can be transplanted. Leave 24 inches (60 cm) between plants and 30 inches (75 cm) between rows. Plant firmly, and water well if the weather is dry at planting time.

The year's work
It saves a lot of weeding time if a mulch is put down between the rows in summer. Give a strawy mulch in winter. Stake firmly against strong winds.

Harvesting
Pick sprouts when they are young and tender, cutting the center head first, usually ready about 95 days after seedlings are planted out. Cut off the side shoots while they are young since constant cutting makes the plant produce more shoots.

GROWING KALE
The year's work
Kale, like all the cabbage family, requires a soil that has been well manured for a previous crop. It must not lack lime since a pH of 6.5 to 6.8 is required for optimum growth.

Sow the curly-leaved types thinly in a seedbed as soon as the ground can be worked. Transplant when danger of frost is past into rows 18 inches (45 cm) apart each way. The plain-leaved types do best if not transplanted. Sow these directly in the ground in early spring. All types of kale are quite cold-hardy and can be sown directly where they are to grow once the ground can be worked. A second sowing in late summer will provide plants for winter harvest. Into Zone 6, kale will often endure frost and if lightly protected will even furnish winter greens as far north as New York.

Harvesting
The flavor of kale improves with cold weather. Many gardeners do not pick the leaves until a frost has occurred, but leaves are more tender when young.

Brassica pests and diseases

The brassicas, apart from some of the stalwart kales, are at risk from more unpleasant pests and diseases than any other common vegetable. It is comparatively easy to cope with birds and slugs, more tiresome to combat cabbage butterflies and moths, and difficult to tackle cabbage root fly. But the real bogy is club root.

Confronted with a heavy infestation of club root, both cabbage and gardener are fairly helpless. The fungus is *Plasmodiophora brassicae*, and in an infected garden thousands of millions of its minute spores can inhabit one square yard. When a spore germinates, triggered off by the presence of a cabbage, it develops a tail which enables it to move toward the root of the plant. It enters the root, loses its tail and produces different spores, causing swelling in the root which then degenerates into a slimy, stinking mess. From this, millions more spores go into the soil to infect other brassica roots. The spores may infect the soil for up to twenty years. So far not enough has been discovered about club root, although it has been around for centuries, to effect a certain cure. It often, but not always, greatly helps if the soil is adequately limed; overliming, however, will lock up essential minerals in the soil, making them unavailable to plants. Growing brassicas in different parts of the garden also helps; but the dormant spores can survive far longer than the usual three-year rotation. Dipping seedlings in Terraclor solution during transplanting is some help in control of club root.

In spite of these depressing facts, there are some useful things an amateur gardener can do:

(1) Raise your own plants from seed or buy them from nurseries, which by law must not grow seedlings on infected land.

(2) See that the brassica patch is not acid, is rich in humus and properly drained. A healthy plant has the best chance of defeating the fungus.

(3) Dig up the stumps as you cut cabbages and finish picking Brussels sprouts. Do not leave them in the ground all winter. Burn all infected roots.

Of course, innumerable gardens never suffer club root. And a swollen root does not always mean the fungus has struck. Slice open the swelling. If there is a maggot inside, the gall weevil is the enemy and you can breathe again (after destroying it).

Protect the seedlings from birds with fine nylon netting supported on sticks. This does not harm the birds as cotton can, but it scares the wits out of them.

Large and Small Cabbage Butterflies. The caterpillars of these two white butterflies eat the leaves of the cabbage. Look under the leaves for the yellow eggs and destroy them by hand or spray the plants with Sevin.

Cabbage Moth. The caterpillar of this gray nocturnal moth is difficult to control because it burrows deeply into the cabbage and eats the heart. As with cabbage butterflies destroy the eggs or spray with Sevin.

Gall Weevil. The gall weevil burrows into the root causing it to swell. Control the weevil by dusting the soil when planting with Diazinon.

Club Root. This dreaded fungus disease attacks many plants of the brassica family. The roots swell and rot and the plants fail to grow properly. Control is difficult if not impossible so follow recommendations on crop rotation and culture mentioned at left.

Cabbage Root Fly. The larvae—small, white grubs—appear from May onward and eat the stem below soil level. Spray around the base of the seedlings with Diazinon.

Spinach

Spinach (*Spinacia oleracea*) can be tricky to grow. The summer varieties do not like hot and dry weather, and the winter ones do not like it when it is cold and wet. Nevertheless,

the satisfaction of eating spinach fresh from the garden, instead of wilted from the market, is worth some gamble in growing it, and proper cultivation of suitable soils will greatly lessen the odds against your success. If you fail, do not despair; you can always turn to the spinach substitutes.

Spinach has a long and respected history. Its origin is vague, like that of many ancient vegetables, but Persia has as strong a claim to being its birthplace as any country. Certainly the Greeks and Romans ate it. The Arabs valued it and in the fourteenth century took it to Spain, from where it quickly spread throughout Europe. Then it was part of a peasant diet. Today it is frequently the gourmet's choice.

Varieties

All-America winner Melody is disease-resistant and adaptable to early-spring or late-summer sowing in the North, also as a winter crop in Zones 8 to 10. Cold Resistant Savoy is a 45-day crop, useful for wintering over in mild regions to provide an early-spring harvest.

GROWING SPINACH
Preparing the soil

For summer spinach choose a site in partial shade and manure it well. Winter spinach will need the same kind of rich soil, but in a sunny, sheltered part of the garden. Both need lime; the pH level should be 6.5 to 6.8. Although a loamy soil is best, it is possible to grow spinach on heavy soil. A light sandy soil, however, will encourage spinach to run to seed, in which case it is better to grow such spinach substitutes as New Zealand spinach and Swiss chard.

Sowing

March to April in North. Sow summer varieties every three weeks in 1-inch (2 cm) drills 12 inches (30 cm) apart. Thin the seedlings as soon as they are big enough to handle to 6 inches (15 cm) apart. August to September. Make two sowings of the winter varieties, one in early August and the other in September. Sow in 1-inch (2 cm) drills 12 inches (30 cm) apart, thinning the seedlings to 6 inches (15 cm) apart.

The year's work

Keep down weeds. Keep the soil moist by watering in dry weather or the plants will bolt and your labor will be wasted. In the middle of summer, spinach seeds can be sown between rows of such other vegetables

as peas, beans and carrots, which will provide shade for the growing plants. Except in the South the winter crop will need some protection—a covering of straw or, better still, cloches—from late fall.

Harvesting

Most of the year. Summer varieties will be ready 8 to 11 weeks after sowing. Pick young and tender leaves, but leave a few on the plant so that it can go on growing. Pick the winter varieties sparingly, particularly in bad weather. They, too, need some covering to keep warm.

Diseases

If there are yellow patches on the leaves and a gray mold on the undersurfaces, downy mildew has struck. Crowding and bad drainage encourage it and a spraying with Maneb may help to check it.

Yellowing of the younger leaves indicates spinach blight due to cucumber mosaic virus. The leaves roll up and gradually die.

Okra

Okra (*Hibiscus esculentus*) originated in the northeastern section of Africa now called Ethiopia. The plant has been cultivated in Egypt for centuries and it was probably the Muslims who transported okra into other areas of the Arab world, then into many Mediterranean countries.

The French settlers in Louisiana were the first to feature okra in cooking, as early as the 1700s. Many present-day gardeners think of okra only as an ingredient in soup, but down South the unique green vegetable is appreciated for the unusual flavor and texture of gumbo pods. The best-known use of okra is to add a thickening substance to soups, especially the famous Southern gumbo dishes. Okra is a warm-weather crop and thrives with the same basic culture given tomatoes.

Varieties

Most okra selections grow 4 to 5 feet (120 to 150 cm) tall so be sure to choose dwarf types if you have limited space. Dwarf Green Long Pod has 7- to 8-inch-long (17 to 20 cm) dark-green ribbed pods on 2- to 2½-foot (60 to 75 cm) plants. All-America winner Clemson Spineless is a heavy-bearing adaptable selection.

GROWING OKRA
Sowing

Sow seed in Jiffy-7 pots 6 weeks before outdoor planting date. Okra, like tomatoes and cucumbers, must not be planted outside until the soil and air are warm.

Planting

Set seedlings 18 to 24 inches (45 to 60 cm) apart in rows 3 feet (90 cm) apart.

Harvesting

Pick pods when they are 3 to 4 inches (8 to 10 cm) long for most tenderness. Harvest just before cooking as okra quickly loses flavor once picked.

New Zealand Spinach

New Zealand spinach (*Tetragonia expansa*) is not a spinach at all, but it does come from New Zealand, where it was found during

Captain Cook's voyage in 1770. Sir Joseph Banks, the great horticulturist, brought it back to England. The virtue of New Zealand spinach is that it will thrive in a hot, dry summer, such as would make ordinary spinach not just run but gallop to seed. It takes up space, but it provides mild-flavored leaves in abundance.

Swiss Chard

The leaves of Swiss chard (*Beta vulgaris*, var. *cicla*) may be substituted in the kitchen for spinach. The stems and midribs may be used

instead of seakale. Swiss chard is easy to grow and handsome enough for the flower garden.

Varieties

Rhubarb Chard is crimson, very flavorful. Lucullus and White King have green foliage, white stems.

Collards

Collards are actually a variety of the same species (*Brassica oleracea*) that contains kale, cabbage and broccoli. The cultivar grown as collards (*B. oleracea acephala cv.*) tolerates more heat than its relatives and is much grown as a cabbage substitute in Southern states. The greens are quite good when picked young and steamed, but all too often the collard leaves are boiled almost beyond recognition. Like okra, collards are little appreciated in the North, but they are easy to grow and well worth trying. Collard greens join kale in being high in vitamin A and in having their flavor improved by exposure to cold weather.

Varieties

Vates is a popular variety with good cold-tolerance and 24- to 36-inch (60 to 90 cm) height. Leaves can be picked after 75 days' growth. Georgia is very adaptable, produces 36-inch-tall (90 cm) plants even in poor soil. The tender greens can be picked starting about 80 days after planting. Flavor is like a mild cabbage. Not all boiling greens used in Southern cooking are collards. Another brassica (*B. juncea*) called leaf mustard is grown for the thin, oval, scalloped-edged foliage. Southern Curled grows a crop in 40 days. More compact and of milder flavor is Burpee's Fordhook Fancy with curled dark-green foliage.

GROWING NEW ZEALAND SPINACH

Preparing the soil
Plenty of humus is needed, as for spinach.

Sowing
May. New Zealand spinach is not hardy. You either raise plants under glass—sowing in March and planting out when all risk of frost is gone—or wait until May to sow out of doors. The skin of the seeds is very hard; to help germination, soak them overnight in water. The seeds are large, so it is simple to sow three together, $\frac{1}{2}$ inch (1 cm) deep and at 36-inch (90 cm) intervals in the row. Allow the sturdiest seedling in each station to grow on and pull up the others.

The year's work
At first, hoe to keep down weeds, but later the thick growth of the plants will keep weeds under control. When the plants are well grown, pinch out the tips to produce branching and more young leaves. Water in dry weather.

Harvesting
Midsummer onward. This is a cut-and-come-again vegetable, so pick regularly, a few leaves from each plant. Cut near to the base of the stalks, although it is only the leaves that will be cooked.

Pests and diseases
Fairly trouble free.

GROWING SWISS CHARD

Preparing the soil
Swiss chard is extremely tolerant about the kind of soil and position it is grown in. It will grow in a light sandy soil, which would be anathema to the true spinach, as well as in heavy clay. Similar to other beets—although this one is grown for its leaves—it needs lime, pH 6.5 to 6.8, and ground manured for a previous crop suits it well. Swiss chard can be sown in shade or sun, but any late sowing under cloches, to get a winter crop, should obviously be in a warm part of the garden.

Sowing
April and July. In April, sow three seeds together $\frac{1}{2}$ inch (1 cm) deep every 15 inches (38 cm) in rows 18 inches (45 cm) apart, thinning the seedlings to the strongest one in each station. Another sowing in July, to be covered by cloches through the winter, will provide greens in spring.

Harvesting
July onward. Always take the stems from the outside of each plant to allow the central stems to develop. Pull them as you do rhubarb; cutting makes them bleed. Swiss chard that has wintered under cloches will provide leaves through the following spring and autumn.

Pests and diseases
Fairly trouble free.

GROWING COLLARD GREENS

Preparing the soil
Collards are tolerant of poor soil but grow best in well-dug soil with full sun exposure. Composted manure or a balanced vegetable fertilizer will increase your yield.

Sowing
Sow seed about 5 per inch $\frac{1}{2}$ inch (1 cm) deep when the soil is warm, usually about June 1 in Northern gardens. Like cabbage, collards may be started indoors in Jiffy-7 pots or flats, then transplanted to the garden after all danger of frost is past.

Mustard
The leafy mustard grown for boiling greens is just as easy to grow as collards and in fact can be sown even earlier in the garden. About 40 days after planting, you can begin to pick the greens. A second sowing in August will provide greens for the fall. The type of mustard grown for tender sprouts, like cress, is described on page 45.

Harvesting
Pick both collards and mustard while they are tender. Older leaves are tough.

Stalks & Shoots

Stalks and shoots are the undoubted aristocrats of the kitchen garden and asparagus is the noblest of them all, even among such competitors as globe artichokes, seakale, cardoons and Florence fennel. The great gardener Arthur Kidner said that asparagus "is somewhat of an acquired taste, and the short natural season does not allow customers time or opportunity to acquire it." Conversely the shortness of the season means that there is no time to get tired of these epicurean vegetables. Rhubarb may seem to be an intruder in these high places, but this is not so. Like many other aristocrats it ages badly, but for its uncommonly beautiful pink youth much may be forgiven it.

1 Celery
2 Seakale
3 Forced rhubarb
4 Globe artichokes
5 Florence fennel
6 Asparagus

Asparagus

Asparagus (*Asparagus officinalis*) has outlived many civilizations. The Egyptians were eating it, or something like it, in the third millennium B.C. The Greeks knew asparagus and, inevitably, invented a myth about it—that it grew from a ram's horn stuck in the

ground; the starting point, perhaps, of later ribaldry associating asparagus with cuckoldry. It advanced with the Roman armies; and when the empire fell, the plant declined, but survived. Asparagus was one of the spoils of war for the Arabs in their North African and Spanish conquests. Then it found its way back into Europe: to France in the fifteenth century and England in the sixteenth century.

Asparagus is a member of the lily family. The edible parts are the immature shoots of the tuberous roots. Those which are not eaten develop into asparagus fern. To grow asparagus you need a fair amount of room, a lot of patience during the first three years, when you must not cut any, and, thereafter, enough will power to curb your greed, so that you do not eat the bed to death.

Varieties

Mary Washington is a favorite for high yield and rust resistance. Viking and Viking 2K, bred from Mary Washington, are even more resistant to rust. Paradise is earliest. Brocks Imperial is a new F_1 hybrid from England, quick to grow from seed.

Pests and diseases

Basically there are three pests and diseases to watch for. Asparagus beetles and grubs may devour, perhaps strip, foliage in summer. Spray with Sevin. To counter rust on foliage, burn diseased tops every fall. Slugs also appreciate asparagus; use baits with methiocarb and metaldehyde.

GROWING ASPARAGUS

Preparing the soil

Choose a sunny part of the garden. In autumn prepare a loamy, well-drained bed with plenty of such organic manure as farmyard manure, old mushroom compost or seaweed. Add lime to achieve pH 5.6 to 5.8. The success of the crops over the next decade will depend on how painstaking you are at this stage.

Planting

March/April. In the prepared bed dig trenches 10 inches (25 cm) deep, 12 inches (30 cm) wide and at least 36 inches (90 cm) apart, for the fleshy roots will spread enormously. Asparagus can be grown from

seed, but buying one- or two-year-old plants cuts time off waiting for crops. One-year-old plants are cheaper and transplant more readily. Plant them in the prepared bed as soon as they arrive so that the roots do not dry out and suffer as little exposure to the air as possible. The crowns should be 24 inches (60 cm) apart in the

rows. Fan the roots out evenly and cover them at once with 3 inches (8 cm) of soil, leaving the rest of the soil to fill in the trench gradually during the first summer.

The year's work

The asparagus fern stalks will turn yellow in the autumn; cut them down near to the

ground. Each February or March give the bed a dressing of general fertilizer, 3 ounces to the square yard (90 g to 1 sq m). Then mound up the soil a few inches deep along

each row. In summer, give the plants a mulch of decayed farmyard manure or compost. Asparagus are male (more productive) and female (berry bearing). Pick off all berries before they ripen or you will be cursed with seedlings of unpredictable parentage.

In about the tenth year, start another bed or, preferably, add another row each year, so that as the original bed declines you do not have that agonizing three-year wait all over again.

Harvesting

May/June. Do not cut at all, not even the fern, for the first two years after planting. In the third year you can take no more than one or two sticks from each plant, stopping altogether in early June and allowing the remaining shoots to produce fern. The time to take a shoot is when it is about 4 inches (10 cm) above the ground and while the tip is still tightly closed. The base of the stick is tough; a special knife makes the job easier. In the fourth year all shoots can

be cut for five weeks after you begin. Then stop. Each year afterwards cut for only six weeks if you want the bed to survive. In the summer, especially if the weather is dry, remember to keep the asparagus bed moist. When they are five years old, a couple of flourishing plants should provide one person with one helping each week for the six weeks of cutting.

Globe Artichokes

The Mediterranean was the original home of the globe artichoke (*Cynara scolymus*). Ancient Greek writings mention it often and the Romans may have introduced it to Britain. It was, however, not until the sixteenth century, again by way of Italy, that globe artichokes became established in Britain. Like many vegetables, the artichoke developed a reputation as an aphrodisiac, which may explain Catherine de Médicis's passion for it.

The globe artichoke has always been considered an epicurean vegetable. It is, however, quite simple to grow. Regard it as a thistle, which it is, rather than as something foreign and exotic. The globe artichoke has absolutely nothing to do with Jerusalem artichokes, the roots of which have a supposedly artichoke flavor.

The delicate bits of the globe artichoke are in the immature flower head, the fleshy scales and the fleshy base, or heart. The hairy center, the choke, is not edible.

When the globes have been harvested, older plants about to be replaced can, in their last autumn, be made to produce another but different crop—the chards or stems. These spring up after the plant has been cut down.

Varieties

Green Globe is the usual variety, but the gourmet's choice is the French Vert de Laon, with pale-green head and plenty of flesh in the scales. Grande Beurre is similar.

Diseases

If the leaves turn brown and the plants begin to die back in warm, humid weather the cause is likely to be artichoke leaf spot. Before the heads form, spray with Maneb.

GROWING GLOBE ARTICHOKES

Preparing the soil

The globe artichoke is hardy only in mild regions, but with special winter protection it sometimes survives as far north as coastal Connecticut. Fortunately a crop can be had in one season by early planting of suckers. Pick a well-drained, sunny location with rich soil. Test for lime (pH 6.5). The plants have a useful life of three years, so at the start dig in plenty of well-rotted manure or compost. Before planting, spread 3 ounces of general fertilizer to the square yard (90 g to 1 sq m).

Planting

April. Grow artichokes from top-quality seed or buy plants (suckers from an estab-

lished plant) and thereafter you will be able to provide your own replacements. Plant them, firmly, at least 3 feet (90 cm) apart and water well.

The year's work
To produce tender heads artichokes need moisture in their roots; each summer apply

a mulch of manure or compost and, occasionally, liquid manure. Each autumn get rid of dying leaves and old stems. Except in the warmest parts of the country, cover the crowns with leaves or straw for winter protection.

Although plants will crop longer, they deteriorate after three years. Renew the bed by taking 6- to 9-inch (15 to 23 cm) suckers, with a few of the roots, from around the crowns of parent plants. And so the cycle starts again.

Harvesting

July to September. Cut the heads when they are plump but still young and tender, and the scales still tight. The terminal bud will

be ready first. If you want very large heads from the terminals, remove the laterals when they are not much more than 1 inch (2 cm) in diameter. These are particularly delicious eaten whole.

Chards

In late September and October, plants which are to be discarded can be made to produce a second, different, crop of chards. After the globe heads are finished, cut down the main stems of these plants to within 1 foot (30 cm) of the ground. Mulch them and water frequently. When the new shoots are about 24 inches (60 cm) high, tie them together and earth them up like celery (see page 63) to blanch them. It is the stems which are eaten, cooked like cardoons, to which the globe artichoke is botanically related. After all the chards have been picked, the parent plant is of no further use, except for compost.

Seakale

Seakale (*Crambe maritima*), growing wild along the coasts of Britain (it is also a native of most of the coastal areas of western Europe), has provided spring greens for country dwellers for centuries. But the cultivation of the forced white shoots, which are sweet and succulent, goes back to the middle of the nineteenth century. Its old name was seacolewort. It belongs to the Cruciferae family and is a relative of the cabbage.

Seakale is easy to grow and to force. It is

remarkably hardy, usually free of all pests and diseases and a fine, wholesome vegetable with a delicate, nutty flavor. Seakale may be forced indoors or in the garden. Although outdoor forcing may provide the better flavor (one of the most esoteric arguments among devotees), there is much to be said for having seakale in the middle of winter. For the outdoor crop you will have to wait until early spring. The curly green leaves of unforced seakale are delicious eaten raw in a salad. The stalks, too, can be eaten raw like celery.

Roots forced indoors are thrown away after all the stems have been used—but they will already have provided cuttings for the next season. Outdoor beds remain productive for four or five years, but do not start forcing them until eighteen months after planting.

For a worthwhile supply of shoots you will need at least fifteen plants. Cut the shoots young, before the leaves have fully developed.

Variety

Lily White provides a good crop of very white, pleasantly sweet shoots. Seeds are offered by Thompson & Morgan, Inc.

Pests and diseases

Fairly trouble free.

GROWING SEAKALE

Preparing the soil

Seakale needs a well-drained soil, rich in humus, especially if you are establishing a five-year bed for outdoor forcing. A maritime plant, seakale appreciates seaweed as a manure. There must also be adequate lime (pH 6.5) in the soil.

Planting

Seakale is easy to raise from seed sown early in the spring. In March plant seeds 1 inch (2 cm) deep in rows, then when plants grow large enough to handle, thin to stand 18 inches (45 cm) apart. In late fall pile earth

around the stem to blanch growth. Harvest in February or March. Plants produce best after two years' growth. Propagate by root cuttings called thongs. Take cuttings in the fall, plant with tops ½ inch (1 cm) below soil surface, mulch with salt hay or well-rotted manure.

The year's work

As the seakale grows, remove all shoots except the strongest one. Keep the weeds down, either by hoeing or, preferably, by giving a mulch of peat or compost. Water in dry weather. Remove any flower stems. In October, remove the foliage as it dies down.

Forcing indoors

November onward. Carefully dig up the roots in November. First cut the thongs from the roots. These are the slim side shoots of the root, about 6 inches (15 cm) long, which will be next year's plants. Cut the top of each one level and the other end slanting.

Tie them in bundles, store in sand and keep in a cool place ready for planting in March.

The roots themselves should also be stored in sand until ready for forcing. Force a few at a time at regular intervals. To

force, plant the roots in rich, loamy soil in boxes or flowerpots—about 3 roots to an 8-inch (20 cm) flowerpot—with the crowns just showing above the surface of the soil.

Cover with boxes or flowerpots—total darkness is vital—and put them in a place where the temperature is a constant 50°F (10°C). In a month to five weeks the shoots will be 6 inches (15 cm) or more long and ready for cutting. Do not cut the shoots, however, until immediately before you use them.

Forcing outdoors

January onward. An outdoor bed should not be forced the first winter after planting. When the bed is established the following winter, either place boxes or flowerpots over the plants or pile up the soil from between the rows to a depth of 10 inches (25 cm) over the plants. Either method, carried out in January, will produce stems for cutting in April.

Celery

Celery (*Apium graveolens*) is such a popular vegetable that it can do without any testimonials from the ancient Greeks, Romans,

Egyptians and Chinese—all of whom held it in high regard as food, flavoring and medicine. The Romans even believed that a celery wreath worn around the head would ease a hangover.

Most probably native to the Mediterranean regions, celery was developed from a plant very similar to the common English weed smallage, which still flourishes in many parts of England, Europe and western Asia.

Celery as we know it today is the result of work done by sixteenth-century Italian gardeners, who developed the finely flavored, succulent stalks from the bitter and foul-tasting weed.

It is regrettable that celery is not easy to grow—being demanding rather than difficult. Celery requires a heavy peaty soil, plenty of moisture and a lot of space. The stalks must be blanched if they are to lose their inherent bitterness, and this takes time and patience. Busy gardeners could settle for the less-demanding self-blanching celery or the much more amenable celeriac, the turniplike root with a celery flavor.

Varieties

White Ice is a vigorous but compact variety bred for flavor and absence of strings. Utah 52–70 Improved has 12-inch (30 cm) dark-green stalks. Burpee's Fordhook is green but blanches silvery white.

GROWING CELERY
Preparing the soil

If you were searching for somewhere to live, with the major aim of growing celery, you would choose an area with peaty soil and a high water table. Failing that, the celery plot must be provided with much well-rotted manure or compost. Do not add too much lime (pH 5.8 to 6). In spring, well before they are needed, dig trenches 12 inches (30 cm) deep and 15 inches (38 cm) wide if planting in a single row, or 18 inches (45 cm) wide for a double row. Single rows are better for small quantities; double rows are space-saving and look nice, but make earthing up more difficult. If there is more than one trench, dig them 3 or even 4 feet (90 or 120 cm) apart. The space in between can profitably be used for such fast-growing catch crops as lettuces and radishes.

When digging out the trenches put half the soil in a ridge on one side of the trench and half on the other. Fork the manure into the soil at the bottom of the trench, treading

it down to make it firm. Then fill the trench with some of the soil from the ridges to within 5 inches (13 cm) of the top. The trenches are now ready for later planting.

Sowing

February/April. The seeds are small, fifty thousand to the ounce, and, since germination is slow, taking three to four weeks, the first batch should be sown early, in February, in a greenhouse heated to 60°F (16°C). Sow the seeds thinly in Jiffy-7 pots or seed compost and cover lightly. When the seedlings are big enough to handle, prick them out into boxes of peat-lite mix. After they have settled down from this upheaval, transfer them to a cold frame and gradually harden them off. The seedlings should be ready for planting out at the beginning of June. Depending on the weather, it should be possible to prick out the seedlings of the March and early-April sowings straight into frames. To avoid this labor, many gardeners sensibly buy plants from a nursery, although this limits the choice of varieties.

Planting

June. Plant celery 12 inches (30 cm) apart. On planting, water liberally unless it is raining heavily at the time.

The year's work

If the summer is at all dry, prodigious watering will be needed throughout. Dilute fish emulsion will help, as will two or three dressings of a general fertilizer, 2 ounces a yard run (60 g to 1 m), between July and September. Remove side shoots (suckers) from the plants.

Earthing up is usually done in three stages. In August, when the plants are 12 inches (30 cm) or more high, loosely tie pieces of newspaper or black plastic around the stalks. This is to prevent soil from getting between the stalks. See that the soil is moist before earthing up. Earth up only a little the first time. The second, more generous earthing up must take place three weeks

later. The final earthing up after three more weeks should completely cover the stalks. Never cover the leaves with soil. Keep the sides of the ridges steep so that rain will run away from the heart of the celery.

A touch of frost improves the crispness and flavor of celery, but late crops often go

rotten after being frozen in the ground. Protect the plants with straw or, better still, by placing cloches over the celery along the top of the ridge.

Harvesting
November onward. The celery should be adequately blanched about nine weeks from the start of earthing up. Dig up the plants as you need them, working from the end of the row and being careful to disturb adjoining plants as little as possible.

Self-blanching Celery
Until celery was developed by Italian

gardeners of the sixteenth century, it had an unpleasant smell and a bitter taste—a fact which supports the theory that it was celery, not parsley, that was the classical and Egyptian funerary plant. In spite of such morbid associations, celery is well worth growing. Gardeners who are not celery addicts, to the point of getting deep satisfaction just out of the labor of growing it, should stick to the yellow and American green self-blanching types, which do not have to be earthed up. Thus the gardener is saved the effort of digging trenches. Self-blanching celery, however, is less hardy than ordinary celery and has a milder flavor. It is ready earlier, and over earlier, than the white, pink and red varieties.

Varieties
Golden Self-Blanching is yellow with compact heads for use from August. American Green is ready from October.

GROWING SELF-BLANCHING CELERY
Preparing the soil
Self-blanching celery needs a well-manured, well-dug soil but no trenches.

Sowing
Sow the seeds in a greenhouse toward the end of March. Prick out the seedlings into boxes and harden them off in cold frames.

Planting
June. Plant in blocks 9 inches (23 cm) apart each way. This is better than planting in rows, for the plants provide shade for one another. Although they are self-blanching, the yellow varieties will be more tender if a piece of black plastic is tied around each plant a few weeks before lifting.

Pests and diseases
Celery fly (*Philophylla heraclei*) attacks celery plants from May throughout the summer. It is the tiny fly that lays the eggs, but the resulting grub that does the damage—tunneling its way through the leaf tissues and raising brown blisters. Dust the soil along the rows with Diazinon and spray the plants with malathion.

Destroy all affected leaves.

Brown patches on leaves and stems, which then wilt, indicate the fungus celery leaf spot. Buy only seed that has been treated against the fungus and at the first sign of the disease spray with Maneb, continuing every two weeks through to October.

Finocchio, or Florence Fennel

Florence fennel (*Foeniculum vulgare*, var. *dulce*) is often difficult to grow in Northern climates, but it is still worth cultivating for its sweet aniseed flavor.

Cardoons

The Americans and the British have less regard for the cardoon (*Cynara cardunculus*) than do others. Admittedly George III liked cardoons as avidly as did the gluttonous

Romans fourteen centuries before him, but he did not have to grow them himself. The cardoon is troublesome to grow, taking as much time and space as celery, and it is cultivated in much the same way. The cardoon, however, is a thistle, closely related to the globe artichoke. The name is derived from the French word *chardon*, meaning a thistle. In Australia, where the cardoon grows like a weed and is regarded as a nuisance, it is known as wild artichoke. It is certainly a tenacious plant—it was introduced into South America and promptly spread over large areas of the pampas.

If the cardoon is allowed to, it will produce similar but smaller heads than the artichoke, but it is for its blanched stems and not for its heads that the cardoon is grown. In the south of Europe it is grown also for its roots, which are thick and fleshy.

Varieties
The Spanish variety, Ivory White, is cold-hardy and does not have spiny leaves, but is liable to run to seed. Tours, from France, tastes better and has longer stems, but the prickly leaves are nasty to handle when earthing up. J. L. Hudson lists cardoon seed.

GROWING FLORENCE FENNEL
Preparing the soil
Florence fennel needs a much richer soil than the herb. Soil rich in humus and decayed manure will keep moist better in summer and encourage the stem base to swell.

Sowing
April to August. Florence fennel needs as much sun as possible to produce a good crop. So sow it in as sunny a position as the garden has to offer. Sow the seeds in ½-inch (1 cm) drills 18 inches (45 cm) apart. Sow a little each month to ensure a continuous supply. As the plant is not large, growing to approximately 24 inches (60 cm) high, thin out the seedlings to only 7 to 8 inches (18 to 20 cm) apart.

The year's work
Florence fennel demands a lot of water, and if it is not watered in dry weather it will certainly not produce bulbous stems. When the swelling is about the size of a golf ball, draw some soil around it, partly covering it. As the bulbs are so small this may be simpler than the alternative method of wrapping paper or black plastic around the bulb, tightly secured with string.

Harvesting
After two or three weeks the bulb will have blanched and grown in size. Pull the bulbs as you need them when they are the size of a tennis ball.

Pests and diseases
Fairly trouble free.

GROWING CARDOONS
Preparing the soil
Dig a trench as for celery, but 18 inches (45 cm) deep. Put plenty of manure or compost in the bottom of the trench. After forking in the manure, the trench should be 12 inches (30 cm) deep. If there is more than one trench, dig them 48 inches (120 cm) apart.

Sowing
April. Although perennial, cardoons are always raised from seed each year, not from suckers, as are globe artichokes. Sow in pots, one seed to a pot, under glass, unheated, in April. Harden off ready for planting out at the end of May.

Planting
May. Disturbing the roots as little as possible, plant firmly 15 to 18 inches (38 to 45 cm) apart. Water the seedlings well after planting.

The year's work
Little needs to be done during the summer except weeding and watering and more watering. If cardoons are not kept moist they will start to produce flower heads—unwanted, although edible, if, like globe artichokes, they are cut before the scales are too open.

Start blanching in September. By then the plants will be fully grown, up to 36 inches (90 cm) or more in height. Remove dead and yellow leaves. Then, either tie the stems together with raffia in two or three places, depending on their height, or tie corrugated paper around the stems. It is best to wear gloves for this job—cardoon leaves are extremely prickly.

Earth up as for celery (see page 63), using the soil from each side of the trench. Cardoons are not hardy and will need a plentiful covering of straw as protection against frost. Place the straw around the earthed-up cardoons and cover with more soil to keep the straw in place.

Harvesting
After five or six weeks the cardoons will be fit to use; at least the crisp hearts will be, the tough outside stems are fit only for the compost heap. By earthing up a number of plants at intervals, a succession of stalks will be ready for cropping.

Pests and diseases
Fairly trouble free.

Rhubarb

Although to many people rhubarb (*Rheum rhaponticum*) may seem a curiously English fruit, it is in fact a vegetable, native to China and Tibet, with a name derived from Latin. As far back as 3000 B.C., the root of the plant was being used medicinally in its countries of

origin. It was put to the same use when it arrived in Britain via the Volga region of Russia. After a period of near oblivion it turned up again in the early 1800s, this time as stalks, forced and blanched, and used as a fruit. Rhubarb has not gathered a literature around it in the way that other ancient vegetables have, but Kingsley Amis's Lucky Jim confessed to a love-hate relationship with it. For most people, however, it is either love or hate. It is easy to grow, very productive and most attractively pink when forced in winter.

Varieties

MacDonald is a brilliant red, has skin so tender that no peeling is required. Valentine, another dark-red sort, grows high-quality, sweet stalks. Victoria, often listed for growing from seed, produces green stalks blushed red, has a delicious, tart flavor when cooked.

Pests and diseases

Occasionally crown rot causes rotting of leaves and stalks. Dig up and burn the affected plants. Any other disasters are unlikely.

GROWING RHUBARB

Preparing the soil

Rhubarb thrives best in fairly heavy soil, given massive organic manuring to produce succulent stalks (pH around 5.8).

Sowing

April. Raising from seed is easy, but you must then wait an extra 18 months for the first crop. Sow 1 inch (2 cm) deep out of doors in April and thin to 6 inches (15 cm) apart. Move the plants to the permanent bed in the autumn.

Planting

It is more reliable to buy roots than to raise from seed. They are planted when buds are dormant, either in October/November or February/March. Allow 3 feet (90 cm) between plants and between rows, and plant to a depth that will leave the buds not more than 2 inches (5 cm) below the surface of the soil. Plant firmly.

The year's work

In the first year the plants will be establishing themselves and no stalks are picked. Pick only a few in the second year and none at all from plants which you intend to force in the winter. After that the bed has five years or more of useful life ahead of it. A rhubarb bed can be forgotten for most of the year. The plants are almost always healthy and their large leaves smother the weeds. However, watch out for and remove all flower heads. Flowering rhubarb is as unproductive as a broody hen. Rhubarb needs feeding—a handful of general fertilizer should be scattered around each plant after pulling finishes each year. A good dressing of compost or manure should be forked into the bed in February. But fork carefully so that the crowns are not damaged.

To keep up a constant supply of three-year-old roots for forcing, divide some of the established clumps each year in October/November or February/March. This is done by digging up the clumps and cutting them into pieces. The pieces can be small, but each must have an undamaged bud. Plant them in the gaps left by the roots removed for forcing, having seized the chance to refresh the soil with more manure.

Harvesting

Mid-April to July. Pull—do not cut—a stick or two from each crown as you need them, balancing your needs with what the plant is capable of producing. If you overpull you will suffer for your greed the following year with a smaller crop from weakened plants. Stop pulling in July.

Forcing outdoors

With a bucket and some straw, outdoor rhubarb can be hurried on for pulling a few weeks earlier. In mid-January or February invert a bucket or box over each of the few crowns you want to force. Over

and around them put plenty of straw (or, ideally, strawy manure for greater warmth). You could gain three weeks this way, but do not overdo it, because the debilitated roots will need time to recuperate. The sensible thing is to force only those plants due to be retired.

Forcing indoors

Preretirement plants—strong clumps at least three years old—are also those you choose for forcing indoors. Dig them up when the leaves die back in late October and November. If you leave the roots exposed to the cold for a couple of weeks they will grow faster when brought into warmth and darkness. Lay the clumps close together in a box, barely cover them with soil and give them a good watering. Put another box on top and cover with black plastic to keep out all light. Keep the covered box in the greenhouse or kitchen

at a temperature of about 50° to 55°F (10° to 13°C). Below 45°F (7°C) growth is very slow; above 60°F (16°C) the stalks will be spindly, anemic and tasteless. Water occasionally to keep the roots moist (not wringing wet), using a watering can with a fine rose. Stalks should be ready for pulling in five to six weeks. By staggering the times when the roots are boxed for forcing, a succession can be obtained. When all the stalks have been pulled, throw the roots away. They will be worn out.

Pods & Seeds

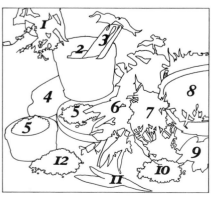

1 *Petits pois*
2 *Dried haricot beans*
3 *Haricots verts*
4 *Sweet corn*
5 *Red and green dried kidney beans*
6 *Garden peas*
7 *Bean shoots*
8 *Bush beans*
9 *Sugar peas (or mangetout peas)*
10 *Soybeans*
11 *Runner beans*
12 *Mung beans*

Once, that dreary period which is neither winter nor spring could be borne by looking ahead to the first broad beans, the first garden peas, the first bush and runner beans. Now, all through the winter you can buy these vegetables—either frozen or "fresh"—brought by air from all over the world. We tend to forget that they taste entirely different when they are picked young from the garden. Surely this is reason enough for growing all kinds of peas and beans. Sweet corn is easy to grow in many parts of the country, so you can know the true flavor of sweet corn picked in its prime and cooked immediately.

Sweet Corn

The forebears of sweet corn (*Zea mays*, var. *saccharata*) may have been growing in Mexico earlier than 5000 B.C. Columbus brought seeds of Indian maize back from Cuba to Spain, from where it spread throughout

the Mediterranean and beyond. The English herbalist Gerard had this to say about it in 1597: "The barbarous Indians, which know no better, thinke it a good food; whereas we may easily judge, that it nourisheth but little, and it is of hard and evill digestion, a more convenient food for swine than for man." In one respect he was right: in many parts of the world it is the food of animals rather than of men. But in defense of the sweet corn of today, it cannot be judged on the weary cobs on sale in markets, for sweet corn goes downhill rapidly, even within the hour of being picked. The only way to know its true character is to grow it. With the new, quick-maturing hybrids, sweet corn can be grown easily in most states.

Varieties

Golden Sweet EH is a supersweet hybrid, very disease resistant; develops full cobs even when grown near other strains. Polar Vee, an extra-early, 53-day corn, has 6-inch (15 cm) golden ears. Bantam Evergreen is a late 87- to 90+-day type with 9- to 10-inch (23 to 25 cm) ears on 8- to 9-foot (about 2 m) plants. Golden Midget has 4-inch (10 cm) golden ears on 30-inch (75 cm) stalks. To dry for decoration, try Rainbow Ornamental (Indian) corn.

Pests

To control earworms and borers, spray with Sevin when silk first shows.

GROWING SWEET CORN

Preparing the soil

Choose an open site for the greatest possible amount of sun. The soil must be rich. Sweet corn also requires lime (pH 6.5 to 6.8).

Sowing

April/May. A balance has to be struck between giving the sweet corn as long a season as possible in which to grow and not exposing it to any danger of frost. You can sow in a greenhouse at a temperature of 55°F (13°C) in April or in cold frames in late April or early May (depending on which part of the country the garden is in), and harden off the young shoots ready for planting out in late May or early June.

Unfortunately, sweet corn hates to be disturbed by transplanting. To get around this use peat pots. Sow two seeds in each pot, 1 inch (2 cm) deep. If both seeds grow, reject the weaker. Alternatively, seeds can be sown out of doors in late May. Sow two seeds together at 16-inch (40 cm) intervals in rows 24 inches (60 cm) apart, later thinning out the weaker of the pair.

Planting

Late May/June. Plant the sweet corn in blocks in a number of short rows 24 inches

(60 cm) apart. This increases the chances of pollination: the male flowers are at the top of the plant and the pollen has to fall or be carried by the wind onto the silks of the female cobs lower down the stem.

The year's work

Weed, hoeing carefully to avoid the roots of the plants. Give the sweet corn a good soaking in dry weather. A mulch will help to keep the soil moist and occasional liquid manure will encourage growth. As the stems grow, support them with stakes.

Harvesting

From mid-July. When the silks wither, press one of the sweet corn seeds to test for

ripeness. If the juice that comes out is clear, you are too early; if it is milky, on time; if dried out, alas, too late. Pull the cobs by giving them a sharp twist and lose no time in delivering them to the kitchen.

Garden Peas

Recently, an archaeological expedition reported finding peas (*Pisum sativum*, var. *hortense*) near the Burma-Thailand border and carbon dated them at approximately 9750 B.C. This is a much earlier finding than the peas found in Bronze Age (approximately 3000 B.C.) lake dwellings in Switzerland and

Savoy. Peas were also cultivated by the Greeks, and they were brought to Britain by the invading Romans, who back home ate them by the plateful at the circus. But to the poor of medieval Britain these dried peas soon became staple fare—unlike the Romans they had to be satisfied with the "bread" but do without the circuses. Not until the sixteenth century did fresh garden peas spread from Italy through northern Europe. A century later they became the fashion in England. Peas have the dubious honor of being the first vegetable to be canned and, later, deep-frozen.

Varieties

Garden peas are either smooth-seeded or wrinkled. For flavor the smooth-seeded are not half as delicious as the wrinkled, but they are hardier, and these are the varieties to sow very early in the North, or in the fall where mild. The sweeter peas are sown from the beginning of March; they are ready in twelve to sixteen weeks.

For autumn sowing in mild regions and extra-early sowing in the north, Alaska (smooth-seeded) is hardiest.

For spring sowing: Wrinkled Little Marvel, 18 inches (45 cm) tall. Improved Laxton's Progress, 18 inches (45 cm) tall, matures in 60 days. Wando is the most tolerant of heat, matures in 68 days, is a compact 30 inches (75 cm) tall. Burpee's Blue Bantam matures in 64 days, grows well in most states. Sparkle is a top-quality early pea, grows 15 inches (38 cm) tall.

GROWING GARDEN PEAS

Preparing the soil

Peas need a rich, loamy soil that has been well manured in the autumn or early winter. If fresh manure is dug in during the spring, too much greenery and too few peas will be produced. Peas also require lime (pH 6.5).

Sowing

March in North, December in South. Successful outdoor sowing at the end of the year depends on a mild winter, but the reward is peas from the end of May. Cloches will be

needed in cold, exposed gardens. Take out a trench (not a drill) a spade's width across and 2 inches (5 cm) deep. Dip the seeds in kerosene, to discourage mice, and sow them along the bottom of the trench 2 inches (5 cm) apart in two rows 4 inches (10 cm) apart. Cover the seeds with the soil taken out of the trench.

By choosing varieties that mature at different times, spring and early-summer sowings will provide peas from the end of June to September. Spring sowings can begin early in December in the South. If you live in the North, be in no hurry—mid-March to mid-April will do if the weather is cold. Sow at two-week intervals. The last sowing, in early June, should be of the quick-

maturing Kelvedon Wonder (available from Thompson & Morgan).

Alternatively, sow seeds in a cold frame in February, in small pots of peat-lite mix, one seed to a pot. Harden off the plants so that they are ready to go outside in late March or in April. Plant the seedlings 3 inches (8 cm) apart, disturbing the roots as little as possible.

Distances between rows of peas should be roughly equal to the height the plants are likely to grow. What may seem to be wide-open spaces between the taller varieties at the start should not be wasted but used for intercropping.

The year's work

When the plants, dwarf varieties included, are about 3 inches (8 cm) high, give them a little support with small twigs or pieces of cane. The taller varieties will soon need much more; use posts and wire or plastic

netting for them to cling to. Mulch to keep down weeds. Water in dry weather. Give a 1-inch (2 cm) mulch of peat or grass mowings between the rows.

Harvesting

June to September. Pick the pods regularly from the bottom of the plants as they fill. When all the peas have been picked do not pull up the plants, but sever them with a hoe at soil level, leaving the roots with their nitrogen-rich nodules in the soil.

Petits Pois

The sweetness of *petits pois* was almost the undoing of Louis XIV—he very nearly stuffed himself to death on them—and it is easy to understand why. They are the most aristocratic of all the peas.

Sugar Peas

The sugar pea (*Pisum sativum*, var. *saccharatum*), also called *mangetout* and snow pea, was praised by Gerard as an "exceeding delicate meate" because it could be eaten "cods and all the rest."

Black-eyed Peas

The black-eyed pea (*Vigna sinensis cv.*) came to America from Jamaica, where it was introduced from Africa by slave traders. This pea thrives in warm climates and has become a favorite food crop in Southern states. Black-eyed peas are often served with boiled collards, corn bread and some form of pork. The smooth-skinned seeds, a type of cowpea, are a light cream color with a dark eye. These tasty peas are useful freshly picked and as a crop to dry for later use. The dried peas are used as one would dried beans.

GROWING PETITS POIS

Gullivert, a 30-inch (75 cm) variety, is a true French type. Cameo is a smooth-seeded type grown commercially. *Petits pois* require a rich, well-drained soil with a fair amount of lime (pH 6.5).

Sow from April to June for a succession of crops. Take out a shallow trench 1 inch (2 cm) deep. Sow the seeds in two rows 6 inches (15 cm) apart each way. The trenches should be 40 inches (100 cm) apart.

Petits pois grow about 40 inches (100 cm) high, so as the plants grow give them some support. Keep the soil moist. A 1-inch (2 cm) mulch of grass mowings or leaf mold between the rows will help retain the moisture. Harvest the pods as they fill.

GROWING SUGAR PEAS

Dwarf Gray Sugar is early, only 24 inches (60 cm) tall. Burpee's Sweetpod and Oregon Sugar Pod grow 36 to 48 inches (90 to 120 cm) tall. Sow the seeds in double rows in spade-wide trenches 2 inches (5 cm) deep and 2 to 3 inches (5 to 8 cm) apart each way. The trenches must be as wide apart as the height of the fully grown plant. Follow the first sowing in April, which produces pods two months later, by sowings in May and June. From early on support the plants. Water well in dry weather, and apply a 1-inch (2 cm) mulch of grass mowings. Occasionally give a feeding of liquid fertilizer. Hoe to keep down weeds.

GROWING BLACK-EYED PEAS

California Blackeye, with 7- to 8-inch (17 to 19 cm) pods, is highly resistant to disease, produces a crop in 75 days. Southern Blackeye is similar. Related but slightly larger are the Southern crowder peas. Mississippi Silver is a good disease-resistant crowder pea which matures in about 8 weeks. To save space you can plant these peas among sweet corn. The pea vines grow up the cornstalks, thus providing two crops in the space of one. Sow seed after the soil is above 70°F (21°C). Black-eyed peas are a warm-growing crop. Otherwise general culture for crowder and black-eyes is similar to garden peas. These warm-growing peas produce a crop in less fertile soil than required for garden or *petits pois* types.

Seed treatments

Since peas are a cool-weather crop the seed should be planted as early as possible. When the soil is cool, seed is more susceptible to rot. In order to prevent rot while seeds are germinating most seed firms now give peas and beans a light dusting of the fungicide Captan. This mild fungicide treatment makes it possible to plant an early crop without the high risk of having most of the seed fail. Some seed catalogs offer a choice of treated or untreated seed in certain varieties.

Inoculation

Peas, beans and other legumes can capture nitrogen from the air, thanks to nitrogen-fixing bacteria that live in the roots. To be sure the legumes have an adequate supply of these beneficial bacteria, dust pea and bean seeds with an inoculant. Local garden centers and mail-order seed catalogs usually carry a powder designed for nitrogen inoculation of legume seed. The bacteria involved live in root nodules and they help plants produce a maximum crop. After legumes die back, the nitrogen left in the roots becomes available to other plants.

Pea pests

Thrips, small black insects, lay eggs on flowers and foliage in May and June, and the eggs hatch into orange nymphs. Aphids may also attack. Spray with malathion to control both insects.

Mice and pigeons eat newly sown peas.

To stop them, dip the seeds in kerosene just before sowing. Sparrows peck the seedlings. Cover them with small-mesh chicken wire or fine nylon netting draped over sticks. (See page 55.)

Pea diseases

Provide good air circulation and drainage to avoid mildew and root rot. Control aphids to prevent spread of virus mosaic.

Bush Beans
Bush beans (*Phaseolus vulgaris* hybrids) are also known as string beans, snap beans, French beans, kidney beans and haricot beans. The original species is the ancient bean of the New World, just as the broad bean is that of the Old World. Sixteenth-century explorers carried bush-bean seeds from Central and South America to Europe. It was the French cooks who first took the bean to their culinary hearts. They called the dried seeds of the beans *haricots*, because they put them in *ragoûts* or *haricots* of mutton. The young pods, eaten whole, were called *haricots verts*, and the shelled beans, eaten extravagantly young, be-

came known as flageolet beans—the name is a corruption of the Latin *phaseolus*, and also relates to the fact that the French imagined the bean resembled a flute known as a flageolet. The dried, mature beans were called *haricots jaunes*. In the nineteenth century, according to *Robinson's Family Herbal*, dried and powdered bush beans were thought to strengthen the kidneys. They were also used to relieve shortness of breath. Today the bush bean is known to be valuable for its vitamin and mineral salt content. Plant breeders have created outstanding types of bush beans. The dwarf self-supporting types sometimes referred to as snap beans are second only to tomatoes in popularity for home gardens according to a Gallup gardening survey.

Varieties
Limelight from Thompson & Morgan is an extra-early, 40-day dwarf green bush bean useful as immature pods and later for dry beans. Greensleeves, a white-seeded green pod, is disease resistant, matures in 56 days. Greencrop is an All-America winner with 6-inch (15 cm) pods after about 50 growing days, popular for French slicing. Royalty has purple pods which turn green when cooked. Waxbean hybrids like yellow Sungold produce 5-inch (12 cm) beans in 56 to 60 days. Green Ruler is an Italian bean hybrid with rich flavor, 50- to 55-day growing season. For seeds to bake, plant White Marrowfat, a 100-day crop.

GROWING BUSH BEANS
Preparing the soil
A light but rich soil is best for bush beans —cold wet clay is deadly to them. Choose an open, sunny part of the garden and, in the autumn, dig in compost or manure. Like all peas and beans they need lime (pH 6.5).

Sowing
Bush beans like getting into a warm bed, indeed, in cold soil the seeds tend to rot. This means that bush beans cannot be sown unprotected out of doors until mid-April or early May, depending on where the garden is and whether spring has come early. Err on the safe side. Rake the bed to a fine tilth some days before you sow. Take out a drill 2 inches (5 cm) deep and plant the beans 10 inches (25 cm) apart. Rows are

18 inches (45 cm) apart, or make them 24 inches (60 cm) apart to give more space for picking later. At the end of the row, sow a few extra beans to fill any gaps in the rows where the beans fail to germinate. A second sowing can follow three weeks later. Another in late June will give a crop in September and October, although cloche protection may then be needed.

To sow beans early—late March in warm areas and mid-April in cold areas —warm up the soil by putting cloches over the rows three weeks before sowing. Or sow indoors in February in pots filled with peat-lite mix and leave to germinate in gentle heat, 55°F (13°C). Harden off the plants. Plant out in June.

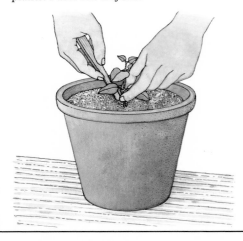

Treated seed
Bean seed often rots when the soil is too cold. To prevent rotting of early-planted seed choose beans that have been treated with a light coating of Captan. With treated seed you can plant an earlier crop in Northern states. When planting untreated seed, wait until soil is fully warm, usually by late May or early June in Zone 5. Dust bean seed with a nitrogen inoculant powder to aid plants in capturing nitrogen with bacteria in the roots, thus increasing crops.

The year's work
Hoe to keep down weeds, and water in dry weather. A mulch of straw or strips of

black plastic in late June will help to smother weeds, keep the ground moist and protect the beans from getting soiled. Dwarf bush beans can be beaten down by heavy rain, so support them with sticks or lines of string. Spraying the plants with water on dry days, when the flowers begin to appear, will help them to set. This is a tedious chore, but one which pays dividends in the resulting crop.

Harvesting
July onward (outdoors). Always pick the beans when the pods are young, about 3 inches (8 cm) long. They taste better then and the plants will be induced to go on producing more beans. When they are picked, bush beans snap off the plant, which is why they are sometimes called snap beans. Take care when harvesting the beans not to loosen the roots of the plants.

*R*unner Beans and Pole Beans

Runner beans (*Phaseolus multiflorus*) followed bush beans from South America. The modern hybrids are usually listed as pole beans but are sometimes still called runner beans as in Scarlet Runner and White Half Runner. Because they are climbers the pole-runner hybrids yield the most beans for any given space. Two ounces (56 g) of seed will grow 20 to 25 pounds (9 to 11 kg) of beans.

Varieties

Tall: Prizewinner; Streamline; Crusader, a red-flowered runner bean; Blue Lake; Desiree (for pods); Kentucky Wonder; Zebra. To treat as non-climber: Kelvedon Marvel; Burpee Golden, a 60-day crop.

Staking

Some varieties of runner and pole beans grow to 12 feet (360 cm) high and they must be sturdily staked. There are several methods.

A batten may be fixed near soil level on the wall of the house and another at 10 or 12 feet (300 or 360 cm). Screw hooks into them at 10-inch (25 cm) intervals and tie tomato string between the hooks for the beans to climb up.

Another method is to make a tent of four canes tied together near the apex.

An inverted "V" frame can be made along the row with bamboo canes or bean poles, if you can get them, one to each plant, reinforced with canes tied horizontally along the top.

To stake runners in flower beds or in large, deep tubs, tie ten poles together at the top. Fan out the poles to make a wigwam and push the ends into the ground. Circle the bottom ends with a wire hoop. Run strings from the hoop to the top of the poles for the beans to swarm up. Dwarf varieties need no staking.

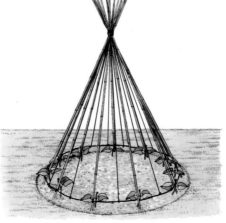

GROWING CLIMBING BEANS

Preparing the soil

Climbing beans must have a rich, deeply dug soil (pH 6.5) in a sheltered part of the garden. If they are to be grown in a row, take out a trench in February or March 18 inches (45 cm) wide to a spade's depth. Dig plenty of compost or well-rotted manure into the soil at the bottom of the trench. If the beans are to be grown in a group, manure a large circle of ground over which the wigwam will be put.

Sowing

Climbing beans are easily damaged by frost. To prevent this, sow in peat pots, one bean to a pot, in the greenhouse at a temperature of 55°F (13°C) in April, and harden off for planting out in late May or June. Alternatively, sow the beans out of doors where they are to grow, but not before the start of May. In warmer areas sow again in June for a late crop. Sow the seeds 2 inches (5 cm) deep and 10 inches (25 cm) apart in double rows 12 inches (30 cm) apart. If there is to be more than one double row of beans and they are to be permitted to grow tall, allow 60 inches (150 cm) between the double rows. If all the plants are to be dwarfed, the double rows need be only 24 inches (60 cm) apart.

The year's work

Put in the stakes for the tall varieties when two leaves have opened out. Hoe to kill weeds and give a mulch of peat. Keep the beans well watered in dry weather, especially if they are being grown against the house, where soil always tends to dry out. A crucial time for watering is when the flowers begin to open. Spray, preferably with rain water, in the evenings. When the beans reach the top of their supports nip out the growing tips.

To avoid staking, plants can be dwarfed as they grow. As soon as they start running, at about 12 inches (30 cm) high, pinch out the main growing shoot. Side shoots will then form. Pinch these out from time to time and the plants will grow bushy and stay low. Kelvedon Marvel is one of the best to treat this way. Dwarfing of tall varieties has the disadvantage of often producing curved pods, but they taste the same. In windy areas dwarfing is the sensible way to grow climbing beans. Bush beans benefit by being supported off the ground, if only to be slightly less accessible to slugs.

Harvesting

July to October. The aim is to grow beans fit to eat, not monsters to boast of with strings in them like old rope. Pick regularly when the beans are young and tender. Young beans are delicious to eat and picking encourages the plants to go on producing.

Broad Beans (Fava Beans)

Beans are as venerable as peas, and in the Old World the broad bean (*Vicia faba*) is the doyen of all. Its prehistoric origin is doubtful. It probably came from the Near East, but it turns up in history, myth and archaeological sites in Europe (especially around the Mediterranean), North Africa and China. Curiously, the broad bean has had less

than its proper share of veneration. The Romans offered it to some of their gods, but for others it was taboo. According to Herodotus (484 B.C.), Egyptian priests regarded the broad bean as unclean, and Pythagoras blamed it for insomnia and bad dreams.

Yet in times of hardship the dried broad bean has been an invaluable source of protein. Bean meal was one ingredient in the hardtack recipe given by God to Ezekiel in the vision of the disasters awaiting Jerusalem. And in medieval England many a peasant owed his survival to the broad bean.

Varieties

Broad Windsor Long Pod matures in 65 days. Long Pod needs an 85-day growing season. Express is cold resistant and fast maturing.

GROWING BROAD BEANS
Preparing the soil

A well-dug, well-manured, fairly heavy soil suits broad beans. Rake the bed to get a fine tilth when you are ready to sow.

Sowing

Broad beans do best where summers are not too warm. Fava broad beans are appreciated by gardeners in Zones 3 and 4 although these beans will also produce a reasonable winter crop in Gulf Coast states. Broad beans are a slow-growing crop and thus need to be sown as early as possible. Fortunately, favas are fairly tolerant of cool soil and can therefore be planted soon after the last spring frosts. Sow seeds 8 inches (20 cm) apart.

The year's work

Maintain soil evenly moist during the growing season. Mulch or hoe to control weeds. Tall varieties need to be supported with poles at intervals along both sides of the row. Tie twine about 12 inches (30 cm) above ground level so that the plants have something to lean against. Add more twine as beans grow. The plastic garden nets are also useful as supports and are almost invisible. Spray with rotenone or malathion to control aphids.

Harvesting

June to September. Use as freshly picked beans (seeds only) or dry for later use.

Lima Beans

The lima bean (*Phaseolus lunatus*) was thus named when Spanish settlers sent the seeds back to Europe via Lima, Peru. However, the species ancestors of our modern lima bean actually came from Guatemala, where Indians cultivated several types long before Europeans came to the New World. Down South the lima bean is called butter bean or butter pea. The variety Dixie Butterpea is actually a delicious bush lima bean.

Lima beans are useful fresh and as a dried-bean crop. Most practical in the home garden are bush limas, which produce pods 3 to 4 inches (8 to 10 cm) long on sturdy plants just slightly taller than bush snap beans. Lima beans are heat resistant and will produce a crop in 65 to 75 days. The tall pole limas need up to 90 days to mature.

Within the bush lima group are small green baby limas and large green mealy limas. Some types, such as Jackson Wonder, have purple-speckled seeds. The types called butter peas are almost round, very meaty.

Varieties

Fordhook 242 is the most famous bush lima and rightly so; this adaptable variety is heat resistant and very productive. Burpee's Fordhook is slightly larger. Henderson Bush produces 3-inch (8 cm) pods with 3 seeds each, of baby lima size. King of the Garden is a vigorous, climbing pole-type lima.

GROWING LIMA BEANS
Sowing

Plant seed after bush beans, usually early to mid-June north of the Ohio River. Soil must be warm for lima beans to succeed. Space seed 4 inches (10 cm) apart, cover 1 inch (2 cm) deep. Germination is often only 50 to 75 percent. Thin plants for 8- to 12-inch (19 to 30 cm) growing space.

The year's work

Mulch around beans with straw or rough compost to reduce weeding chores and to hold moisture. Provide support for climbing pole limas.

Harvesting

Begin harvest when pods are full but before they turn yellow. Picking young pods is best for tender green beans you wish to cook. Older, fully mature beans are preferred for drying.

*S*oybeans

The soybean (*Glycine hispida*) is, economically, the most important bean in the world. It has been cultivated in China for centuries, but was not known at all in Europe until the seventeenth century.

*B*ean Sprouts

The mung bean (*Phaseolus mungo*), the bean most commonly used for producing bean sprouts, is native to India, where the beans are cooked, puréed and eaten as part of the daily diet. In China, however, the beans are cultivated for their crisp, refreshing, delicately flavored young shoots.

*H*aricot Beans

Haricot beans are the ripe seeds of bush beans. Napoleon was so fond of them that when he was imprisoned he ate haricot-bean salad every alternate day. Both the French and Italians so enjoy haricots that they have invented many bean dishes.

GROWING SOYBEANS

Select a variety bred for home garden use; the commercial types raised for oil are not tasty. Akita Early is a recent Japanese variety which produces 2 to 3 yellow beans per pod in a 95- to 100-day period. Early Green Bush matures in 85 days, grows 16 inches (40 cm) tall. Fiskeby V has more protein than steak! Sow seeds when soil is warm; mid-June in Northern states. For fast start, plant seed April to May in 2- to 3-inch (4 to 8 cm) peat pots. Grow seedlings under lights or in a bright greenhouse, transplant outdoors 5 inches (12 cm) apart when all danger of frost is past. Use beans cooked like limas or roasted like peanuts.

GROWING BEAN SPROUTS

All you need is somewhere warm, about 70°F (21°C), mung beans and total darkness. Rinse the beans and soak them in a bowl of water for a day or two. When the skins begin to burst, spread the beans on a piece of damp toweling or blanket and put them in a warm, dark cupboard. They will have to be watered several times a day to keep them constantly damp. You will quickly learn how much water they need, for if they are too wet and too warm they will get moldy. All being well, however, in a week to nine days the fat shoots will be about 2 inches (5 cm) long and ready to pull or cut with scissors.

GROWING HARICOT BEANS

Haricot beans need a warm, sheltered garden to mature in and a lot of space to produce a sizable crop. Leave all the pods on the plants until early autumn, when they turn yellow. Then pull up the plants on a day when there is no rain on them. Hang the plants up in a well-ventilated shed to dry thoroughly. Shell, and store the beans in perforated cardboard boxes. If stored in tins or sealed jars the beans will perspire and will deteriorate in quality. Comtesse de Chambord is a good variety to grow for drying. It produces thin-skinned beans, which will need less soaking than other varieties before cooking.

Bean pests

Aphids that adore broad beans attack in April (if the weather is good), May and June. Spray with malathion, not waiting for the infestation to build up and weaken the plant. When using malathion and pyrethrum always spray in the evening when the bees are back in the hive. By the next morning, when they are out and busy pollinating again, the bees will no longer be poisoned by the sprays. Repeat the spraying each week, if necessary, during the dangerous months. Aphids usually choose the succulent growing tips of the spring-grown plant. Remove this temptation by cutting off about 6 inches (15 cm) of stem with the growing shoots as soon as a good number of flowers have set and pods are forming. If bush beans are attacked by aphids, as sometimes they are, unfortunately, spray them similarly with rotenone or malathion.

Bean diseases

Brown spots and marks on broad-bean leaves and stems mean an attack of chocolate leaf spot, a form of botrytis. Attacks in early summer, especially in damp weather, are more likely to be serious and may kill the plant. Spray with Maneb.

Semitransparent spots surrounded by a yellow ring on the leaves and pods of bush (and sometimes runner) beans is halo blight, a bacterial seed-borne disease which can kill

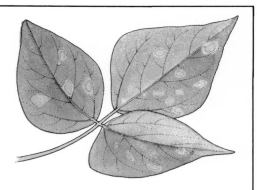

the plant. The practice of soaking beans in water before sowing to help them to germinate spreads the disease from infected to healthy seeds. Spray with Maneb.

Stunted growth, yellowing leaves and a quickly dying plant may be caused by the fusarium wilt fungus attacking the root. It is less evident on well-cultivated land. Wilt-resistant varieties are hard to find.

Onions

The onion is one of 450 species of allium. Regrettably, most of the rest, although highly ornamental in the garden, are not for eating. Nonetheless, there is a whole range of onion flavors which are worth cultivating, from the gentle chive to the strong-flavored garlic. Home-grown scallions (salad onions) are cheaper than those bought in the market. Home-grown garlic is absurdly cheap and much juicier. Leeks taste much better when just taken out of the ground, and since they are incredibly hardy there is no excuse for not growing them. Some of the other onions included in this section are unusual, but interesting.

1 String of onions
2 Scallions
3 Onions
4 Garlic
5 Shallots
6 Pickling onions
7 Leeks

*L*eeks

The Emperor Nero believed that leeks (*Allium porrum*) were good for his singing voice. Romany Leon Petulengro believes that they are good for his hair. Most of us are content that they are just good to eat. Juvenal, a contemporary of Pliny, must have been of the same opinion, since he complained so bitterly at their being adopted as divine: ". . . to injure the leek and onion is wicked, and to crush them with the teeth—O Holy race! Whose gods are born in the kitchen garden!" Never are leeks better to eat than in the grim days of February, although it means going out into the garden to dig them up.

Growing leeks is a good introduction to other members of the onion family. You are hardly ever likely to fail, even in the coldest parts of the country. Disaster with main crop onions is far more likely, and can sour a novice for years.

There are two common ways of growing leeks. One, for the ordinary gardener, is simple. The other, for the gardener whose principal aim is to win medals and cups, is tedious and arduous. But the gardener who is as concerned with eating leeks as with cultivating them, can adopt something of both approaches.

Varieties
The Lyon and Artico are flavorful, hardy varieties. Musselburgh, long, thick stems, very hardy, resistant to frost, with excellent flavor.

Pests and diseases
Although leeks can suffer the pests and diseases to which the onion family is prone (see page 79), they seldom do. This is a worthy plant.

GROWING LEEKS
Preparing the soil
Although leeks are not as greedy as onions, no harm is done by giving them the same treatment—digging in compost or rotted manure the previous autumn—and the same place in the rotation, although they are planted later in the year. Add lime to achieve pH 6 to 6.5.

Sowing
Late January indoors. Leeks can be sown in flats of a peat-lite mix 1 inch (2 cm) apart each way. Keep in a greenhouse at 55°F (13°C). Prick out to 2 inches (5 cm) apart each way when the seedlings are 1 inch (2 cm) high and then harden off for planting out in April or early May by moving them into frames in late March.

March/April. Leeks meant only for the kitchen and not for show are sown out of doors in 1-inch (2 cm) drills in a brassica-type seedbed. (See page 48.) The earlier the sowing the better, between late February and mid-April, depending upon where the garden is and the earliness of spring. On the day before transplanting, water the bed well.

Planting
Late June. Lightly fork over the rows where the leeks are to go and then rake them. Using a garden line to get the row straight, makes holes with a large dibble 6 inches (15 cm) deep and 8 inches (20 cm) apart. Leave 12 inches (30 cm) between the rows. Lift the leek seedlings carefully from the seedbed. A handfork is the least

likely to damage them. By this time they will be 6 to 8 inches (15 to 20 cm) high. Reject the weaklings. Lower a leek seedling into each hole, but do not fill the hole up with soil. Instead, pour water into it gently, for the purpose is to anchor the roots without drowning or floating the seedling.

Another method is to take out two drills 4 inches (10 cm) deep and 6 inches (15 cm) apart, using a trowel for making a hole for the roots. Stagger the seedlings 10 inches (25 cm) apart along the two drills. Do not plant too deeply; only the roots and the base of the bulblet should be below the

surface. Allow 24 inches (60 cm) between these double rows. This will give room for earthing up later, to produce longer, whiter leeks.

The year's work
Hoe occasionally to keep down weeds. In dry weather in July and August water may be needed. Afterward, all that remains to be done with those leeks which were merely dropped into holes in the ground is to dig them up through the winter as you want them.

Earthing up and blanching of leeks sown in double rows begins in September or October. The tedious part of this operation is to ensure that soil does not get into the leek. Tie paper or plastic around the stems to the base of the leaves before drawing up the soil (with a garden hoe) from between the rows. Further earthings up until the plants stop growing around November may make it necessary to add another collar.

Harvesting
November/April. Dig up the plants with a fork as you want them. They are very hardy. Any plants left in the ground when it is needed for the new season's crop can be heeled in in a small trench until needed.

Onion

The onion (*Allium cepa*) goes farther back in time than historians can. A Turkish fable, attributing the onion's creation to the devil, dates it from the time when he was thrown out of paradise and landed on Earth.

Other more reliable authorities have surmised that it originated in Central Asia and record it as being invested with divinity, not devilry.

Fortunately, however highly the onion has since been honored, no one has regarded it as too sacred to eat, as the Egyptians came to do two thousand years ago. There was no hesitation about eating it among the Greeks or the Romans, who brought it to Britain.

In Britain the history of the onion has been occupied more with its medicinal than its magical properties. Among the more notable observations is the notion in Gerard's *Herbal* that the juice of the onion "anointed upon a bald head in the sun bringeth the haire again very speedily." Gerard was less enthusiastic about the onion's culinary qualities: "The onion being eaten, yea though it be boiled, causeth head ache, hurteth the eyes, and maketh a man dim sighted, dulleth the senses, and provoketh overmuch sleep, especially being eaten raw." In spite of Gerard's damnation of the onion, its culinary reputation increased as surely as the faith in its magical properties declined.

Varieties

For sowing in August where mild: Sturon, mild-flavored yellow. Express Yellow F₁, dark-yellow globe, one of the new Japanese varieties.

For sowing in January under glass: Ailsa Craig, the old faithful, large golden globe.

For sowing in spring: Bedfordshire Champion, large, well-flavored globe and a good keeper. Giant Zittau, medium-sized, semiflat bulbs and an exceptional keeper. Yellow Sweet Spanish matures in 115 days.

GROWING ONIONS FROM SEED
Preparing the soil

Once upon a time everyone was advised to make a permanent onion bed and, by heavy manuring every year, build up a soil of incredible fertility, which would produce monster onions. For the gardener who grows onions to eat it is both unnecessary (because an ordinary-sized and tasty onion does not need force-feeding like an Alsace goose) and dangerous (because the plot is as likely to build up disease as fertility). So let the onion bed rotate with the rest of the vegetable garden. It usually goes along in the cycle with the peas and beans.

Add lime to achieve pH 6 to 6.3. Dig in compost or well-rotted manure in the autumn, to give the soil time to settle, and let the winter break down the soil to a fine tilth. Rake in the spring. Onions prefer a medium soil, but it must be firm—hence the ritual of treading up and down the bed before sowing or transplanting. But wait until the soil is dry and friable enough not to stick in great clods on your boots.

Sowing

Early spring in North; fall in warm South: sowings in shallow drills 12 inches (30 cm) apart can be made where the onions are to grow (in ground, for example, that was cleared of the crop of early potatoes). It is better, however, to

prepare a seedbed in a very sheltered part of the garden, leaving the seedlings unthinned over the winter and transplanting them in March or early April. Autumn sowings are worthwhile only in warm gardens, and even then losses will be heavy, although covering the seedlings with cloches by the end of October will help to reduce them. Only certain varieties are suitable for autumn sowing; Ailsa Craig is the most popular.

January, under glass: Sow in January in seed trays in a heated greenhouse—60°F (16°C) to ensure adequate germination, thereafter dropping the temperature to around 50°F (10°C) by daytime and 45°F (7°C) at night. Or sow in peat pots, 3 or 4 seeds to the pot, removing all but the strongest seedling. Harden off in a cold frame toward the end of March, ready for transplanting in early April. Seeds can also be sown in frames or under cloches, but obviously germinate more slowly.

March/April, out of doors: In the bed that is all ready and waiting, take out shallow drills 12 inches (30 cm) apart. If you have large or clumsy feet allow more space between rows so that you can later weed in comfort. Sow thinly and just cover the seeds with soil or sifted compost, firming the rows with the back of a rake. Since the seeds are black and not very large it is a good idea to give them a pre-sowing dusting of flour. This makes it easy for you to see whether you are sowing them as thinly as you should be. The less thinning that has to be done later the better, for the disturbance of the roots and the soil during thinning is an odorous invitation to the onion fly to get to work. (See pests, page 79.) Thinning is usually done in two stages, the first to 2 inches (5 cm) apart and the second to 4 to 6 inches (10 to 15 cm) apart.

Planting

March/April. Autumn-sown seedlings will be transplanted in March or April, according to the state of the soil and the weather. Allow 12 inches (30 cm), or more for those large feet, between rows and 6 inches (15 cm) between plants. Planting must be done with care.

Do not plant too deeply. Make a hole with a trowel deep enough for the roots of the seedling to go their full depth in the soil, but the bottom of the bulblet should be not more than ½ inch (1 cm) below the surface of the soil. And plant firmly.

Try not to damage the leaves of the seedlings. Even if you do not notice the smell of a bruised leaf the female onion fly may, and will come homing in to lay her eggs.

Seedlings raised under glass will be ready for transplanting from the middle of April.

The year's work

Weed, preferably by hand, because onions resent you digging around their roots with a hoe. In dry weather water may be needed. A peat sedge mulch will inhibit weeds and conserve moisture, but it should not bury any part of the swelling bulb, which needs the sun. Stop watering as soon as the bulbs begin to ripen, from late July to August. In a dry summer the leaves will topple over on their own. In a wet summer you may have to help by bending the leaves over. (In a very wet summer the onion may go on producing foliage when it should be swelling into a bulb, and bull-necked onions which will not ripen or keep will be the result.) When, after two or three weeks, the leaves have turned yellow and shriveled, the onions are ready for harvesting.

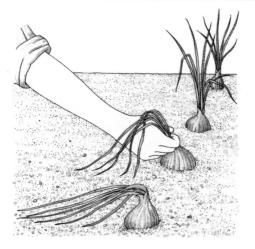

Harvesting

August/September. Choose a dry day. If the bulbs are ripe they can be pulled by hand or eased up with a fork. If the weather is thoroughly settled they can be laid on burlap or, better still, on a raised wire netting frame, and

left in the garden with their roots facing south to the sun. If the weather is uncertain, spread the bulbs out in a greenhouse or in a well-ventilated covered frame.

When the leaves are brittle the onions are ready for storing. Store them where they will be dry and cool, but safe from hard frost. Wooden crates can probably be acquired from supermarkets. Fill each crate with one layer of onions, and stack. Ropes of onions take up less room, and there is a certain satisfaction in being able to rope at all, and much pride in being able to do it well.

Store only sound, firm bulbs, and inspect them frequently during the winter, removing any which have gone soft. By May even the longest-keeping varieties will have abandoned the effort to live up to their name.

Stringing onions

When the onions are properly dry they can be strung as a rope, which is the most convenient way to store them. This method has the advantages of taking up less room than stacking in crates and of allowing a flow of air around the onions.

To string onions, take a length of stout string or twine and tie it to form a loop. Hang the loop over a hook at a convenient height for working and proceed as shown below.

Onion Sets

Some gardeners, especially those who live where the summers are short and wet, will never be able to grow satisfactory main crop onions from seed. Their alternative is to grow onions from sets. These are small immature onions raised from seed one year (usually by

specialist growers) and planted by gardeners the following spring to grow into full-sized onions. The young onion having, as it were, borrowed time from the previous year has a chance to grow to maturity and ripeness before the onset of autumn. Years ago, the varieties available as sets were, alas, limited, sources of supply dubious and sets were given to bolting after replanting. Now sets are available from many reliable mail-order firms. The onion set has a further advantage; it is generally regarded by the onion fly as too tough and unattractive a target. The only drawback is that sets are more expensive than seed, but not prohibitively so, considering that one pound of sets should produce fifty times that weight of onions.

Varieties

Ebenezer is offered as a white or a yellow variety. Golden Mosque combines the earliness of Ebenezer with the long-keeping qualities of Stuttgarter, another good type, noted for flattened form. Spartan Sleeper, developed at Michigan State University, keeps 15 to 18 months without sprouting. Many growers now heat treat onion sets to kill the dormant flower stem in the bulb and so prevent bolting. If the bulbs arrive before planting time, unpack them and spread them out in a cool place and in full light so that they do not sprout.

GROWING ONIONS FROM SETS

Preparing the soil

Sets are not as demanding as onions grown from seed. Do not manure the ground for this crop, but apply a dressing of general fertilizer, 4 ounces to the square yard (120 g to 1 sq m), ten to fourteen days before planting. Onions need a firm soil.

Planting

March/April. The bulbs should be of a fairly uniform size about ½ inch (1 cm) in diameter. Any much smaller are not worth planting because they will not grow into decent-sized bulbs. Before planting, trim

the old dry stems of the bulbs, but do not cut back into the flesh of the onion or it may rot. The purpose of this trimming is to leave less purchase for birds trying to tug them out of the ground, as they will. (Trimming is even more advisable for shallots, which tend to have more stem on

them.) Plant the sets just deep enough for the tips to show. Do not plant more deeply, even to cheat the birds. The bulbs should be 6 inches (15 cm) apart in rows 12 inches (30 cm) or more apart. Make the soil firm around them.

The year's work

Except for the difference in planting, onions grown from sets need the same treatment as those grown from seed. It is unlikely, however, that there will be any trouble from onion-fly maggots.

Harvesting

Harvesting and storing are the same as for seed-grown onions. The problem is to provide enough sun to dry the onions out for storing, and this is not altogether in your hands. Northern gardeners, however, will find that onions from sets ripen more readily.

Shallots

Shallots (*Allium ascalonicum*) may be grown as a milder alternative, or as an addition, to onions. They are planted as offsets, but instead of growing bigger—for they are

already mature—they produce a new generation of clusters of bulbs, anything from six to a dozen.

Varieties

Dutch Yellow is productive and stores well. Hative de Niort has round bulbs, but they do not keep well.

GROWING SHALLOTS

Preparing the soil

Grow shallots in a bed prepared as for onions. Shallots prefer a soil which has been manured the previous autumn and which has had time to settle. The soil must be firm, but do not tread it down until it is dry enough not to stick to your boots.

Planting

February/March. Planting should be done as early in the year as possible. Trim back any dead, long leaves which birds might fancy for their nests or worms for their burrows. Push the bulbs into the soil, leaving the tips just showing. Since shallots have a way of pushing themselves out of the soil, or being pushed out by frost, watch out for any which may need replanting.

The year's work

Weed, with care. In June, draw the soil slightly away from the clusters of bulbs which will have developed, to help them to ripen.

Harvesting

June/July. When the leaves turn yellow dig up the shallots and leave them in the sun to dry. When dried, rub them with your hands to remove brittle foliage and loose skin. Put to one side enough healthy-looking small bulbs for next year's planting. Hang the rest in a cool place in string bags for use in the winter. Look at the bulbs occasionally. Remove any going bad.

Pests and diseases

The onion-fly maggot is the curse of the onion family, especially in May and June, although the plants may be attacked by later generations right up until September. Main crop onions from spring sowings are those most likely to be attacked. Onions planted in light soil are also in danger of attack.

Onion sets, shallots and leeks are less vulnerable. The onion fly, which resembles the house fly, lays eggs in the soil. When the destructive off-white maggots emerge, they burrow into the bulbs and eat them away. The first sign above ground of their presence below—yellowing and dying of leaves—comes too late for action. Dusting the soil with Diazinon immediately after planting and again in two weeks discourages the flies. Above all, take great care when you are thinning out your onion bed. Disturbed roots, damaged leaves and thinnings left lying about put the onion fly on the scent of your crop.

Eelworms (nematodes, see page 24) look like minute, transparent eels. However, they are invisible to the naked eye. Their rate of propagation is phenomenal—an infected bulb could contain literally millions of these pests. Of the thousands of species of eelworm there is one parasitic form which is attracted to onions. Secretions from the roots make the dormant

cysts burst into life and the microscopic eelworms burrow into the bulbs and then into the stems, which swell and go soft. Burn all affected plants. After an outbreak you must abandon growing any of the onion family on that ground for at least five years. Chickweed is a host to the same eelworm, hence the importance of keeping a weed-free onion bed.

Cool, wet autumns may produce ideal conditions for downy mildew. This fungus grows deep into the onion plant. The leaves become velvety, die back from the tips, then finally collapse. If there has been a fair amount of rain, the leaves may also turn purple.

Warm summers may encourage white rot in onions, particularly in White Lisbon. The leaves turn yellow, the bulbs rot and are covered with a growth of white-gray fungus. Burn affected plants, and do not use that ground again for onions for at least eight years. There is less danger of an attack

on fertile, organically manured soil. Leeks and some varieties of onion, especially Bedfordshire Champion, are less likely to be attacked by white rot; however, Bedfordshire Champion is very susceptible to downy mildew.

Neck rot and bulb rot are caused by one

of the botrytis fungi, producing masses of white and gray mold or brown rot on onions in store. The fungus is most likely to develop if the bulbs have been damaged, for example by hoeing, or have not been dried thoroughly when harvested and are stored in a damp and ill-ventilated place. Do not try to store onions with green, fleshy necks.

Shallot virus yellows produces yellow streaks on the leaves of shallots and causes dwarfing of the plants. Onions are only occasionally affected. Burn the diseased plants as soon as you notice the signs. The virus is spread by aphids so control begins there with sprayings of malathion.

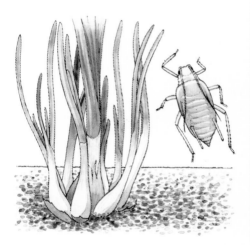

Onion smut is easily recognizable: the diseased young onion leaves are covered with blisters, which contain black, powdery spores. The blisters also appear on the bulbs. To avoid onion smut, dust seed and furrow with Thiram or Captan.

These are the main pests and diseases, and there are more than a dozen others that could be mentioned. But by maintaining a fertile soil and not making life too easy for the onion fly, you have a good chance of avoiding all of them. It is important that you should recognize the symptoms so that you may always be on your guard.

Chives

The chive (*Allium schoenoprasum*) fills a spring gap in the onion year. It has been grown in Britain and throughout Europe for centuries, and in China for thousands of years.

Scallions

Not satisfied with thinnings from main crop onions, the true onion lover demands "spring" onions all year around, and with a little bit of care he can almost get them. White Lisbon is the variety usually chosen.

Welsh Onions

The perennial Welsh onion (*Allium fistulosum*) is a native of Siberia, being correctly not "Welsh," but *walsch*, meaning foreign. Its hardiness makes the scallions it produces a substitute for spring onions in winter and early spring.

GROWING CHIVES

Preparing the soil
In the garden, chives are fairly tolerant about soil and position, but produce far more succulent grass in humus-rich, moisture-holding soil. In poor soil the leaves quickly yellow at the tips.

Sowing and planting
Chives can easily be grown from April-sown seed, but germination is slow and the first year is fairly unproductive. Buying clumps in spring is better, for cutting can begin less than two months later when the shoots are about 3 inches (8 cm) high. Divide them into clumps of up to half a dozen bulbs and plant them 8 inches (20 cm) apart in a row. They can be planted as an edging in the vegetable, flower or herb garden. Every third year divide the clumps and replant them in another part of the garden. Given good soil and not allowed to get dry, chives are also excellent for windowsill pots or window boxes.

The year's work
Although a hardy perennial like the Welsh onion, chives are not evergreen. If you want early chives, however, they can be grown indoors. Dig up a few clumps in late autumn, divide them up, plant in pots and then cut the foliage to within a couple of inches of the soil. Keep them moist and cut and use the new shoots before they get too tall and tough. Constant cutting, both indoors and out, is essential if you are to keep up a supply of leaves. They should certainly be cut back when they flower—if you can bear to do so, for the flowers are particularly attractive.

GROWING SCALLIONS

Preparing the soil
Prepare the ground as for other onions—raking to a fine tilth soil that has been manured for a previous crop.

Sowing
For the earliest spring crop sow under cloches in August or early September in ½-inch (1 cm) drills 10 inches (25 cm) apart. Sow fairly thickly.

For a later crop (June onward) sow under cloches in February or in the open in March/April. Sow again in May/June for pulling in the autumn.

The year's work
Weed carefully by hand in the early growing period and regularly thereafter—the young plants are delicate and can be easily enveloped by weeds.

Harvesting
Pull the onions as they get big enough to use.

Japanese Bunching Onions

The Japanese bunching onion is sometimes called Hardy White Bunching. Sakata's Evergreen is an excellent hardy selection. It is untroubled by pests and diseases. If growing Japanese bunching onions from seed, sow in April and thin to 10 inches (25 cm) apart. By the following year each bulb will have produced a considerable number of scallions, with crisp, tender leaves and stems for use in salads. It can be divided to provide further clumps. After several years it benefits from division, only the younger bulbs being planted and the rest eaten.

GROWING WELSH ONIONS

Preparing the soil
There is no need for any special preparation as these hardy, non-bulbous onions thrive in any convenient part of the garden as long as it is fertile and well drained.

Planting
Although Welsh onions can be raised from seed by sowing in April in a shallow drill, it is preferable to buy a few plants. Plant 10 inches (25 cm) apart as an edging in the vegetable garden or in the herb garden. They do not need pampering, but give them a sheltered spot if you plan to dig them up in the depth of winter.

The year's work
Welsh onions require little attention. After harvesting, leave some of the scallions in each clump to multiply again. The next year, each plant will have produced a couple of dozen more. After three years, divide the clumps, giving them a change of ground.

Harvesting
From June onward. Cut whole clumps—both the leaves and shoots are good to eat.

Sources
This unusual onion is not easy to find and in fact most of the vegetable catalogs do not list Welsh onions. However, seed is offered by some firms, such as J. L. Hudson, where it may be found along with flower seeds, listed as *Allium fistulosum*. Once you grow a clump, you will have this unique species available for years as clump divisions.

Onion Seedlings

As an alternative to planting sets or seeds try growing a crop of onions from seedlings. Several firms now offer onion seedlings every spring. The plants are sold in bunches which may contain 50 to 75 plants each. The seedlings are inexpensive and thus provide a fine source of healthy onions to get your crop off

to an early start. Another advantage to planting seedlings is that some varieties not available as sets (small bulbs) are offered as seedlings. For example, you can obtain seedlings of the big Bermuda White hybrid and Giant Red Hamburger hybrid. The started onion seedlings need a growing season of about 65 days before they reach harvest size. Some dealers, such as R. H. Shumway, offer onion seedlings in the fall and spring. This is an advantage if you live in a mild region and wish to get a crop in after the main summer growing season.

Varieties

The onions most often sold as seedlings are the Spanish Yellow hybrid, a large globe-type onion with a mild, sweet flavor; Bermuda White hybrid, an onion famous for large size, semiflat shape, very mild taste, a favorite raw in salads and on hamburgers; Red Burgundy, for crisp, sweet red-green flesh; and Giant Red Hamburger hybrid, a big, semiflat onion with red skin and an inside of red alternated with white, attractive raw in salads.

PLANTING ONION SEEDLINGS

The onion seedlings will come to you with good root systems, looking like a small bunch of scallions. As soon as they come put the plants into a bucket of lukewarm water which just covers the root system. For an added push to the plants use a transplanting solution instead of a water soak. Mix a water-soluble fertilizer such as Miracle-Gro or Hyponex at one-third strength. Add several drops of a root-stimulating hormone such as SuperThrive or some Transplantone powder according to package directions. This solution will provide both a weak fertilizer and a root stimulant. After giving the seedlings a soak of several hours, plant them out in well-prepared soil as explained on page 76. Water the seedlings well with a fine mist. If you have a very small garden you may wish to order the onion seedlings with a neighbor since most firms will ship a minimum of 2 bunches, which usually total more than 150 plants!

Garlic

Garlic (*Allium sativum*) is one of the oldest and certainly the strongest of the edible alliums. The Romans, believing that it gave strength, fed it to their soldiers to fight the better and to their laborers to work the harder,

as the Egyptians did to the slaves building the pyramids. Today, the widely held theory is that garlic originated in the Kirghiz region of central Asia. In spite of its long history there is still much prejudice against garlic, but nowhere is it so evident as in parts of India, where it is associated with the devil. There is no need to buy garlic, because it is extraordinarily easy to grow.

GROWING GARLIC
Preparing the soil
A row or part of a row in full sun in the ground prepared for the onions would suit garlic, but it does not need the same firmness. The sun, however, is vital.

Planting
November to March. Plant the cloves, pointed end up, in holes 1 inch (2 cm) deep and 6 inches (15 cm) apart.

The year's work
Weed well, preferably by hand to avoid hoe damage. If there is a lot of top growth, support the stems with lengths of string between stakes.

Harvesting
July/August. When the stems and leaves lose their greenness and topple over, it is time to take up the bulbs. Do not tug them up; you may damage the stems and make them rot. Ease them out of the ground with a fork. Let the bulbs dry outside in the sun if possible, but dry them indoors if there is any danger of their getting wet. After a few days drying, hang them up in a string bag. Save as many as you need of the sturdy, outside cloves for planting the next year.

Pickling Onions

The onions specially grown for pickling are the mild-flavored varieties, which are lifted before they are fully grown. The best of these are Silver Queen and Barletta White.

GROWING PICKLING ONIONS
Preparing the soil
Pickling onions are modest and convenient vegetables to cultivate: they actually prefer to grow in poor soil, so they can be planted in any corner of the garden that has been rejected by other fussier vegetables. All that is necessary for the gardener to do is to rake the ground to a fine tilth before sowing the seeds. Pickling onions can also be grown in soil that had been manured for a previous crop.

Sowing
April. Broadcast the seeds fairly thickly or sow them in shallow drills 10 inches (25 cm) apart. Seeds sown shallowly produce round onion bulbs. Those which are planted about an inch (2 cm) deep produce oval-shaped onions.

The year's work
All that is required is to keep the plot free of weeds, which, if allowed to thrive, will dominate the pickling onions. Remove the weeds by hand. Pickling onions do not require thinning. Allow them to grow without interference until the tops have begun to die down. They will then be ready for lifting.

Harvesting
Because the onions have not been heavily manured and have grown in crowded conditions they mature early and should be ready for lifting by about the end of August. Fork up the onions, and if the weather is good, leave them on the ground for a week to ten days, turning them over occasionally so that they can ripen and dry.

Roots

"**T**he roots have a peculiar flavor" was the catalog recommendation, many years ago, for some obscure Chinese vegetable. The same can be said of any of the roots in this section. Which roots you grow depends on which peculiar flavors appeal to you. My own prejudices are against all of them except rutabagas, celeriac and cold beets. The common objection is that roots are too sweet. Only the radish escapes being condemned for that; instead it is blamed for being indigestible. It is a pity about the prejudices, for, in the barren winter months, roots are invaluable as vegetables in their own right, and as ingredients in other dishes they are indispensable.

1 Carrots
2 Rutabagas
3 Turnips
4 Beets
5 Parsnips
6 Celeriac
7 Radishes
8 Kohlrabi

Carrots

The carrot (*Daucus carota*), a native of Afghanistan, grows wild in Europe and in the United States. As a cultivated vegetable it was well established in the Mediterranean region two thousand years ago, and spread east to China and north to Europe six hundred years ago. The Flemings brought garden carrots to England in the reign of Elizabeth I, and to this day Dutch varieties are among the best.

The carrot has long had a reputation as a breaker of wind. Athenaeus, in *The Sophists at Dinner*, included this tribute to the carrot from Diphilus, one of the diners: "This is pungent, very nourishing and fairly wholesome, with a tendency to loosening and windiness; not easy to digest, very diuretic, calculated to rouse sexual desire, hence by some it is called 'love philter.'"

Varieties

For sowing in frames or under cloches and early out of doors: Coreless Amsterdam and Nantes Half Long both produce 6- to 7-inch (15 to 17 cm) roots of good orange color. For heavy soil and excellent cooking try the small types such as Baby-Finger Nantes, a 2- to 3-inch (4 to 8 cm) root, or Tiny Sweet, a similar golden-orange, 3-inch (8 cm) midget root. Where soil is deeply prepared, the large carrots will do well. Royal Cross is a new bright-orange cylindrical type which grows 6 to 7 inches (16 to 17 cm) long. Pioneer is a similar, deeply colored hybrid.

Pests and diseases

On rare occasions carrot-fly maggots may attack. These can be controlled by spraying seedling tops with Sevin and dusting the ground with Diazinon later in the season. Sevin will also control leafhoppers which sometimes suck plant juices and carry virus diseases.

GROWING CARROTS

Preparing the soil

The ideal soil is sandy loam and it will also have to be deep for the long-rooted varieties. In heavier soils the stumpier and intermediate varieties are better. Heavier soil should be dug before winter so that frost can make it friable. The ground must not be manured for carrots; freshly manured land encourages the roots to fork. Apply lime to get a pH of 6.3 to 6.4. Just before sowing spread a general fertilizer, 4 ounces to the square yard (120 g to 1 sq m), and rake the soil to a fine tilth.

Sowing

March to July. The most desired carrots—the early ones—are the most trouble to grow. The earliest to be harvested would be those sown in February in a frame over a hotbed, but manure is too scarce for old-fashioned hotbeds and electricity too expensive to pamper carrots with soil-warming cables. With a little patience, however, a start can be made in March under cloches. Sow in ½-inch (1 cm) drills in rows 10 inches (25 cm) apart. As with all early sowings the cloches are put in position some weeks—at least two—before sowing, to warm up the soil.

The first main crop sowing can be made in April, and again in May, June and early July. Because the seeds are small, it is better to use pelleted seeds, if you can get them in the varieties you want. This allows you to space out the seeds and eliminates thinning.

For extra-easy-to-harvest, well-shaped carrots, plant in a raised bed filled with a humus-rich soil or a peat-lite mixture such as Terralite planting mix, which contains nutrients. Raised beds can be quickly constructed with lumber (redwood), railroad

ties or cement patio blocks sold at garden centers.

The year's work

Once the seedlings are well through, water if the soil is dry. When they are 1 inch (2 cm) or so high, start thinning. Do not leave the thinnings lying around on the soil. Bury them in the compost heap instead of just leaving them on the top.

The first thinning should be to 2 inches (5 cm) apart and the second, two weeks or so later, 4 to 6 inches (10 to 15 cm)—the long-rooted varieties need more room to spread than the others. Hoe to keep weeds under control.

Harvesting

Summer and October. Pull the early carrots when they are young and tender, as wanted during the summer. Those for storing are lifted, eased out of the ground with a fork, in October before the first frosts occur. If they are left in the ground too long in wet weather the roots will start to split. Store only the healthy undamaged carrots. Twist off the leaves and store the roots (not touching each other) between layers of sand or peat in boxes or plastic bins in a cool, frostproof place.

Turnips

Turnips (*Brassica campestris*, var. *rapa*) were a staple food of the poor of northern Europe until they were ousted by potatoes. Viscount "Turnip" Townshend, advocate of

the concept of the rotation of crops in Britain in the eighteenth century, made them the food of sheep. But, in the first century A.D., they were not beneath the notice of Gavius Apicius, Roman man about town and ostentatious *bon viveur*, who preserved them with myrtle berries, honey and vinegar. Sir Thomas Elyot, in 1539, in his *Castel of Helth*, wrote that not only were boiled turnips nourishing, but they "augmenteth the sede of man, provoketh carnall lust," a considerable claim for a vegetable which is more than 90 percent water. Those who wish to can have turnips for a large part of the year, but the turnips picked in their infancy in early summer are the most delicious.

Varieties
Tokyo Cross hybrid gives 2-inch (4 cm), round white turnips in 35 days but plants keep growing for larger roots later. Just Right hybrid needs 60 days for roots, has round white turnips, tasty greens. Purple-Top White Globe is purple above soil line, is good fresh and stores well.

Pests and diseases
The flea beetle is a menace. It is small and black and noted for its jumping ability and voracious appetite. The young leaves are particularly vulnerable to attack in dry weather and are quickly reduced to lacework if the pest is not checked. Do this with Sevin.

Club root is the commonest disease, as with cabbages. (See page 55.) In autumn, watch for mildew on the leaves, and if it appears spray the plants with Zineb or Captan.

GROWING TURNIPS
Preparing the soil
Turnips to be at their best must be grown quickly. This means a fertile, moisture-holding soil manured the year before. Winter turnips can be grown on ground vacated by other early crops. Turnips require a dressing of general fertilizer, 2 to 3 ounces to the square yard (60 to 90 g to 1 sq m). Turnips need a firm brassicalike seedbed or they may bolt. The soil must be adequately limed (pH 6.5 to 6.8).

Sowing
Late February to late July. The early sowings will have to be made under cloches or in frames. In early April, sowing can begin in the open and continue every three weeks until the beginning of July. In late July, sow seed of late-variety turnips, to be stored for use in winter. All varieties are sown in $\frac{1}{2}$-inch (1 cm) drills. Space the rows 12 to 16 inches (30 to 40 cm) apart.

The year's work
The first thinning, to 3 inches (8 cm) apart, is done when the seedlings have grown their first rough leaves. The second, a couple of weeks later, reduces them to 6 inches (15 cm) apart. Hoe constantly and water well if the weather is at all dry. Never, at any stage, must they go short of moisture.

Harvesting
Pull the early varieties as you need them. The turnips should be no smaller than a golf ball and no larger than a tennis ball. In October, the late varieties will be ready for lifting—use a fork. Twist off the tops,

and store the roots in sand-filled or peat-filled boxes in a cool, frostproof place. Do not try to store any which are damaged or diseased.

Rutabagas

Rutabagas (*Brassica campestris*, var. *ruta-baga*), or Swedish turnips, were once confused with turnips, but they are in fact larger and

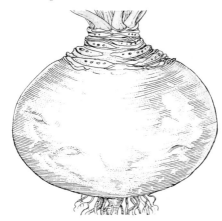

sweeter. They are much hardier than turnips and are particularly good for storing. Rutabagas grow best above the Mason-Dixon line.

Varieties
Purple Top, either to store or eat young, is the usual garden variety. Altasweet is a good hybrid with yellow flesh.

GROWING RUTABAGAS
Preparing the soil
Rutabagas, like turnips, need a fertile, adequately limed soil (pH 6.5 to 6.8) that does not dry out quickly in summer.

Sowing
May/June. Rutabagas, slower maturing than turnips, are sown early in May in the North. In the South, sowing is delayed until mid-June; there is then less chance that the leaves will be attacked by mildew. Sow in $\frac{1}{2}$-inch (1 cm) drills 18 inches (45 cm) apart.

The year's work
Thin the seedlings to 12 inches (30 cm) apart as soon as they are big enough to handle. Keep the rows free of weeds. In dry weather give the plants a thorough watering.

Harvesting
September/October. Immature rutabagas can be pulled in late summer, and excellent they are, too. But the main virtue of rutabagas is as a winter vegetable. They will be mature in October and can be lifted and stored like turnips. In milder areas they can be left in the ground and dug up as required.

Pests and diseases
Use Sevin, especially when the seedlings start coming through the soil, to deal with the flea beetle. Rutabagas are affected by brassica diseases generally, but more particularly by brown heart—the heart turns brown and glassy-looking—which is usually recognized only when the root is cut open. The cause is a deficiency of boron. Water lightly with a borax solution—$\frac{1}{2}$ ounce to a gallon of water (15 g to $4\frac{1}{2}$ liters).

Kohlrabi

Kohlrabi (*Brassica oleracea caulorapa*, var. *gougyloides*) is a cabbage with a swollen stem. It looks like the root of a turnip growing out of the ground. Kohlrabi can be grown in

places where the summers are hot and dry and turnips are, therefore, likely to fail. It can stand drought and heat without losing its flavor.

Varieties
Early White Vienna and the slightly later maturing Early Purple Vienna.

GROWING KOHLRABI
Preparing the soil
Kohlrabi prefers a light soil, but to achieve the fast growth necessary for tender roots, well-rotted compost or manure should be dug in well before sowing. Because kohlrabi is actually a brassica, make sure the soil is adequately limed (pH 6.5 to 6.8).

Sowing
April to July. Make small successional sowings every three weeks from April to July. Sow in drills 1 inch (2 cm) deep and 16 inches (40 cm) apart. Sow three seeds every 8 inches (20 cm) along a row and leave one seedling at each station when thinning. Late sowings should be of the purple variety if you want to have some for winter. They will produce large and coarser stems, and they will not have the quality of the summer variety.

The year's work
It is important to thin the seedlings as soon as they are large enough to handle. When hoeing take great care not to hit and damage the roots.

Harvesting
June onward. In summer, kohlrabi is pulled as needed when the roots are about 2 inches (5 cm) in diameter. Although the remaining produce of the late sowings can be lifted in October and stored in peat, they shrivel more than other stored roots.

Pests and diseases
For a brassica, kohlrabi is remarkably free of pests and diseases.

Celeriac

Celeriac (*Apium graveolens*), often called turnip-rooted celery, is, in spite of its shape, a true celery and has, both raw and cooked, the authentic celery taste. The texture is different, however, for it is the swollen base, not the stalks, for which celeriac is grown. In fact, the celerylike tops can be eaten—the leaves themselves as celery-flavored spinach and the leaf stalks as celery-flavored seakale. Unlike kohlrabi, the celeriac root should be allowed to swell to a decent size. This calls for a long growing season, but otherwise the plant has much to commend it. It is as hardy as celery, but less tiresome to grow because it requires no earthing up. It is surprising that this versatile vegetable has not gained more popularity.

Varieties
Globus has a good flavor. Balder has large roots and produces few side roots. Alabaster is useful fresh or stored.

GROWING CELERIAC
Preparing the soil
Celeriac is a Mediterranean plant and should have as much sun as possible. Dig in as much rotted manure or compost as you can spare. Do not overlime, a pH of 5.8 to 6 is quite adequate.

Sowing
March. Since celeriac plants, unlike celery, can seldom be bought from nurserymen, you will have to raise them from seed. For this, if the growing season is to be long enough, heat will be needed. If you do not have a heated greenhouse use an electric seed propagator. Sow early in March at a temperature of 65°F (18°C). Failing that, try raising the plants in good light indoors, sowing the seeds in pots in a peat-lite mix at the end of March. Press down the soil firmly and sprinkle the seed thinly over the top. Cover with a fine sifting of compost

and water lightly. Seedlings should begin to show through within two to three weeks. When they are large enough, transplant to a frame and gradually harden off.

Planting
End May to early June. Plant the seedlings 12 inches (30 cm) apart in rows 16 inches

(40 cm) apart. Make sure that the little bulbous swelling at the base of the plant is not buried in the process, but stays at soil level. Then water gently.

The year's work
Keep the ground reasonably moist, although celeriac does not need such prodigious watering in dry weather as does celery. Celeriac responds well to liquid fertilizer applied every 14 days from July, or to a mulch of well-rotted manure. If the plants

put out any side shoots cut them off. In late September, draw some soil around the swollen roots to keep them white.

Harvesting
From October. Dig the celeriac as needed. Cover the roots with straw for protection. In November, however, especially in cold areas, it is safer to lift them for storing. Left in the ground they are vulnerable to frost. They store well. Remove the foliage and keep the roots packed in boxes with sand or peat in a cool, frostproof room.

Pests and diseases
Both pests and diseases usually avoid celeriac.

*B*eets

Beets (*Beta vulgaris*) are a very ancient vegetable, but the Greeks and Romans grew them for leaves and not for roots. Pliny credited beet leaves with the virtue of restoring

to its original flavor wine which had deteriorated in the vat. The gourmandizing Apicius recommended beets as a laxative. In Britain, Robinson's nineteenth-century *Family Herbal* prescribed snuffing beet juice up the nose to promote sneezing as a cure for toothache. Three hundred years earlier, Gerard also recommended inhaling the juice up into the nostrils to draw forth phlegm and purge the head. He did not, however, think much of the leaves, which "nourisheth little or nothing, and is not as wholesome as Lettuce." But of the red and beautiful root it "is to be preferred before the leaves, as well as in beautie as in goodness."

The long-rooted varieties of beet have been cultivated since the sixteenth century, but the globe varieties, now the most popular, both to grow and to eat, are a late development. Although the leaves are now generally thrown away, they are perfectly wholesome to eat as a substitute for spinach.

Varieties

Early globe: Boltardy has good color and flavor. Pacemaker II is fine flavored, deep red.

Main season: Ruby Queen is adaptable red All-America selection. Detroit Dark Red is a favorite for excellent flavor. Burpee's Golden Beet is fine for greens and non-bleeding roots. Albino and Snowhite are flavorful pale roots.

Long-rooted: Long Season and Formanova are carrot-shaped red beets which store well.

Pests and diseases

Beets are usually remarkably free from pests and diseases, but keep half an eye open for mildew.

GROWING BEETS
Preparing the soil

Like the other root vegetables, beets should not be grown on recently manured ground. Yet they need a soil which is fertile and friable—one, therefore, which has been well manured and cultivated for a previous crop. If you dig the soil in the autumn and let winter work on it, you will have to labor less in the spring to get it to a fine tilth. Add lime to achieve pH 6 to 6.4.

Sowing

March to June. To have small and tender beets in June, seed will have to be sown under cloches. Using a globe variety, Boltardy for choice, a start can be made in March in the South and at the end of the month in the North. Beet seed is large, in fact in all varieties except one it is a little cluster of seeds, so station sowing is possible. This cuts down on thinning, an especially tiresome operation when crops are under cloches. Make two drills 1 inch (2 cm) deep and 8 inches (20 cm) apart, and place two clusters of seeds (or three for extra insurance against failure) every 6 inches (15 cm) along each row. Germination is helped

if the seed is soaked overnight before sowing. To thin, just remove all but the strongest seedling when the first rough leaves appear. Because they grow from clusters make sure that only one seedling is left. The one variety that produces a single seed and not a cluster is Mono King Explorer. Sow these seeds 2 inches (5 cm) apart, thinning to 6 inches (15 cm). Globe varieties are also used for early sowings in open ground in April or early May. These will produce large beets, so the spacing should be 12 inches (30 cm) between rows and 8 inches (20 cm) between the stations of seeds.

The long-rooting varieties, which are used only as a main crop, are not sown until late May or early June. Many gardeners stick to globe varieties as the main crop for winter storage as well as for early summer use. A final sowing of the globe variety Early Wonder in July will provide salad-size beets in late autumn.

The year's work

Hoeing will be needed while the seedlings are young, but the fully grown beet leaves will themselves suppress most weeds. This

is as well, for careless hoeing can damage the beets and make them bleed. If the leaves do not succeed in keeping down the weeds, apply a peat mulch, which will also stop the roots from going hard. But—to repeat an earlier warning—never put a mulch down when the soil is dry. Keep the soil moist. Denied water in warm weather the plants tend to run to seed prematurely. Pull the beets you need for current use as soon as they are big enough—the smaller they are the sweeter they taste.

Harvesting

October. The main crop is lifted for storing on dry days at the end of September and early October. After working hard to grow the beets it pays to take extra care at this stage to ensure that they will be successfully stored through winter and spring. The roots are best pulled up by hand, since there is always the risk of damaging them if a fork

is used. Twist off the tops, not too near the crown; if they are cut they will bleed. Reject any roots which have been attacked by pests. Damaged roots will rot in storage; do not bruise them by careless handling. Wooden crates, if you can get them, are ideal for storing beets, but any large box or plastic bin will do. Starting with peat, layer the beets (not touching each other) and peat until the box is filled. Store in a cool, frostproof room.

Radishes

The radish (*Raphanus sativus*) is by any standards an ancient vegetable. It was being cultivated in China, where it may have originated, in the seventh century B.C. The pyramids of Egypt are, in a sense, built on a foundation of radishes, onions and garlic for, according to Herodotus, this was the staple diet of the slaves working there. The Greeks were fond

of radishes. Pliny slightingly commented, "Such is the frivolity of the Greeks that in the temple of Apollo at Delphi, it is said, the radish is so greatly preferred to all other articles of diet as to be represented there in gold, the beet in silver and the rape in lead." The Romans, however, were more down to earth; they used to hurl radishes at politicians. Culpeper, the seventeenth-century English herbalist, was not enamored of them. "Garden radishes," he wrote, "are in wantoness eaten as a sallad, but they breed scurvy humours in the stomach, and corrupt the blood."

Modern Japanese would certainly not agree. They are very fond of radishes, especially pickled, and grow quantities of them, some to monstrous sizes. Japanese, Chinese and Spanish radishes, the winter radishes, are usually eaten cooked. The summer radish, however, is essentially a raw salad plant.

Varieties

Salad radishes: Round: Cherry Belle remains crisp longer than most varieties. Sparkler, scarlet tipped with white; sweet.

Cylindrical: French Breakfast, fast growing and mild. Icicle is a white, tapering sort. Yellow Gold has white flesh. Red Prince lasts well in the garden.

Winter radishes: Japanese: Mino Early produces a mild-flavored parsnip-shaped root 2 inches (5 cm) in diameter and 12 inches (30 cm) long.

Chinese: Chinese Rose, red and white radish-looking roots, but about 6 inches (15 cm) long.

Spanish: Black Spanish Round (turnip shaped) and Black Spanish Long (stumpy carrot shaped) have black skins, which must be peeled, and white flesh.

GROWING SUMMER RADISHES
Preparing the soil

Unless salad radishes are grown quickly they are not worth growing. A slow-grown radish will be hot on the tongue and as unpleasant to chew as cotton wool. For rapid growth, a rich, moisture-holding soil, adequately limed (pH 6.5), is essential. Radishes, however, seldom have a patch of ground specially cultivated for them. They are the catch crop above all catch crops, taking only three to four weeks from sowing to eating. Their needs, therefore, come second to those of the crops alongside them. But at least the soil must be fertile, and before sowing the radishes 2 ounces of general fertilizer should be applied along each yard (60 g to 1 m) of row. The soil should also be broken down to a fine tilth. In high summer, radishes must be given a moist, shady place in which to grow.

Sowing

February to August. The earliest sowings are in frames or cloches in February and early March. Sow the seed thinly in the shallowest of drills, with a fine covering of soil, allowing 6 inches (15 cm) between rows.

First sowings out of doors can follow from early March in similar shallow drills. Always sow thinly; thick sowing produces a lot of leaves and miserably small roots. If you choose the cylindrical French Breakfast or the round Scarlet Globe or Sparkler, intervals between sowings should be as little as ten days or two weeks. This is because they not only grow quickly, but are soon past their best. Cherry Belle stays crisper longer, so the intervals between sowings can be stretched to three weeks or more. Times of sowings will also be dictated by the time at which space becomes available after other crops—for example, after clearing a row, or part of a row, of lettuce. Slip in a short row of radishes whenever and wherever you can.

The year's work

Radishes are scarcely in the ground long enough for them to need, or to be given,

Pests and diseases

Radishes are liable to get all the diseases that attack turnips and brassicas generally, but they seldom do and even more seldom suffer seriously. Because winter radishes are in the

any attention. Birds, however, enjoy the young leaves and may have to be kept off with nylon netting. In a hot, dry spell the radishes should be watered or given up as lost.

Harvesting

Pull radishes young, when they are about the size of a quarter or smaller.

GROWING WINTER RADISHES
Preparing the soil

Winter radishes should not be sown in freshly manured ground, but, like other roots, should follow a crop which had manure or compost. They also need lime—pH 6.5. Before sowing make the seedbed firm and rake to a fine tilth.

Sowing

Japanese varieties are sown in March for use in summer, and again at the end of July for roots to store for winter. The seeds are large enough to be sown in twos or threes in stations 6 inches (15 cm) apart and ½ inch (1 cm) deep in rows 12 inches (30 cm) apart. Leave only the strongest seedling to grow on. Chinese and Spanish varieties run to seed if sown early. The best time to sow them is from the middle of July in the North to late August in the South. Sow in ½-inch (1 cm) drills in stations 8 inches (20 cm) apart.

The year's work

The soil must be kept moist and free of weeds.

Harvesting

Winter radishes will be ready to eat two or three months after sowing. The late-sown Japanese radishes can be lifted and stored in peat at the end of October. The Chinese and Spanish radishes are sometimes left in the ground and dug up as needed during the winter. But they, too, are better stored in peat.

ground longer than the summer varieties, it is somewhat more at risk from club root, but generally escapes.

Parsnips

Parsnips (*Peucedanum sativum*) have been eaten in Britain for some two thousand years, and may even be native. Their distinctive

sweetness is an acquired taste, and in the last few decades fewer people have been acquiring it. Although parsnips are outstandingly hardy and could, therefore, be grown in any part of the country, they do need a depth of soil, especially for the long-rooted varieties, which many gardens lack. Other gardens may be too stony to grow straight roots, and forked roots are infuriating to lift. Devotees of the parsnip, however, can overcome these obstacles. Gerard, the sixteenth-century herbalist, was evidently not an addict. He reported that his friend Mr. Plat had made a pleasant bread from parsnip roots, but Gerard tartly added "which I have made no tryall of, nor meane to do." People who do not enjoy eating the roots often relish them in the form of parsnip wine, however.

Varieties

Avon Resister is resistant to canker, has small roots and can be grown just 3 inches (8 cm) apart. Hollow Crown Improved has large, clear-white root about 10 inches (25 cm) long. Harris' Model is longer and thinner than Hollow Crown, has excellent flavor. All types grow to maximum size with deeply dug soil.

Pests and diseases

The main trouble is canker. Some cankers are caused by a fungus, but the more common orange-brown canker occurs when there is cracking of the roots. The cause may be lack of lime or excess nitrogen, therefore add dolomite lime and avoid digging in fresh manure. A wet autumn after a dry spell encourages canker. Late-grown crops are less liable to suffer from canker.

GROWING PARSNIPS

Preparing the soil

A parsnip is capable of thrusting 3 feet (90 cm) or more into the soil. Although this is not to be encouraged, deep, well-cultivated soil is vital. Like other roots, parsnips are also liable to fork in newly manured ground. Grow them where manure was given to the previous crop. Canker is encouraged by soil which is too rich in nitrogen or deficient in lime. Aim at pH 6.3. Before sowing, spread 4 ounces of general fertilizer to the square yard (120 g to 1 sq m).

If the ground is stony the roots will fork. To provide a stone-free environment for each root, push a crowbar 18 inches (45 cm) or more into the soil and rotate it to make a hole about 3 inches (8 cm) in diameter at the top. Fill this with sifted soil mixed with a little peat and mark with sticks.

Alternatively, stand 4-inch-diameter (10 cm) drain-pipes on end, about 8 inches (20 cm) apart and sunk 2 inches (5 cm) or so into the soil, make firm and fill in the same way.

Sowing

Parsnips take a long time to grow. If the weather allows, begin sowing in February, otherwise leave it until March. Sowings in April are less susceptible to canker. Take out 1-inch (2 cm) drills 18 inches (45 cm) apart. Sow three seeds in stations 8 inches (20 cm) apart or sow in bore holes or drain-pipes. Parsnip seeds are painfully slow to germinate. To mark the rows before the seedlings appear—so that you do not hoe through them—sow quick-germinating radishes between each station. Buy fresh parsnip seed each year.

The year's work

There is little to do except harvest the radishes and thin the parsnips to the strongest in each group. Hoe carefully or give them a mulch. The roots in the drain-pipes, if they are used, will need frequent watering.

Harvesting

October onward. Dig the parsnips as needed, but in cold areas lift the roots in November.

Salsify

The true salsify (*Tragopogon porrifolius*), like black salsify (scorzonera) and Spanish salsify (scolymus), belongs to the daisy (Compositae) family and so escapes the diseases of the brassica roots. Salsify is grown not only for its long, white roots but also for its chards.

Varieties

Mammoth Sandwich Island and Giant.

GROWING SALSIFY

Preparing the soil

Salsify prefers a light soil that is deeply cultivated and free from stones. It must not be grown in freshly manured ground. Adequate lime (pH 6.5) is essential.

Sowing

Early April. Sow in ½-inch (1 cm) drills in rows 12 inches (30 cm) apart. The seeds are quite large, so they can be easily sown in stations, three to a station, 8 inches (20 cm) apart, the distance to which they will be thinned if you sow continuously along the drill.

The year's work

The plants need little attention beyond being kept moist and weed free. A mulch of peat or compost is better than hoeing, because a hoe can easily and fatally damage the roots, which readily bleed.

Harvesting

Mid-October onward. The roots are deep in the ground and must be lifted with great care. They are hardy and in many regions can be left in the ground all winter and taken up as needed.

April to June. Salsify is biennial and roots left in the ground will begin to put up shoots in April. In January or February, remove dead foliage and ridge up the soil 6 to 8 inches (15 to 20 cm) over the roots, and the shoots will be blanched as they grow. Cut them just above root level to use raw in salads.

Alternatively, do not cover the roots with soil, but cut the shoots (chards) when they are about 5 inches (13 cm) long and cook them as spinach. By frequent cutting the root can be induced to send up shoots still fit to eat until late May.

Pests and diseases

Fairly trouble free.

Scorzonera

Scorzonera (*Scorzonera hispanica*) looks like a black-skinned version of salsify, hence one of its names—black salsify. Although the

skin is black, which makes it look unappetizing, the flesh is white and of a better, more pronounced flavor than salsify. Duplex is a good Dutch strain.

GROWING SCORZONERA

Scorzonera needs rich, moist soil which has been deeply cultivated, for the roots often go down 18 inches (45 cm). Sow the seeds in shallow drills in late April. Thin the seedlings to 4 inches (10 cm) apart. In November, lift the roots—take care because they snap easily. In warm areas leave them in the ground, because freshly dug roots have a better flavor. Scorzonera left in the ground will provide spring shoots.

Chervil

The biennial turnip-rooted chervil (*Chaerophyllum bulbosum*) must not be confused with the annual chervil, the aniseed-flavored herb. Chervil is fairly common in

France and Italy. The slightly yellow roots are sweet and nutty, and rather floury when cooked.

GROWING CHERVIL

Once the seed has germinated, growing the plant is not difficult. Seed sown in shallow drills in October does not germinate until the following spring, and if it is sown in April it takes a year to germinate. The seedlings should be thinned to 6 inches (15 cm) apart. Growth thereafter is rapid, if the plants are kept moist. By July the leaves will begin to die and then dry. The roots are then ready for lifting and storing in peat. They store well.

Hamburg Parsley

Hamburg parsley (*Petroselinum crispum*) has parsley-flavored leaves and a parsnip-like root up to 6 inches (15 cm) long, with a

hint of a taste of celeriac. Hamburg parsley is hardy and needs a long growing season.

GROWING HAMBURG PARSLEY

Sow in shallow drills from mid-March to April in soil manured for a previous crop. Thin the seedlings to 8 inches (20 cm) apart. Water well in summer. Harvest late because the rate of root growth is greatest in the autumn and, unlike most vegetables, the largest roots taste best. Leave them in the ground all winter, but it is safer to lift them in late October or November and store them in the same way as beets.

Sweet Potatoes

The sweet potato (*Ipomoea batatas*) was first mentioned in European history in accounts made by Columbus after the vegetable was found being cultivated by Central American Indians. The potato was taken back to Spain and was grown there as a crop starting in the sixteenth century. Spanish explorers later took the sweet potato to the Philippines, and from those islands it was exported to Asia. Today the sweet potato is popular in Africa, Japan and the southern United States. Of all garden crops the sweet potato requires the most heat, and in fact it thrives where the growing season is long and warm. You can grow sweet potatoes in Northern areas but only where there will be 150 to 170 warm growing days. Among the cultivated sweet potatoes are a dry-fleshed type and a moist, orange sort. The moist types are the only ones generally available to home gardeners, usually as started plants. In Northern areas order small sweet-potato plants for planting outside in late May to early June. In Southern states local garden centers frequently offer small, rooted cuttings at planting time.

Varieties

Sweet potatoes are sometimes called yams, but the true yam is from another tropical genus, *Dioscorea*. For home gardens the most popular are true sweet potatoes that take up a minimum of space, such as the vineless Bunch Puerto Rico, which has copper-colored skin and dark-orange flesh. Centennial, another popular moist, orange variety, is the one most often found in local supermarkets. Allgold,

a variety bred by the Oklahoma Agricultural Experiment Station for high vitamins A and C content, thrives for Midwest gardeners. Allgold has excellent flavor and stores well. Rose and Golden Jewel are similar orange types but with only average vitamin content. Sometimes offered is a rare white tuber called Triumph or White Yam, a very sweet tasting, pure-white-fleshed variety.

Any of these sweet potatoes makes an attractive houseplant when grown indoors during winter months. Small shoots can be rooted from a houseplant sweet potato for planting outside in the spring, but the plants sold by commercial growers are so reasonably priced that producing your own is not necessary, except for fun.

GROWING SWEET POTATOES
Preparing the soil

A light, well-drained soil is best. Mix in perlite or sand if the soil is heavy. Roots are shallow so there is no need to dig deeply. Two weeks before planting, dig in a 5-10-10 fertilizer. Excessive nitrogen is not good for sweet potatoes so avoid heavy applications of fertilizer, especially manures.

Planting

Set out started plants (called slips or cuttings) after the soil is warm and all danger of frost has passed. Plant each potato on a slight rise or atop a long, 8-inch-high (20 cm) ridge. Make ridges 36 to 48 inches (90 to 120 cm) apart if you want more than one row. Set plants 12 inches (30 cm) apart. Mulch to prevent weeds taking over. Sweet potatoes need lots of sun and warmth but they do not require heavy watering. In the North, some gardeners enjoy growing a few plants in big outdoor containers set in a protected location to provide a full growing season.

Harvesting

Just before frost, harvest the tubers by digging them up with a garden fork, taking care not to bruise the potatoes. Let the tubers lie out in the sun for several hours until they are quite dry. Cure the potatoes in a room at about 85°F (29°C) for 10 days. Further storage is best at 50° to 55°F (10° to 13°C).

Tubers

The potato is the most versatile vegetable of the Western World and the most widely eaten.

Many varieties with superior texture and flavor, however, have gone out of commercial cultivation altogether because they crop less profitably. If you want first-rate potatoes you will probably have to grow them yourself. If you have no room in your garden that is the end of the matter, but consider carefully whether there are other vegetables that it might be better to abandon.

The other tubers of note—light-years behind the potato in popularity—are Jerusalem and Chinese artichokes. They make a welcome addition to winter diets.

1 Main crop potatoes
2 Chinese artichokes
3 Jerusalem artichokes
4 Seed potatoes
5 New potatoes

Potatoes

The potato (*Solanum tuberosum*) came to Europe as recently as the sixteenth century, brought back by Spanish explorers from South America. There it had been cultivated since the beginning of the Christian era. The sweet

potato came first, and the common potato followed it to Europe. For a long time the potato was eaten only by the wealthy, and then as a delicacy. Not until the nineteenth century did it become the staple diet of the poor. In Scotland and Ireland the potato had to battle against the prejudice that it was not mentioned in the Bible. In Burgundy it was held to cause leprosy. The Swiss blamed it for tuberculosis. The English thought it induced lust. Now they blame it for inducing overweight. But the potato survives. It is hard to imagine a world without it.

Varieties

The flavor of a variety can vary greatly depending on the nature of the soil in which it is grown and the fertilizer treatment which the soil has had. It is, therefore, wise to experiment each year with a few plants of a variety not previously grown. The following varieties are suggested for their above-average flavor.

Anoka is an early, smooth-skinned white with round tubers, excellent for French fries or baking. All Blue is a unique sort with blue skin and light-blue flesh, interesting in summer salads. Kennebec is a blight- and mosaic-resistant late white type which also stores well. New Norland is an early, heavy-yielding red-skinned type that is resistant to scab. Norchip, an early white potato, is excellent baked. Norgold Russet is quite resistant to scab, produces an early crop of large, white oblong potatoes, much appreciated for baking. A similar midseason russet-toned white baking type is Bake King. Green Mountain, introduced in Vermont in 1878, is still grown by many Northern gardeners. The flavor is excellent fried, baked or boiled, but this variety is not resistant to scab. Potato sets (seed potatoes) should be purchased from dealers who offer certified stock. By planting only certified potato "seed," you will greatly minimize problems from diseases like blight and scab.

GROWING POTATOES

Preparing the soil

In the autumn, dig in plenty of well-rotted manure or compost. Add peat to lighten heavy soil and to give body to light soil. Do not lime. Potatoes prefer a slightly acid soil (pH 5.6).

Sprouting the tubers

Encouraging the tubers (usually called seed potatoes) to sprout before planting has the same effect as adding a few weeks to the growing season. If, however, you tried to gain the same time by planting them earlier, they would be damaged by frost. Order the seed potatoes early so that sprouting can be started some six weeks before planting. Use plastic flats or egg cartons and place the tubers in them "rose end" up—the rose end is the end which has the most eyes and is usually the widest. Place the boxes in the

light, but not in the sun, in a room which is frostproof but not warm. Warmth will produce weak, spindly growth, whereas the aim is sturdy shoots $\frac{3}{4}$ to 1 inch (1 to 2 cm) long.

Planting under glass

January/February. If you cannot bear to wait for the first outdoor new potatoes a few can be raised under glass. In a greenhouse which has a little heat, plant sprouted tubers in January, three to an 8-inch (20 cm) pot, in a peat-lite potting compost. Remember to use fertilizer in soil-free mixes. By the middle of April the young potatoes should be ready for eating. In an unheated greenhouse, plant late in February and expect to eat the potatoes during May.

Planting outdoors

February to May. Because the young shoots of potatoes are easily damaged by frost as they appear above the soil, the time of planting depends on when your garden usually gets its last spring frosts.

The usual method of planting is to take out flat or V-shaped drills at least 5 inches (13 cm) deep and 24 inches (60 cm) apart for the first early varieties, and 30 inches (75 cm) apart for the later varieties, which make more top and root growth. The first

earlies are planted not more than 12 inches (30 cm) apart, but the others need 15 inches (38 cm). Plant the tubers with care, rose end up, rejecting and burning any which are weaklings or diseased. After setting out the potatoes along the drill, cover each with a handful of peat or soil to

protect the tender shoots from damage as you draw the soil back into the drill. The tubers should finish with a covering of 3 inches (8 cm) of soil, perhaps leaving a slight ridge the length of the row. Alternatively, if the soil is reasonably light, it saves time to make holes with a dibble and drop the tubers in.

After planting, scatter general fertilizer over the rows, 2 ounces to the square yard (60 g to 1 sq m).

The year's work

If the shoots emerge into late frosts, draw a little soil over them or cover them with straw. If you intend to earth up, loosen the surface soil between the rows with a fork when the plants are 6 to 8 inches (15 to 20 cm) high. Then, with a hoe, draw the soil toward the plants from each side of the row. If after three weeks the potato foliage

has not grown dense enough to smother any weeds, a second minor earthing up can be done. In dry weather, potatoes need water. Give it to them by flooding the trenches formed by earthing up. Spray against blight with Maneb early in July and once every 7 to 10 days until the middle of September.

Harvesting

June to October. The first early varieties will be ready 10 to 12 weeks from planting. Once the flowers are fully open, dig up a root to see whether the potatoes are large enough to eat. If they are not, wait another week. Never dig up more potatoes than you need for one or two meals. The longer they are out of the ground the harder they will be to scrape. And while they are still in the ground they are still growing.

Potatoes for storing, whether second earlies or main crop, are left in the ground until the foliage has died down. Choose a dry day for harvesting. Use a fork to lever the potatoes out of the ground so as not to spear them. Damaged potatoes cannot be stored. Work along the sides of the ridges, not head on along the rows. Root systems vary, but when you have carefully forked up a few roots you will have found how that particular variety grows and where most of the tubers lie. Pick up all tubers, however small. Any left in the ground will be a nuisance when they grow next year, and will help perpetuate eelworms and the fungus that causes blight. After lifting, dry the potatoes on sacks or trays in the sun. Sort out diseased tubers and burn them. Pick out the damaged and small potatoes for using first. The rest of the crop is then ready for storing.

Storing

Avoid sacks; one potato rotting away unseen can infect dozens. Use trays, for they make inspection easy. It is vital, however, to cover the trays—preferably with sheets of black plastic—to exclude all light or the potatoes will become green and dangerous to eat. Alternatively, apple boxes or grape boxes can be used. These also must be covered.

Stored potatoes will be ruined by frost. They must not be warm or they will sprout, or sweat and rot. Inspect them from time to time and remove any which are diseased. From January, when going through the potatoes each month, remove all the small shoots that they will have started producing.

Growing potatoes under plastic sheeting

Another simple way to grow potatoes, which involves no weeding and no earthing up, is to grow them through holes in black polyethylene sheeting. This method, however, adds to the cost and possibly encourages slugs.

Prepare the ground as for conventionally grown potatoes and plant the tubers in the same way. Then, 12 inches (30 cm) on each side of the planted row, mark parallel lines with string and with a spade make a

slit in the ground along the length of each line. Similarly make slits at each end of the row to join the lengthwise slits. Take a roll of 150-gauge polyethylene sheeting, 36 inches (90 cm) wide, and tuck the short edge of the sheeting into the slit at one end of the row and make it firm in the soil. Unroll the sheeting to the other end of the row and cut it to length, leaving 6 inches (15 cm) over, which you tuck into the soil at that end. Then tuck the sheeting into the ground along both lengths of the row, weighting the edges down with some soil. If there is more than one row, leave 6 inches (15 cm) space between the polyethylene strips to give you access. To avoid having to weed that bit of bare soil, cover it with a peat mulch up to 2 inches (5 cm) deep.

In May, bumps will be seen along the plastic strips. These are the potato shoots demanding to be let out. Cut holes in the sheeting just large enough to pull them through, taking care not to damage the shoots. For harvesting, fold back the sheeting. Unlike earthed-up potatoes, most of the tubers underneath will be near the surface of the soil.

Jerusalem Artichokes

The Jerusalem artichoke (*Helianthus tuberosus*) is confusingly named. The tubers for which it is grown have something of the flavor of a globe artichoke, but the plant is a relative of the sunflower. It certainly has

nothing to do with Jerusalem, for it is a native of North America. Jerusalem, the theories go, is either a corruption of *girasole*, the Italian name for sunflower, or of Ter Heusen, the Dutch village where the vegetable was cultivated. The Jerusalem artichoke is easy to grow—indeed it is often more difficult to get rid of than to establish.

Varieties

White-skinned varieties are superior to the purple-skinned varieties.

GROWING JERUSALEM ARTICHOKES
Preparing the soil

Although the Jerusalem artichoke will tolerate poor conditions, it will then produce miserably small tubers. Therefore, dig in as much compost or manure as can be spared. Add lime if the pH is below 5.8. Lift all the tubers each year, replanting in new ground, for even the smallest tuber left in the soil will shoot up the following year.

Planting

February/March. Jerusalem artichokes should be planted as early as possible—according to local weather. Plant the tubers 6 inches (15 cm) deep and 12 inches (30 cm) apart, using either a trowel or a dibble, or spacing them along a drill. Leave up to 36 inches (90 cm) between the rows.

The year's work

Hoe if necessary and give liquid fertilizer occasionally. In May, earth up the plants a little. Staking will be needed, for if the stems break, the crop will suffer. Cut off just the top of each plant in August to limit further growth.

Harvesting

October/November. The tubers will be ready for lifting from the end of October, but they taste better if they are left in the ground and lifted as needed through the winter. Save and store some of the smaller ($1\frac{1}{2}$ inch, 3 cm), smoother, healthy tubers for replanting next season.

*C*hinese Artichokes

The Chinese artichoke (*Stachys sieboldii* syn. *S. affinis*) is not an artichoke but it is from the Far East. It arrived in Europe in 1882, when Dr. Bretschneider, doctor to the Russian ambassador in Peking, sent tubers to M.

Pailleuz of Crosnes, and *crosnes* is the name of the vegetable in France today. Chinese artichokes are grown for their ivory-white tubers. Basic culture is similar to that listed for Jerusalem artichokes, although *Stachys* can use more humus in the soil and fertilizer during growing. Plants need no staking, but they are great colonizers, so be sure to clear the ground of tubers at the end of each year. You will have to hunt for Chinese artichokes because they are carried by very few firms in the United States.

*P*eanuts

The peanut (*Arachis hypogaea*), a legume from Brazil, grows best in a warm, humid climate. Peanuts thrive in loose, sandy soil with 4 to 5 months of warm growing weather. Where seasons are short, grow peanuts in large containers of Jiffy-Mix on a sunny terrace or

other sheltered location. Two types are offered home gardeners. The Spanish variety has small nuts, 2 to 3 per pod, and matures fastest. The Virginia variety is available as a Jumbo strain, and as a more compact Bunch strain. With at least 120 warm growing days, Virginia types will crop well. To sow remove kernels from pod, dust with nitrogen inoculant. Plant 3 kernels 2 inches (4 cm) deep in a small hill, spacing hills 18 inches (45 cm) apart. Peanuts have small yellow flowers that form pegs on the end of a thin aboveground root. The pegs burrow into the soil and ripen into pods, thus the need for a loose soil. Just before frost, dig up entire bush to harvest. Hang plant upside down to air-dry for 2 to 3 weeks, then roast pods at 350°F (180°C) for about 20 minutes.

Pests and diseases of tubers

Jerusalem artichokes and Chinese artichokes are troubled by scarcely a pest or disease, but potatoes are besieged on all sides, at least by the threat of them. However, with constant care and occasional luck it is possible to escape disaster for years or even for a lifetime. There are two evil pests—the Colorado beetle and the eelworm, or nematode. These are matched by two evil diseases—wart disease, which is now not common, and blight, which is.

The Colorado beetle is $\frac{1}{2}$ inch (1 cm) long, has orange and black striped wings and lays orange eggs, which turn into destructive orange grubs. Spray with Sevin weekly from the time grubs (larvae) are first seen.

The home of the potato root eelworm (*Heterodera rostochiensis*) is Peru. Cysts containing hundreds of eggs can stay dormant in the soil for ten years or so. Excretions from a growing potato activate the eggs and the minute larvae burrow into the root. Healthy potatoes can withstand the attacks of thousands of eelworms, but there comes a point when enough is too much, and the foliage dies and the crop is poor. No way has been found to destroy the cysts, and if the land is heavily infested the gardener has to give up growing potatoes for years. To help to avoid a build-up, do not grow potatoes on the same ground two years running. Fertile soil is the greatest ally against this enemy.

Wireworms are the yellow, tough-skinned larvae of the click beetle which bore into the tubers. They are encountered most in new gardens which were previously grassland, and there may be trouble for a couple of years if you dig up a lawn to make a vegetable garden. Trap them with the millipede trap described on page 43. Slugs usually damage only main crops. Use methiocarb or metaldehyde baits.

Some of the newer varieties of potatoes have been bred for their greater resistance to attacks of blight. Blight is caused by the fungus *Phytophthora infestans*, the culprit of the Irish potato famine in the mid-1840s. The fungus is carried forward from one year to the next in infected tubers, and the build-up starts in the spring. Given certain well-defined warm and moist weather

conditions, usually occurring in July and August, it can spread like wildfire. If over wide areas there are two days when the temperature has not fallen below 50°F (10°C) and relative humidity stays above 75 percent, watch out for blight in the next week or two. The danger is greater in the wetter regions of the country. The first outward signs are dark-brown marks on the leaves and stems. The foliage dies, and affected tubers later rot. There is no cure, so take precautions. Always, as a matter of course, burn affected tubers—they are the source of next year's infection. As an insurance, spray with Maneb early in July and thereafter every 7 to 10 days until the middle of September. After an attack burn all foliage. And to repeat, never grow potatoes on the same ground two years running.

Common scab looks nasty, but the damage is only skin deep. The fungus which causes it, *Actinomyces scabies*, is encouraged by liming (never lime land which is to be cropped with potatoes that season) and is discouraged by the presence of humus.

Aphids spread viruses. The five species of aphids which descend on potatoes can be destroyed by malathion spray.

Remember that potato roots exposed to sunlight during growth will develop green tubers which contain a dangerous poison (solanine). Be sure that all developing tubers are fully covered with earth or a mulch. During the harvest throw out any green potatoes.

Vegetable Fruits

Vegetable fruits are the exotics of the kitchen garden. Many of them come from the tropics. That they grow in the North as successfully as they do is largely because of the immense work that has gone into raising new varieties. To grow these vegetable fruits, a greenhouse and a cold frame are very useful. In the Northern zones these warm-growing crops are best sown indoors 3 to 8 weeks before the first safe outdoor planting date, in order that plants can fruit before fall frosts. Some of the compact selections can be grown indoors under lights during winter months. In the summer, vegetable fruits succeed outdoors in most regions of the United States.

1 Crenshaw melon
2 Cucumbers
3 Eggplants
4 Cantaloupe
5 Tomatoes
6 Sweet peppers
7 Summer squash
8 Golden winter squash
9 Zucchini

Tomatoes

The tomato (*Lycopersicon esculentum*) arrived in Europe from South America less than four centuries ago. It was then regarded as decorative but dangerous, for it is a relative of poisonous and narcotic plants of the Solanaceae family, one of which is deadly nightshade. The tomato's bright color did nothing to allay people's suspicions.

After two centuries, the fear of eating tomatoes had been largely overcome, but it is only in the last fifty years that tomatoes have become universally popular. But while the tomato has risen in popularity, it has declined in flavor and texture. The reasons are commercial; if the professional grower is not to go bankrupt he must plant varieties which crop heavily and travel well to market.

The amateur gardener, however, can still grow tomatoes for flavor. He can follow long-established practices or adapt some of the newer methods used by the professionals. Anyone who can provide a reasonable amount of sun can grow tomatoes, with or without a garden. The letters after tomato names refer to inbred disease resistance (see page 103).

Varieties

Early: Spring Giant-VF, Ultra Girl-VFN, semibush type, and Springset-VF, a bush type, are all adaptable sorts which need minimum support. They bear about 65 days after transplanting.

Midseason (75 days): Super Fantastic-VF, Better Boy-VFN and Big Girl-VF are indeterminate types widely grown for vigor, flavor, long bearing. Manapal is best in warm, humid Southern states.

Late: Ramapo-VF and Vineripe-VFN are vigorous, flavorful indeterminate hybrids.

For small fruit grow Small Fry-VFN, a 36-inch (90 cm) plant with clusters of 1-inch (2 cm) red fruit, or Sweet 100, a similar type but having up to 20 fruit per cluster.

GROWING TOMATOES OUTDOORS

Preparing the soil

The most important thing is the choice of a site for the outdoor tomato bed, especially in colder areas. More of the crop is likely to ripen if the plants are grown along a sheltered south-facing wall. The soil must be rich in humus. Early in the year dig in well-rotted manure or compost at the rate of 1 cwt to 10 square yards (50 kg to 10 sq m), plus plenty of peat. The pH to aim at is 6.5, but if lime is needed to bring it to this it must not be applied with the manure. Two weeks before planting out apply a general fertilizer at 4 ounces to the square yard (120 g to 1 sq m).

Sowing

As described for indoor tomatoes. (See page 96.)

Planting

Late May/June. If cloches are used to warm up the soil and to give early protection, planting will be possible about two weeks earlier than without them. The plants, raised in pots under glass or bought from a nurseryman, will be about 8 inches (20 cm) high and the first flower truss will be forming. Water the plants the day before they are to go out. Mark out a row and, at 18-inch (45 cm) intervals, make holes with a trowel as big as the size of the pot. To get the plant out of the pot, spread your fingers over the surface of the soil, turn the pot upside down and hit the base sharply with the back of the trowel. Without disturbing the roots put the plant in the hole and fill any gap with sifted soil, firming it with your hand. Set plants several inches deeper than previous soil level. Cover peat pots or Jiffy-7s completely. If cloches are being used, put them back in place until the plants are well established. All tomatoes need adequate support, especially those out of doors.

Although not all seed catalogs mention it, tomatoes have two basic growing styles. The bushy types are called determinate. Determinate types often grow well without staking, although a support will help keep

fruit off soil. Indeterminate tomatoes grow as a vine, with the tip of each plant continuing to bloom and bear until season's end. Determinate types are ideal in containers and very small gardens. The indeterminate hybrids are best for long-season production and for training on fences or the new plastic Gro-Nets.

The year's work

Ensuring that the plants are adequately supported as they grow is a job not to be neglected. Cut out or snap off cleanly side shoots when they are about 2 inches (5 cm) long. The main stem itself has to be cut (this is known as pinching out), so that the plant's energies can be concentrated on fruiting, not growing, one leaf beyond a flower truss. This will be the third truss in cooler areas or in cool summers elsewhere. Otherwise it should be possible to ripen four or, exceptionally, five trusses. Do not let the plants go short of water; a peat mulch helps.

Harvesting

Pick tomatoes when they are red and ripe. At the end of the summer spread straw along the row, cut the string supporting the plants and lay the plants along the row. Cover with cloches and many of the still green tomatoes will ripen.

Starting tomatoes indoors

Start tomato seeds in a bright window, a heated frame or a greenhouse 6 to 8 weeks before the last frost in your region. Be sure that you can provide adequate light and heat before trying to start tomatoes inside. Remember that if light is a problem you can grow excellent seedlings under fluorescent lamps. (See pages 14 and 15.)

Purchase top-quality seeds of varieties adapted to your growing conditions. See page 95 for the names of tomatoes that are successful over a wide range of growing conditions.

Plant seeds in Jiffy-7 peat pellets or in plastic compartmentalized flats so that each seedling can later be transplanted without root trauma. To be sure that each pot or compartment produces at least one healthy seedling sow 2 or 3 seeds together. Later use sharp scissors to snip away all but the biggest plant. (If you prefer, each seedling can be transplanted to individual 3- to 4-inch (8 to 10 cm) pots once they have two sets of leaves.) After planting seeds, cover them with $\frac{1}{4}$ inch (1 cm) of milled sphagnum moss or vermiculite. Moisten the covering with warm water. Place the seed flat or tray of Jiffy-7s in a warm (75°F to 80°F [24°C to 27°C]), moist location. As soon as the seeds germinate provide bright light for 12 to 18 hours per day, with care that the seedlings never dry out. Under fluorescent lights keep the seedling foliage about 3 to 4 inches (8 to 10 cm) below the tubes.

The optimum growing temperature for seedlings is 65°F to 70°F (17°C to 21°C). Fertilize the seedlings with half-strength water-soluble fertilizer if they are growing in a soil-free mix such as peat-lite. Read package directions for the sowing mix you use because some, such as Terralite planting soil, although peat-lite formulas, *do* contain added nutrients which make additional fertilizer unnecessary.

Harden off plants

When danger of hard frosts has passed begin to put the tomato seedlings outdoors each day. Bring the plants inside each night for the first 10 to 14 days. Finally, after this gradual hardening process, you will be able to transplant the young tomatoes directly to garden locations, or to large containers for mature growth. If there is any doubt about the weather remaining warm provide night protection in the form of hotkaps or A-frames over the transplants. By late May to early June in the North this extra protection should no longer be required.

Container growing

Tomatoes will thrive in containers filled with one of the new commercially prepared peat-lite formulas such as Jiffy-Mix, Burpee Tomato Growing Formula or Terralite planting soil. Read directions on the planting-mix bags to determine how much, if any, additional fertilizer will be required during the growing season. Timed-release products such as Osmocote (14-14-14), MagAmp (7-40-6) and Precise Tomato Food (6-18-6) need be applied only once, at final transplanting.

Excellent crops can be obtained by planting a seedling of some modern hybrid such as Better Boy in about $\frac{1}{2}$ cubic foot (.01 cubic meter) of soil or in a container of about 5-gallon (18 liter) size. Train the vines on a wooden trellis, spreading the branches in a fan shape. Hold branches in place with plastic plant ties or by training the growing shoots in and out of the

support. The new plastic Gro-Nets are also useful supports for container-grown tomatoes but the plastic net must be well supported by sturdy stakes. The small-fruited tomatoes, such as Small Fry, are especially attractive in terrace containers.

Greenhouse culture

In the greenhouse you can obtain a maximum crop by using a combination of peat-lite growing mix and a loose bench filling of sand or clay aggregate. Plant seedlings in 5-gallon (18 liter) bottomless containers of plastic or tar paper set on top of the bench filling. Roots will escape into the moist bench sand or aggregate and will pick up fertilizer solution which you provide at every watering. The vines are supported in the peat-lite mix and containers, yet the root system is given free run. This system provides maximum top growth and fruiting. Support the vines with wire cages or train them up plastic mesh run along the greenhouse bench, with sturdy pole supports every 3 feet (90 cm).

The year's work

To help pollination, spray the plants with water in the mornings, but only on bright days. On indeterminate, or long-vine, types, take out side shoots when they are 2 inches (5 cm) long. Spray plants with a fungicide such as Maneb every 7 to 10 days if blight or anthracnose fungus attacks. Malathion will control aphids. Spray with Sevin for beetles and cutworms.

Harvesting

Pick tomatoes as they ripen by snapping the stalk from the main stem. Remember that determinate (bush) types bear on side shoots, with most of the crop coming during a short time. The indeterminate (vining) types keep growing, with fruit developing for many months so long as growing conditions are favorable.

More on varieties

The tomatoes listed on page 95 are the favorite hybrids in American gardens throughout the various zones. These can be grown in a greenhouse but some hybrids are especially adapted to greenhouse growing. Michigan-Ohio, developed by the Michigan Agricultural Experiment Station, is an indeterminate hybrid which begins producing fruit after about 75 days of growing, then continues for the whole season. Vendor is a medium-sized, bright-red tomato that is a favorite for greenhouse soil or hydroponic culture. Outdoor selections worth growing for something unusual, in the garden or under glass, are often seen in catalogs of tomato specialists.

The largest selection for home gardeners is found in the catalog from Burgess Seed and Plant Company (see page 41), which offers more than 25 kinds. Among the unusual sorts are White Beauty, a 100-percent-white, very sweet fruit, and Burgess Stuffing Tomato, bred to have a hollow core.

For extra vitamins grow Caro-Red, a yellow-red variety with 10 times the level of vitamin A found in other tomatoes, or Doublerich, a red fruit with as much vitamin C as citrus fruit. Finally, if you prefer to have tomatoes for sauce and paste, you can grow the oblong, easy-peeling kinds, such as Italian Canner, Roma, Red Top, San Marzano and Veeroma. Those giant tomatoes often pictured with gardeners in hometown newspapers are usually Beefmaster hybrid-VFN, a Beefsteak type which can exceed 2 pounds (1 kg).

Tomato aids

One modern aid to help you grow the best tomatoes is the Automator, a 12 × 12 inch (30 × 30 cm) plastic device somewhat resembling a square baking pan but with holes. The Automator acts as stem support, mulch and soil warmer, and provides protection against cutworm. The tomato grows through a center hole where there is also room to insert a stake. A wire cage can also be pushed in the ground around the Automator to support taller tomatoes. Pour water and fertilizing solution into the plastic tray to directly feed each plant.

Blossom-Set is a hormone spray which causes flowers to set more fruit, especially during unfavorable weather.

Muskmelons

The muskmelon (*Cucumis melo*) most favored by gardeners is the round, netted sort we call cantaloupe, but within the cultivated muskmelon group are several other important fruits. The honeydew, casaba and long banana melons are all cultivars of the original Persian *Cucumis melo* species. Thanks to advances in modern plant breeding we now have many melons that can be easily grown in the average home garden. Most of the commercially grown melons are crops from the Imperial Valley in California, where growing conditions are perfect. The muskmelons, including garden cantaloupes, need a sunny, warm, not-too-humid growing season of about 90 days after being transplanted. In the North, gardeners should start melon seeds indoors 3 to 4 weeks before the outdoor planting date, or buy started seedlings at local garden centers for planting outdoors about June 1. In milder areas outdoor planting can be done earlier, but everywhere the melons should be protected from damp, cool weather. Temperatures below 65°F (13°C) encourage a slow start and rot diseases. Portable plastic protectors or waxed hotkaps are a good investment for protecting melons planted out toward the beginning of a growing season. To maximize your chances for success choose the new hybrids which mature quickly and have inbred resistance to disease. Some of the small-growing melons, including a few new hybrids from Japan, are adaptable to being grown in peat bags or in large containers of a peat-lite formula such as Jiffy-Mix. With container culture the melons can be moved to a warm location if an early fall occurs.

Cantaloupes and related melons need warm, sunny weather to produce tasty fruit. If the growing season is damp, cool or too humid, fruit is likely to be small and poorly flavored. Planting near warm rocks or training vines up a Gro-Net in a warm, sunny southern exposure are good techniques where summers are likely to be cool and damp.

Varieties

Among the cantaloupe-type muskmelons choose the short-season, disease-resistant varieties such as Sweet Granite or the new Ambrosia, a salmon-fleshed, firm hybrid cantaloupe which crops about 86 days after transplanting. Similar but with slightly deeper color is Gold Star, another new hybrid. Minnesota Midget has 4-inch (10 cm) fruit but they start after only 60 days and form on a compact 36-inch (90 cm) vine. Ball 1776 is an F_1 hybrid very tolerant of wilt and mildew, has heavily netted fruit up to 5-pound (2 kg) size. Started seedlings of Ball 1776 are often sold at local garden centers. Burpee's Early Hybrid Crenshaw has melons up to 14 pounds (6 kg) each. This hybrid will crop with a 90- to 100-day growing season from the time transplants are set out. Honey Mist, a honeydew type with greenish-white flesh, will also produce a satisfactory crop in about 100 days. The casaba and the true honeydew are satisfactory only in warm areas such as California. The small melons satisfactory with short growing times of 70 to 80 days include Ha-Ogen, a new mini-melon from Israel with rich, aromatic flavor, baseball-sized round fruit, and the Japanese hybrids which have skin thin enough to eat. Sakata's Sweet has 10-ounce (280 g) soft, green fruit with flesh like a honeydew melon. Takii's Honey is oblong with silvery skin striped green. Honey Gold has egg-shaped, bright-yellow fruit with crisp, applelike flesh. All of these small melons can be grown in a peat bag, with the vine trailing over a sunny terrace or up a small trellis.

Peat bags

Heavy plastic bags filled with a peat-lite-type mix and a small supplement of complete fertilizer can be used for growing melons, small cucumber hybrids and tomatoes. Since there is no drainage from the bag you must use care that the mix does not become waterlogged nor fully dry. This method of growing has been used for years in England but has only recently

been practiced by gardeners in the United States. Commercially manufactured peat bags may soon be offered at local garden centers.

Preparing the soil

Choose a planting bed in full sun, well away from tree roots. Prepare the soil by digging in compost, peat moss or well-rotted manure. Sprinkle 4 to 5 pounds (about 2 kg) of a complete vegetable fertilizer, such as Scott's 18-24-6, over every 100 square feet of growing space. If the soil is heavy clay, sprinkle agricultural gypsum and perlite over the bed and dig in to a depth of 12 inches (30 cm). For the ultimate in easy culture grow melons through a black plastic mulch. Spread the plastic over the well-prepared soil about 2 weeks before planting time (last frost date). Put rocks or soil over the edges of the plastic to hold it in place.

Planting

Punch or cut holes in the plastic for each melon plant. Melons planted through a plastic mulch or without the mulch should be spaced according to seed package directions since each variety has a different growth pattern. In general, a spacing of 12 inches (30 cm) between plants in rows 48 to 72 inches (120 to 180 cm) apart is good for standard growing types. Some of the newer compact hybrids need less room. If no plastic mulch is used spread some other type of mulch around the plants to preserve soil moisture and to protect the fruit when it starts to form. Salt hay or straw are both suitable melon mulches.

Harvesting

Cantaloupes turn yellowish when ripe, but an even surer test for full maturity is how each fruit slips from the vine. A fruit ready to eat will break away from the vine as you lift it up. Pick melons as you need them until just before frost, then harvest any that are ready before they are hit by cold. Melons not needed for immediate use can be made into melon balls for freezing.

Watermelons

The watermelon (*Citrullus vulgaris*) was thought for many years to belong to only home gardeners with huge back yards or a true farm because the vines grew so big. Now, thanks to the plant breeders, you can grow very compact watermelons which produce sweet fruit in an average-sized garden. Some of the smaller hybrids, such as Burpee's Sugar Bush, need only 6 square feet (.5 square meters) of growing room per plant. Culture of watermelons is similar to that of muskmelons except that watermelons are even more sensitive to dark days. For the best fruit, watermelons need a bright, warm season of at least 80 to 100 days after transplanting. In the North, start watermelon seed indoors about 3 weeks before outdoor planting time. Sow seed in 3-inch (8 cm) Jiffy peat pots or in Jiffy-7s. Start seed as described for tomatoes (see page 96), with a 75°F to 80°F (24°C to 27°C) germination temperature. Harvest watermelons when the bottom turns a rich golden-yellow and the powdery, slick top surface starts to look dull.

Greenhouse Cucumbers

Cucumbers, Pliny records, were "a wonderful favorite" with the Emperor Tiberius, who ate them every day, thanks to the skill of his gardeners, who "forced" cucumbers in winter. Tiberius' devotion to the cucumber

was not shared by the egregious Dr. Samuel Johnson, who wrote, "A cucumber should be well sliced, and dressed with pepper and vinegar, and then thrown out, as good for nothing." The verdict of history is against him. The cucumber (*Cucumis sativus*) has been grown for thousands of years. It is probably a native of northwest India, but it traveled west long before the Christian era.

The Roman Apicius had a recipe for boiling cucumber with brains, honey, cumin, celery seed, oil and eggs. The English herbalist Gerard advocated boiling it with mutton and mixing it with oatmeal. This, he said, "doth perfectly cure all manner of sauce flegme and copper faces, red and shining fierie noses."

Greenhouse cucumbers, mainly European hybrids, are bred for growing under glass. The garden cucumbers do best outside and are most popular for home gardens. Unfortunately, tomatoes and cucumbers are bad companions in the greenhouse. Both like warmth, but the cucumber likes steamy heat, which would be disastrous for tomatoes. However, tomatoes and cucumbers grow well together outdoors. The amateur gardener would probably do better to leave the greenhouse to tomatoes and grow cucumbers under frames, heated or cold, and cloches.

Varieties

Gourmet has long, bitter-free fruit. Toska has dark-green, 14-inch (34 cm) fruit which are seedless and smooth, with about 6 percent male blooms, which should be removed. Uniflora is an F_1 hybrid with all female flowers, 14- to 15-inch (34 to 35 cm) smooth fruit. La Reine is a gynoecious hybrid with 15-inch (38 cm) ridged, medium fruit on vines resistant to leaf spot and scab.

GROWING GREENHOUSE CUCUMBERS

Preparing the soil

In the center of each frame dig a hole 12 inches (30 cm) square and 12 inches (30 cm) deep and fill it in with a mixture of well-rotted manure or compost and peat. (This method—digging a hole in preference to a trench—economizes on precious manure and compost.) For cucumbers under cloches the enriched holes should be 36 inches (90 cm) apart down the center of a row.

Sowing

The time of sowing will depend on whether your garden is situated in a warm or cold area. It also depends on whether you are planting out to a frame with some heat, or to a cold frame, cold greenhouse or cloche. Allow about five weeks from sowing to planting out. If you are using a heated frame in a Southern area, sow in mid-March. The seedlings will be ready for planting out in late April. For an unheated frame in the South, sow toward the end of April to plant out in May or early June. In the North, sowing and planting dates are at least two weeks later.

Cucumbers thoroughly dislike root disturbance, therefore they should be sown in individual 3-inch (8 cm) pots or in Jiffy-7 pellets. Push two seeds, on their edges, ¾ inch (2 cm) into the compost, which must not be pressed down; the cucumber is an exception to the general rule of firm

planting. Water the mix using a watering can with a fine rose, and put the pots in the propagator. For quick germination the temperature should be 65°F to 70°F (18°C to 21°C). When the seedlings show through in two or three days make sure they have plenty of light, but not direct sunlight, and keep them moist. Temperatures should be about 65°F (18°C) by day and not less than 60°F (16°C) at night. They will be ready for planting out when the third or fourth true leaves have appeared.

To grow vines in a greenhouse, transplant seedlings to beds or large containers of peat-lite mix with slow-release fertilizer. Support as suggested for tomatoes on a trellis or with a wire cage.

Planting

Set one plant in a slight mound of soil in the center of each frame. (The mound is to help to prevent water from collecting at the base of the plant's stem and causing stem rot.) Under cloches the cucumber plants should be 36 inches (90 cm) apart.

The year's work

Cucumbers need a lot of attention. The soil must be kept moist, but not sodden, and the atmosphere in the frame must be humid. Shading may be needed against scorching sun to ensure that the temperature in the frame does not soar above 85°F (29°C). Training and pinching back of shoots is essential for a decent crop. The male flowers must be removed so that they do not pollinate the fruiting females. Fortunately, it is easy to spot the difference: the incipient cucumber can be seen behind the flower of the female. If the male flower is not removed the result will be bitter cucumbers full of large seeds. This chore can be avoided, however, by choosing only the female-flowering (gynoecious) varieties.

Training

In frames. When the plant has six leaves, pinch out the growing point. When laterals appear, select the best four and lightly peg them down, one toward each corner of the frame. Pinch out the growing shoot of these laterals when they near the corners.

Under cloches, pinching back is done to just above the fourth leaf. Keep two laterals to train in opposite directions along the cloche row. Thereafter, in frames and cloches, non-fruit-bearing shoots are stopped at the fourth leaf. Fruit-bearing shoots are stopped two leaves beyond the developing cucumber. Male flowers must be picked off to prevent pollination. Liquid fertilizer should be given every week when the fruits begin to develop. As a cucumber develops, place a shingle or piece of wood under it to keep it off the soil.

Harvesting

July onward. Pick the cucumbers before they get old and large. The young ones taste better, and removing them induces the plant to go on producing more.

Garden Cucumbers

For a long time the smaller garden cucumbers were regarded as the poor relations of the greenhouse cucumber, but not any longer. There has been a vast improvement in quality among new varieties, and there is a far wider choice. Garden cucumbers are much

easier to grow than greenhouse cucumbers; they can be sown and grown out of doors in most parts of the country with only a minimum of protection at the start. They are also wildly prolific if they are planted in very rich soil. Even people without gardens could well grow them in boxes or tubs on patios or balconies, as long as the soil is rich to begin with and kept moist all along. Peat bags can be used instead of boxes, in the same way as they are for tomatoes.

It is not necessary to be content with only the green varieties. The white cucumber, a great favorite on the Continent, has a delicately flavored, juicy flesh, which is not indigestible as is the case with most cucumbers. And because the plant does not trail as vigorously as most cucumbers it takes up far less room in the garden. The prejudice against it must be because its skin is creamy-white and not the regulation green—the kind of prejudice felt against yellow tomatoes and raspberries for not being red.

Another delicious-tasting cucumber is conventionally wrong both in shape (slightly oval) and color (yellow). This is the apple cucumber which, if it is picked when it is the size of a small apple, is the juiciest and crispest of all.

The Japanese climbing cucumber can be grown up a trellis or netting against a sunny wall. It really does better, however, in an unheated greenhouse which, unlike most cucumbers, it will share amicably with tomatoes.

Varieties

Pot Luck is a unique new hybrid which has 6-inch (15 cm), dark-green fruit on vines only 18 inches (45 cm) long. Pot Luck is ideal for terrace plantings or in greenhouse containers. Burpless (F_1) has all the indigestibility bred out of it. Burpee Hybrid (F_1) produces a heavy crop of flavorful, white-fleshed fruits. For gherkin pickles grow Early Hycrop. For larger pickles use Spartan Dawn hybrid, a 4- to 6-inch (10 to 15 cm) fruit.

GROWING CUCUMBERS OUTDOORS

Preparing the soil

The simplest way to grow cucumbers is to sow them where they are to grow. This labor-saving method also suits them, for they dislike having their roots disturbed. Give them a warm, sunny and well-drained position and exceptionally humus-rich soil. This is most economically done by making holes 12 inches (30 cm) deep and 12 inches (30 cm) square at 36-inch (90 cm) intervals along a row. Almost completely fill the holes with a mixture of compost or manure and peat and cover it with soil. Mark the centers of the holes to show where the seeds have later to be sown. If cloches are available put them in position along the row two weeks before sowing to give the soil a chance to warm up.

Sowing

Sow in early May in the South, but later as you go North—up to the end of May or early June—so that there will be no danger of the young plants being damaged by late frosts. Plant two seeds, edgewise and 1 inch (2 cm) deep, at the center of the prepared holes, the weaker seedling to be discarded later. Cover with cloches. If cloches are not available some other cover must be devised—a small plastic bag over wires, or a sheet of glass on top of a support formed by four bricks. Remove these when the two seed leaves have opened. Cloches would remain longer.

Alternatively, seeds can be sown in a greenhouse or propagator from the end of April for planting out at the end of May or early June. Sow seeds singly in peat pots or Jiffy-7 pellets—to avoid root disturbance—and raise them in the same way as green-

house cucumbers. The plants must be thoroughly hardened off before they are put out of doors.

Gherkin varieties should always be sown where they are to grow and be treated as above. However, the distance between the plants need be only 24 inches (60 cm).

Planting

June. Plants grown in pots should be set out in the garden 36 inches (90 cm) apart in early June, or earlier if cloches are being used.

The year's work

Cloches can be removed as soon as the plants are established and when the weather is good. When the plant has seven leaves, pinch out the growing tip to encourage

side shoots. That is all that is needed in the way of training. Unlike some greenhouse cucumbers, which grow bitter if they are pollinated, garden cucumbers have to be pollinated if they are to fruit at all. This task can safely be left to the bees. Keep the soil moist; a mulch of peat or lawn mowings will help. Black plastic mulch will hold moisture and protect fruits too. Water

should be given around the plants and not over them. As the fruits appear lay a shingle or a piece of wood under them to keep them off the soil or use a black plastic mulch.

Harvesting

July onward. Cucumbers are prolific if well fed, some plants producing up to forty cucumbers. But if the plants are to provide anything like this number of cucumbers it is essential to keep picking and not to let the cucumbers grow big. Gherkins especially should be picked young, when they are 2 to 3 inches (5 to 8 cm) long. When the first frosts of autumn are imminent pick the rest of the cucumbers before they are ruined.

Squashes and Pumpkins

Squashes, pumpkins and gourds are all cucurbits, but there is not much precision about which name should be attached to which species. They are one of the very ancient vegetables of the world—dating from 7000 B.C. in Central and South America, and from 1000 B.C. in North America.

Squashes and pumpkins are regarded as American. Winter squashes have a more solid texture than summer types. The name pump-

kin dates only to the seventeenth century and comes from the Greek—*sikuos pepon*. The sun is certainly an important factor in growing all cucurbits, and with good culture it is possible to produce pumpkins weighing seventy-five pounds (34 kg).

As the taste for growing large squashes is at last waning, so the popularity of the young, small fruits increases. A large squash is particularly tasteless, not surprisingly, since up to 99 percent of it may be water. The Romans made squash palatable by smothering it with pungent sauces—one recipe by Apicius contains thirteen ingredients, including pepper, cumin, coriander, mint, honey, vinegar and oil—and it was again sprinkled with pepper when served.

Squashes take up a lot of room in the garden. Beware of planting large, vine-type squashes close to other vegetables because the squash leaves will cover their neighbors by midsummer. Fortunately, you can grow some compact bush squashes or train the vine squashes on a fence or up a plastic mesh Gro-Net supported by stout stakes. The winter squashes, such as Gold Nugget, Hubbard types and acorn varieties, are most often grown for winter storage, although the young fruits are good steamed. Summer squashes, including zucchini and the yellow crookneck, are best picked young, for flavor and to keep vines

producing all summer. Pumpkins grow like other squashes but need room. A more compact type than usual is All-America winner Spirit, a 10- to 15-pound (4 to 7 kg) type produced on semibush vines which need about 4 feet (120 cm) of space.

Varieties

Summer squashes: Burpee Golden zucchini has lovely yellow fruits with typical zucchini flavor on bush-type plants. The All-America winner Scallopini is a new hybrid bush variety with a 36- to 48-inch (90 to 120 cm) spread and bears flattened, fluted patty-pan-shaped green fruits, good in salads, steamed, fried or baked. For green zucchini, plant one of the hybrid types such as Aristocrat. Yellow Butterbar is a productive bush with smooth, tender crookneck-type fruits but with a straight shape.

Winter squashes: Waltham Butternut, an All-America selection, has straight, deep-orange fruits that store well. Burpee's Butter Bush is a new dwarf butternut type that grows 36 to 48 inches (90 to 120 cm) long and has 4 to 5 butternut-style fruits about $1\frac{1}{2}$ pounds (.6 kg) each. Table King is an adaptable, productive acorn squash with smooth, dark-green skin, pale-orange flesh. Gold Nugget is a compact bush with 5 to 8 orange football-shaped fruits about 3 pounds (1 kg) each. Vegetable Spaghetti is a curious, easy-to-grow squash. It has bright-yellow fruits, about 8 inches (20 cm) long, and the flesh when boiled looks like spaghetti, with the advantage that it is non-fattening.

Trailing varieties grown on the ground take up a lot of room, for the shoots can be several yards long. But they can successfully be grown up fences or trained up tripods made of 7- to 8-foot (2 to 2.5 m) poles tied together at the top. One squash plant is grown up each pole. A tripod is a good way of planting squashes in a flower border.

GROWING SQUASHES
Preparing the soil

Rich soil and sun are essential. To make precious compost or manure go farther, concentrate it at the points where each squash is to be planted. Dig holes 12 inches square (30 cm sq) 36 inches (90 cm) apart for bush squashes and 48 inches (120 cm) apart for trailers, and fill them with a mixture of well-

rotted manure or compost, peat and soil. Squash roots do not go very deep, so do not bury this richness out of reach. The pH should be close to 6.

Sowing

April/May. Sow seeds in small pots or Jiffy-7s because squashes hate having their roots disturbed in transplanting. Sow two seeds to a pot, the weaker seedling to be

discarded later. In a heated greenhouse, sowing can be done early in April in a temperature of 65°F (18°C). In an unheated greenhouse or frame wait to sow until the end of April or early May. Outdoor seed can be sown from mid-May in the prepared positions where the plants are to grow. It will help outdoor sowings, of course, if the soil has been warmed under cloches or black plastic for a few weeks.

Planting

Late May to June. Plants raised indoors can be put out, properly hardened off, from late May to early June. Water before transplanting; disturb roots as little as poosible.

The year's work

Slugs are greatly attracted to young squash plants, so if your garden is a haunt of slugs lay down bait. Be ready always to water the plants when needed. Give liquid fertilizer weekly after the first fruits begin to form. When the shoots of the trailing varieties are about 36 inches (90 cm) long the growing points can be pinched out to encourage fruit-bearing side shoots. Squashes trained up fences or tripods should have their growing points pinched out when the vines are about 60 inches (152 cm) high. Bush varieties will need no stopping.

Insects pollinate the flowers, but human help may be needed. The female has a squashlike swelling behind the flower, the male flower has not. Dust pollen from the

male flower into the fully open female flower with a stick tipped with cotton wool. Or pick one of the male flowers, turn back the petals, and gently press it into the center of the female flower.

Harvesting

Start picking summer squashes and zucchini when the fruits are 1 to 2 inches in diameter, or 3 to 4 inches across for scallop-type squashes. Winter squashes grown for storage must mature completely and are better if left to ripen during cool fall days. The butternut types should turn a rich tan; green kinds blush bronze.

Zucchini

Zucchini are best picked when they are very young, when they have a delicate taste. They have become increasingly popular in the last decade, perhaps as a result of the increase in the numbers of people who go abroad for their vacations. Zucchini have long been favorites in France, and are even more popular in Italy, which is where we get the popular name.

Varieties

Although zucchini are basically small squashes, special varieties have been bred to bear numerous small fruits instead of the one-time monsters.

Zucchini Select F_1 is an early variety, has slender, dark-green fruits. Golden Zucchini is similar, but the fruits are a rich yellow. Aristocrat is a compact All-America selection.

GROWING ZUCCHINI
Preparing the soil
The zucchini needs the same kind of soil as the other varieties of squash.

Sowing and planting
The methods are the same as for other squashes, but the zucchini varieties need to be planted only 20 inches (50 cm) or so apart. They grow and fruit particularly well if started under cloches.

The year's work
The aim is to grow zucchini quickly; this means keeping them moist but not sodden. Water the soil around the plants regularly, particularly during dry weather. If you water over the plants the fruit may rot. Regular watering helps prevent mildew. Give them a weekly feed of liquid fertilizer as soon as the first fruits form. Lay down bait against slugs, which unfortunately have an inordinate fondness for both the leaves and the young fruit. Using a hoe, weed between the rows of plants as often as is necessary. Taking great care not to bruise

the fruits or damage the plants, pick the zucchini when they are not more than 4 inches (10 cm) long if they are to be used whole in cooking. They could be allowed to grow up to 8 inches (20 cm) if they are to be sliced, as for ratatouille, the French vegetable casserole. But the longer the fruits are left on the plant the fewer female flowers will grow, and the more the later crop will be reduced.

Eggplants

The eggplant (*Solanum melongena*, var. *esculentum*) is another tropical vegetable fruit, a native of southern Asia, which was regarded with deep suspicion when it was first imported to Europe in the thirteenth century. It was grown only for its ornamental value until the late-fourteenth century, when doubts were overcome and people began to eat it. Outside Europe, however, it was the Arabs who first dared to eat it as long ago as the fourth century. The eggplant, which has become increasingly popular, belongs to the potato family and, therefore, is related to the sweet pepper. Eggplants, however, are somewhat harder to grow than peppers and are best started in greenhouses or under tall cloches. On a sunny patio, eggplants can be raised in pots, as they are in the greenhouse.

Varieties

Burpee Hybrid (F_1) and Dusky F_1 are disease-resistant, reliable varieties and they both have very good flavor.

Sweet Peppers

The sweet pepper (*Capsicum annuum*) is a relative of the potato and the tomato, and cultivation is much the same as for the tomato. The green peppers are the unripened fruit, and are usually picked at that stage. They are slow to turn red and taste no better for it.

Varieties

New Ace (F_1) is early and prolific. Burpee's Tasty Hybrid matures in 70 days, has big yield of dark-green fruits turning red when fully ripe. California Wonder is similar. For hot peppers you can select red, green or yellow. Anaheim M is a long, green type which gradually turns red. Long Red Cayenne has 5-inch-long (13 cm) curled and twisted fruits which are easily dried. Hungarian Wax is bright yellow, 6 to 8 inches (15 to 20 cm) long, matures to bright red. For a large, red hot pepper grow Hot Portugal, which produces 6-inch-long (15 cm) fruits in 65 to 70 days.

GROWING EGGPLANTS

Preparing the soil
If the plants are to be grown under cloches dig in plenty of mature compost.

Sowing
February. For greenhouse plants sow seeds in early February in pots or Jiffy-7s. Keep in a temperature of 60°F (16°C). The seeds may take two weeks or more to germinate. Move the seedlings to larger pots of peat-lite mix and later to 8-inch (20 cm) pots

with additional fertilizer if required. Plants destined to go outside should be sown in late March, similarly repotted, and later hardened off for planting out in late May or early June.

Planting
May/June. Plant the seedlings 24 inches (60 cm) apart in a single row under large barn cloches, which will later have to be raised.

The year's work
When the plant is 6 inches (15 cm) high, pinch out the growing tip. After four fruits have set, remove the rest of the flowers and pinch out all the side shoots. Water well and give two or three liquid-fertilizer feeds at intervals in July.

Harvesting
August onward. Take care to pick the fruits while the bloom is still on them. As the shine goes, bitterness creeps in.

GROWING PEPPERS

Preparing the soil
Add well-rotted compost but no fresh manure as too rich a soil encourages leaf growth, not fruit.

Sowing
Peppers need a warm growing season. Start with plants from mail-order sources or local garden centers for maximum success. To grow your own plants sow seed in Jiffy-7 pots or individual pots of a peat-lite mix 8 to 10 weeks before outdoor planting date. Pepper seedlings should be planted outside only after weather is settled and warm, for like eggplants they are quite easily damaged by cool, wet periods.

Planting
Set plants in the garden 18 to 24 inches (45 to 60 cm) apart in rows 24 to 36 inches (60 to 90 cm) apart. Mulch to keep down weeds. Push a stake down next to the plant as support in windy areas.

Harvesting
Begin picking fruits from late summer onward, while they are still green.

PESTS AND DISEASES OF TOMATOES, EGGPLANTS AND PEPPERS

Tomatoes are liable to more than their fair share of pests and diseases, but fertile soil and thoroughly clean greenhouses will help in escaping them. Eggplants and peppers, of the same family as tomatoes, are liable to suffer tomato pests and diseases, but in fact do so less frequently. Aphids spread virus diseases. Spray with malathion.

Red spiders (shown below 55 times life size) are especially the bane of peppers. The

mites suck the sap of the plants, particularly in hot, dry weather. It is important, therefore, to keep the atmosphere of the greenhouse humid. It may involve spraying once or twice a day. Do not, however, let too much water fall on the leaves of the plants.

The nymphs of whitefly suck the sap and excrete unpleasant honeydew. The nymphs are very resistant to chemicals, but thorough cleaning of the greenhouse will get rid of the overwintering fly. Or control them with Diazinon.

Potato blight can also affect tomatoes, mainly those grown outdoors.

The control measures are the same as for potatoes. (See page 93.)

Verticillium wilt is caused by a fungus which cuts down the flow of sap to mature plants when they are laden with fruit. The disease is often associated with low temperatures, but the wilting itself occurs on hot days, and the plant may appear to recover in the cooler evenings. Badly affected plants should be burned. For the less badly

affected plants heat the greenhouse to 77°F (25°C) for 14 days. This will kill the fungus and may enable plants to survive.

To avoid major problems with disease,

plant only varieties bred for resistance to verticillium and fusarium wilts and to soil nematodes. Seed catalogs show which selections are resistant to diseases by the code letters V, F, N after the variety name. Better Boy VFN tomato is resistant to all three problems, as is dwarf cherry tomato Small Fry.

Botrytis stem rot usually affects plants in the greenhouse, in humid surroundings. Avoid crowding. Keep the greenhouse ventilated. Above all take care not to damage the plants—for instance, when removing side shoots cut cleanly with a sharp knife, and when picking the fruit do not leave the calyx on the stem. These are the danger points at which the spores enter. Do not let the lower leaves rot on the plant or leave any lying around on the soil.

Virus diseases are legion; the most common serious one is tomato mosaic

(yellow mottling of the leaves and stunted growth). There is no cure. Handle the diseased plants only after dealing with other plants, or you will pass the infection on. Some viruses are common to tomatoes and tobacco, so smokers would be advised not to handle the plants after smoking.

PESTS AND DISEASES OF CUCUMBERS, MELONS AND SQUASHES

Cucumbers, melons and squashes share a number of pests and diseases. The pests are slugs (use methiocarb baits) and aphids (spray with malathion).

Many varieties are susceptible to cucumber mosaic virus. There is no cure, but aphids are the main carriers of the disease

and should be destroyed. The symptoms of the disease are yellow mottling and shriveling of the leaves, stunted growth and fruits which die before they develop. Burn infected plants.

Cucumbers are available in varieties resistant to scab (S), anthracnose (A), mosaic (M), downy mildew (DM) and powdery mildew (PM).

Mildew often attacks in the autumn, showing as white powdery patches on the leaves and stems. It is encouraged by a combination of humid air and dry soil. Beds should never be allowed to get dry. Reduce the risk of mildew in greenhouses by being careful to prevent drafts or sharp changes in humidity. Karathane, used when the temperature is below 80°F (27°C) helps control mildew.

Mushrooms

Mushrooms have been growing and have been eaten for thousands of years, but it was less than three centuries ago that man discovered how to cultivate them as we do today. We have the French to thank for that advance, while Americans are responsible for many of the scientific developments in mushroom growing in the twentieth century. But there are still enormous gaps in our knowledge of this mysterious, lowly form of plant life

(*Psalliotra campestris*), and a vast amount of research continues in Europe and the United States to fill them.

The mushroom is a fungus and, therefore, obtains its food in an entirely different way from any other vegetable in the kitchen garden.

A fungus has no leaves and no chlorophyll and cannot absorb and use carbon dioxide from the air. Some fungi are parasitic, feeding on living matter, but the mushroom is a saprophytic fungus, that is it lives on dead matter. It starts life as a spore from the parent mushroom. On germination the spore puts out minute threads called hyphae, which branch out in all directions and form the mycelium. (An example of mycelium that can be seen in the kitchen is the white fluff on moldy bread.) The mushroom's mycelium produces enzymes, which break down the organic matter in which they are growing to provide food for the mushroom itself, the fruiting head, to grow.

The amateur gardener starts his cultivation of mushrooms by buying mycelium as spawn—either composted manure or grains inoculated with mycelium. As the spawn grows, the fruiting head develops—the mushroom-to-be. It emerges above the surface of the soil as a small white ball, then a stalk appears and lastly a cap develops. When the cap opens, pink gills can be seen inside it. These turn brown as the spores growing on them mature. (The black spots on that moldy bread in the kitchen are spores.) Before the mushroom dies it will have produced and shed five to six thousand million minute spores. Fortunately for the future of mankind few of the spores even get a chance to grow—if they did the whole world would soon be taken over by mushrooms. But mushrooms have many enemies to keep them firmly in check—far too many for the good of his crop, the gardener may think.

Mushrooms are curiously exciting things to grow, but they are unpredictable. Although

you will have no difficulty in finding a place for them to grow—you could even have a box of them under the bed—do not be too surprised, or too bitterly disappointed, if sometimes they do not come up.

Reduced to deceptive simplicity, mushrooms grow in compost which has a covering of soil (called a casing in mushroom jargon). They will grow in the dark or in light, but avoid direct sunlight. The optimum temperatures for growth are between 50° and 55°F (10° and 13°C); and none will grow if the temperature is below 40°F (4°C). Ventilation must be good, for an excess of carbon dioxide in the air will stop growth.

A program for mushroom growing indoors without heat might be: Composting, March. Spawning, April. Cropping, May to August. Then disinfect boxes. Composting, August. Spawning, September. Cropping, October to November. After a break, when it is too cold for growing, it starts up again from March to April with the return of the warmer weather. Then disinfect boxes.

Varieties and spawns

Brown mushrooms grow more vigorously, are more disease resistant and taste better than white mushrooms. But the white are more popular merely because they look more attractive—before they are cooked. A cream variety is halfway between the white and the brown in its qualities.

Manure spawn is made from composted manure, grain spawn from crushed rye, wheat or barley grains. Grain spawn is growing in popularity, but, on balance, manure spawn is probably the safest for the beginner.

Pests and diseases

The larvae of the prolific sciarid flies eat both the compost and the spawn and burrow into the stems and caps of the mushrooms, ruining

them. Dust the boxes or beds with pyrethrum every 10 to 14 days after the spawn has been put in the compost, but do it between flushes in the crop.

The phorid, or manure fly, is an equal menace—its shiny yellow larvae devouring the

growing spawn. Dust the boxes or beds every 10 to 14 days with pyrethrum.

Mushroom mites, too small to be seen, breed at a fantastic rate. They feed on the mycelium

and damage the mushroom caps. To try to prevent a build-up, dust the compost once with Lindane while turning it. Do not use Lindane on growing mushrooms.

Eelworms also feed on the mycelium, but

the danger from them is less if the compost has been well made and is not soggy.

Bubbles is the innocent-sounding name of the worst fungus disease to attack mushrooms; the Latin name, *Mycogone perniciosa*, is far more suggestive of its evil effects. These are distorted, moldy mushrooms from which oozes a brown, foul-smelling substance. Burn them and disinfect your hands. The casing is probably the source of the disease, so amateurs growing mushrooms on a small scale would do well to buy sterilized soil for the casing.

Two molds, well described by their names —white plaster mold and brown plaster mold—are diseases usually associated with improperly made or wet compost.

GROWING MUSHROOMS

Some simple ways to grow mushrooms:

Anyone who is keen to cultivate mushrooms will almost certainly be able to find a suitable place to put them while they are growing. Mushrooms do not require daylight and can be grown indoors in a kitchen cupboard or in a cupboard under the stairs. Buy buckets or sacks of prepared compost, complete with spawn. Water, cover with the casing provided and wait. Or fill 9-inch (23 cm) pots with compost, plant with spawn and cover. (For methods of composting, spawning and casing, see below.)

Growing mushrooms in sheds, garages or cellars: The spawn is planted in 9-inch-deep (23 cm) compost in boxes which are stacked to give good ventilation and room for picking.

Growing mushrooms outdoors in boxes fixed to walls: Choose a sunless wall. The boxes must be at least deep enough to hold 9 inches (23 cm) of compost and 1½ to 2 inches (3 to 5 cm) of soil covering.

Growing on beds in sheds or cellars: The compost in the bed should be 18 inches (45 cm) deep.

Preparing the compost

The one tedious operation in mushroom growing is making the compost in which the mushroom spawn is planted. It can be avoided by buying prepared compost, but if you have time, energy and room it is worth doing, because after the mushroom crop is finished you are left with a supply of good humus which can be used in the garden. Experience makes it easier than it sounds.

The ideal compost is made from the wheat straw of hard-working (and presumably well-fed) horses. But these days not only will you not be able to be choosy about your horses, you may well have to do without any horse manure at all. The alternative is to use a proprietary compost activator. Try, however, to get wheat straw, because it composts best. 200 lb (100 kg) of straw treated with activator will produce enough compost for about 60 square feet (6 sq m) to a depth of 9 inches (23 cm).

The straw must first be thoroughly saturated with water; it takes a lot. Make the heap as compact and tall as possible or you will lose a lot of heat. Start with a layer of shaken-out straw 6 inches (15 cm) or more deep. Sprinkle the activator, according to the instructions, on top of it. Then add another layer of straw and activator, and so on. The addition of even a little manure—horse, pig or dry poultry manure—makes a better compost, which produces a bigger crop.

In a few days the heap will get hot, and after a week turn it so that the colder outside is put to the center of the heap to heat up. Shake the straw in turning, and water if it has dried out. At this stage gypsum should be added, at least 1 pound to each cwt (½ kg to 50 kg) of straw, to prevent the compost from becoming sticky. Turn the heap again after a week, and again after another week. By then the compost should be a rich brown with a

pleasantly earthy smell, not black and greasy, and moist but not wet. The pH of the compost, which varies greatly while it is being made, should now be 7.6 (slightly alkaline). If the pH and the texture are correct and the temperature of the compost in the heap, taken with a soil thermometer, has fallen below 80°F (27°C), the compost is now ready for transferring to the boxes or beds in which the mushrooms are to be grown.

Spawning and casing

Put the compost into the boxes, pressing it down hard with a brick to an even depth of 9 inches (23 cm). When the temperature of the

compost has fallen to 70° to 75°F (21° to 24°C) plant the spawn. Manure spawn is broken into ¾-inch (2 cm) lumps and pushed 2 inches (5 cm) into the compost. Use staggered formation planting, 10 inches (25 cm) apart each way. Grain spawn is usually scattered on the

surface. Do not water the compost, but cover the boxes with black plastic sheeting to keep the surface moist. If all goes well the mycelium will be spreading through the compost

by the end of one week.

After 10 to 14 days the bed is cased. This means covering the compost evenly with a 1½- to 2-inch (3 to 5 cm) layer of moist, sterilized soil (pH 7)—other materials are often used commercially. Do not use soil from the garden, which may be seething with enemies of the mushroom. Do not firm the covering. It must be kept moist, but never given so much water that any soaks into the compost below; that will kill the spawn. Water evenly, using a watering can with a fine rose. If the air temperature is about 65°F (18°C), which is hot for mushrooms, watering may have to be done every other day; with temperatures about 50°F (10°C), perhaps once a week. You will quickly learn to judge when the casing appears to be drying out.

The first pinhead mushrooms may begin to appear three weeks after casing. A week or ten days later they will reach maturity. Most people pick them too soon—before they are open. Big open mushrooms have a far better taste than the buttons. When picking, never pull the mushrooms out of the soil, but give

a twisting upward movement. Fill the holes left with some casing. Mushrooms, if thriving, tend to crop in flushes, at intervals of ten days or so, and may continue for two months. Then the beds have to be renewed. The exhausted compost provides valuable humus for the garden.

Fruits

Galen, the Greco-Roman "prince of physicians" who died in A.D. 200 a stripling of only seventy years, was of the opinion that his father had lived to be a hundred because he never ate fruit. Even if we accepted the young Galen's theory, we could still wonder whether those extra years were worth his father's sacrifice. It is hard to imagine a life deprived of such experiences as the heady aroma of strawberries, the hint of earthiness in ripe blackberries, or the sensuous juiciness of pears. Since we now believe that fruit is good for us, there is no reason why we should not raise our own, since many are not difficult to grow.

The kitchen garden is not an orchard, but there is often room for soft fruit. Strawberries give the quickest return—they will bear fruit in less than a year. Raspberries can be picked within eighteen months and give bigger crops over the years for the space they occupy than any other soft fruits. Currants and gooseberries take longer to come to full cropping, but they then have a longer fruiting life.

Apples and pears take up little room if grown as cordons against a wall facing south, and they give a reasonable return. Almost double the crops could be expected if they were grown as dwarf pyramids, but then they would take up more space.

Vines have been growing in Europe since Roman times, through both warm and bitterly cold centuries, and are much hardier than many people imagine. There are now varieties of grapes which combine hardy American types with European grapes.

Only the easier and the hardiest fruits have been included in this section, but after gaining a little experience and more confidence you could turn to the intricacies of espalier-trained apples and pears and to fan-trained plums, peaches and morello cherries. Figs are undemanding, except for sun, and for winter protection in the North.

Melons are an exciting fruit for the amateur gardener. If you wish to live to be a centenarian, however, it might be as well to avoid an excess of melons, for a surfeit of them is reported to have been responsible for the deaths of Pope Paul II in 1417, of the German King Frederick the Peaceful in 1493 and of his son Maximilian I in 1519. On the other hand, Catherine de Médicis, immoderate in so many things, was inordinately fond of melons without apparent harm.

Although many varieties of melons have to be greenhouse grown, new cantaloupe hybrids will crop well outside, although the seeds have to be sown indoors, as mentioned on page 97. The following are hardy perennial fruits.

1 Dessert apples
2 Pears
3 Black grapes
4 Strawberries
5 Black currants
6 Blackberries
7 Raspberries
8 White grapes

Raspberries

After strawberries, the soft fruits which show the quickest return are raspberries (*Rubus idaeus*), blackberries (*Rubus fruticosus*) and loganberries (*Rubus × loganobaccus*). A year and a half after planting the canes you will be eating the fruit.

The most popular is the raspberry. Eastern Asia is probably its original home. Pliny describes it growing wild on Mount Ida, and it still grows wild in much of the northern hemisphere. The raspberry has been cultivated in American gardens since colonial times, although few varieties of raspberry grown today go back more than twenty-five years.

Varieties

Reds: Giant Newburgh and Latham are adaptable heavy fruiters. Indian Summer and Heritage are good for summer and fall crops once established.

Blacks: Cumberland and Bristol are productive black types. Black Treasure is a new, dark, everbearing hybrid which fruits from June until frost.

Yellow: Fall Gold is a summer- and fall-bearing yellow hybrid.

Pests and diseases

Where there are raspberries there are usually the little white maggots that lurk in the plug of the fruit. Attack the beetle, not the maggot. Spray the flowers with Sevin about a week after flowering begins and again two weeks later. This will be approximately from the middle to the end of June.

Raspberries are prone to virus diseases, which eventually kill them. There is no cure. Buy healthy stock.

GROWING RASPBERRIES

Preparing the soil

The ideal soil for raspberries is loam, well drained but moisture holding and rich in humus. It should also be slightly acid with a pH around 6. Many gardens will fall short of the ideal yet still grow raspberries well. But you will inevitably be disappointed if you expect raspberries to thrive in poor or waterlogged soil. In August or early September, dig a trench 12 inches (30 cm) deep and 30 inches (75 cm) wide and put in the bottom as much manure or compost as you can find, or spare, remembering that the raspberries (viruses permitting) will be there for eight to ten years. Raspberries have a mass of surface roots as well as their deeper roots, so you cannot hope to dig in manure in later years to make up for a bad start. If you cannot be extravagant with manuring, $\frac{1}{4}$ pound of bone meal to the square yard (120 g to 1 sq m) should be raked in a few weeks before planting.

Raspberries (and blackberries and loganberries) are less liable to be damaged by frosts than gooseberries or currants. However, they need protection from winds, which all too easily snap off shoots laden with fruits. Raspberries will tolerate some shade, but for the finest flavor give them sun. If rows run north to south all the canes get an equal share of sunshine.

Planting

Raspberries, like most soft fruits, are plagued by debilitating virus diseases. It is essential, therefore, that the raspberry canes you buy should be certified; then, at least, they will be healthy when you get them.

Try to plant them as soon as canes are available, which will be from late October. Plant the canes 18 inches (45 cm) apart in rows 60 inches (150 cm) or more apart. They should go about 3 inches (8 cm) deep in the soil. Firm the soil around each cane. A week or two after planting, cut back the canes to 8 to 10 inches (20 to 25 cm) above the ground, for they are not allowed to fruit in the summer after planting. That first

year has to be spent in building up a strong root system and healthy canes for the following year.

The year's work

Give a dressing of $\frac{1}{2}$ ounce to the square yard (15 g to 1 sq m) of sulfate of potash in March and a thin mulch of lawn mowings in May, when the bed is moist. Support must be provided for the growing canes. Fasten three rows of wire to strong, supporting posts at each end of the row, at

24 inches (60 cm), 40 inches (100 cm) and 60 inches (150 cm) from the ground. Tie the canes to this as they grow to keep them straight and to help to protect them from damage by the wind. Water when necessary with a perforated hose on the ground along the row. At the end of the summer cut away the stumps of the original canes, remove any weak new canes, and tie the rest, spaced out, to the wires, to withstand the autumn gales.

The following year's work

Cut 6 inches (15 cm) from the top of the strongest canes and 3 inches (8 cm) from the smaller, in February, to encourage fruiting. Dress the soil with potash in March and mulch in May as in the first year. Temporarily tie the canes as they grow. Prune as soon as the crop is finished. First cut down the canes which have fruited to just above the soil. Then cut away all but the five or six stronger new canes, spacing them out to 3 to 4 inches (8 to 10 cm) along the wires—retying where necessary.

Autumn-fruiting raspberries are grown in the same way, but the system of pruning is different. They fruit on canes which have grown the same year. After fruiting they are left unpruned until the end of February, when all the canes are cut to ground level. New canes then grow.

Harvesting

Summer fruiting, July to August. Autumn fruiting, September to October. Try not to pick when the fruit is wet—they go moldy rapidly. Pick the berries and leave the cores.

Propagation

Raspberries are easily propagated, but it would be folly to reproduce any but the healthiest stock. October is the best time but it can also be done in spring. Simply lift some of the strongest suckers that have come up some distance from the row, along with some root, and replant them in new beds. (If suckers that stray from the rows are not wanted for propagation, dig them up and throw them away.)

Blackberries

The wild blackberry grows widely, and often rampantly, in the temperate regions of both the Old and New World. The cultivated blackberry scores over its bramble forebears in size, sweetness and juiciness, if not in flavor. Now it has been grown without thorns, and is tame enough for even small gardens, especially when well trained against a tall fence or wall.

Varieties

Blackberries are hardier than loganberries or boysenberries, and more compact. Thornfree is a vining type, hardy only to Zone 5. Darrow has excellent flavor and is hardy into Zone 5, with ripe fruit by mid-June. In warm Southern areas grow hybrid Thornless loganberries or boysenberries, but remember that these require more space, often growing 7 feet (210 cm) tall.

Loganberries

The loganberry, which has a rather more acid taste than the blackberry, began its life in California in 1881. The man who raised and gave his name to it was an amateur gardener, Judge Logan, of Santa Cruz. The loganberry got itself a bad reputation when virus ruined many plantings. However, with the raising of a virus-free variety, and the arrival of American Thornless loganberries, it has now started the climb back into favor.

Varieties

Loganberries are listed by Gurney's and a few other catalogs. More popular are the Thornless boysenberry hybrids, which, like the loganberry, need winter protection anywhere that temperatures drop below 5°F (—15°C). They are best in Zones 7 and 8.

GROWING BLACKBERRIES AND LOGANBERRIES

Preparing the soil

Blackberries and loganberries are less demanding than raspberries. A reasonably good soil will do for most varieties, and a certain amount of shade will be accepted. The soil should be slightly acid (pH 6). But the better the treatment they get the better they will crop over the twelve or more fruitful years you can expect of them. Blackberries flower later than raspberries, and loganberries even later, so they usually escape spring frosts. But loganberry canes can be damaged or even killed by severe winter frosts, so choose a sheltered site.

Planting

October or early spring. Plant the canes, spreading the roots out well and firming the soil. They should go as deep in the soil

as they were in the nursery. Even the less vigorous varieties need a lot of room: each blackberry plant should have at least 96 inches (240 cm) of space to spread in, and a loganberry at least 120 inches (300 cm). Cut back the canes to not more than 12 inches (30 cm) above the ground.

Support and training

Blackberries and loganberries grow long, trailing canes, which need supporting and training. Galvanized or plastic netting, 72

inches (180 cm) high, can be fixed against walls, or lines of galvanized wire, 12 inches (30 cm) apart, can be strung between sturdy, long-lasting posts of galvanized iron or concrete. Fan-training on the wires is probably the most straightforward for the amateur gardener, although it does involve a lot of tying. Fruiting canes are trained left and right along the wire, leaving the center open for new canes, which are loosely bunched together and tied to the wires with string as they grow. (As shown below

without leaves.) When the old canes have fruited and been cut down to the ground, the new canes are securely tied fanwise to the wires, as the old canes were. The center is left empty for the next year's growth of cane. Or the new canes can be left bunched together during the winter and fanned out later, in February or early in March.

The year's work

Give a dressing of rotted manure or compost around the roots each spring. This will produce better fruit that year and healthier canes to fruit the following year. For the same reason, water well if the soil is at all dry, as it may well be if the plants are being grown against a wall. In the first summer few canes will be produced, but the sooner

the planting has been done after October the more canes will grow. Tie them carefully, fanwise, to the wires. The beetles which put the maggots into raspberries may also be attracted to loganberries. Spray the flowers with Sevin a week or so after flowering begins and repeat the spraying in two weeks.

Birds prefer raspberries to blackberries and loganberries, so while raspberries must be protected if you are to have any, blackberries and loganberries need not be netted if you are willing to lose a few to the birds. But be prepared with nets in case they are needed.

Harvesting

Mid-June/September. Pick carefully or really ripe berries will go to mush between your fingers, and pick the berries, if possible, when they are dry. The core usually comes away with the fruit. Loganberries fruit for only two or three weeks, but blackberries go on bearing and ripening much longer.

Pruning

The time to prune is when all fruit has been picked. The principle of the operation is simple—remove all the old canes (those which have fruited). Carrying out the operation can be appalling unless you have, wisely, chosen a thornless variety. If you have inherited one with thorns, wear leather gloves and try to persuade someone to help you. Cut back all the old canes to ground level. (Burn them. You will bitterly regret it if you try to compost them.) Only when the old canes have been removed and cleared away, make a start on tying the new canes to the wire. Cut out the weaklings and the damaged canes, but keep as many healthy canes as you can, even if they seem crowded. The unripe canes, especially of loganberries, are liable to be killed by frost or damaged by wind, so it is sensible to have a reserve of canes against such losses.

If there are no losses, surplus canes can be removed at the end of the winter. In late February or March, cut back any dead tips of canes to the first live bud.

Strawberries

"Doubtless God could have made a better berry, but doubtless God never did." This tribute by Dr. Butler, the sixteenth-century physician, first quoted by Izaak Walton in *The Compleat Angler* and requoted endlessly since, was in praise of the wild strawberry, which still grows all over the northern hemisphere. The fruits are minute, but the flavor is outstanding. The fat, juicy and less tasty commercially grown strawberries (*Fragaria × Ananassa*) of today have as their ancestors two species from the New World: one from the eastern states of America and a larger West

Coast Pine strawberry. Large numbers of hybrids were produced and cultivated throughout Europe during the nineteenth century. The most notable hybrid was raised by Thomas Laxton in 1892. It is still one of the most truly strawberry-flavored varieties, but is susceptible to debilitating virus disease.

In the last fifty years breeders have concentrated on heavy-cropping, disease-resistant varieties, often at the expense of flavor. The discerning amateur gardener, however, will be concerned more with quality than quantity, and it is still available.

By using cloches for an early crop and again for the autumn-fruiting varieties, the normal, all too short, strawberry season can be ex-

tended somewhat.

Everbearing strawberries send up flower trusses from late spring to late autumn. Geneva is a good example.

Alpine strawberries (*Fragaria vesca*, var. *semperflorens*) are small, fragrant and bright red in color. They make the best jam because they have a higher pectin content than other strawberries.

Alpines are raised from seed, as the plant does not produce runners. Although they are perennials, alpines fruit profusely for only one year and are, therefore, best treated as annuals.

Sow the seeds in seed compost in a greenhouse at a temperature of 50° to 60°F (10° to 16°C) in January or February. Prick out the seedlings into boxes, and transplant them in late May or June. Plants from later sowings without heat will produce a little fruit the same year, but will have a long fruiting season the following year.

Varieties

Earlidawn is a productive first-of-the-season crop. Redchief has medium to large fruit with firm substance, deep-red color, and is disease resistant. Sweet Surprise has a red, wedge-shaped berry with flavor somewhat like a raspberry. Marlate is a very late selection from the Maryland Agricultural Experiment Station. Guardian is a midseason selection with high resistance to disease. Superfection, Sunburst and Geneva are productive, adaptable everbearing types.

Alpine strawberries: Baron Solemacher is the most widely grown, but Alexandria has larger fruits. Yellow Alpine is a good yellow variety.

Pests and diseases

Birds and slugs are two of the most obvious threats to strawberries. Net the plants against the birds, and put down poison bait against the slugs.

Aphids are less obvious but dangerous, because they are carriers of virus diseases. Kill them relentlessly, using malathion.

Red spider mite may be a nuisance under cloches. Spray with malathion if needed.

Botrytis (gray mold) may cause great damage to fruit in warm, humid weather. Do not crowd the plants, keep the bed weed free and remove rotting fruit.

Strawberry mildew may occur in dry weather and mainly affects the leaves. There are sprays to combat both these diseases; some however, create problems of taint or

cannot be used under cloches.

Virus diseases are the curse of strawberries, and of some varieties more than others. All you can do is to buy healthy, certified runners and wage constant war on aphids.

GROWING SUMMER STRAWBERRIES

Preparing the soil

Strawberries prefer loamy and slightly acid soil, but will prosper in other soils when the ground is prepared with rotted manure or coarse peat moss. The bed must be sunny and well drained. If soil disease is a problem, plant crowns in sunken, drained 5-gallon (18 liter) containers filled with pasteurized soil mix or a peat-lite formula with added slow-release fertilizer.

Planting

In the open. August/September or April/May. Buy only runners which have been officially certified as virus tested. Plant in August or early September for a good crop the following summer. Runners planted in late autumn and in spring should not be allowed to crop in their first season, and must be deblossomed to ensure that there is a heavy crop the following year.

Plants should be about 15 to 18 inches (38 to 45 cm) apart and the rows 30 inches (75 cm) apart. To ensure that the crown is not buried,

make two adjacent holes with a trowel. Put the plant on the ridge between the holes, with half the roots in one hole and half in the other. Firm the soil; the crown should now be level with the surface. Water well.

Alternatively, grow the strawberries through holes in black plastic sheeting. Make the surface of the soil convex so that rain will not collect on the sheeting, making the plants rot. Roll out a length of 150-gauge black plastic

sheeting and bury the edges firmly in the soil.

Make a row of slits, 15 to 18 inches (38 to

45 cm) apart, in the plastic through which the runners will be planted. The soil must be moist before the plastic is put down. Plastic tubing can be laid under the sheeting to give trickle irrigation for summer watering.

The year's work

If the autumn-planted runners are pushed out of the soil by frost, make the roots firm again. Toward the end of winter a light dressing of sulfate of potash, up to 1 ounce to the square yard (30 g to 1 sq m), can be given. Do not give the plants nitrogen (sulfate of ammonia); it will produce leaves at the expense of fruit. Spring frosts are a problem, since the flowers are easily killed. If frost is forecast, cover the rows lightly with straw or strips of black plastic, but remove the covering during the day. Never put down a straw mulch at this early stage because, on frosty nights, it insulates the plant from the comparative warmth of the soil. (The purpose of a straw mulch is to prevent the strawberries from being splashed by soil, so it need not be put down until fruiting is well under way.)

Remove new runners as they appear. Water when the weather is hot, especially when fruiting begins. Early watering produces more foliage, but late watering swells the fruit, which is largely water. Stop watering when the fruit is ripening fast.

Birds like strawberries, so cover the rows with nets to keep them off. The nets are far more effective slung over 48-inch (120 cm) poles than draped over the plants themselves. A jam jar over the top of each pole prevents snagging the net when you lift it to pick the crop.

After the harvesting is over, cut back the dying foliage and generally clean up the bed. The plants can be cut back quite drastically as long as the crowns are not touched. New growth will then start.

For an earlier crop use cloches—hotkaps or tunnels of plastic sheeting. The cloches are put over the rows in February or early March (earlier in the North). The strawberries remain under the cloches until fruiting is over. When the plants start flowering, give them some ventilation on warm days, and more during the hot, fruiting days. Move the barn cloches a little apart, but not far enough to let the birds

in. Do not take away the end glasses of the row. Lift up the sides of the plastic tunnels.

Strawberries grown with black plastic mulch do well under cloches. The cloches are placed over the plastic. Trickle irrigation is then a great advantage.

Production tails off in the third year, and the bed should then be renewed. Some gardeners, especially if they are growing strawberries under cloches to get early fruit, prefer to treat the plant as an annual. The runners are planted as early as possible, in August, and they fruit the next year. Some plants, preferably grown in a separate part of the garden, may be used solely to produce replacement runners. These plants must not be

allowed to flower, and the runners they produce are pegged down in the soil or pots. By August the stalks from the parent plants can be cut and the young runner plants put in a new bed. Save some to provide the next year's runners. After three years it is wise to buy new certified plants so that disease does not build up.

Harvesting

June/July. The fruiting season of the summer varieties is short—as little as two weeks in a hot spell and three or more if the weather is dull. Pick the fruit when it is dry, pick frequently and carefully. Less damage to both berries and plants will be done by picking fruit with calyx and some stalk.

GROWING EVERBEARING STRAWBERRIES
Preparing the soil

Many everbearing hybrids crop more heavily than summer strawberries and correspondingly need even more generous fertilizing.

Planting

March/May. Plant from late March, in the South, to May, in the extreme North. Plant them 18 to 24 inches (45 to 60 cm) apart in rows 36 inches (90 cm) apart. Water copiously until they are well established, and afterward whenever the weather is dry.

The year's work

All blossom must be removed until the end, or almost the end, of May. The first fruit will come some six weeks after deblossoming ends

and may be poor. This does not matter, as a later crop occurs, which is the important one. In the second year, cropping is not as heavy as in the first year, so the best results will be achieved by treating everbearers as annuals. Everbearers are propagated by runners, or by splitting up the original roots, or both. The best runners will come from plants that have not been allowed to fruit.

Runners taken in October can be planted for the winter in loose bunches of six or so, 6 inches (15 cm) apart. Mark them with small sticks in order not to lose track of them, for they die back completely. In colder districts, cloches help to get the runners established, but they must not be encouraged to grow. They are hardy, and although they may look unbelievably dead they will start some growth in March. Thereafter, when the weather permits, they can be set out in their fruiting bed. Runners produced very late in the year should be left attached to the parent plant during the winter and planted out direct in the spring.

Harvesting

August/mid-October, or November if the crop is grown under cloches or in mild parts of the country. Only a small amount of fruit will be available at any one time, but over a long period. Stop picking the fruit in November or the plant will be too weak to survive the winter.

Currants and Gooseberries

Currants and gooseberries are closely related in what, in botanical terms, is a very small family, the Grossulariaceae. It is a talented family, indeed, which can produce such beautiful fruits as the red currant (*Ribes sativum*), whose ancestors came from western Europe, Scandinavia and Russia; its variant,

the white currant; and the gooseberry (*Ribes grossularia*, var. *uvacrispa*), another native of all Europe. Yet all too seldom are these berries found in gardens. Red currants and gooseberries can be trained as cordons. It is, therefore, possible to grow them even in small gardens.

Protecting soft fruit from the onslaught of birds can be a major problem. A temporary covering of netting can be devised for a few cordons or bushes, but if a great deal of fruit is to be grown it is best grouped within a permanent fruit cage. Ready-made cages are sold in sections. Alternatively, a cage can be built with a framework of strong wooden posts 7 feet (210 cm) high. The sides are permanently covered with ¾-inch (2 cm) mesh wire netting. The cotton or plastic netting on the top of the cage should be removable so that pollinating insects are not discouraged from entering the cage during blossom time.

Varieties

Red currant: Red Lake, a prolific American variety.

White currants: White Grape, a heavy cropper, and the very sweet White Versailles are both midseason varieties.

Gooseberries: Burgess Colossal has big fruit on 5-foot (150 cm) bushes. Welcome has medium-sized fruit that is pink, on an almost thornless, mildew-resistant bush.

Pests and diseases

Spray against aphids in late spring or early summer.

GROWING CURRANTS AND GOOSEBERRIES

Preparing the soil

Currants and gooseberries must be fed generously. The more manure and compost you dig into the soil the more you will be repaid over many years. If cordons are being grown against a house wall, the soil there is often very poor and needs particularly heavy manuring. The soil should be slightly acid; aim for a pH of about 6.

Currants and gooseberries must be planted where they are sheltered from winds and can be protected from spring frosts. They flower early (March/April) and the flowers are easily damaged by frost. Cold northerly or easterly winds in spring discourage pollinating insects and also damage the flowers. Currants and gooseberries will tolerate a certain amount of shade, but the fruits of all will taste better if grown in full sun.

Planting

Always buy bushes, preferably two-year-olds, from reliable sources. Red and white currants: From the end of October—the sooner the better—plant bushes 5 feet (150 cm) apart with 6 feet (180 cm) between rows. Red currant bushes are grown on a stem. Plant at the depth of the nursery soil mark. Single cordons are planted 16 inches (40 cm) apart and double cordons not less than 24 inches (60 cm).

Gooseberries: As soon as possible from October onward, plant the bushes at least 60 inches (150 cm) apart, with at least 90 inches (230 cm) between rows, partly for your own comfort. Gooseberry bushes should be planted at nursery soil level, or even slightly above. Single cordon gooseberries are planted 16 inches (40 cm) apart and double cordons at 24 inches (60 cm).

The year's work

Pruning, however tedious, must be attended to regularly every year, summer and winter. (See opposite page.)

Weeding must be done with the greatest care. All these soft fruits have shallow roots and a hoe can cause havoc. Strawy manure mulches in late spring each year are both a weed-deterrent and the food the bushes need. Red currants and gooseberries particularly need potash: give a dressing in February each year of sulfate of potash (not muriate), ½ ounce to the square yard (15 g to 1 sq m). Water liberally. Net the fruit, particularly red currants, and also gooseberries, if they are allowed to ripen, against birds.

The green-and-black caterpillars of the gooseberry sawfly, if allowed to get a hold, can defoliate currant as well as gooseberry bushes in a few days. Spray with Sevin at the first sign of the caterpillars and repeat two weeks later.

Currants and gooseberries are hosts to the white-pine blister rot and their planting is restricted in some states where the white pine is economically important.

The most dreaded pest is the mite. (Red currants are less affected.) The mites both destroy the buds (thousands of them will be found in one bud) and spread incurable virus disease, which spells the end of the bush's

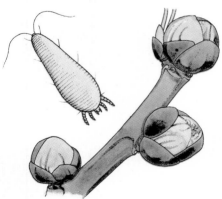

productive life. Every spring, as a routine measure, a 1 percent lime sulfur spray should be used, first as the flowers begin to open and again three weeks later. This may help to keep the mite away. Bushes affected must be dug up and burned.

American gooseberry mildew is the worst of the gooseberry diseases, causing powdery areas on young leaves and berries. Spraying regularly from March with a solution of all-purpose orchard fungicide will control the attack.

Pruning currant and gooseberry bushes

Red currant, white currant and gooseberry bushes are pruned in much the same way in winter and summer. In the first few years the aim must be to establish the framework of the bushes—sturdy main branches around an open center. As the bushes grow older there will be more and more side shoots and these will have to be pruned back hard, while the leaders (the new growth of the branch) will need cutting back only a little. A two-year-old bush will have six or more strong shoots. In November, cut these back by half or more to an outward-pointing bud. Gooseberries which have drooping habits should be pruned back to an upward-pointing bud. Summer pruning consists of cutting the side shoots back to five leaves. But do not summer prune bushes which are not growing vigorously; summer pruning is to inhibit growth and to encourage fruit-forming buds.

This three-year-old bush is now establishing its shape. Cut back the eight or so leading shoots to half their length to an outward-pointing bud. Cut back the side shoots to leave two buds. In summer, cut back the side shoots to five leaves.

In later years the increasingly numerous side shoots should be cut back to a bud within 1 inch (2 cm) of the main branch. Later still, strong new growths from the base of the bush should be allowed to grow to replace the aging branches, which can be cut away.

Pruning currant and gooseberry cordons

Gooseberries and red currants grown as cordons are pruned in similar ways. In winter pruning, however, the laterals of red currants are shortened more drastically than those of gooseberries. Pruning must be done regularly each year, summer and winter, or the cordon will get out of hand and be very difficult to retrain.

Summer pruning

From mid to late June cut back all side shoots to five leaves. Do this each year. The leader, which is the new growth on the main stem, is not cut in summer until it is as tall as you want it to be.

A gooseberry cordon shown without leaves, before summer pruning, above. Below, the side shoots have been pruned to only 5 leaves.

Winter pruning

Shorten the side shoots of the gooseberry cordons to three buds. The side shoots of red currants are shortened to one or two buds. The new growth on the leading shoot should be reduced by a third, or more if it has been racing ahead.

Blueberries

Blueberry species are widely distributed, growing naturally in Asia, Europe and North and South America. Plants can be selected to provide ripe fruit over a period

of two months. Cultivated blueberries in temperate climates are bred from the low-bush *Vaccinium angustifolium* and the high-bush mid-Atlantic species *V. corymbosum*. In warmer Southern states the small-fruited *V. ashei* is grown. Blueberry bushes must have an acid soil rich in humus. To obtain the maximum crop, you should plant at least two varieties near each other.

Varieties

Blueray and Earliblue are prolific early-season types. Southland and Homebell are small-fruited types best grown in the South. Bluecrop and Pemberton are midseason, adaptable, hardy types. Herbert is one of the best new hybrids, has large fruit from mid to late season. Coville is a very late, tall variety. Blueberry shrubs have attractive, glossy foliage which turns yellow and red in the fall. In spring the fragrant white flowers provide another show; then come the berries, soon followed by the birds! Some gardeners grow blueberry shrubs inside big walk-in wire cages to keep birds away or cover the bushes in midsummer with light-weight plastic mesh.

Preparing the soil

Unless you live in a region with very acid soil you must dig in about half a bale of coarse sphagnum peat moss per blueberry bush planting area. The pH should be at least 4.8. If you live in an area with very alkaline soil it would be best not to attempt blueberries. If wild blueberries live near your home you can be sure that your garden will grow a good crop if soil is prepared correctly. Ammonium sulfate is the most effective source of nitrogen fertilizer for blueberry bushes, but they will also respond well to cottonseed meal and the gradual release of nutrients from rotted pine needles or oak-leaf compost. Water-soluble micronized iron corrects yellow foliage. Acid fertilizer such as Stern's Miracid is excellent. On very sandy soils more fertilizer will be needed than on heavier clay/humus soils.

Grapes

The vine has provided man with food and drink from time immemorial. Once the flood was safely behind him, Noah planted a vineyard, and in tending it, in spite of an occasional drunken bout, lived to the ripe old age of 950. The Romans brought vines to Britain, but it was the monks who most assiduously cultivated them. Missionaries, traveling with Spanish conquistadors, brought European wine grapes

to America. Later settlers, especially those from Mediterranean countries, planted table grapes in their home gardens. Recently improved hybrids, some crossing American and European stock, have produced new grapes with improved yields, unique taste and disease resistance.

Varieties

Hybrid No. 35814, a blue grape introduced in 1977 by the New York Agricultural Experiment Station, is a highly flavored, completely seedless table grape from vines with a very cold-hardy constitution. Traditional American Concord is fine for jelly and juice. Golden Muscat and dark-blue Steuben are suitable anywhere grapes grow. These vines should be planted 8 feet (2 m) apart. In warm, humid areas of Zones 7 to 9, try Higgins for a white wine or juice grape, or Hunt, a juicy black hybrid.

Pests and diseases

Vines grown outdoors are remarkably free from pests, but may be affected by two unpleasant, destructive mildews caused by fungi.

Powdery mildew, or oidium, shows as gray powdery patches on leaves, young canes and grapes, any time from spring to autumn. Dust with sulfur early in June and again during flowering, or spray with Karathane.

Downy mildew—a thick white down on the underside of the leaves—spreads at a great rate once the vine is infected. It cannot be cured, but it can be avoided by regular preventive spraying with Bordeaux mixture. Begin spraying when flowering has finished and continue every two weeks or so until early September.

GROWING GRAPES
Preparing the soil

In the Northern states some fancy table grapes may need a sheltered place in the sun if they are to ripen properly: against a south-facing wall is best. The soil should not be too rich or the vine will produce too much leaf. Often, however, soil alongside walls will be too poor. A simple way to provide adequate soil and the good drainage that is vital for the vine is to dig a hole by the wall 12 inches (30 cm) deep and 36 inches (90 cm) square. At the bottom of the hole put a layer of stones or broken bricks to drain away surplus water. On top of the rubble

put a layer of compost or rotted manure and a covering of soil. Leave the rest of the soil to go back into the hole at planting time. The soil must not be acid, with a pH not lower than 6.5.

If several vines are to be planted, the distances apart will depend on the vigor of the variety and the method of pruning. For the single Guyot system illustrated on the opposite page allow at least 30 inches (75 cm) between the vines.

Planting

October or March. Buy a vine from a nursery and plant it as soon as possible. Before planting, water the vine in the pot in which it has been grown. Soak bare-root vines in water overnight. Gently spread the roots, 5 inches (13 cm) deep, in the prepared hole so that the vine itself is about 10 inches (25 cm) from the wall. Cover the roots with sifted soil. Then fill up the hole, making the soil firm.

The year's work

The yearly winter pruning is best done in late December or January when the vine is dormant—otherwise there may be bleeding from the cuts, and the loss of sap will weaken the vine.

Give a mulch of compost each spring, unless the vine is producing vast quantities of leaf.

Water well in dry spells, in late spring and summer, particularly if the vines are growing against walls, where the soil dries out rapidly. Stop watering as the grapes swell.

For fancy-quality table grapes begin thinning of the bunches soon after they form. Using special vine scissors, start thinning the

moment the larger grapes on the bunch are the size of peas. The first to be cut are those grapes which are seedless (they have not been fertilized), followed by those growing awkwardly into the bunch. After that, aim for a well-balanced shape: reckon to remove two weaklings for every larger one you leave to grow. The more grapes that form the more severe the thinning must be.

As the grapes ripen, net the vines to keep off marauding birds.

Wasps can do immense damage to early-ripening grapes. To tempt and drown them, sink jam jars, partly filled with sweetened water, in the ground around the vines.

Harvesting

When the grapes are ripe use clippers to cut the lateral bearing the bunch of grapes about 2 inches (5 cm) on each side of the bunch. Hold them by this "handle"; do not touch the grapes themselves or you will rub off the bloom (that soft, dusty covering) and they will look less attractive. They can be eaten immediately, but will keep for a week or two in a cool, dark place.

Training and pruning the vines

There are many rival methods of pruning vines. The one considered best for the amateur gardener, however, is called the single Guyot system, in which the vines are pruned to produce one fruiting cane each year and replacement canes for the following year. The single Guyot system can be used for vines grown on walls or under cloches and is suitable for colder parts of the country.

A wire support to which the vines can be tied must be provided. Fix three horizontal wires to "vine eyes" (long nails with eyes) driven into the wall. The lowest wire will be 18 inches (45 cm) from the ground, the middle one 30 inches (75 cm) and the third 48 inches (120 cm).

Alongside the vine, a 60-inch (150 cm) bamboo cane tied vertically to the wires will provide extra support.

If vines are to be grown under tall cloches, run wires between posts firmly driven into the ground at the ends of the row of cloches. Fix the lowest wire 3 inches (8 cm) above the soil, the second wire just below the top of the cloches, and the third wire outside the cloches at a height of 48 inches (120 cm).

After planting, cut back the cane to leave no more than three buds.

Minimum care system

The precise training of vines is required for maximum fruit quality and size, but grapes are tough vines which will thrive without constant care if planted correctly. To grow grapes on an arbor or along a fence for shade, privacy and some medium-quality fruit, you need only thin the vines of very old wood late every winter and provide some balanced fertilizer. Grapes grown with this low-maintenance system will be smaller but quite satisfactory for jelly, wine and snacks (for you AND the birds!).

The first year's growth

When the three buds begin to grow in the following spring (April or May), remove the weakest shoot and let the other two grow. A few weeks later, when it is obvious which is the stronger of the two canes, the weaker of the pair may be cut back to a few inches. Many gardeners, however, let both canes grow throughout the summer. In any event, nip off all lateral shoots as they appear about 1 inch (2 cm) from the main stem.

In January, cut back both canes to three buds.

Single Guyot System

The third year's growth

Let two replacement canes grow. Pinch out the laterals on these two canes. On the fruiting cane wait to thin the laterals until the flower trusses show. Keep only the strongest-looking laterals, only two or three in the first year of fruiting, four the next, and in later years six or more. Never overcrop or you will suffer poor crops in later years.

Having chosen which laterals are to be allowed to fruit, pinch out all the others.

In January, cut away the cane which fruited during the previous summer. Choose the stronger of the two replacement canes to take its place, bending it over gently and tying it down along the bottom wire. Cut the other replacement cane back to two or three buds. This is the pattern for winter pruning in all succeeding years. As the vine matures and flourishes, the fruiting cane need not be cut back as far.

The second year's growth

In the spring of the second year remove all but two of the strongest shoots. The most vigorous one will be that chosen to fruit in the third year; the other will produce replacement canes. Pinch out lateral shoots as they appear and any flower clusters which develop. (The vine must establish a strong root system before it is allowed to fruit.)

In January, gently tie down the stronger cane along the bottom wire and cut it back to about eight buds. The lesser cane is cut back to two or three buds.

Double Guyot System

Double Guyot system

This system produces two shorter fruiting canes instead of one longer one (but do not expect a heavier crop). One bearing stem is trained to the right of the vine and one to the left along the bottom wire. Therefore, three replacement canes instead of two have to be grown each year, tied to the middle support. They need not be allowed to grow so tall as under the single Guyot system—36 inches (90 cm) is enough, or 30 inches (75 cm) if the vines are being grown under cloches.

When cloches are used, the fruiting canes grow under the glass, and thus have a better chance of ripening. The replacement canes, however, are trained up the supporting stakes through gaps between the cloches; in order to conserve the warmth inside the cloches, the gaps should be no wider than is necessary.

Apples

According to Genesis the apple (*Malus pumila*) was created three days before man, but, unlike man, it has never fallen from grace —it is the world's most cultivated tree fruit.

For a kitchen garden, choose rigorously trained trees grafted on dwarf rootstock. The cordon has a single stem with short side shoots and a mass of fruit spurs. The dwarf pyramid takes up more room, but needs no support and crops more heavily.

Varieties

Choose at least two varieties which blossom at the same time so they will pollinate each other. If your garden is liable to spring frosts choose varieties which flower late or whose blossom can tolerate some frost.

An excellent combination for Zones 5 to 8 is a Red Delicious planted with a Yellow Delicious. In colder areas choose fully hardy McIntosh, the favorite red for September harvest, and Lodi, a summer greenish apple good for cooking. A recent development is patio fruit trees, selections of very dwarf types suitable in Zones 5 to 8. The Burpee catalog lists Garden Delicious, a yellow apple which is self-pollinating, produces full-sized apples by mid-September, grows 5 to 6 feet (150 to 180 cm) tall. A recently introduced hybrid from Burgess is August Delicious, a dwarf variety that ripens red fruit by mid-August. If you have room for a 10- to 15-foot (300 to 450 cm) semidwarf tree, try a 5-N-1 apple tree, which has five different kinds grafted onto a single semidwarf understock. The 5-N-1 apple is self-pollinating.

Pests and diseases

Apples and pears have a frightening number of pests and diseases, but in a small garden with a few trees, lovingly cultivated and constantly watched, there is little danger of them getting out of hand. You should, however, be aware of some of the signs and take certain counter-measures.

Net pear cordons or bushes against birds or cover each fruit with a paper bag.

To prevent codling moth caterpillars boring into apples, tie bands of sacking around the trunks near the ground early in July. Burn the bands and the caterpillars lurking in them in October.

Pears

Until a hundred years ago it would have been unwise to grow pears (*Pyrus communis*) in a small garden. Up to that time most pears were grown on pear stock, which produced

huge trees. Today, pears are grown on quince stock and can be trained as cordons or dwarf pyramids.

Pears are vulnerable to spring frosts, so in the North grow them as cordons against a south-facing wall. In warmer areas, dwarf pyramids will thrive and provide more fruit.

Varieties

The pollination needs of pears are vital and complicated. Most varieties are diploid and need to be cross-pollinated by another variety; some are triploid and should have two pollinators which will also pollinate each other.

Catalogs listing dwarf pears give clear directions regarding which of their pears will pollinate one another. One available late-September variety, Duchesse d'Angoulême, is self-pollinating. Bartlett has golden-yellow fruit on very adaptable trees, can be well pollinated by Clapp's Favorite, a large, pale-yellow pear which ripens in mid-August, or Moonglow, a mid-August variety best picked while slightly green, then kept in a cool place to develop a full, sweet flavor. For a wide selection of pears check specialists' catalogs of Henry Leuthardt and Stark Bros. Nursery. (See page 41.)

A combination fruit-tree dust or spray such as Ortho Home Orchard Spray will solve most problems.

Grease bands put around the trunks 12 inches (30 cm) above ground from October to June stop moths climbing the trees to lay eggs.

Aphids can be sprayed with oil in winter. But this is a classic example of how one remedy creates another evil. (See page 24.)

Scab begins as blisters on apple or pear tree shoots and spreads to leaves and fruits. Remove the shoots at once. The fungus which causes brown rot in apples and pears enters through wounds on the fruits both on the tree and in store. Burn the affected fruits.

GROWING APPLES AND PEARS
Preparing the soil

Avoid choosing a site in the garden where frost collects, for spring frosts damage blossoms. Pears are even more susceptible to frost than apples. The soil should be well drained but not rich, or too much foliage will be produced at the expense of fruit.

Planting

Plant cordon apples and pears 30 to 36 inches (75 to 90 cm) apart, and dwarf pyramids 40 inches (100 cm) apart. Planting time is from November to March, but better early in winter than late. If the trees arrive from the nursery in frosty weather, put them, unpacked, in a frostproof place until the frost has gone. When planting, it is vital to leave the join between rootstock and scion 5 to 6 inches (13 to 15 cm) above soil level. If the scion is covered, roots will grow from it. Plant firmly.

The year's work

Each spring the trees can be given a mulch of compost or rotted manure—apples sparingly, pears less so. On no account must the mulch touch the trunk, or rooting from the scion will be encouraged. The rest of the year's work is pruning, thinning if needed, protecting ripening fruit from birds and watching for pests and diseases.

Thinning

No heavy thinning of apples will be needed on cordons or dwarf pyramids. If the crop is light, leave doubles to develop. If the crop is heavy, thin to singles. Pears usually need even less thinning.

Harvesting

An apple is ready to pick when, if held gently and given the slightest twist, it leaves the fruit spur. Early varieties must be eaten soon after picking. Late varieties can be stored for weeks or even months, according to the variety. Handle each apple gently and wrap it in newspaper. Store the apples in slatted wooden boxes or trays. A moist, cool room is best for storage; 40°F (4°C) is the ideal. Look the apples over from time to time and remove any that are starting to rot.

A pear is ready to pull when it comes away easily when lifted and twisted slightly. Early varieties are best picked when unripe. Later ones stay on the tree longer. Do not wrap pears for storage. The temperature for storing can be a little lower than for apples.

Cordons are tied to bamboo canes fixed at an angle of 45 degrees to wires tightly stretched between strong posts. The posts should be at least 72 inches (180 cm) above soil level.

The pruning of a maiden cordon in the summer after planting. The cordon is shown before pruning, above, and after pruning, right. Pruning continues in the same way in subsequent summers.

It is usual to train cordons, grown against wires, at a 45-degree angle. This will save space only if a large number of trees are to be grown. One or two trees are best grown upright against a wall.

Pruning apples and pears as cordons

Apples and pears grown as cordons are pruned in the same way. Cordons are pruned in summer every year, but at left alone in winter.

Prune apples in late July in the South and later in the North. Prune pears from mid-July. Cut back the laterals growing from the main stem to four leaves (not counting the cluster of leaves growing at the stem itself). Laterals growing from side shoots or spurs are cut back to one leaf beyond that basal cluster. Any secondary shoots which grow from shoots pruned in July should be cut back in late September or October to one bud.

Prune in the same way in succeeding summers. When the leader has grown as long as the supports will take, cut it back in May. If spurs become crowded, thin them out during winter.

Pruning apples and pears as dwarf pyramids

Cordons are pruned to produce fruit spurs on very short shoots: dwarf pyramids are pruned to allow fruit spurs to grow on much longer shoots.

A maiden tree is a single vertical stem. In the spring after planting, when the buds begin to grow, cut the stem back to about 20 inches (50 cm) above the ground, to an upward- and outward-pointing bud. Cut back to four buds any side shoots more than 6 inches (15 cm) long.

During the second winter, cut about 8 inches (20 cm) off the leader. Cut to immediately above a bud, which will grow in the opposite direction to the topmost bud you chose the year before. Cut the laterals back to about 8 inches (20 cm) to an outward-facing bud.

In summer, leave pear trees alone. In late July or August, cut back apple tree side shoots to four leaves from the basal cluster.

In the third and later winters, cut back the central leader by one-third of its new growth, always cutting back to a bud facing in the opposite direction to the one chosen the year before. Also cut back the main branches by one-third of their new growth.

When the pyramid approaches 7 feet (2 m) cut back by half the central leader and long

Skeleton drawing of apple or pear trees grown as cordons, above, and dwarf pyramids, below. The illustrations show the main stem and laterals of the trees without leaves and what has been cut away during the first, second and third summers.

Cordons are pruned only in summer and their leaders are left to grow until they are the required height. The pruning of dwarf pyramids is more complicated and the leader is first trimmed in its second winter.

branches at the top of the tree, in May. Each May therafter cut back the new growth on these branches to ½ inch (1 cm).

Many gardeners use a pruning knife on apples and pears, but prefer pruners for soft fruits. Whichever you choose, the blades must be kept sharp. If you have to hack away at a branch you are inviting disease.

Herbs

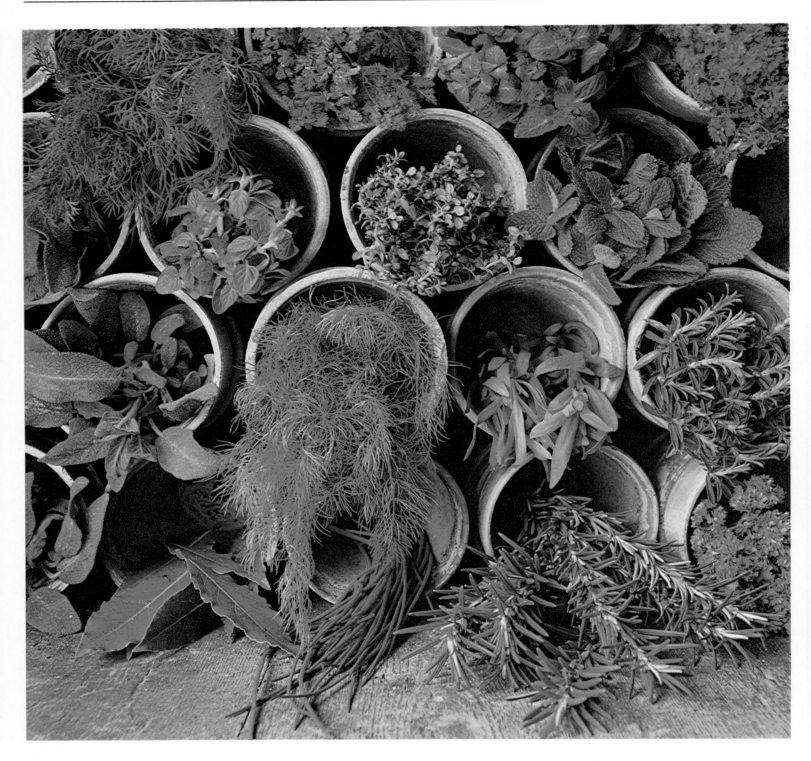

There is room in every garden for herbs. If there is no garden, there is room for some herbs on a patio, in window boxes or indoors in pots in the kitchen. On the whole, herbs are easy to grow. Most of them need sun for at least half the day. Mint, parsley, chervil, sorrel and horseradish will grow in shade. The annual herbs can often be grown in the vegetable garden, either between rows of vegetables or after early crops have been cleared. Many a neglected front garden could be dug up and converted into a perfumed herb garden by planting herbs and such flowers as lavender, mignonette, alyssum, candytuft and sweet william, stocks and nicotiana (to smell, not to smoke).

1 Dill
2 Chervil
3 Mint
4 Parsley
5 Sage
6 Marjoram
7 Thyme
8 Fennel
9 Tarragon
10 Summer savory
11 Bay leaves
12 Chives
13 Rosemary

Parsley *Rosemary* *Sorrel* *Sage* *Bay*

Parsley

Parsley (*Petroselinum crispum*) in its long existence has been credited with many virtues. The ancient Greeks thought parsley worthy of being fed to chariot horses; now it is used as a tonic for pet dogs. Victors at Greek games were garlanded with parsley; now it is the universal garnish in cookery. It is reputed to drive away the onion fly from onions grown near it and to protect humans from fleas. In addition to all that, parsley is the most widely accepted culinary herb.

Treat parsley as an annual or biennial. The moss curled varieties are the most attractive, but French parsley, with plain leaves, has a superior flavor and survives the winter better. The leaves of Hamburg parsley (see page 89) can also be used.

GROWING PARSLEY

Parsley should be given a rich soil with rotted manure or compost dug in. It needs moisture, so a shady position should be chosen for spring sowing. For a late-summer sowing, to crop in winter, choose a sunnier part of the garden. Sow at intervals from April, in drills ½ inch (1 cm) deep, and cover only lightly with soil. Germination is painfully slow—it may take one month or two. Throughout, the soil must be kept moist or the seed will not germinate at all. In order not to lose track of the row, sow fast-growing radish seed with the parsley seed. The appearance of something green will at least curb your impatience.

Thin the seedlings, when at last they appear, to 3 inches (8 cm) apart. Keep picking the parsley during summer to maintain a constant supply of young leaves.

A late sowing can be made in August. Cover at least some of the plants with cloches for winter picking or carefully uproot some of the smaller plants (the taproots of larger plants are long and easily damaged) and transplant them into pots to take indoors.

Parsley is an excellent herb for growing indoors (special parsley pots are available from gardening shops and centers) or in containers in yards and on patios.

Rosemary

Rosemary (*Rosmarinus officinalis*) is one of the most beautiful herbs to grow. Although it has been grown in Britain since the Middle Ages it is not one of the most popular in the kitchen. Rosemary is rampant around the Mediterranean ("dew of the sea" is the meaning of its Latin name), but the cold, wet and windy winters of northern regions are often more than it can take. Its uses have been ritual, at solemn occasions in ancient Greece, and medicinal, a brain strengthener and a disinfectant, as well as culinary.

GROWING ROSEMARY

Rosemary, a perennial shrub growing 24 to 48 inches (60 to 120 cm) high, must have sun and shelter, and a soil that is well drained and well limed. Growing rosemary from seed is slow; it is better to buy young plants for putting out in May, 36 inches (90 cm) apart. Protection will be needed in winter. Alternatively, plants can be raised in pots to spend the summer outdoors and the winter indoors. Rosemary is easily grown from cuttings, either to grow more or to replace winter casualties. Take cuttings of new growth from the main stem in spring or early summer and plant in a frame or greenhouse, where they will spend the winter. Plant them out in May.

Sorrel

In the past, French, or buckler-leaved, sorrel (*Rumex acetosa*) was cooked in the same way as spinach and eaten as a vegetable. Today, the leaves are usually made into soup or eaten raw in salads. Do not gorge on sorrel, especially if you have gout, because of the oxalic acid it contains.

GROWING SORREL

Sorrel is a sharp-tasting perennial that likes an acid soil and can accept partial shade. It can be raised from seed (sow in April) or planted, from division of roots, in spring or autumn. Allow 12 inches (30 cm) between plants. Remove all flowering stems to encourage new leaf growth.

Sage

There is nothing that sage (*Salvia officinalis*) cannot do for you, if you accept all the claims made for it over the last two thousand years. It was supposed to give long life, cure the palsy, strengthen the sinews, fortify the memory, stop hair falling out, turn gray hair dark and, when used in brewing ale, make you "dead, or foolish or madde drunke." It is also useful in the kitchen.

Sage is an evergreen perennial. There is a broad-leaved variety and a more tangy, hardier, narrow-leaved variety.

GROWING SAGE

A moderately rich, well-drained, well-limed soil and sun are the needs of sage. Sow at the end of April and seedlings will appear toward the end of May. Thin the seedlings to 16 inches (40 cm) apart. Although perennial, sage wears itself out in a few years and some of the plants should be replaced each year. Take cuttings (with a heel) in April or May, root them in a frame and then plant them out.

Sage can easily be grown in containers or pots, but is best renewed regularly.

Bay

Sweet bay (*Laurus nobilis*) is one of the more literary herbs. It is also one of the classic herbs of *bouquet garni*, which is found more often today in cookery books than in use in the kitchen.

The bay is a native of the Mediterranean, where, in Roman times, it was made into garlands and placed on the heads of poets and victorious soldiers and athletes.

The bay has also been reputed to ward off thunder and witches, encourage elves and fairies and ameliorate wasp stings.

GROWING BAY

Bay trees can be grown out of doors in full sun in the South. It is an excellent tub plant, spending the summer in the garden and the winter indoors—always handy for when you need a few aromatic leaves. Bay can easily be increased with cuttings of that year's shoots.

Horseradish

Thyme

Dill

Savory

Marjoram

Dill

Dill (*Peucedarium graveolens*) is a Mediterranean plant, but its name is Norse. It comes from *dilla*, to lull, so called because of its soporific effects. The ancient Egyptians and Romans used it as a cure for insomnia. Generations of mothers have given dill water to their fractious infants.

Dill is an annual, some 24 to 36 inches (60 to 90 cm) tall. Its graceful blue-green, feathery leaves are like those of fennel, but it grows more compactly. The flowers are yellow.

GROWING DILL

Dill needs sun, but is tolerant of almost any kind of soil as long as it does not dry out in summer. Sow shallowly out of doors from April to June to get a continuing supply of leaves for salads or fish dishes. Seedlings should be thinned to 8 inches (20 cm) apart. They cannot be successfully transplanted. Dill matures in less than two months. and the strongly flavored seed for use in pickling will be ready in July from early sowings. Pick them when there are both flowers and seed heads on the plant.

Dill can easily be grown in window boxes or pots.

Thyme

The smell of thyme meant both grace and courage to the Greeks, for thyme was the herb of Venus as well as of Mars. Common thyme (*Thymus vulgaris*), which grows about 10 inches (25 cm) high, is hardier than the beautifully scented lemon thyme (*Thymus* × *citriodorus*).

GROWING THYME

The soil should be light, well drained and well limed. Plant 12 inches (30 cm) apart in April. Cut the shoots hard back in June to encourage new, young, bushy growth. Stock can be increased by dividing the roots or by taking cuttings of 2-inch (5 cm) new shoots with a heel from the old stem. Root them in sandy soil in a frame, and plant out in September.

Thyme grows well in containers.

Horseradish

Horseradish (*Cochlearia Armoracia*), which has its origins in eastern Europe, has been grown for centuries. The leaves and stems of the plant contain certain poisonous substances, but the root is safe in amounts that even the most confirmed horseradish-sauce addict would be unlikely to exceed. For years horseradish was regarded only as a medicine, notably to prevent scurvy and alleviate rheumatism and chilblains. Now the roots are used mainly as a condiment. Horseradish is absolutely no trouble to grow; indeed, the greater trouble may be to stop it from taking over the garden in the same way that mint can.

GROWING HORSERADISH

Horseradish plants are usually consigned to some otherwise useless part of the garden and left to themselves to spread and spread. This is the totally wrong approach and quickly turns horseradish into a weed. Instead, give it a sunny spot, with deeply cultivated soil and plenty of manure or compost worked in. Such treatment will make all the difference to the flavor of the roots.

The best method of keeping a horseradish bed under control is to dig it up every autumn, instead of the usually recommended three or four years. This way the plants never get a chance to run amok, and the quality of the roots will be greatly improved.

To start a horseradish bed, early in the year buy root cuttings or "thongs" that are about 8 inches (20 cm) long and store them in sand. They will be sprouting by March. Make holes for them 12 inches (30 cm) apart by ramming the dibble into the soil at an angle of 45 degrees and far enough down to take the roots with the thicker end just showing. Make them firm. Keep the bed weed free while the horseradish leaves are still small.

Lift all the roots in October. The smaller, slimmer roots (thongs) are stored in sand during the winter for planting in a new bed in spring. The larger roots are stored for use as needed.

Marjoram

Marjoram is not one but three related herbs. There is wild marjoram (*Origanum vulgare*); pot marjoram (*Origanum onites*), an easy-to-grow perennial; and the more subtly flavored sweet marjoram (*Origanum majorana*), another perennial, which in the North must be treated as a half-hardy annual.

GROWING MARJORAM

Sow sweet marjoram in a fairly rich, well-limed, finely sifted soil in a frame in March. Transplant in May, 6 inches (15 cm) apart. Or sow out of doors in late May. Germination may be slow; growth certainly is. Keep seedlings weed free and watered. If the leaves are to be dried, cut the plant, which grows about 8 inches (20 cm) tall, down to about 2 inches (5 cm) when flowers begin to appear, from July.

Pot marjoram, which is more reliable, needs sun and a light soil. It grows about 24 inches (60 cm) high and will produce for several years. Growing from seed is slow; plants can be put out in spring. In following years they are easy to increase by cuttings (early summer) or by dividing the roots (spring or autumn). Harvest for drying as for sweet marjoram.

Pot marjoram dies back in winter. If in late summer a plant is cut back hard, put in a pot and taken indoors, it will produce new leaves for flavoring winter dishes.

Savory

There is a choice of savories; summer savory (*Satureia hortensia*), a tender annual, and winter savory (*Satureia montana*), which has a stronger flavor and is a perennial.

GROWING WINTER SAVORY

Winter savory thrives best in rather poor, limy soil. Sow in August, but do not cover the seeds—they germinate in the light. Thin to 12 inches (30 cm) apart. Cutting can begin the following spring. In late autumn cut the plants back hard and give them some protection in cold areas. In early spring cut the plants back to 3 inches (8 cm) from the ground.

Mint

Chervil

Tarragon

Basil

Fennel

Basil

Basil (*Ocimum basilicum*) is a native of India. Even the mention of the word "frost" appears to kill it. Planting it indoors in pots or containers will be easier than coaxing it outside. Basil has the added virtue of driving away flies.

GROWING BASIL

Sweet basil must be treated as an annual. Sow the seeds in peat pots, at 55° to 60°F (13° to 16°C), in a greenhouse or propagator during March. Harden off for planting out. Plant out 8 inches (20 cm) apart at the end of May or early June. The soil must be rich, the position sunny and sheltered. Cut leaves for use as needed. At the beginning of September, pot a few plants to go indoors. Cut back hard and for a month or two you will have fresh green leaves to pick.

If basil is to be grown in containers throughout the year, choose the dwarf varieties—bush basil and Dark Opal basil. These grow about 6 inches (15 cm) high instead of the 24 inches (60 cm) of sweet basil, and can be planted more closely.

Tarragon

Tarragon (*Artemisia dracunculus*) is an herb with a great reputation in *haute cuisine*. The French variety has an indubitably finer flavor than the Russian.

GROWING TARRAGON

Tarragon needs sun and a thoroughly well-drained but not rich soil. It is usually described as a hardy, evergreen perennial, but often sheds its leaves. In colder parts of the country it will benefit from protection in winter. Plant in early spring or September, 24 inches (60 cm) apart—tarragon grows 24 inches (60 cm) tall and as wide. Friends can be given underground runners in early spring or cuttings in late spring. It is customary to transplant tarragon to fresh ground after four or five years.

Mint

In mythology, the nymph Minthe, beloved by Pluto, was, out of jealousy, changed by Proserpine into mint. The Greeks associated the smell of the herb with strength and rubbed themselves with mint leaves—an early male deodorant that had the added virtue, it was thought, of frightening mice. The Romans brought the plant—and possibly the sauce—to Britain, so the British have been consuming mint sauce since the third century.

In the sixteenth century, John Gerard wrote in his famous herbal: "Mint is marvellous wholesome for the stomacke. It is good against watering eies. It is poured into the eares with honied water." Mint julep is a famous way to use this refreshing herb.

Spearmint (*Mentha spicata*) is the variety most commonly grown, but the woolly-leaved Bowles mint (*Mentha rotundifolia*, var. *Bowles*) is better flavored, taller—it grows from 24 to 48 inches (60 to 120 cm)—and resistant to the widespread virus that causes mint rust. Apple mint and pineapple mint are also popular.

GROWING MINT

Mint should be grown in a fertile, moist soil, in partial shade. In April and May take out 2-inch (5 cm) drills and lay the roots horizontally in them. Little can be pulled the first year. In the autumn, cut the stalks to the ground and cover the bed with a mixture of soil and manure. Mint spreads avidly. To keep it under control take up the bed every three years in March, divide the roots and replant them. This also improves the quality of the crop.

Mint can be forced for use in winter. Fork up some mint runners in November and put them 1 inch (2 cm) apart on a layer of soil in a box. Cover them with soil. If the boxes are put in the warmth, about 60°F (16°C), in greenhouse or kitchen and kept moist, shoots should be ready for cutting in three to four weeks. More roots can be forced as winter goes on.

Mint is easily grown in containers. Give it a container to itself, or you will find it overwhelming the other herbs.

Fennel

Fennel (*Foeniculum vulgare*) has been grown for thousands of years. During that time it has been variously credited with curing blindness in serpents, increasing courage and the flow of mother's milk and making the fat grow "gaunt and lank."

Fennel is a hardy perennial which grows 60 inches (150 cm) or more tall, with beautiful, feathery leaves of yellowy green. There is also a decorative bronze variety.

GROWING FENNEL

Fennel needs sun, but is otherwise not demanding; even a town garden suits it. However, the soil should be reasonably fertile because the plants have a useful life of up to five years. Sow the seeds in shallow drills in April or May and thin to 16 inches (40 cm) apart. When fully grown they will need support against wind. Remove all flower stems as they develop. Harvesting can be prolonged by transplanting a few plants into pots in late autumn and taking them indoors. In early spring, roots can be divided to replace those taken indoors.

Chervil

Chervil (*Anthriseus cerefolium*), one of the *fines herbes* which can be harvested fresh almost all the year around, has been grown since Roman times.

GROWING CHERVIL

A wet, heavy soil is the only one in which chervil will not flourish. Summer sowings should be in partial shade: sow at other times in a sunny part of the garden. Sow every few weeks in spring, in drills 12 inches (30 cm) apart, and thin to 8 inches (20 cm). Do not transplant. Always keep the soil moist. Pick off any flowers. Cutting can begin in six to eight weeks. Take the leaves from the outside of the plant. An August sowing will provide a crop in late autumn and again in spring in warmer parts of the country or if the plants have been cloched during the winter. Chervil can also be grown in containers.

Gardening Calendar

January

J. C. Loudon wrote in 1822 in his *Encyclopedia of Gardening*, "Perform every operation in the proper season." There is, unfortunately, no "proper season" which applies to all gardens; it can differ even in neighboring gardens. In this garden calendar the suggested dates are for a broad Zone 5 to 6 range, except as mentioned. In Southern regions many vegetables can be raised during winter months, while in the coldest Northern states, gardeners must wait until June before planting outdoors. Common sense plus experience—yours and your neighbors'—must ultimately be your guide.

The calendar merely outlines what to do and when. How to do it will be found in the sections on individual vegetables. Also check pages 34 and 35 for helpful sowing charts.

Sowing
In a heated greenhouse you can sow cauliflowers (early varieties), onion, leeks and alpine strawberries. Pixie tomato sown now will have fruit by April.

Crops
In the South there will be cabbages, Brussels sprouts, kale and possibly winter cauliflowers to gather, and celery, leeks, parsnips and Jerusalem artichokes to dig up. From store there will be roots, onions, potatoes, apples and pears. Seakale and chicory forced indoors will be ready.

Work
Start forcing rhubarb, salsify and seakale out of doors. Look over stored crops and throw away any going rotten. Prune outdoor vines.

This is an ideal month to enjoy seed catalogs and to plan your new garden.

If you have not already done so order seeds; popular varieties are quickly sold out.

February

The year begins to stir a little, but do not be impatient. Even the hardiest seeds germinate only slowly in cold soil, and if it is also wet they will rot.

Sowing
Brussels sprouts, broad beans, peas and carrots may be sown in frames, and turnips and radishes in frames or under cloches. To warm up the soil always put cloches in place two weeks before sowing. In a heated greenhouse sow tomatoes, cauliflowers, celery, bush beans and eggplants.

Planting
Out of doors in California or the South plant Jerusalem artichokes, rhubarb, garlic and shallots.

Crops
In the protected garden there will be brassicas (including sprouting broccoli), leeks, parsnips and celery. In the heated greenhouse, lettuce will be cropping. Variety can be added by curly chicory forced indoors and "kitchen crops"—mustard and cress, bean shoots and mushrooms. There are roots and onions from store.

Work
Seed potatoes intended for planting in April should be placed in trays in the light to sprout.

Toward the end of the winter it is most important to go through fruit and vegetables in store to pick out the rotten ones. Rub any sprouts off potatoes.

Lime those parts of the garden where soil tests show lime will be needed by the crop to be grown.

Dress the asparagus bed with a general fertilizer. Lightly fork in compost or manure on the rhubarb bed. Top-dress gooseberries and currants with sulfate of potash. Prune fruit trees.

Cut down to ground level the canes of autumn-fruiting raspberries.

This is a fine time to try one of the Gourmet or Windowsill Herb Garden kits offered at seed stores. The kits come complete with pots, seed and Jiffy-Mix.

March

In the mid-South, March is the first of three busy months of sowing and planting. Farther north it will be April before a real start can be made.

Sowing
Out of doors, sow peas, leeks, onions, Brussels sprouts, round-seeded spinach (and every three weeks to the end of July), parsnips, Hamburg parsley, Japanese radishes, and more broad beans. For salads, sow lettuce and scallions. Under cloches or in frames sow summer cabbages, radishes, carrots, turnips and bush beans.

In the heated greenhouse, sow celery, self-blanching celery, celeriac, peppers, cucumbers and tomatoes for planting outside in May.

Planting
Plant Jerusalem artichokes, onion sets, autumn-sown onions, shallots and garlic (if not already done), seakale and horseradish; also potatoes at the end of the month in warm, sheltered gardens. Asparagus and strawberries may be planted this month or next. In a heated greenhouse, plant tomatoes.

Crops
Brussels sprouts will be past their best, but spring greens, sprouting broccoli and Swiss chard should be in good shape. In store, roots will be deteriorating, but still usable. Corn salad can supplement lettuce in salads. A mushroom bed dormant in winter should be starting to crop again.

Work
Make compost for mushrooms.

Give a boost to spring cabbage with 1 ounce of sulfate of ammonia to each yard (30 g to 1 m) of row cultivated. Top-dress raspberries with sulfate of potash.

As the gardener becomes more active so do his foes. Hoe weeds before they become large and put down bait for ravaging slugs.

Read planting suggestions on seed envelopes and in catalogs for the most up-to-date information.

April

North or South, April is the most heartening month of the gardening year. In March, after a vicious winter, it can be hard to believe that anything will ever grow again. In April, we can see that it will.

Sowing
Continue the little-and-often sowings of lettuces, radishes and scallions (and mustard and cress in the kitchen). Make a start with sowing winter cauliflower, broccoli, salsify, Swiss chard, kohlrabi and Florence fennel. Sow more broad beans, peas (including sugar peas and *petits pois*), cabbages, Brussels sprouts, cauliflowers for autumn, curly-leaved kale, globe beets, carrots, turnips, parsnips, leeks and onions. Harden seedlings started indoors by placing them outside on mild days for two weeks before transplanting. In the North still use hotkaps for warm-weather vegetables! Spawn mushrooms on compost made in March.

Planting
Plant potatoes, globe artichokes, asparagus and onion sets. Transplant red cabbage and cauliflowers sown in autumn, and onions, leeks and broad beans raised under glass.

Crops
There will be lettuces ready from autumn sowings, radishes, scallions, perhaps a stick or two of asparagus, the shoots of seakale forced outdoors and salsify. Add to these the continuing cabbages, cauliflowers, sprouting broccoli, kale and the last leeks from the garden. There will be more forced rhubarb and some from outdoors. Dwindling stores may still include some usable roots and onions.

Work
Dig and manure the celery trench ready for planting in June. Spray currant and gooseberry bushes because red spider mites, aphids and sawfly are at work.

May

In the South, May is the last of the big sowing months and transplanting has begun.

Sowing
A start can be made with sowing savoy cabbages, New Zealand spinach, and—at the end of the month—rutabagas, bush beans, runner beans, soybeans, long-rooted beets and sweet corn. Sow garden cucumbers under cloches and greenhouse cucumbers and squashes in a frame. (At the end of the month, squashes can also be sown out of doors.) For follow-on crops continue to sow lettuce, scallions, globe beets and radishes. Winter cauliflowers, broccoli, cabbages, carrots, peas, broad beans, spinach, turnips and kohlrabi can still be sown.

Planting
Plant out Brussels sprouts, cardoons, sweet corn (late in the month), leeks and celeriac. Tomatoes, peppers, eggplants and okra go out under cloches. Transplant alpine strawberries.

Crops
May, although a good month for growing, is a bleak one for harvesting. Established asparagus beds will be bearing well, but exercise great restraint with young beds. Lettuce, radishes and onions will provide salads. The vegetable stand-bys will be cabbage, sprouting broccoli and spinach. There may be mushrooms from April-spawned beds.

Work
Do not delay thinning early crops. Weed, or mulch where you can. Earth up early potatoes. In the far North be ready to protect (with straw or another covering) any tender crops if late frosts are forecast.

Blackfly will descend on broad beans, and carrot fly, onion fly and the turnip flea beetle are other possible visitors. Be ready to spray.

June

June is a busy month—some sowing still to be done, and planting, thinning, weeding, watering, staking and waging war against pests and diseases. As a reward there will be broad beans, peas, early potatoes and berries to eat.

Sowing
Sow curly chicory in the middle of the month (earlier in the North) and Brussels chicory toward the end of the month. Further sowings may be made of bush and runner beans, peas (an early variety), beets, carrots, turnips, kohlrabi, spinach, Swiss chard, Florence fennel and lettuces and onions.

Planting
The month's transplanting includes leeks, Brussels sprouts, cabbages, autumn cauliflowers, sprouting broccoli, celery and self-blanching celery, celeriac, cucumbers, summer squashes, runner beans sown under glass, eggplants and outdoor tomatoes.

Crops
Stop cutting asparagus by the middle of the month. To take its place there will be broad beans, peas, early potatoes and kohlrabi to supplement the cabbages, cauliflower, spinach and salad crops. Shallots may be ready for harvesting.

Work
Mulch where possible. Although mulching will cut down the amount of watering and weeding you will have to do, never let the vegetables go short of water in hot, dry weather, and hoe when necessary to keep down weeds. Stake peas and runner beans—indeed, stake anything that grows tall or climbs. Tomatoes, raspberry canes and vines will regularly need tying. Net berries against birds. Prune currant and gooseberry cordons.

Apply a balanced fertilizer for crops that need rich soil. A timed-release-type fertilizer needs to be applied only once.

Gardening Calendar

July

July is a wonderful month in the vegetable garden, if all has gone well. Like a child at a Christmas or birthday party you can become bemused by the superabundance of things to eat. In the middle of this euphoria do not forget that pests and diseases may also be having a fine feast. And in this month's sowing program there is a reminder of winter ahead. Such is gardening.

Sowing
For the winter, sow turnips and beets for storing, kale and Swiss chard. For cropping this year, sow curly chicory, Chinese cabbage and Sutton broad beans. Further sowings can be made of fennel, purple kohlrabi, summer spinach, main crop carrots, summer and winter radishes and lettuces (in cool Northern areas).

Crops
Bush beans and runner beans will be taking over from broad beans and peas. Other eagerly awaited crops are tomatoes, cucumbers, zucchini, globe artichokes and potatoes. There will be berries—strawberries, raspberries, red and white currants and gooseberries. There will also be beautiful broccoli, cauliflowers, as well as cabbages, New Zealand spinach, carrots and turnips. Dig up shallots and dry them for storing.

Work
Hoe. Water. Stake and tie tall plants.

Earth up main crop potatoes and start earthing up celery.

Cut down raspberry canes after they have fruited. Prune cordon pears (mid-month) and apples (late month). Thin grapes.

As a preventive measure, spray Maneb on celery (against celery leaf spot) every two weeks from early July to October, and on potatoes (against potato blight) every two weeks until September.

August

This is often a vacation month and the garden is neglected. Try to find a friend who will at least keep crops picked—both to avoid waste and to induce the plants to go on producing until you return.

Sowing
Looking forward now to next year, sow cabbages for spring (around the middle of the month in the South), red cabbage, winter spinach, lettuces and onions (at the end of the month and in warm gardens only, and be prepared to cloche them in October).

Try sowing scallions fairly thickly under cloches for an early spring crop.

For autumn and winter cropping sow Batavian chicory and parsley.

Planting
Plant out rooted cuttings of strawberries. Rosemary, sage and mint can be propagated from cuttings.

Crops
Some vegetables will be past their peak, but new ones coming along are sweet corn, peppers, eggplants and onions. There will still be beans, even broad beans, peas, broccoli, cauliflowers, cabbages, globe artichokes, carrots, turnips, summer squashes, potatoes and okra.

Everbearing strawberries and autumn-fruiting raspberries take over from the summer varieties. Blackberries help to fill the gap left by the finished currants.

Autumn-sown onions may be ripe enough for storing; garlic certainly will. Pickling onions will be ready by the end of the month. (August is certainly not the best time to be away.)

Work
If you have to go away get as far ahead as you can with the obvious work. For example, do not leave the garden already choking with weeds, and make sure that tall plants are securely staked and tied.

As the days shorten, remove the stakes from outdoor tomatoes and lay the plants on straw under cloches to help the fruit to ripen.

Make mushroom compost.

Prune dwarf pyramid apples.

September

There is nothing much to sow or plant, but plenty to harvest in September.

Sowing
Sow summer cauliflowers for transplanting to a frame next month and planting out next April. The last sowing of winter spinach can be made out of doors.

Spawn mushrooms on compost made last month.

Planting
Transplant seedlings of spring cabbages, and transplant the lettuces sown last month to frames or cloches.

Crops
For immediate use there will be the bush beans, broad beans and peas sown in summer, runner beans, sweet corn, globe artichokes, carrots, squashes, cucumbers, tomatoes, broccoli, cauliflowers, cabbages, the first Brussels sprouts and savoys, self-blanching celery and potatoes. All outdoor tomatoes, cucumbers and squashes should be picked before the frosts begin. Ripen the tomatoes indoors.

Onions should be lifted, dried off and stored for winter. Toward the end of the month potatoes may also be ready for lifting and storing. Dig peanuts.

Everbearing strawberries are still fruiting, along with late raspberries and blackberries. The earlier apples and pears will be ready for picking.

Work
Start blanching cardoons. Earth up celery for the second time and leeks for the first. Draw soil around celeriac roots. Cut off blackberry canes after they have finished fruiting and tie in the new canes. Put greasebands on apple and pear trees to trap or deter various pests in winter and spring.

October

The gardener turns squirrel this month, wisely storing against the winter ahead. Roots are dug up and the healthy ones carefully packed in sand or peat to keep their plumpness. Potatoes also go into store. Apples and pears need particular care in handling and storing. These are tedious chores, but if you skimp on them your punishment will be shriveled and rotten vegetables and fruit when you come to use them.

Sowing
In mild areas sow lettuce in frames, and peas either out of doors or under cloches.

Planting
Vines and such soft fruits as gooseberries, red and white currants, and blackberries and loganberries can be planted from the end of October. The earlier they are planted the better chance they will have in the following year. Divide and plant rhubarb.

Crops
This is the month for lifting many of the roots for storing for the winter: carrots, beets, turnips, rutabagas and winter radishes. Other roots can be left in the ground longer and pulled as required—celeriac, Jerusalem artichokes, salsify, Hamburg parsley and horseradish. There will be cauliflowers and cabbages, and the Brussels sprouts will be improving in quality. There may also be mushrooms from last month's spawning.

Pick apples and pears for storing. Everbearing strawberries may still be fruiting, especially if they have been cloched. Also the last of the raspberries and blackberries should be picked.

Work
Start forcing Brussels chicory and blanching curly chicory. Earth up celery and leeks again. Put cloches over winter spinach. Remove dead foliage from seakale. Cut down yellowing stems of asparagus and mulch the bed. Cut down Jerusalem artichoke stems to prevent the wind from blowing them over. Store winter squashes.

November

With scarcely anything to sow or plant, November is the time for digging and spring cleaning; do not wait until spring.

Sowing
Peas and long-pod broad beans can be sown in warm, sheltered gardens.

Planting
Berries and rhubarb can still be planted if the ground is not wet and sticky or frozen.

Crops
There are still a lot of vegetables to be taken from the garden, as well as those in store. Blanched celery, leeks, parsnips and scorzonera join Jerusalem artichokes, cauliflowers, Brussels sprouts and cabbages. Lift and store July-sown turnips and beets, Hamburg parsley, celeriac and, in very cold areas, parsnips.

The first forced curly chicory will be ready. Now lift all remaining curly chicory roots to store and force them as wanted. Use Brussels chicory from last month's blanching.

There will be onions, potatoes, beets, carrots, rutabagas and turnips from store. Some apples and pears will be ready for use.

Work
Lift seakale roots for storing and forcing indoors as needed. Put mint roots in a box of soil for forcing in a warm kitchen.

Clean up the garden; a dirty garden can harbor disease. Take the yellowing leaves off Brussels sprouts. Fallen leaves of fruit trees may be diseased and are best burned.

Dig whenever you can if the soil is fit to work. Dig in farmyard manure or compost where next year's peas and beans, onions and leeks, celery and spinach are to grow.

Cover rows of root crops with straw if you "store" produce in the garden. Protect cardoons and globe artichokes in the North.

December

This is the dead time of the year for doing, but you need to be thoroughly alive to your plans for next year. Write for seed catalogs and study and compare them well. Even the most reliable seedsmen tend to over-fertilize their catalog prose. But while remaining suitably skeptical, do experiment each year with something new—perhaps a previously untried vegetable or a new variety of a favorite one. You may find it ideal both for your garden and your taste. Having decided, order quickly. Because of the vast increase in vegetable growing, only the early orders will catch the popular varieties.

Planting
In the mid to deep South transplant to frames or cloches the lettuces sown in frames in October. In the North grow salad greens and herbs under lights or in a greenhouse.

Crops
For this year you still have celery, leeks, parsnips, Jerusalem artichokes, cabbages, Brussels sprouts and broccoli in the garden. Blanched Brussels chicory and forced curly chicory are available for salads, as well as the mustard and cress you grow indoors. Indoor chives and outdoor Welsh onions are there to add flavor. From store you can choose potatoes, onions, turnips, carrots, rutabagas, beets and salsify. There are still good-keeping apples and some pears.

Work
Protection against frost can include covering celery trenches with straw. Marjoram and rosemary also need protecting.

Everything in store should be in a frost-proof, but not warm, place. Go through stored crops to make sure that nothing is rotting and spoiling the others.

Recycle holiday evergreens and Christmas trees as winter protection and mulch. Send for catalogs. Feed wild birds.

In the Kitchen

There are few things more rewarding than gathering in the vegetables and fruits that you have grown in your own kitchen garden. The feeling of achievement is much the same as when you bake bread—a satisfying sense of fulfillment. Equally satisfying is the task of preparing and cooking the vegetables so that the taste is enhanced, the texture is preserved and the nutrients are not lost.

Vegetables are the richest and cheapest source of vitamins and mineral salts. To preserve the nutrients, as well as the flavor, it is best to pick vegetables when they are young and to put them in the pot as quickly as you can, pausing only to trim and wash them. Vegetables should be steamed, simmered in a little water, or cooked in butter or oil for the shortest possible time until they are just tender. They should then be served immediately.

Some people consider it more economical to allow vegetables to grow large before picking them. They do not realize that the longer vegetables are left to mature, the coarser they will be and the more time it will take to cook them. Longer cooking not only destroys the flavor of vegetables but also their nutrients.

If vegetables require washing, wash them just before they are to be cooked or used. Never soak vegetables unless it is recommended in a particular recipe.

The less a vegetable is "prepared"—peeled and cut—the fewer nutrients it loses during cooking. In most vegetables the vitamins lie just under the skin, so if a vegetable must be peeled do it thinly.

The simplest methods of cooking vegetables are usually the best. Steaming is undoubtedly the most satisfactory way of cooking delicate young vegetables, which will lose goodness and flavor if boiled in water. You may need to buy either a steamer to fit one of your larger pans or a smaller, flower-shaped French steamer which will fit almost any pan. Be sure that the water is boiling before putting the vegetables in the steamer. For "tougher" vegetables, such as beets and potatoes, it will be more economical of time and money to use a pressure cooker, but do not overcook the vegetables.

Steam-boiling is suitable for many vegetables, particularly asparagus, cauliflower and broccoli. The vegetable is put upright into a small amount of simmering water in a tightly covered pan. The more delicate heads cook in steam while the tougher stalks simmer in the water. Do not throw the water away after the vegetables are cooked. Use it to make soups or sauces.

If vegetables are cooked in water, add a little lemon juice or vinegar—2 teaspoons to 1 pint of water—to preserve the color.

The Chinese method of stir-frying is the quickest and tastiest way to cook vegetables. The time saved in cooking, however, is often spent instead in preparation, as most vegetables must be cut into small, even-sized pieces.

When equipping the kitchen, good stainless-steel knives are one of the first priorities. They should be regarded as an investment and will probably last a lifetime provided that they are looked after sensibly, are sharpened regularly on a steel, and are used in conjunction with a wooden chopping board. Only two knives are needed for vegetables: a 3-inch blade for peeling and paring, and a 9- to 12-inch blade for chopping and slicing.

Many recipes for both vegetables and fruit either start or end with a purée. To make a purée, you will need a fine nylon sieve and a wooden spoon. There is nothing, however, to match the versatility and convenience of an electric blender. It will not only blend, but will also grind bread crumbs and nuts and chop herbs to a fineness that would take some time to achieve by hand.

The food mill (French *mouli*), which does not have the wide application of an electric blender but is considerably less expensive, is a fine compromise between a sieve and a blender. Best of all, though most expensive, is the amazing new appliance—the food processor.

Growing your own vegetables and fruits gives you the opportunity to discover flavors and textures which many of us have either never experienced or have long since forgotten. Who could resist what the French call a *bouquet jardinière*, a platter of garden-fresh young vegetables, each one poached or steamed separately until just tender and served with either butter, coarse salt and freshly ground black pepper, with crisp buttered bread crumbs, or with a meltingly smooth hollandaise sauce? Nothing could be simpler or more delightful in its simplicity, and this is precisely what growing your own vegetables is all about.

Motter 75

Salad Plants

Green salads have enjoyed a reputation as gastronomic delicacies for thousands of years. They were served at Roman banquets as part of the first course, and the guests' gustatory pleasure was doubtless heightened at the thought of the aphrodisiac—and medicinal—benefits they believed would result.

But aphrodisiac and medicinal considerations aside, a green salad makes a welcome accompaniment to practically any dish of meat, fish or fowl. After a rich main dish, a tossed green salad is particularly refreshing, or it can add the finishing touch to an informal meal of soup and bread and cheese.

Salad greens picked just before they are to be eaten have a fine, sweet crispness, as every gardening cook knows. Another advantage of growing your own vegetables is the diversity of salad plants available.

Besides the familiar lettuce, there is curly, mop-headed chicory, which has an interesting, faintly bitter flavor. Pale whitish-green Brussels chicory (endive) adds interest to winter salads to which, for variety, bright, firm-textured corn salad leaves may be added. Celtuce is a cross between lettuce and celery and is rich in vitamin C. The leaves are used in salads or they may be cooked like spinach. The stems may be eaten raw, chopped or grated, or cooked like celery.

Even young, cultivated dandelion leaves, peppery and tasty, make excellent salad greens. They should be washed quickly, trimmed and dressed with a light vinaigrette, or wilted in a hot bacon-and-vinegar dressing. Watercress, which is often thought of only as a garnish, also makes a fine salad, particularly when it is combined with thin slices of orange and tossed with a vinaigrette dressing to which has been added finely chopped shallots and a dash of cayenne pepper. Both American cress and mustard and cress can be used raw in salads, sandwiches and as a garnish.

Salad greens must be carefully washed and dried. The leaves should be torn into small pieces. Never use a knife as this will bruise the delicate leaves.

When preparing a salad, both the texture and the flavor of the ingredients should be considered. Add crunch with large pieces of Brussels chicory, chopped celery, cucumber or sweet pepper, slices of mild, sweet onion or shreds of crisp cabbage. Vary the color with wedges of tomato, black olives or a few slices of anise-flavored Florence fennel.

A salad is only as good as its dressing and a salad dressing is only as good as its ingredients. Experiment with various types of olive oil until you find the one that suits your taste. Dark, strong olive oil can be given a less heavy flavor if it is mixed with a light vegetable oil, such as corn or peanut oil. Walnut oil, now rare and expensive, goes particularly well with Brussels chicory.

Good-quality red or matured white wine vinegar is essential for a good dressing. For a change try an herb vinegar, but never use malt vinegar, which is too strong and acid. Use lemon juice or a good cider vinegar for a milder dressing. Sea salt is preferable to ordinary table salt: its taste is somehow rounder and saltier. Pepper should always be freshly ground.

The classic proportions of a vinaigrette, or French dressing, are three parts oil to one part vinegar. If this seems too sharp, try four or five parts oil to one part vinegar. Mix the vinegar with salt, a good grinding of black pepper and/or a little dry or French mustard. A pinch of sugar, anathema to purists, helps to tone down excess acidity. Add the oil, a tablespoon at a time, beating vigorously with a fork until the dressing is smooth and creamy.

Fresh herbs transform a salad dressing. Try coarsely chopped chervil, chives, tarragon, savory or parsley. For a light garlic flavor, rub the salad bowl with a cut garlic clove. If a stronger flavor is desired, chop the garlic finely, crush it in a garlic press or mash it well with a little salt, using the side of a knife blade. Then blend it thoroughly with the dressing. Another way to flavor a salad with garlic is to make a *chapon*. Rub a slice of stale French bread all over with a bruised garlic clove. Drop it in among the salad greens shortly before tossing them. Soaked with dressing, a *chapon* is a delicacy in its own right.

For a mustard dressing, dilute a heaped teaspoon of a coarse, mild French mustard, such as *Moutarde de Meaux*, with a tablespoon of cold water. Beat in 4 tablespoons of olive oil and season to taste with salt and a generous pinch of sugar. A mustard cream dressing, which is particularly good with curly chicory, is made by beating 2 tablespoons of good-quality prepared mustard with 4 tablespoons of cream, seasoned to taste with lemon juice, salt and freshly ground pepper.

A sour-cream dressing, a central European classic, is traditionally used for salads served with baked or broiled poultry or pork. To make enough dressing for a large head of lettuce, beat $\frac{2}{3}$ cup of thick, commercial sour cream with 2 tablespoons of finely chopped chives, a good pinch of sugar, salt and freshly ground pepper to taste.

Do not toss a salad until just before serving. If the leaves are coated with the dressing for any length of time, the acid will wilt them.

Lettuce

"Lettuce maketh a pleasant sallad, being eaten with vinegar, oile, and a little salt: but if it be boiled it is sooner digested and nourisheth more." So said John Gerard, the sixteenth-century herbalist. Although the value of boiled lettuce may be disputed, most people will agree that lettuce makes a pleasant salad, particularly when it is gathered minutes before it is eaten. It is only when there are more lettuces in the garden than can possibly be eaten in salads that the cooked lettuce comes into its own—for soup, soufflé, casserole or purée.

To prepare a lettuce for salad, wash it carefully leaf by leaf. Shake the leaves free of moisture in a salad basket or gently pat them dry. If the lettuce is not required immediately, roll the leaves loosely in a cloth and refrigerate.

Corn salad, curly chicory and dandelion leaves may be substituted for lettuce in salads or used in lettuce salads to add color and flavor.

Green Salad with Roquefort Dressing

An excellent accompaniment for steak. Brussels chicory should be included in this salad because it adds flavor and crispness. Gorgonzola or blue cheese can be substituted for Roquefort if desired.

SERVES EIGHT
3 tablespoons vinegar
10 tablespoons olive oil
Salt
Freshly ground black pepper
French mustard
Sugar
2 heads Brussels chicory
1 romaine lettuce
1 curly chicory
12 dandelion leaves
3 oz Roquefort cheese
Lemon juice, Tabasco sauce or
*   cayenne pepper*

Pour the vinegar into a small bowl and add the oil 1 tablespoon at a time, beating the mixture vigorously with a fork at each addition. Add salt, pepper, mustard and sugar to taste and beat again. Set aside.

Slice the Brussels chicory thinly crosswise and place in a salad bowl. Tear the lettuce, curly chicory and dandelion leaves into bite-size pieces and add to the Brussels chicory. Set aside.

In a small bowl, mash the cheese to a paste with a fork. Add the prepared dressing and beat until blended. Flavor with a little lemon juice or a drop or two of Tabasco or a pinch of cayenne, and season to taste.

Pour the dressing over the greens and toss thoroughly. Serve immediately.

Caesar Salad

Caesar Salad is one of America's greatest culinary triumphs. A brilliant combination of flavor and texture, it has become a classic. Serve it as a first course or as a main luncheon dish.

SERVES SIX
Olive oil
3 garlic cloves
4 large, thick slices of bread, trimmed
*   and cut into ½-inch cubes*
2 romaine lettuces, washed, dried
*   and chilled*
1 egg
Juice of 1 lemon
16 anchovy fillets, cut into pieces
½ cup Parmesan cheese, grated
Salt
Freshly ground black pepper

Heat 4 tablespoons of olive oil in a frying pan with 2 crushed garlic cloves. Fry the bread cubes until crisp and golden on all sides, adding more oil as needed. Drain the croutons thoroughly on paper toweling. Discard the garlic and oil. Crush the remaining garlic clove and rub it around a salad bowl.

Tear the lettuce into bite-size pieces and place in the salad bowl. Add 8 tablespoons of olive oil and toss until every leaf is thoroughly coated. Cook the egg in a pan of boiling water for 1 minute. Break the egg over the lettuce, add the lemon juice, anchovies, cheese, and salt and pepper to taste.

Toss gently until well mixed. Taste for seasoning and add salt if needed. Add the croutons, toss again and serve immediately, while the croutons are still crisp.

Wilted Salad with Hot Bacon Dressing

A hot dressing is used to wilt the greens for this salad. Romaine is the best lettuce for a wilted salad, although head lettuce will stand up well to a hot dressing if it is fresh from the garden. This recipe is also good for curly chicory or dandelion greens.

SERVES FOUR
1 garlic clove, halved
1 romaine lettuce, washed and dried
1 teaspoon butter
4 thick slices streaky bacon, diced
1 tablespoon wine vinegar
1 hard-boiled egg, chopped
2 tablespoons finely chopped parsley
Salt
Freshly ground black pepper

Rub a warmed salad bowl with the garlic. Tear the lettuce into the bowl in bite-size pieces. Set aside.

Melt the butter in a small frying pan. Add the bacon and cook gently, stirring, for 10 minutes, or until the fat runs. Pour the contents of the pan over the greens. Add the vinegar to the pan, swirl to heat it and sprinkle over the salad in the bowl.

Toss the salad thoroughly. Add the chopped egg, parsley, and salt and pepper to taste. Toss again and serve.

Lettuce

An English Salad

This recipe comes from a famous English cookery book, *The Cook's Oracle*, by Dr. Kitchiner, which was published in 1817 and went through five editions in six years. In the words of Dr. Kitchiner: "Boil a couple of Eggs for twelve minutes, and put them in a basin of cold water for a few minutes,—*the Yolks must be quite cold and hard, or they will not incorporate with the ingredients.* Rub them [the yolks] through a sieve with a wooden spoon, and mix them with a tablespoonful of water, or fine double cream, then add two tablespoonsful of Oil or melted Butter; when these are well mixed, add by degrees, a teaspoonful of Salt, or powdered lump Sugar, and the same of made Mustard; when these are smoothly united, add very gradually three tablespoonsful of Vinegar, rub it with the other ingredients till thoroughly incorporated with them; cut up the white of the egg, and garnish the top of the salad with it."

We can only guess at the size of Dr. Kitchiner's teaspoons and tablespoons, but using standard measuring spoons the following quantities make a very good dressing indeed, enough for quite a large head of lettuce: 2 eggs, 2 tablespoons heavy cream, 2 tablespoons olive oil, $\frac{1}{4}$ teaspoon salt (more or less according to taste, but sugar is not a good idea in this case), $\frac{1}{2}$ teaspoon Dijon mustard and 2 tablespoons wine vinegar.

Lettuce Soup

This is an ideal dish to make in early autumn when there is a glut of lettuce and the weather is chilly.

SERVES FOUR
4 head lettuces, washed
2 tablespoons butter
1 small onion, finely chopped
2 tablespoons flour
4 cups milk or chicken stock
Salt
Freshly grated nutmeg
2 tablespoons grated Parmesan cheese

Put the lettuce in a saucepan and cover it with water. Bring the water to the boil and cook for 5 minutes. Drain, rinse the lettuce in cold water, drain again and set aside.

Melt the butter in a large saucepan, add the chopped onion and cook, stirring frequently, for 3 minutes. Stir in the flour with a wooden spoon. Gradually add the milk or stock and, stirring constantly, bring to the boil. Add the lettuce to the soup. Reduce the heat and simmer for 3 minutes.

Liquefy the soup in a blender or put it through a food mill. Return the soup to the pan, season to taste with salt and nutmeg. Reheat the soup to just under boiling point. Serve sprinkled with Parmesan cheese.

Souffléed Lettuce

This is another delicious way of using up surplus lettuce. It makes an unusual accompaniment to broiled or roast lamb, or can be served as a luncheon dish with poached eggs.

SERVES THREE TO FOUR
2 large or 3 small head lettuces
2 tablespoons butter
2 tablespoons flour
3 scallions, finely chopped
$\frac{1}{2}$ cup ham, diced (optional)
1 lb floury potatoes,
  cooked and puréed
2 eggs, separated
Salt
Freshly ground black pepper
Lemon juice
2 tablespoons grated Parmesan or any
  good, hard, melting cheese

Preheat the oven to 375°F. Wash the lettuces, keeping the heads whole. Shake off as much moisture as possible. Place them in a heavy pan and cover tightly. Cook over high heat for 5 minutes.

Drain and press out as much moisture as possible with the back of a wooden spoon. Chop the lettuce very finely or purée in a blender or food processor.

In another pan, melt the butter. Gradually blend in the flour and cook over low heat, stirring constantly, for 2 to 3 minutes to make a pale roux. Beat in the lettuce purée, the onions and diced ham, if used, and, stirring, cook over moderate heat for 1 minute longer.

Remove from the heat. Beat in the potato purée, then the egg yolks. Season to taste with salt, pepper and a few drops of lemon juice.

Whisk the egg whites until stiff but not dry. With a large metal spoon fold them gently but thoroughly into the lettuce-and-potato mixture.

Spoon the mixture into a deep, buttered baking dish or soufflé dish. Sprinkle with the grated cheese and bake for 30 minutes, or until puffed and golden. Serve immediately.

Lettuce Casserole

This lettuce casserole goes well with lamb or boiled beef. Serve each person with a whole head of lettuce.

SERVES FOUR
5 teaspoons butter
4 slices streaky bacon, diced
1 medium-sized Spanish onion, thinly
  sliced
2 carrots, quartered lengthwise and
  thinly sliced
4 tomatoes, blanched, peeled and chopped
Salt
Freshly ground black pepper
4 large head lettuces
4 tablespoons water or stock

Melt 2 teaspoons of butter in a saucepan and simmer the bacon in it until the fat runs. Add the onion and carrots and fry until soft and lightly colored, stirring frequently. Stir in the tomatoes and cook gently for 2 to 3 minutes, or until the tomatoes are slightly softened. Season with salt and pepper to taste. Set aside.

Wash the lettuces without separating the leaves. Trim the stems. Fill a large pan with salted water and bring to the boil. Blanch the lettuces, two at a time if necessary, by lowering them into the boiling water and, as they wilt, pressing them down gently with the back of a wooden spoon so that they are totally submerged. When the water returns to the boil, remove the lettuces and drop them into a large bowl of ice-cold water.

When the lettuces are cool enough to handle, squeeze them gently, extracting as much moisture as possible without spoiling their shape. Cut each lettuce in half vertically.

Melt the remaining butter in a heavy pan large enough to take the lettuces in one layer, swirling the butter around to coat the pan. Put the lettuce halves in the pan and sprinkle them with salt and pepper. Spoon the tomato mixture over them.

Moisten with 4 tablespoons of water or stock, bring to a simmer, cover, and cook gently for 20 minutes, or until the lettuces are tender.

To dry lettuce leaves without bruising them, use a salad basket. Twirl or shake thoroughly.

Brussels Chicory (Endive)

Brussels chicory is a remarkably versatile member of the salad family. Some people shy away from it because of its bitterness. But so long as this is cleverly partnered by other flavors it can be turned into an advantage.

Equally good raw or cooked, Brussels chicory adds a juicy crunchiness to winter salads and also provides a subtly flavored, bittersweet vegetable to serve as a separate course or as an accompaniment to meat dishes.

When serving Brussels chicory in a raw salad, you will need one large head per person; for a cooked dish, two heads will be required.

The preparation of Brussels chicory is the same whether it is to be used raw or cooked. Pull off a layer of outer leaves. Trim the stem and carefully remove the core with the point of a sharp knife. Rinse under cold water or wipe with a damp cloth. Use the Brussels chicory immediately, as the cut surfaces soon discolor. Never leave the heads soaking in water, as this tends to make them more bitter.

Brussels Chicory-and-Orange Salad

A Brussels chicory-and-orange salad makes a wonderful accompaniment to roast duck or ham.

SERVES FOUR

1 tablespoon lemon juice
Salt
Freshly ground black pepper
French mustard
Cayenne pepper or Tabasco sauce
1 teaspoon honey
3 tablespoons olive oil
1 orange
4 heads Brussels chicory, prepared, washed and thinly sliced crosswise
12 black olives, to garnish

In a salad bowl, mix the lemon juice with a little salt, pepper, mustard, cayenne or Tabasco and the honey. Add the oil a tablespoon at a time, beating the mixture vigorously with a fork at each addition until it is smooth and creamy. Taste and add more lemon juice, seasoning or honey if necessary. Set aside.

Peel the orange and remove the pith. Slice the orange thinly on a plate and quarter each slice. Put the Brussels chicory, the orange slices and any orange juice left on the plate into the salad bowl. Toss gently but well. Serve immediately, garnished with black olives.

Braised Brussels Chicory

This dish may be garnished with chopped parsley, buttered bread crumbs or finely chopped hard-boiled egg heated through in butter. Or serve with a hollandaise sauce, which sets off the bittersweet flavor well.

If the endive is going to accompany a roast, substitute a few tablespoons of the juices from the roasting pan for some of the butter in the final braising.

SERVES FOUR

8 heads Brussels chicory, prepared and washed
Juice of 1 lemon
Salt
4 tablespoons butter
Freshly ground black pepper
Freshly grated nutmeg

Arrange the whole Brussels chicory heads in a large saucepan. Sprinkle each layer with a little lemon juice and salt. Pour over enough boiling water to cover the Brussels chicory. Partly cover the pan and simmer over low heat for 10 to 15 minutes. Drain in a colander and squeeze out as much moisture as possible, using a clean cloth to protect your hands.

In a pan wide enough to hold the Brussels chicory in one layer, melt the butter without letting it color. Add the Brussels chicory, turning each head to coat it well. Sprinkle with salt, pepper and nutmeg and a little more lemon juice to taste. Cover the pan and cook for 15 to 20 minutes longer, or until tender when pierced through the thickest part over a thin skewer. Turn the heads occasionally so that they color evenly.

Brussels Chicory and Ham Mornay

Serve one head of Brussels chicory per portion as an hors d'oeuvre, two per person as a luncheon dish. Accompany with fresh crusty bread to mop up the delicious sauce.

SERVES FOUR

8 heads Brussels chicory, prepared and washed
Salt
Lemon juice
2⅔ cups milk
1 chicken stock cube
1 small onion, coarsely chopped
4 black peppercorns
1 small bay leaf
8 slices ham, about 1 oz each
Butter
4 tablespoons flour
⅔ cup light cream
5 tablespoons freshly grated Parmesan cheese
5 tablespoons freshly grated Gruyère cheese
1 egg yolk
Freshly ground black pepper
Freshly ground nutmeg

Put the Brussels chicory heads in a pan of salted water. Add 2 tablespoons of lemon juice to each pint of water and bring to the boil. Cook for 15 minutes.

Meanwhile, pour the milk into a pan and add the stock cube, the onion, peppercorns and bay leaf. Heat, stirring until the stock cube has dissolved and the liquid comes to the boil. Remove the pan from the heat. Cover the pan and set aside for 15 minutes.

Drain the Brussels chicory. Squeeze each head between the folds of a cloth to extract as much moisture as possible, taking care not to spoil its shape. Wrap each head in a slice of ham. Pack them tightly head to tail in a buttered, oblong *gratin* dish just large enough to hold them.

Preheat the oven to 400°F.

To prepare the sauce, melt 3 tablespoons of butter in a heavy pan without letting it color. Blend in the flour smoothly with a wooden spoon and stir over low heat for 2 to 3 minutes to make a pale roux. Strain the infused milk into the roux gradually, stirring vigorously to prevent lumps forming. Stir in the cream. Bring the sauce to simmering point and cook gently, stirring frequently, for 15 minutes.

Remove the pan from the heat. Beat in 4 tablespoons each of the grated Parmesan and Gruyère, and the egg yolk. Season to taste with salt, pepper, a grating of nutmeg and a few drops of lemon juice.

Spoon the sauce over the Brussels chicory-and-ham rolls and sprinkle with the remaining cheese. Bake for 25 minutes, or until the sauce is bubbling and golden brown on top.

Let the dish rest for a few minutes before serving.

Brassicas

George Bernard Shaw had the right attitude to the brassica family. In *The Apple Cart*, King Magnus is being tempted by his rather tediously exalted mistress Orinthia to share her concept of the regal life. "Heaven," she complains, "is offering you a rose; and you cling to a cabbage." His answer is one which both the kitchen gardener and the cook would applaud: "But what wise man, if you force him to choose between doing without roses and doing without cabbages, would not secure the cabbages?"

There are more than forty species of the genus *Brassica*, yet only one, *B. oleracea*, has found such favor in the kitchen. Even so, the variety of subspecies that are descended from it are without doubt one of the Old World's most valuable contributions to the kitchen garden—a rainbow of cabbages, green, white and red, smooth-leaved and curly; kale (borecole), to all appearances a cabbage that has not quite made it; and the Brussels sprout, which admirably succeeds in reproducing handfuls of tiny replicas of its cabbage cousins. Kale may be cooked like cabbage, but its stronger flavor and coarser texture make it unsuitable for any but the simplest dishes.

Cauliflowers, cultivated for their undeveloped flowers, were missing from the European culinary scene during the Dark Ages. When they reappeared in western Europe in the sixteenth century—seeds were brought from Cyprus via Italy to reach France in the seventeenth century—they were hailed as a great culinary novelty. The cooks of Louis XIV boiled them in stock flavored with mace and presented them to the king topped with fresh butter.

Even today, cauliflowers are prized for their delicate flavor and are considered by many to be the aristocrats of the brassica family. They are particularly fine when gathered from the garden early in the day, with the dew still sparkling on the curds, the correct name for their knobbly white heads.

Like all the brassicas, broccoli, one of the many candidates for the title "poor man's asparagus," has been cultivated for thousands of years. One legacy of the Romans' love for both broccoli and cauliflower remains in the fact that even today you can never be quite sure which of the two is meant when an Italian recipe calls for "broccoli."

Most cooks could list the brassicas in order of preference, as likely as not influenced by their price at the supermarket. For kitchen gardeners, however, this is not a consideration, and they can concentrate on the goodness of the vegetables themselves.

One of the greatest crimes perpetrated on all the brassicas, but particularly on cabbage, is overcooking, which deprives these vegetables not only of most of their vitamins and mineral salts, but also of flavor and texture.

The nutritional value of brassicas also depends to some extent on the sulfur they contain, which, unfortunately, can cause them to give off a somewhat unpleasant odor during cooking.

Sauerkraut was considered one of the best ways to use white cabbage as long ago as 200 B.C., when it was served to the laborers working on the Great Wall of China. Sauerkraut is an excellent way to preserve cabbage to last the whole year. To make it you need a large, glazed earthenware crock and a plate or board that just fits into the top of the crock. A 2-gallon crock holds about 15 pounds of sauerkraut.

Shred the cabbages finely, cores and all. A knife will do the job well, although the shredding ability of the magical new food processor is a great boon.

Layer the cabbage in the crock with salt; 6 tablespoons is ample for 10 pounds of cabbage. Flavor it with two or three crumbled bay leaves, a little cumin seed and dill seed to taste. Chopped carrots and apples can be added if desired. Pack the cabbage down firmly until it is within 2 inches of the top of the crock. Cover the surface with a piece of scalded cloth. Lay the upturned plate or board on top of the cloth and weight it down with a scrubbed stone which is heavy enough to force the brine to come up and wet the cloth. Keep the crock in a warm place (65°F) to start the fermentation, then store it in a cool place (about 50°F) for at least a month until the fermentation process is complete. Skim the scum off daily and regularly scald the cloth and scrub the stone clean. Be sure that the surface is always covered with liquid, otherwise the sauerkraut may go bad. If you use canned sauerkraut, make sure that it is in brine not vinegar.

Cabbage

For economy and versatility, cabbages are difficult to surpass, although, all too often, they have suffered badly at the hands of incompetent or impatient cooks. Yet the peasant cuisines of Europe are a treasure house of imaginative dishes based on cabbage.

For most dishes either white or green cabbages may be used, although the looser green heads are easier to take apart for rolling and stuffing. Red cabbage is in a class of its own. It is most often used for salads, casseroles or pickles. When cooking red cabbage, always add a little vinegar or lemon juice. This will prevent it turning purple.

The best cabbage is heavy for its size. Strip off damaged or wilted outer leaves and trim the stem. Cut the head in half from tip to stem.

Then cut each half into thirds. Slice out the core and, if the cabbage is to be shredded, make a slit lengthwise down the middle of the thickest part of each piece, then shred it crosswise.

Cabbage may simply be cooked in a small amount of salted water—or chicken stock with a little chopped onion for extra flavor—until just tender, then thoroughly drained, seasoned and served with butter, or in a creamy white sauce. A good way to cook shredded cabbage is to wilt the shreds by pouring boiling water over them in a colander, then simmer the shreds in a little butter until soft and golden. Another way to cook shredded cabbage is to stir-fry it in a little oil with thinly sliced onion and slivered fresh root ginger. It takes only a few minutes to cook and it retains its color and crispness.

Sauerkraut Salad

Sauerkraut salad goes well with pork dishes of all kinds. Try it, too, with fried fish. This recipe can be varied by substituting 1 tart eating apple and 2 raw carrots, both coarsely grated, for the finely chopped onion.

Sauerkraut (pickled cabbage) can be bought in cans or from the barrel at delicatessens. To make your own sauerkraut, see the recipe on page 132.

SERVES FOUR
¾ lb (2 cups) sauerkraut in brine
1 medium-sized onion, finely chopped
3 tablespoons olive oil
Sugar
Freshly ground black pepper
Salt
GARNISH
Onion rings
Finely chopped parsley

Drain the sauerkraut and chop it coarsely. Put it in a bowl. Add the onion, olive oil and sugar to taste. Toss thoroughly with a fork to separate the shreds. Season with pepper and a little salt, if necessary.

Heap the sauerkraut in a serving dish. Garnish with paper-thin rings of sweet onion and a sprinkling of chopped parsley and serve.

Coleslaw

Originally a plain cabbage salad, coleslaw (the name is a corruption of the Dutch *koolsla*) now often includes such varied ingredients as pineapple, carrots and apples.

Celery seed, a traditional ingredient, is not always available. Celery salt makes an acceptable substitute, although it does not add the same interesting variety to the texture.

SERVES FOUR TO SIX
1 lb (3½ cups) shredded cabbage
2 carrots, coarsely grated
1 crisp, tart apple, coarsely grated
2 shallots, finely chopped
3 tablespoons cider vinegar
1⅓ cups thick homemade mayonnaise
⅔ cup thick sour cream
1 tablespoon sugar
1 teaspoon celery seed or celery salt
6 drops Tabasco sauce
Salt (not necessary if celery salt is used)
Freshly ground black pepper

Put the cabbage in a large bowl. Add the carrots, apple, shallots and cider vinegar. Toss thoroughly.

In a small bowl mix the mayonnaise and sour cream together. Mix in the sugar, celery salt or seed, the Tabasco, salt and pepper, balancing flavors to suit your own taste. Pour the dressing over the salad and toss again until every shred of cabbage is coated.

Chill before serving.

Swedish Red Cabbage

This is an excellent dish served either as part of a vegetarian meal or with rich meats and such poultry as roast duck, as well as with all kinds of game. It also reheats and freezes well.

SERVES EIGHT
1 head red cabbage, about 3 lb,
   finely shredded
½ lb (about 1½ cups) tart eating apples,
   peeled, cored and chopped
2 Spanish onions, thinly sliced
4 tablespoons brown sugar
½ lb (about 1½ cups) tart eating apples,
   peeled, cored and chopped
⅔ cup well-flavored chicken stock
⅔ cup red wine
3 tablespoons wine or cider vinegar
Salt
Freshly ground black pepper
1 small, raw beet, coarsely grated

Put the shredded cabbage in a large bowl. Pour over enough boiling water to cover the cabbage. Set aside.

In a large, heavy, enameled pan or casserole, sauté the diced salt pork until the fat runs. If using bacon fat it need only be melted. Add the onions and fry, stirring frequently, over moderate heat until soft and transparent. Stir in the sugar and continue to fry gently until the onions are caramelized and a rich golden color. Take great care not to let the sugar burn.

Drain the cabbage thoroughly. Add it to the casserole, together with the apples, stock, wine and vinegar. Mix well. Season generously with salt and pepper. Cover tightly and cook gently for 1½ hours, stirring occasionally.

Mix in the grated beet—this transforms the color—and continue to cook, covered, for 30 minutes longer, or until the cabbage is soft. Correct seasoning and serve very hot.

Cabbage Quiche

This is an unusual and delicious quiche. The same mixture baked without the crust in a dish set in a pan of hot water makes a fine side dish with meat.

SERVES FOUR AS A MAIN DISH
Dough for 9-inch pie or tart shell
1 lb (3½ cups) finely shredded cabbage
¼ lb (1 stick) butter
3 eggs
1⅓ cups light cream and milk, mixed
4 tablespoons freshly grated
   Gruyère cheese
3 tablespoons freshly grated
   Parmesan cheese
Salt
Freshly ground black pepper
Freshly grated nutmeg

Preheat the oven to 425°F. Roll out the dough and line a 9-inch pie pan with a removable base. Line the crust with greaseproof paper or foil, fill with dried beans and bake "blind" for 15 minutes. Remove the paper and beans, and let the base dry out for a further 5 minutes in the oven.

Reduce the oven temperature to 350°F.

Meanwhile, put the cabbage in a colander and slowly pour a kettle of boiling water over it. Shake off excess moisture.

In a large, heavy saucepan melt the butter. Add the cabbage, cover tightly and cook over moderate heat until the cabbage is soft and golden, shaking the pan to prevent the cabbage burning. The cooking time will depend on the type of cabbage used, but firm white cabbage takes about 30 minutes.

In a small bowl, beat the eggs with the cream and milk. Remove the pan from the heat. Let the cabbage cool slightly, then stir in the egg mixture and 2 tablespoons each of the Gruyère and Parmesan. Add salt, pepper and nutmeg to taste.

Carefully spoon the mixture into the baked pie shell. Sprinkle the remaining cheese over the top. Bake for 30 minutes, or until the filling is set and a rich golden color on top.

Cabbage Casserole

Like so many cabbage dishes, this one improves when cooked ahead of time and reheated. It also freezes well.

SERVES SIX TO EIGHT
1 tablespoon dried mushrooms
1 head cabbage, about 3 lb, shredded
Salt
4 tablespoons butter
4 slices fat bacon, finely chopped
1 large onion, finely chopped
2 tablespoons flour
2 carrots, diced
1 small parsnip, diced
1 large cooking apple
2 tablespoons chopped parsley
3 allspice berries
1 small bay leaf
Freshly ground black pepper
3 ripe tomatoes, blanched,
   peeled and sieved
⅔ cup light stock

To shred cabbage, remove the stem and outer leaves. Cut the cabbage in half from tip to stem, then cut each half into three.

Put the dried mushrooms in a small bowl. Pour over 1⅓ cups of boiling water and set aside to soak for 30 minutes.

Meanwhile, put the cabbage in a large pan. Sprinkle with salt. Pour over boiling water to cover. Cover the pan and bring the water to the boil again over high heat. Remove the lid for 1 to 2 seconds; replace it, lower the heat and simmer for 5 minutes. Drain the cabbage in a colander.

Pour the mushrooms and the soaking water into a small saucepan and boil them, uncovered, until they are very soft. Drain the mushrooms and reserve the remaining liquor. Chop the mushrooms finely and set aside.

Melt the butter in another large pan. Add the bacon and cook until the fat runs. The add the onion and cook over low heat until it is soft and a rich golden color. Blend in the flour and stir over moderate heat to make a nutty brown roux.

Add the parboiled cabbage, the carrots and parsnip. Peel and core the apple, and grate it coarsely into the mixture. Add the mushrooms and their reserved liquor, the parsley, allspice berries and bay leaf. Season to taste with salt and pepper. Add the sieved tomatoes and stock and, stirring, bring to simmering point over moderate heat.

Cover the pan tightly and cook gently for 1½ hours, stirring occasionally, particularly at the beginning, to prevent the cabbage sticking to the bottom of the pan. Serve hot.

Stuffed Cabbage Rolls

This classic dish requires very little meat, not more than 2 ounces per portion, even less if the amount of rice is increased.

SERVES FOUR TO SIX
1 large head cabbage, white or green
½ cup short-grain rice
3 tablespoons butter
2 Spanish onions, finely chopped
¾ lb lean lamb or pork, minced
2 tablespoons chopped parsley
4 tablespoons tomato paste
Salt
Freshly ground black pepper
Worcestershire sauce (optional)
About 4 cups hot chicken or beef stock

Make a slit along the thickest part of each piece, then cut out the core of the cabbage.

Finally, shred the cabbage thinly, cutting it crosswise.

Trim the cabbage. Remove damaged outer leaves and carefully hollow out the stem end with a potato peeler. Plunge the cabbage into a large pan of boiling water. When the water comes to the boil again remove the pan from the heat. Cover the pan tightly and set aside.

Put the rice in a small bowl. Pour over enough boiling water to cover the rice and let it soak for 5 minutes. Drain and rinse well.

Melt the butter in a large frying pan. Add the onions and cook gently until they are soft and richly colored. Scrape the onions and the butter into a large bowl. Mix in the minced meat, rice, parsley and half of the tomato paste diluted with ⅔ cup of water. Season generously with salt, pepper and a few drops of Worcestershire sauce, if desired.

Drain the cabbage. As soon as it is cool enough to handle take the leaves apart, cutting them free at the stem end and carefully separating them from the head. If the inner leaves are still too crisp to handle, cover the head with more boiling water and let it stand for a few minutes longer. Stop taking the cabbage apart when the very small leaves that make up the heart are reached.

Use only the best and biggest leaves for making the cabbage rolls. Lay each leaf on a board and with a sharp knife pare down the thick central rib so that the leaf lies flat. Put a roll of filling at the stem end. Fold in the two sides over the filling and roll up the leaf firmly to make a neat packet.

Line the bottom of a large, wide pan with some of the leftover cabbage leaves. Arrange the cabbage rolls in the pan side by side as tightly as possible so that they do not unwind—use pieces of cabbage heart to plug any spaces. Try to fit all the rolls in two, or at most three, layers. Cover with the remaining leaves.

Weight the cabbage rolls down with an upturned heatproof plate slightly smaller in diameter than the top of the pan. Blend the remaining tomato paste with the hot stock and pour it into the pan so that it just shows around the sides of the plate.

Over moderate heat bring the liquid to the boil. Cover the pan tightly and cook very gently for 1½ hours.

Serve the cabbage rolls with the pan juices or drain the pan juices and use them to make a light lemon or tomato sauce to spoon over the top.

Kulebiak

This Russian cabbage-and-mushroom pie is a party dish to serve on its own as part of a hot buffet or, with hot melted butter, as a first course. It may also be served as a main dish accompanied by a rich mushroom sauce.

Kulebiak may be time-consuming to prepare but it can be made in advance, baked and quick-frozen. Transfer it straight from the freezer to a fairly hot oven, 425°F, fo. 35 to 40 minutes, covered with foil for the first 20 minutes to prevent the crust from becoming too brown.

If it is more convenient to prepare the *kulebiak* in two stages, start with the cabbage filling.

SERVES EIGHT TO TWELVE
CABBAGE FILLING
2 lb (7 cups) finely shredded cabbage
Salt
4 tablespoons butter
1 large Spanish onion, finely chopped
1¼ cups small button mushrooms, thinly sliced
1 large cooking apple, peeled, cored and coarsely grated
Freshly ground black pepper
2 large eggs, hard-boiled and finely chopped
YEAST DOUGH
4½ cups all-purpose flour
1 teaspoon salt
1 oz fresh yeast or 1 tablespoon dried yeast
1⅓ cups lukewarm milk and water, mixed
2 teaspoons sugar
1 egg and 2 egg yolks, beaten
6 tablespoons butter, melted and cooled

Put the cabbage in a large pan. Sprinkle it with salt and pour over enough boiling water to cover. Put the pan on the heat and when the water returns to the boil reduce the heat and simmer the cabbage steadily for 5 minutes. Drain the cabbage in a colander, pressing out as much moisture as possible with the back of a spoon.

Rinse and dry the pan and return it to the heat. Add the butter. When it is hot, stir in the onion and cook until soft and golden brown. Add the mushrooms and continue to cook gently until they have softened.

Stir in the parboiled cabbage and the apple. Mix well and season generously with salt and pepper. Cover the pan and cook over low heat, stirring occasionally. When the cabbage is very soft, remove the pan from the heat, adjust the seasoning and leave to cool.

Meanwhile, make the yeast dough. Sift the flour and salt into a large bowl, and warm it gently over the pilot light of a gas stove or in a 90°F oven.

In a small bowl blend the fresh yeast smoothly with the milk and water and the sugar. Beat in enough of the flour to make a thick cream. Put the bowl in a warm place for 15 to 20 minutes until the mixture becomes spongy. (Dried yeast should be reconstituted according to the directions on the packet.)

Make a well in the center of the flour. Pour in the yeast mixture and the eggs, reserving a tablespoon or two of the egg to glaze the top of the pie later. Using your hands, work the ingredients to a smooth dough. Depending on the flour, a little more milk and water or a handful of flour may have to be added. When the dough leaves the sides of the bowl, work in the melted butter.

When the dough is smooth again, turn it out onto a floured board and knead vigorously for about 10 minutes until it is silky soft and elastic. Rinse and dry the bowl and oil it lightly. Roll the dough into a ball and put it back in the bowl. Cover the bowl with a cloth and leave it in a warm place until the dough has doubled in bulk.

Deflate the dough, knead it lightly and divide it into two pieces, one double the size of the other. Roll out the larger piece and use it to line the base and sides of a deep, buttered baking dish 10 × 12 inches. Spoon the cabbage filling into the baking dish and sprinkle the top evenly with the chopped hard-boiled eggs. Roll out the other piece of dough and cover the pie, sealing the edges. Make slits in the top to allow steam to escape. Put the pie in a warm place for about 30 minutes, or until the top is puffy.

Preheat the oven to 400°F. Brush the top of the pie with the reserved egg and bake for 15 minutes. Reduce the heat to 350°F and continue to bake for 45 minutes longer, or until the pie is well risen and a rich golden brown on top. Serve hot.

To make cabbage rolls, place some of the stuffing at the root end of each blanched cabbage leaf.

Fold the sides of the leaf toward the center and begin to roll up the leaf, starting at the root end.

Cabbage Dumplings

The excellent partnership of cabbage and pasta can be found in many culinary traditions from the Mediterranean to as far north as Poland. Cooked shredded cabbage simply tossed with buttered noodles makes a fine side dish for pork. Or try the same mixture dotted with butter, sprinkled with a little cheese and browned in the oven. Cabbage dumplings are a more elaborate variation on the same theme. The cabbage filling is made in the same way as in the recipe for *kulebiak*. Leftover dumplings are delicious fried in butter.

MAKES ABOUT FORTY-EIGHT DUMPLINGS,
SERVES FOUR TO SIX
½ recipe cabbage filling
2 cups all-purpose flour
½ teaspoon salt
1 egg
Dry bread crumbs, fried in butter, to garnish

Chop the cabbage filling very finely or, if necessary, put it through the coarse blade of a grinder. Mix in the hard-boiled eggs.

The noodle dough should be prepared in advance to give it at least an hour to "relax" before it is rolled out. Sift the flour and salt into a bowl. Make a well in the center and drop in the egg. Work the egg into the flour with your fingertips, together with enough lukewarm water—6 to 8 tablespoons—to make a firm dough. When the dough holds together, transfer it to a board dusted with flour and knead it vigorously until it is satin-smooth and elastic. When little blisters of air start forming just under the surface of the dough, stop kneading.

Roll the dough into a ball and put it into a plastic bag. Leave the dough for at least 1 hour to relax and soften. Roll the dough out very thinly. Stamp out 2½-inch rounds with a plain pastry cutter. Taking one round at a

time, put it in the palm of one hand and stretch it out slightly. Put a small heap of filling in the center. Fold the circle in half and pinch the edges firmly to seal them. Arrange the plump little dumplings on a lightly floured board. Collect all the trimmings in the plastic bag as you work to prevent them drying out. Then roll them out to make more dumplings.

Bring a large pan of salted water to the boil. Drop in a batch of dumplings (about 20 at a time in a large pan). When the water comes back to the boil and the dumplings rise to the surface, stir once, cover the pan, reduce the heat and cook gently for 5 to 6 minutes. Using a slotted spoon, transfer the dumplings to a colander. Rinse the dumplings with boiling water and drain thoroughly.

Serve the dumplings very hot, with buttered bread crumbs spooned over each portion.

The leaf should be rolled up tightly, right to the end.

The cabbage roll is now ready to be cooked. It may be held together with a toothpick if necessary.

Cauliflower

Although a much-loved vegetable, the cauliflower, in common with other brassicas, is often overcooked and unimaginatively served. With a little care, however, it can provide a satisfying main dish, as well as a tasty accompaniment to meat, fish and egg dishes.

To prepare cauliflower for cooking, first cut all around the base, removing all but the tiniest green leaves nestling around the head. Trim the stem so that the cauliflower will stand level. If there are any blemishes or bruised spots among the flowerets, cut them out. With an apple corer, hollow out about 2 inches of the stem. Wash the cauliflower carefully and leave it to soak for 10 to 15 minutes in a large bowl of cold water to which a handful of salt has been added. This will extract any grubs hiding in the interior.

Cooking a cauliflower calls for care. It must not be allowed to get even slightly mushy. The simplest way to avoid this is to cook it in a pan just large enough to hold the head comfortably. Pour in 1 inch of water, add salt and bring it to the boil. Put the cauliflower in the pan stem downward. As soon as the water returns to the boil, cover with a tight-fitting lid. Cook over high heat for 15 minutes, a little longer if the head is very large. Using this method the flowerets cook in steam while the tougher stem end is

boiled in water. Carefully transfer the cauliflower to a colander and drain it thoroughly. It may now be used whole or divided into flowerets.

A perfectly cooked head of cauliflower makes a marvelous dish with a sprinkling of coarse salt, a grinding of pepper and a few tablespoons of hot melted butter spooned over the top. Try sprinkling 3 or 4 tablespoons each of chopped parsley and chives over the dressed cauliflower just before serving. Or sauté a handful of slivered almonds in butter before pouring it all, sizzling hot, over the top. Or serve it *à la polonaise*, sprinkled with 3 tablespoons of fine, dry bread crumbs that have been fried in butter until crisp and golden.

For special occasions, make a hollandaise sauce and pour it over the entire head just before serving. Mayonnaise is also extremely good spread over a chilled, cooked head of cauliflower and served as part of a cold buffet. For extra flavor, spoon a little vinaigrette over the cauliflower and let it soak in thoroughly before masking it with mayonnaise.

In Italy, tiny raw cauliflowerets are included in a basket of raw vegetables for dipping into *bagna cauda*, a hot oil-and-butter sauce flavored with anchovies and garlic. Raw cauliflower also makes an unusual addition and provides a delicious crunchiness to a tossed green salad.

Cauliflower Appetizer Salad

As an alternative to this salad, serve the flowerets, raw or cooked, with sour-cream cheese dip—sour cream blended with mild blue cheese, 1 teaspoon of finely chopped shallot or chives and a few drops of Tabasco sauce.

SERVES FOUR TO SIX
1 large cauliflower
Salt
8 tablespoons olive oil
3 tablespoons lemon juice
8 anchovy fillets, finely chopped
2 shallots, finely chopped or crushed in a garlic press
½ teaspoon French mustard
Freshly ground black pepper
1 canned pimento, finely chopped
3 tablespoons finely chopped parsley
Pitted black olives, to garnish

Parboil the cauliflower in 1 inch of salted water for 8 minutes. It should remain distinctly crisp. Drain the cauliflower in a colander. As soon as it is cool enough to handle, divide it into flowerets and put them in a bowl.

In a small pan, combine the olive oil with the lemon juice, anchovy fillets, shallots, mustard and a grinding of pepper. Put the pan on the heat and slowly bring the dressing to the boil, stirring. Immediately pour it over the cauliflower. Add the chopped pimento and parsley. Toss lightly and season to taste with salt. Chill and serve garnished with olives.

Cream of Cauliflower Soup

Cauliflower makes a satisfying soup, delicate in flavor and creamy in texture.

SERVES FOUR TO SIX
1 medium-sized cauliflower
2⅔ cups milk
Salt
4 cups chicken stock
2 tablespoons butter
2 tablespoons flour
Freshly ground black pepper
Sharp Cheddar cheese, grated

Cut off a handful of tiny flowerets no bigger than daisy heads from the cauliflower. Bring ⅔ cup of the milk to the boil in a small pan with ⅔ cup of water and a pinch of salt. Add the flowerets and poach them for 6 to 7 minutes, until they are cooked but still very firm. Drain them, reserving the liquor, and set aside.

Chop the remainder of the cauliflower into chunks. Put them in a pan with 2⅔ cups of the chicken stock, the rest of the milk and the reserved cauliflower liquor. Bring to the boil and cook, covered, until the cauliflower is soft. Purée the contents of the pan in a blender or through the finest plate of a food mill.

In another pan melt the butter. Blend in the flour and stir over low heat for 1 minute to make a pale roux. Gradually add the remaining stock, beating vigorously to make a smooth sauce. Stir in the puréed cauliflower mixture and bring to the boil, stirring. Season to taste with salt and pepper and simmer for 5 minutes.

Taste the soup. If it seems too bland, stir in 2 or 3 tablespoons of cheese. Add the poached flowerets and heat them through. Serve the soup with a bowl of cheese for sprinkling over each portion.

*"... In the midst of which Leaves,
sometimes in the middle of autumn,
and sometimes sooner, there rises up a
great white Head of white hard Flowers
closely thrust together, sometimes
they are of a Milk, or Cream,
or yellowish White color."*

The English Herbal *by William Salmon, M.D., 1710*

*Cauliflowers are considered by many
to be the aristocrats of the brassica
family. They are particularly fine
when they are gathered from the garden early in the day, with the dew
still sparkling on the curds.*

"... Note also, That being boiled in Milk, and then eaten with Sweet fresh Butter and Salt, and Juice of Limons they have been found to restore admirably in Consumptions."

The English Herbal *by William Salmon, M.D., 1710*

Cauliflower

Cauliflower au Gratin

A family lunch or supper dish, this can be very good indeed, so long as the sauce is not too thick, the cheese flavor not too mild and the cauliflower underneath firm enough to stand upright. In spite of its French-sounding name this is a very English dish, so use a sharp Cheddar or crumbly Lancashire cheese for the sauce.

SERVES FOUR
3 tablespoons butter
3 tablespoons flour
2 cups hot milk
About 1¼ cups grated cheese
1 egg yolk
Dry mustard or cayenne pepper
Salt
Freshly ground black pepper
Lemon juice (optional)
1 large cauliflower, steam-boiled
3 tablespoons fresh white bread crumbs

Preheat the oven to 375°F. Melt the butter in a small saucepan. Blend in the flour and stir over low heat for 1 minute to make a pale roux. Gradually add the milk, stirring constantly, to make a smooth sauce. Simmer for 6 to 8 minutes, stirring occasionally, to cook out the raw flour taste. Remove the pan from the heat. Beat in 1 cup of the cheese, followed by the egg yolk. Season to taste with a pinch of dry mustard or cayenne, salt and pepper, and, if necessary, intensify the flavor of the cheese with a few drops of lemon juice.

Drain the cauliflower and put it in a buttered baking dish. Pour the sauce over the top and sprinkle with the remaining cheese lightly mixed with the bread crumbs. Bake the cauliflower in the upper part of the oven for 10 to 15 minutes, or until the cheese on top has melted and the sauce is bubbling.

Serve immediately.

Cauliflower in Cider Sauce

Unusual and delicious, this sauce is ideal for cauliflower which is to be served with chicken or other delicate meats.

SERVES FOUR TO SIX
2 tablespoons butter
2 tablespoons flour
1⅓ cups cider
⅔ cup heavy cream
Salt
Sugar
Freshly ground black pepper
Freshly grated nutmeg
1 large cauliflower, steam-boiled

Melt the butter in a heavy pan. Blend in the flour and cook over a low heat, stirring, for 1 to 2 minutes to make a pale roux. Gradually add the cider, beating vigorously to prevent lumps forming. Beat in the cream and bring to the boil, stirring constantly. Simmer the sauce for 5 minutes. Season to taste with salt, sugar, pepper and nutmeg. Simmer for 2 to 3 minutes longer.

Drain the cauliflower thoroughly and place it in a hot serving dish. Pour the creamy cider sauce over the cauliflower and serve immediately.

Cauliflower Cheese, Italian Style

This is another version of cauliflower au gratin that is even easier to make.

SERVES FOUR
1 medium-sized cauliflower, steam-boiled
8 tablespoons freshly grated Gruyère or Swiss cheese
2 tablespoons freshly grated Parmesan cheese
2 tablespoons fine dry bread crumbs
4 tablespoons melted butter

Preheat the oven to 400°F.

Drain the cauliflower carefully in a colander and put it in a buttered baking dish.

In a bowl, toss the cheeses with the bread crumbs and the melted butter. Sprinkle this mixture over the cauliflower and bake it for 10 to 15 minutes, or until the cheese has melted and the topping is sizzling and golden.

To prepare cauliflower, cut off the stalk and the leaves. Soak in cold, salted water for 10 minutes.

Cauliflower Fritters

Serve these crisp, light fritters with coarse salt, grated cheese or a sprinkling of soy sauce. Another way to make simple but delicious cauliflower fritters is this Turkish recipe: dip the cooked flowerets in seasoned beaten egg and then in flour. Deep-fry them in olive oil until crisp and golden. Serve the fritters very hot with a bowl of yogurt or fresh tomato sauce.

SERVES FOUR
1 medium-sized cauliflower
Salt
Oil for deep-frying
FRITTER BATTER
1⅛ cups all-purpose flour
½ teaspoon salt
2 tablespoons olive oil
2 egg whites

Make the fritter batter at least 1 hour before it is to be used. Sift the flour and salt into a bowl, and make a well in the center. Pour in ⅔ cup of luke-warm water. Gradually beat the flour into the liquid until the mixture forms a smooth batter. Beat in the oil. Set aside.

Steam-boil the cauliflower in 1 inch of salted water for 12 minutes. It should remain crisp. Drain the cauliflower well and divide it into bite-size flowerets. Leave to cool.

When ready to make the fritters, whisk the egg whites until stiff but not dry, and fold them into the batter. Heat a pan of oil for deep-frying to 350°F.

Dip the flowerets individually into the batter and deep-fry them, a few at a time, turning them over once, until they are crisply puffed and golden. Drain the fritters on paper toweling and serve immediately.

Cauliflower may be cooked whole or broken into flowerets, which will cook in half the time.

Place the cauliflower in very little boiling salted water. Cook, covered, until tender but not mushy.

Broccoli

The culinary confusion that arises over what qualifies as "broccoli" is not surprising, for there are many varieties. They are, however, all cooked and eaten in the same way.

Select tender, young broccoli. Do not break the stalks more than 4 or 5 inches long. Divide the heads into flowerets about 2 inches in diameter. If the stalks are thick, cut them in half lengthwise and peel them thinly.

Broccoli spears are fragile and 8 to 10 minutes' fast boiling in salted water should be ample to make them tender. They may also be steam-boiled in the same way as cauliflower or asparagus, with the heads above the surface of the simmering water.

Eaten hot, broccoli is delicious with a sauce of melted butter, with brown butter mixed with capers or with butter in which flaked almonds have been sautéed. The hot spears may also be served with hollandaise or Mornay sauce. Cold broccoli is excellent with a vinaigrette dressing or mayonnaise.

Broccoli-and-Cheese Soufflé

This delicious soufflé may be served as a main dish, a first course or as an accompaniment to any meat or fish dish.

SERVES THREE
Ground almonds or fine dry bread crumbs
1 lb fresh broccoli
⅞ cup chicken stock, boiling
Milk
2 tablespoons butter
2 tablespoons flour
2 egg yolks (from large eggs)
1½ teaspoons lemon juice
1 small garlic clove, crushed
Salt
Freshly ground black pepper
Freshly grated nutmeg
¼ cup Gruyère or sharp Cheddar cheese, grated
4 egg whites (from large eggs)

Butter a 1-quart soufflé dish and dust it with ground almonds or fine dry bread crumbs. Pour 1½ inches of hot water into a deep roasting pan and put it on a rack just below the center of the oven. Set the oven to 400°F.

Peel the stems of the broccoli if necessary. Put the broccoli into a pan, stems downward, and pour in the boiling stock. Put the pan on the heat and as soon as the stock returns to the boil cover the pan and reduce the heat to moderate. Cook the broccoli for about 10 minutes, or until tender.

Drain the broccoli in a strainer set over a bowl. Then pour the drained liquor into a measuring cup and add milk to make it up to ⅔ cup.

Put the cooked broccoli into the bowl and mash it with a fork. It does not matter if a few coarse pieces remain. Leave to cool.

Melt the butter in a medium-sized pan. Blend in the flour and stir over low heat for 1 minute. Gradually add the broccoli liquor, beating vigorously to prevent lumps forming, and stir over moderate heat until it starts to bubble thickly. Remove the pan from the heat. Beat in the egg yolks, lemon juice and crushed garlic. Season to taste with salt, pepper and nutmeg. Cool the mixture, then beat in the cheese and the mashed broccoli.

Whisk the egg whites until stiff but not dry. Stir a heaped tablespoonful into the broccoli mixture. Then, with a large metal spoon, lightly but thoroughly fold in the remainder.

Gently transfer the mixture to the prepared soufflé dish. Set the dish in the roasting pan of water and bake for 45 to 50 minutes, or until the soufflé is well risen but still slightly creamy in the center. Serve immediately.

Cream of Broccoli Soup

When there is plenty of broccoli in the garden this is an excellent way to use it up. This soup is also delicious cold, with chopped chives sprinkled over each portion.

SERVES FOUR TO SIX
2 tablespoons butter
1 leek, white part only, thinly sliced
1 celery stalk, thinly sliced
1 lb broccoli
1 small potato, thickly sliced
4 cups chicken stock
⅔ cup light cream
Salt
Freshly ground black pepper
Lemon juice
Small croutons, to garnish

Melt the butter in a large pan. Add the leek and celery, cover the pan and simmer until the vegetables are soft but not colored. Add the broccoli and the potato. Pour in the chicken stock, cover the pan and simmer gently until the vegetables are soft.

Blend the contents of the pan to a purée in an electric blender, or rub through the fine plate of a food mill. Pour the purée back into the pan. Stir in the cream. Season to taste with salt and pepper, and intensify the flavor with a few drops of lemon juice.

Bring the soup to boiling point, but do not let it boil. Serve hot, garnished with tiny, crisp croutons.

Broccoli alla Siciliana

Broccoli is a great Italian favorite. Serve this classic dish with roast chicken and such meats as beef, lamb or ham.

SERVES SIX
2 tablespoons olive oil
1 Spanish onion, finely chopped
12 black olives, pitted and sliced
6 canned anchovy fillets, chopped, and the oil reserved
2 lb fresh broccoli
⅔ cup chicken stock
⅔ cup red wine
Freshly ground black pepper
1 teaspoon butter
1 teaspoon flour
Salt

Heat the olive oil in a large, flameproof casserole. Stir in the onion, olives and anchovy fillets. Simmer gently, uncovered, for 5 minutes.

Add the broccoli, turning the pieces over to coat them with the oil. Add the stock and wine. Sprinkle with 1 tablespoon of oil drained from the can of anchovy fillets and season with a generous grinding of pepper. Cover the casserole and cook over moderate heat for 15 minutes. Stir occasionally to prevent the mixture sticking to the pan.

When the broccoli is tender, uncover the pan and continue simmering for 3 minutes longer. Using a slotted spoon, transfer the broccoli to a heated serving dish and keep hot.

Thicken the sauce in the pan with a beurre manié made by mashing the butter and flour to a smooth paste and stirring it in in small pieces. Add salt if necessary. Stir the sauce until it comes to the boil. Pour it over the broccoli and serve.

Brussels Sprouts

When Brussels sprouts are at their peak they need not be cooked at all. Shredded raw, they make a deliciously crisp and nutty-flavored addition to a salad.

Sprouts should be picked while they are still very small, plumply rounded and hard between the fingers. Strip off any damaged, wilted or worm-eaten outer leaves and trim the stems. Then—this is important—nick a small cross in the stem to help the sprout to cook evenly. Wash the sprouts quickly in cold water and drain them thoroughly. Speed is the secret of cooking sprouts. Bring a large pan of salted water to a fast boil. Drop in the sprouts and cook them at a rolling boil until their stems can easily be pierced with a skewer. Boil them for no longer than 10 minutes or 6 to 7 minutes if they are to be cooked further with other ingredients.

Poached sprouts are best served with a knob of fresh butter, or tossed with buttered bread crumbs or a slice or two of crumbled, crisply fried bacon.

Brussels Sprouts with Chestnuts

This dish is an English accompaniment for the Christmas turkey. If fresh chestnuts are not in season, canned ones make a perfectly good substitute.

SERVES FOUR
1 lb Brussels sprouts
Salt
2 tablespoons butter
¼ lb fat bacon, diced
½ lb peeled, cooked chestnuts
4 tablespoons poultry stock or water
Buttered bread crumbs, to garnish
   (optional)

Poach the sprouts in salted water for 6 to 7 minutes. They should remain crisp. Drain well and keep hot.

Melt the butter in a deep frying pan. Add the bacon and sauté until the fat runs. Add the chestnuts and toss over fairly high heat until they are thoroughly hot and lightly colored.

Gently mix in the Brussels sprouts and moisten with stock or water. Cook gently, stirring frequently, until the liquid has evaporated.

Garnish if desired with buttered bread crumbs and serve.

Brussels Sprouts with Mushrooms

Brussels sprouts cooked in this way make a good dish to serve with meat and poultry.

SERVES FOUR
1 lb Brussels sprouts
Salt
4 tablespoons butter
2 shallots, finely chopped
¼ lb button mushrooms, thickly sliced
Lemon juice
Freshly ground black pepper

Poach the sprouts in salted water for 6 to 7 minutes. They should remain slightly crisp.

While the sprouts are cooking, melt the butter in a wide pan. Add the shallots and cook gently until they are soft and richly colored. Add the mushrooms, tossing them to coat them with the buttery juices. Squeeze a few drops of lemon juice over them to help preserve their color and cook gently until the mushrooms have softened and the excess moisture has evaporated, leaving the butter clear again.

Drain the sprouts thoroughly. Mix them gently with the mushrooms and shallots and season generously with salt and freshly ground pepper. Cook for 2 to 3 minutes longer, stirring frequently. Serve immediately.

Brussels Sprouts Baked in Cream

This dish is well worth the effort of preparation.

SERVES FOUR
1 lb Brussels sprouts
Salt
2 oz lean ham, in one piece
2 tablespoons butter
Freshly ground black pepper
1 tablespoon flour
8 tablespoons heavy cream
¼ cup grated Gruyère cheese

Preheat the oven to 375°F.

Poach the sprouts in salted water for 5 minutes. Drain them and toss them in the pan over low heat to dry them. Cut the ham into tiny dice and toss it with the hot sprouts.

Melt the butter in a baking dish that will hold the sprouts in a single layer. Turn the sprouts and ham into the dish. Season to taste with salt and pepper. Cover the dish with a lid or aluminum foil and bake for 10 minutes.

In a small bowl, blend the flour smoothly with the cream. Fold the mixture gently into the hot sprouts. Sprinkle with the grated cheese and continue to bake, uncovered, for 15 to 20 minutes, or until the sauce is bubbling and golden brown on top. Serve from the baking dish.

Puréed Brussels Sprouts

This is one of the nicest ways to serve Brussels sprouts. The purée has a lovely green color and an excellent flavor. It can also be used as a base for making a soufflé—1 pound of purée will require 3 egg yolks and 4 egg whites.

SERVES FOUR TO SIX
1½ lb Brussels sprouts
⅔ cup light cream
½ lb puréed potatoes
4 tablespoons butter, melted
Salt
Freshly ground black pepper
Nutmeg

Poach the sprouts in salted water for 5 minutes. Drain them well.

Purée the sprouts with the cream in an electric blender. Pour the purée into a large bowl. Add the puréed potato and the butter and beat well until the mixture is light and fluffy. Season to taste with salt, pepper and a grating of nutmeg.

Return the purée to the pan and reheat gently, adding more cream if necessary.

Serve hot.

To prepare Brussels sprouts, use a sharp knife to slice off the stem of each sprout.

Remove the outer leaves and wash the sprouts thoroughly or soak them for 10 minutes in salted water.

Drain well, then cut a cross in the base of each sprout so that they will cook more quickly.

Spinach & Other Greens

Even the simplest dish of spinach cooked for 3 to 4 minutes, drained, seasoned with salt, pepper, a touch of nutmeg, or perhaps a squeeze of lemon or a pinch of rosemary or basil, and topped with a generous pat of butter is delicious, particularly when it is served with such meats as roast lamb, veal or broiled chicken.

Spinach has traveled a long way to reach our tables. Some say it came from Persia, others that it originated in the Far East. And as it traveled, it was welcomed by every cuisine along the way, adopting a variety of guises, in salads and soups, pastries and pies of all kinds, soufflés, omelets and creams, proving its versatility in all but the dessert course.

True spinach is more delicate than any of the other leafy vegetables that are used as spinach substitutes. Swiss chard was known to the botanists of the classical world. Its stems, particularly those of the red chard, which are rather sweet, are attractive enough to plant in the flower garden.

New Zealand spinach, turnip greens, collards and the other leaves cooked in the South as "greens" can be prepared in many of the same ways as spinach. However, greens are most commonly simmered for a long time with bacon, salt pork or ham hocks.

Like all low-growing leaves, spinach must be washed with great care; the slightest suspicion of grit in the finished dish will ruin it. The old custom of washing spinach in seven waters may be taking things too far, but two or three changes of water are necessary. There is less danger of leaving specks of grit among the leaves if they are lifted individually out of the rinse water, rather than drained in a colander, which allows any remaining grit to seep back in.

Very young spinach leaves make an interesting salad, washed, dried and chilled, then tossed with a sherry dressing—for ½ pound of spinach leaves mix 4 to 6 tablespoons of dry sherry, a tablespoon or two of light wine vinegar, 4 tablespoons of olive oil, salt, pepper, a pinch of sugar and a little chopped fresh basil or marjoram. Or shred the leaves, dress them with lemon mayonnaise and serve the salad garnished with chopped hard-boiled eggs.

To cook spinach, drop the leaves into a pan of boiling salted water—add a pinch of sugar for flavor—and simmer, uncovered, for 10 to 15 minutes, or until tender. Drain in a colander and refresh the leaves under cold running water. Gently squeeze the leaves as dry as possible and either reheat them in butter or chop or mince them, as your recipe demands. This method of cooking spinach makes it more digestible and ensures that it never has an unpleasant, metallic aftertaste.

Another way to cook spinach is to put it in a pan over high heat without adding water—the water trapped in the leaves is sufficient to cook them. Cover the pan and cook the spinach for 7 to 10 minutes, or until the leaves are tender.

Spinach may also be pan-fried in oil or in a mixture of oil and butter. For 1 to 1½ pounds of spinach, 3 tablespoons of oil or 2 tablespoons of oil and 1 tablespoon of butter will be sufficient. Add any flavoring, such as onion, garlic or root ginger. Fry the spinach in a large, deep frying pan for 7 to 10 minutes and serve immediately.

Because spinach can be frozen successfully it is well worth freezing a part of the crop. For however efficiently you manage your patch there will be times when there are no fresh spinach or chard leaves in the garden ready to be harvested. When using frozen spinach allow just over half the weight specified in recipes for fresh spinach. Frozen spinach may be thawed in a pan over low heat. Then stir it over high heat for a minute or two to evaporate excess moisture.

Spinach & Other Greens

Summer Spinach Soup

This is a light soup subtly flavored with fresh dill. If fresh dill is not available, substitute half the quantity of the dried herb.

SERVES SIX

1 lb fresh spinach, cooked and finely chopped
6 cups chicken or light meat stock
⅔ cup puréed tomatoes
2 medium-sized carrots, diced
1 large potato, peeled and diced
1 tablespoon chopped fresh dill
Lemon juice
Sugar
Salt
Freshly ground black pepper
Finely chopped hard-boiled eggs or thick sour cream, to garnish

In a large pan, combine the spinach with the stock, puréed tomatoes, carrots, potato and dill. Bring the soup to simmering point and cook gently, uncovered, for 25 to 30 minutes, or until the carrots and potato are soft.

Flavor the soup to taste with lemon juice and sugar and season with salt and pepper.

Serve each portion garnished with a sprinkling of chopped hard-boiled egg or a spoonful of sour cream.

Spinach-and-Cheese Quiche

Serve wedges of hot or warm quiche with drinks or as a first course.

SERVES SIX TO EIGHT

Dough to line a 9-inch pie pan
2 tablespoons butter
2 lb fresh spinach, cooked and finely chopped
1 cup cottage cheese
½ cup freshly grated Gruyère cheese
¼ cup freshly grated Parmesan cheese
⅔ cup heavy cream
3 eggs, beaten
Salt
Freshly ground black pepper
Freshly grated nutmeg

Preheat the oven to 425°F. Line a 9-inch pie pan with the dough. Line the pie shell with greaseproof paper or foil and fill it with dried beans. Bake the shell "blind" for 15 minutes. Remove the paper and beans, and let the base dry out in the oven for a further 5 minutes.

Reduce the oven temperature to 350°F. Melt the butter in a saucepan. Add the spinach and, stirring, heat it through. Remove the pan from the heat and beat in the cheeses, cream and eggs. Season to taste with salt, pepper and nutmeg.

Spoon the spinach mixture into the hot pie shell and bake it for 30 to 40 minutes, or until the filling is set and is lightly colored on top.

Spinach Börek

The filling used in making the quiche can also be used for making little Middle Eastern pastries called börek. Börek are made with filo, a fine, strudel-like pastry, which can be bought in Greek grocery shops. One pound of filo will be required for one recipe of spinach filling.

Working with one sheet of filo at a time (they dry out rapidly when exposed to the air and should be kept wrapped in a damp cloth to prevent them becoming brittle), cut it lengthwise into 3-inch strips. Brush a strip with melted butter. Put a rounded teaspoonful of filling about 1 inch in from one of the shorter ends. Fold the end over the filling, then fold the strip over and over to make a fat little triangular packet.

Butter baking sheets and arrange the pastries on them. Brush the tops of the pastries with more melted butter.

Bake the pastries in a moderately hot oven, 400°F, for 20 to 30 minutes, until they are puffed and a crisp golden brown. Serve them hot from the oven.

Spinach Cutlets

Served with fried or boiled new potatoes and a fresh green salad, spinach cutlets make a satisfying meal.

SERVES FOUR

2 tablespoons butter
1 medium-sized onion, finely chopped
2 lb fresh spinach, cooked and finely chopped or minced
1 large egg
Fine dry bread crumbs
Salt
Freshly grated nutmeg
Freshly ground black pepper
Oil or bacon fat, for frying

Melt the butter in a large pan. Add the onion and cook gently until it is soft and lightly colored. Remove the pan from the heat and add the spinach, egg and 2 ounces bread crumbs. Mix the ingredients together with a wooden spoon until smoothly blended. Season to taste with salt, nutmeg and pepper.

Shape the mixture into eight flat, oval cakes and coat them with dry bread crumbs. In a large frying pan, heat the oil or bacon fat. Add the cakes and fry them on both sides until the crumbs are golden and the cutlets are heated through.

Greens with Ham Hocks

The recent popularity of soul food has revealed to all Americans the rich tradition of love and ingenuity which Southern black cooks lavished on the simple meals they made for their families. Using leftovers from the pigs slaughtered for plantation dinners and any available cultivated or wild leaves, each woman evolved her own version of the basic recipe for greens which has influenced Southern white cooking too. In this recipe the blandness of the collards is enhanced by the sharper tang of mustard greens.

SERVES FOUR

4 fresh ham hocks
2 quarts cold water
1 teaspoon salt
Freshly ground black pepper
1 crushed red pepper (optional)
2 lb collard greens
1 lb mustard greens
Vinegar
1 onion or 4 scallions, minced

Simmer the ham hocks in a large kettle with water for 1 hour, or until the meat is tender and starting to come away from the bones. Add the collard greens, salt and pepper, and boil another 30 minutes. Then add the more tender mustard greens and cook a final 30 minutes. A crushed red pepper may be added to the kettle with the greens. Serve with more black pepper, a touch of vinegar and a sprinkling of onion or scallions. The "pot likker" may be served in cups or bowls, along with corn bread or biscuits.

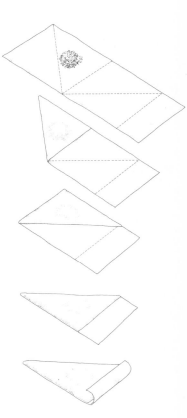

Cut a sheet of filo pastry into strips 3 inches wide. Brush a strip with melted butter. Place a rounded teaspoonful of filling at one of the shorter ends. Fold one corner of the pastry diagonally over the filling to form a triangle. Continue folding the triangle over and over until the strip of pastry is completely used up. Brush the triangular packet with more melted butter.

Stalks & Shoots

Stalks and shoots are a mixed bouquet—asparagus, artichokes and cardoons, celery and Florence fennel, seakale and rhubarb. To all appearances they have little in common except, perhaps, that most of them have enjoyed, at one stage or another in their history, a reputation as aphrodisiacs.

Some stalks and shoots are a luxury in the garden in terms of time, space and effort, but once in the kitchen, patience and effort are rewarded. The unmistakable aroma of asparagus steaming on the stove is like a breath of spring—although Louis XIV, a great vegetable enthusiast, bullied his gardeners into providing him with asparagus in January.

The artichoke, once a strong contender in the aphrodisiac stakes, is a culinary enthusiasm that not all gourmets share; for some people, all those leaves represent a lot of work for little return. To them it is small consolation to be told that in southern countries, where artichokes flourish, the leaves are thrown away together with the chokes and only the delectable hearts are eaten. In Turkey, the hearts are quickly dropped into a bowl of acidulated water to preserve their color. Then they are usually simmered in oil with a handful of baby broad beans, two or three sour green plums and a touch of chopped dill for flavoring. Sometimes they are coated with batter and deep-fried in olive oil.

When globe artichoke plants are about to be replaced they can be made to produce their last crop—of chards. These tender, blanched stalks may be cooked and served like cardoons.

Cardoons grow wild in Turkey, free for the picking, and children chew the stalks raw. But in America cardoons are regarded as vegetable curiosities. In spite of their resemblance to the artichoke (they are called "prickly artichokes" and are closely related), cardoons are grown not for the flower but for the leaf stem. Its flavor is a cross between artichoke and celery. To prepare cardoons, discard the tough outer stalks. Remove the "strings" of the remaining stalks and cut into 5-inch or 2-inch lengths, depending on the recipe. Boil the stalks in salted water with a little lemon juice, to preserve their color, for 20 minutes, or until just tender. Then drain the cardoons and either serve them cold with a vinaigrette dressing, hot with melted butter or in a light cream sauce.

Raw or boiled cardoon stalks are also delicious served with a *bagna cauda*, hot garlic-and-anchovy dip. To make the dip, melt ¼ pound of butter in 8 tablespoons of olive oil in a heavy saucepan. Stir in 6 crushed garlic cloves and 8 anchovy fillets which have been drained, rinsed and finely chopped.

The root of the cardoon is also eaten. It is boiled until tender, sliced and served cold with a vinaigrette dressing.

Unlike cardoons, asparagus and artichokes, celery is an everyday vegetable. It would be sorely missed in the kitchen if the cook were deprived of it, be it in the form of stalks, seeds or salt. Celery can be used not only as a flavoring or garnish, or as part of a *bouquet garni*, but as a vegetable in its own right.

The blanched, bulbous stems of Florence fennel, sweet cousin of the seeds and green fronds of the pungent herb fennel, are rather similar to celery in texture, but very different in flavor. Because fennel has a pungent aniseed taste it is important that it be handled with discretion. Raw or parboiled, it can be grated into a salad, or it can be braised Italian style and served with butter. Fennel can also be baked with tomatoes and grated Parmesan, or frittered, and served with a wedge of lemon to squeeze over the top.

Unlike fennel, which prefers a warm climate, seakale grows wild on the coasts of northern Europe, but is an exotic in America. The leaves are delicious when cooked like spinach or served raw in a salad. The leaves, washed and dried, are torn into pieces, dressed with a vinaigrette sauce and garnished with a sprinkling of finely chopped scallions. The stalks, when blanched like celery and chicory and forced like rhubarb, are a welcome winter vegetable. Many people, however, prefer the flavor of seakale which is not forced and is picked in late spring.

Seakale stalks may be steamed—it takes about 25 minutes; be careful as overcooking toughens the stalks—or simmered gently in stock. Serve the steamed stalks with melted butter or hollandaise sauce or cover them with a good cheese sauce and bake in a 375°F oven for 40 minutes, or until bubbling and golden brown on top.

Forcing plants is the gardener's way of extending their season, particularly through the winter months, when the garden has comparatively little to offer. When forced rhubarb comes on the scene, sour and sharp, it is a refreshing change from the winter's apples and pears, and from imported citrus fruits. Once a weed in Asia, rhubarb is today a very American vegetable. Its crisp pink stalks are used to make compotes, pies and fools, chutneys and jams. The unforced, deeper-hued rhubarb of summer is often combined with other fruits to make more economical but delicious jams.

Rhubarb

Although rhubarb is botanically classed as a vegetable, it is usually thought of as a fruit for stewing, making pies, preserving and making wine. But it can also be substituted for gooseberries to make a mock gooseberry sauce for such oily fish as mackerel, or used to make a sweet soup, a favorite in northeastern Europe.

Make the most of rhubarb, especially in the early days. First to arrive toward the end of winter are the thin, pink stalks of forced rhubarb, to be followed by the thicker outdoor rhubarb, dark red and juicy. More sugar will be needed to sweeten the rhubarb as the season progresses. Some of its acidity can be toned down by blanching the stalks before cooking them with sugar. To blanch rhubarb, pour boiling water over the cut stalks in a pan. Bring the water to the boil again and immediately drain the stalks. Rhubarb cooks quickly and is liable to disintegrate if it is overcooked by even a minute.

The simplest of desserts is a rhubarb compote, 1-inch chunks quickly and gently poached in an orange- or spice-flavored syrup. An unusual and delicious touch can be added by stirring a tablespoonful or two of gin into the ice-cold compote just before serving.

In late spring and early summer, rhubarb combines splendidly with fresh strawberries in a pie, an open tart or stewed in a sauce to serve over pound cake or custard.

Rhubarb will make a particularly delicious crisp. Use 4 tablespoons of butter rubbed into 1 cup of self-rising flour and mix with about ⅔ cup of granulated sugar. Mix 2 or 3 tablespoonfuls in with 2 cups of rhubarb. Heap the rest lightly on top. Bake in a moderate oven for about 1 hour. Or make rhubarb conserve or jam to store in the cupboard. And remember that rhubarb's greatest allies are orange, lemon, preserved or ground ginger, and cinnamon.

Rhubarb Fool

An old English favorite for a late-winter party. Some people like the taste of ginger in rhubarb fool. To try this, add 1 ounce of chopped preserved ginger to the fruit while it is cooking and leave out the orange liqueur.

The same mixture can also be frozen (stir it once or twice as it freezes) to make an unusual ice cream.

Rhubarb fool is delicious served with ladyfingers.

SERVES SIX
1 lb rhubarb
⅔ cup brown sugar
2 tablespoons butter
Grated rind of ½ large orange
1⅓ cups heavy cream
2 tablespoons orange liqueur (optional)

Cut the rhubarb into chunks. Put them in a heavy, enameled pan with the sugar, butter and grated orange rind. Cover the pan tightly and cook over the lowest possible heat for 7 to 10 minutes, or until the rhubarb disintegrates. Mash the rhubarb with the back of a wooden spoon, mixing it with the buttery juices. Set aside to cool.

In a bowl, whisk the cream lightly with the orange liqueur, if used. Fold in the crushed rhubarb, and more sugar if necessary, although the flavor should be rather sharp.

Spoon the fool into small individual glasses and chill thoroughly before serving.

Rhubarb Kissel

This is a simple, refreshing dessert, delicious served with a vanilla custard sauce or light cream.

SERVES FOUR
1 lb rhubarb
1 cup sugar
Juice of 1 large orange
4 tablespoons cornstarch

Cut the rhubarb into chunks and put in an enameled pan. Add the sugar and the orange juice made up to 1⅓ cups with water. Cover tightly and cook over low heat for 10 minutes, or until the rhubarb has disintegrated. Mash the rhubarb with a wooden spoon and mix it with the juices.

Blend the cornstarch to a smooth paste with 6 tablespoons of cold water. Stir it into the hot rhubarb purée. Bring to the boil and cook over low heat, stirring constantly, for 4 minutes, or until the mixture is thick and has lost its floury opaqueness.

Divide between four dishes or pour into a decorative mold rinsed out with cold water. (The pudding will be firm enough to turn out.) Serve very cold.

Rhubarb Pie

Rhubarb varies in the amount of sugar that it needs. Forced pink rhubarb, for example, usually requires less sugar than mature stalks. The 1¼ cups suggested here is an approximation and may need to be adjusted.

SERVES SIX
1 lb rhubarb
Pastry for an 8- or 9-inch two-crust pie
1 egg plus 1 egg yolk
1¼ cups sugar
Grated rind of ½ orange
2 tablespoons flour
Salt
1 tablespoon softened butter
Powdered sugar

Put a baking sheet on the middle shelf of the oven and set the oven to 450°F.

Chop the rhubarb stalks into 1-inch lengths, shorter if they are thick.

Roll half of the pastry out to make a lid for the pie, and the other half to line the bottom and sides of a 2-pint pie pan. Capacity is as important as diameter, but the pan should measure 8 or 9 inches across.

In a bowl, beat the egg and egg yolk with the sugar and grated orange rind until fluffy. Sift in the flour and a generous pinch of salt. Beat until smoothly blended. Fold in the prepared rhubarb.

Spread the mixture in the pastry-lined pie pan and dot with the butter. Brush the rim with water. Place the lid in position and seal the edges, crimping them attractively. Cut slits in the lid to allow steam to escape and brush the top with water.

Put the pie pan on the heated baking sheet and bake the pie for 15 to 20 minutes. Turn the heat down to 350°F and continue to bake it for a further 30 minutes, or until the pastry is puffed and golden brown and the rhubarb feels soft when pierced (through one of the slits) with a skewer.

Serve the pie lukewarm dusted with powdered sugar, with cream or a custard sauce.

Asparagus

Many people would insist that there is only one way to eat fresh asparagus—steamed or boiled and served with melted butter. Those lucky enough to have a superabundance of asparagus, however, may want to try other ways of cooking and serving it.

Fresh young asparagus is tender for most of its length, especially if the stem has been carefully peeled. Bend each stem until it snaps—the break will come at the point where the stem starts to become woody or fibrous. Rinse the stalk carefully, especially around the tight little green buds, which can harbor soil or grit, and nick off any stray buds or leaf points farther down the stem. Then, using a knife or a potato peeler, shave the stalk all the way down, starting below the buds and gradually digging deeper into the stalk as the knife progresses toward the butt. Drop the stalks into a bowl of cold water as you prepare them. Finally, grade the stalks according to thickness. Line up the tips and tie them into neat bundles in two places, under the tips and near the bottom. Trim all the butts to the same length. This will ensure that all the stalks in a bundle are ready at the same time. It is a good idea to leave one stalk loose so that it can be tested without disturbing the bundle.

To cook asparagus requires care. It should be steam-boiled or steamed, but preferably not boiled. This is because the tips are tender but the stalks are less so. The Romans always cooked asparagus upright and this is still considered one of the best ways of cooking it. An asparagus pan, deep and narrow, fitted with a perforated basket, allows the tender tips to cook in steam while the stems boil gently in water. Another special asparagus pan is a steamer fitted with a liner on which the stalks lie flat. The liner can be lifted out easily when the asparagus is ready.

Failing a special steamer, you can improvise with a large saucepan. Stand the bundle of stalks upright in the pan with boiling, lightly salted water to come about three-quarters of the way up, supporting the tips with crumpled foil if necessary to keep them clear of the water. Use more foil to make a "cap" for the tips. Bring the water back to a gentle boil and keep it there for 10 to 15 minutes or until a stalk feels tender when pierced through the butt with the tip of a knife. A little flour worked to a smooth, thin paste with cold water and a tablespoon of white wine vinegar may be added to the cooking water to preserve the color and enhance the delicate flavor.

When the asparagus is tender—and it cooks very quickly indeed (the Romans had a saying about doing something "as quickly as it takes to cook asparagus")—drain the stalks and serve them hot either with melted butter or a buttery sauce (see below). Alternatively, drain them dry on a clean napkin and chill them until required.

Properly cooked, asparagus should be neither crunchy nor so limp that their heads droop right over. Never throw out the cooking water or the trimmings. They make excellent soup.

How much asparagus you allow per portion will depend on the state of your asparagus bed, but $\frac{1}{2}$ pound for each person is a generous and satisfying amount.

Asparagus with Scrambled Eggs
A delicately flavored first course or light luncheon dish. Serve on hot toast or in little pastry shells.

SERVES TWO TO THREE
6 eggs
2 tablespoons heavy cream
Salt
Freshly ground black pepper
2 tablespoons butter
12 asparagus spears, cooked and sliced
2 tablespoons grated Parmesan cheese

In a bowl, beat the eggs and the cream together with a fork until just mixed. Season to taste with the salt and pepper.

Melt the butter in a heavy saucepan. Add the asparagus and cook gently, stirring, for 1 minute. Pour in the egg mixture and, stirring constantly, cook over the lowest possible heat until the eggs begin to set in creamy curds. Stir in the cheese and, as soon as the eggs have set to the right consistency, remove the pan from the heat and serve.

Clear Asparagus Soup
Based on a Chinese recipe, this soup may be made more filling with the addition of rice or fine noodles. Make the stock from $1\frac{1}{2}$ pounds of mixed vegetables—use cabbage stalks, carrots, runner beans, potato peel or any vegetables that are available and simmer for $1\frac{1}{2}$ to 2 hours.

SERVES FOUR
2 oz Chinese dried mushrooms
2 lb asparagus, cut into 2-inch pieces
4 cups clear, strong vegetable or chicken
  stock, strained
1 tablespoon butter
1 tablespoon light soy sauce
$\frac{1}{4}$ teaspoon monosodium glutamate
  (optional)
Salt
Freshly ground pepper

Preheat the oven to 300°F.

In a small bowl, soak the mushrooms in warm water for 30 minutes. Drain them and remove and discard the stems. Cut the mushrooms into quarters.

Put the tougher asparagus pieces and the mushrooms into a casserole. Bring the stock to the boil and pour it into the casserole. Put the casserole into the oven for 30 minutes.

Add the asparagus tips and butter. Stir in the soy sauce and monosodium glutamate, if used. Season to taste with salt, if needed, and pepper. Reduce the oven temperature to 275°F and continue to cook for a further 30 minutes.

Asparagus

Crème d'Asperges

Making soup is a good way of using asparagus which is no longer at its succulent best.

SERVES FOUR TO SIX
1 lb mature asparagus
Salt
1 potato, peeled and sliced
1 small, mild onion, coarsely chopped
2 tablespoons butter
1 tablespoon flour
4 cups hot chicken stock
2 egg yolks
⅔ cup light cream
White pepper

Wash and trim the asparagus and cut it into chunks. Snip off a handful of the best tips to use as a garnish. Put the pieces of asparagus in a pan. Pour in just enough lightly salted water to cover. Add the potato and onion and bring to the boil. Cover the pan, reduce the heat and cook gently for 15 to 20 minutes, or until the vegetables are very soft.

Steam the reserved asparagus tips separately and put them aside until they are needed.

In another pan melt the butter. Blend in the flour and stir over low heat for 1 minute to make a pale roux. Gradually add the chicken stock, stirring vigorously to prevent lumps from forming. Bring the mixture to the boil and pour it into the pan of undrained vegetables.

Purée the contents of the pan in an electric blender or put it through the fine plate of a food mill. If there are any woody fibers still in evidence, rub the purée through a fine sieve. Then pour the mixture back into the rinsed and dried pan.

Beat the egg yolks and cream together just enough to mix them. Stir them into the soup. Season with pepper and a little more salt if necessary. Add the reserved asparagus tips and reheat gently, stirring. Do not let the soup reach boiling point again, or the egg yolks may start to curdle.

If the soup is too thick, thin it down with more hot chicken stock or cream.

Serve immediately.

Asparagus with Hot Butter Sauce

This is a classic first course, the simplest and best way of serving the pick of the crop.

SERVES FOUR
2 lb asparagus, cooked and drained
¼ lb (2 sticks) butter
Lemon juice
4 tablespoons finely chopped parsley
Coarse salt
Freshly ground black pepper

While the asparagus is cooking, melt the butter in a saucepan. Take great care not to let the butter sizzle or color. If you cannot keep an eye on it all the time, put the pan of butter in a larger pan of simmering water until the butter has melted and is very hot. Add lemon juice to taste and stir in the parsley.

Serve the hot asparagus sprinkled with coarse salt and black pepper, and accompanied by individual dishes of butter sauce for dipping.

To prepare asparagus, use a knife to peel each stalk. Peel thickly at the butt end and thinly near the tip.

Asparagus Hollandaise

Sauce hollandaise is another fine accompaniment for asparagus. Hollandaise can be transformed into a sauce mousseline by folding 4 to 6 tablespoons of whipped cream, 1 tablespoon at a time, into the hot hollandaise just before serving. Alternatively, it may be turned into a delicious sauce maltaise by substituting the strained juice of 1 or 2 oranges for the water and lemon juice, and adding the blanched grated rind of 1 orange to enrich its flavor.

SERVES FOUR
2 lb asparagus, cooked and drained
SAUCE HOLLANDAISE
¼ lb (2 sticks) butter
2 teaspoons lemon juice
Salt
White pepper
4 egg yolks

Let the butter stand at room temperature until it is soft but not oily. Divide it into four equal portions.

In the top of a double saucepan, dilute the lemon juice with 1 tablespoon of cold water. Add a pinch each of salt and pepper. Fit the top of the pan over hot but not boiling water. Add the egg yolks and a portion of butter. Stir vigorously with a wire whisk for 5 minutes, or until the ingredients are thoroughly blended and the sauce begins to thicken.

Continue adding the butter, a portion at a time, whisking constantly until it is completely incorporated. (Do not neglect the corners of the pan.) Then continue whisking rapidly until the sauce is very thick.

Taste for seasoning, adding more salt, pepper or lemon juice as necessary, and serve with the hot asparagus.

Using string, make bundles of about ten stalks. Line up the tips and cut off the ends of the stalks.

Baked Asparagus with Pasta

This is an economical way of making a little asparagus go a long way. Served as it is, this dish makes a good accompaniment for all white meats and poultry. It can also be turned into a main dish by the addition of some diced lean ham.

SERVES FOUR
¼ lb macaroni
Salt
½ lb fresh or frozen asparagus
1½ cups hot light cream
Freshly ground black pepper
2 eggs, beaten
5 tablespoons freshly grated
  Parmesan cheese
1 tablespoon butter

Boil the macaroni in a large pan of salted water, following the timing recommended on the package.

Meanwhile, cut the asparagus into ¾-inch lengths and parboil them in just enough salted water to cover until half done—6 to 8 minutes in the case of fresh asparagus, only 4 minutes for frozen asparagus.

Preheat the oven to 400°F.

Drain the asparagus in a strainer held over the pot of boiling macaroni. Then drop the asparagus into a pan containing the hot cream and simmer for 2 minutes. Season to taste with salt and pepper. Cover and put aside.

Drain the macaroni in a colander. Return it to the pan and stir with a wooden spoon over low heat for a minute or two to evaporate any remaining moisture. Cool slightly. Then carefully mix in the asparagus and cream, followed by the eggs and 3 tablespoons of grated Parmesan cheese. Correct seasoning.

Pour the mixture into a well-buttered baking dish. Sprinkle with the remaining Parmesan cheese and dot with butter.

Bake for 20 to 25 minutes, or until the mixture has set and the top is golden and bubbling. Serve hot.

If you do not have an asparagus pan, improvise with a Mason jar. Stand the bundles in a Mason jar almost filled with boiling water. Cover with perforated foil secured with a rubber band. Stand the jar in a pan half-filled with boiling water. After 30 minutes, lift the asparagus from the jar, drain and remove the strings.

Artichokes

With the arrival of spring, the vegetable markets of Rome are piled high with the most exquisite *primizie*, baby vegetables of all kinds, a glorious sight to gladden the heart of the artist as well as the cook. Among them are stacks of tiny globe artichokes so young that they have not yet had a chance to develop their fuzzy chokes. Consequently, they may be cooked and served whole, boiled, braised, deep-fried or baked.

When the choke has developed, true to its name it will be inedible and must be removed either before or after cooking. Before trimming an artichoke, prepare a bowl of water acidulated with lemon juice—1 tablespoon of lemon juice to 1 pint of water—so that the artichoke can be swished around in it each time any cuts are made. The cut surfaces rapidly turn brown if they are not treated in this way. When the artichoke has been prepared, drop the globe, head down, into the bowl of acidulated water and leave it to soak until needed.

The most delectable part of this extraordinary vegetable is the heart, also known as the *fond*, or bottom. Shaped like a little round saucer, it is completely edible. Artichoke hearts discolor easily so rub them well all over with a cut lemon as they are trimmed and then drop them into a bowl of acidulated water until you are ready to cook them. Parboil artichoke hearts in lightly salted, acidulated water for 10 to 15 minutes (to set the color). The hearts are now ready to be cooked further according to the recipe.

To cook the heads, select a pan large enough to allow them plenty of room. Fill the pan with lightly salted water and bring it to a rolling boil. Drop the artichokes into the water and boil them gently, uncovered, for 35 to 45 minutes, or until a leaf can be pulled out easily and the base feels tender when pierced with a skewer. Drain the artichokes thoroughly, heads down, in a colander.

Another way to cook artichokes is to steam them—either in a steamer or on a rack placed in a pan. If neither steamer nor rack is available, place the artichoke heads right way up in 1 to 2 inches of boiling acidulated water and cook, covered, for 40 to 45 minutes or until tender.

A tender globe artichoke makes a fine and simple first course served hot with melted butter or hollandaise, or cold with vinaigrette or an herb-flavored mayonnaise.

To prepare artichoke hearts, break off the tough outer leaves of the artichoke.

With a sharp knife, slice off the artichoke stalk.

The remaining leaves should be cut off above the white base, or heart.

Rub lemon juice over the heart. Finally, slice off the green leaf bases.

Artichokes, Greek Style

These tiny artichokes, picked before the chokes have formed and cooked whole *à la grecque*, may be served as an hors d'oeuvre or added to mixed salad.

SERVES FOUR
20 baby artichokes
Juice of 3 lemons
⅔ cup olive oil
1 teaspoon fennel seeds
1 teaspoon chopped fresh dill
10 peppercorns
Bouquet garni, *consisting of 1 celery stalk, 1 bay leaf, 1 thyme sprig*
1 teaspoon salt

Parboil the artichokes for 5 minutes in enough acidulated water (using the juice of 1 lemon) to cover.

Drain the artichokes in a colander and rinse under cold running water. Drain and set aside.

Put the remaining ingredients in a saucepan and add 2⅔ cups of water. Place the pan over high heat and bring to the boil. Add the artichokes. When the liquid returns to the boil, reduce the heat, cover the pan and simmer for 8 minutes, or until the artichokes are tender.

Remove the artichokes from the pan with a slotted spoon and put them in a bowl. Increase the heat to high and boil the liquid in the pan until it is reduced by half. Pour the liquid, through a strainer, over the artichokes. When the artichokes are cold, cover the bowl and put it in the refrigerator until required.

Artichoke Hearts with Sherried Mushrooms

Artichoke hearts make a particularly luxurious appetizer. Whole artichokes, boiled until they are quite tender, make an equally delicious but less extravagant dish. Spoon the mushrooms and cream into the cavity left by the choke and serve hot. Serve with crusty French bread to mop up the sauce.

SERVES FOUR
8 large artichoke hearts, parboiled
2 cups chicken stock
Lemon juice
½ lb button mushrooms, trimmed
4 tablespoons butter
1 tablespoon cornstarch
1⅓ cups light cream
Salt
Freshly ground black pepper
4 tablespoons dry sherry

Drain the artichoke hearts. Rinse them in cold water and put them in a pan. Pour in the chicken stock and 1 tablespoon of lemon juice and bring to the boil. Cover the pan, reduce the heat and simmer gently for 30 minutes, or until the hearts are tender. Drain and keep hot. Reserve the stock.

If the mushrooms are very small leave them whole. Otherwise, halve or quarter them, or slice them thickly. Melt the butter in a heavy pan. Add the mushrooms and sauté for 2 to 3 minutes, or until lightly colored.

In a small bowl, blend the cornstarch smoothly with the cream and ⅔ cup of the reserved stock. Season to taste with salt and pepper. Stir the mixture into the mushrooms. Bring the mixture to the boil and stir in the sherry. Simmer the sauce over low heat, stirring, for 5 minutes, or until it has thickened and is slightly reduced.

Fold in the artichoke hearts and serve as soon as they are thoroughly hot.

Artichokes

Casserole of Artichokes with Vegetables

This casserole includes a number of summer vegetables which enhance the flavor of the artichokes. Serve the casserole as a separate course or with a main dish of poultry or ham.

SERVES FOUR

8 small tender artichokes or 4 large
    artichokes
Salt
Lemon juice
¼ lb (1 stick) butter
2 Spanish onions, thinly sliced
2 garlic cloves, crushed
8 baby carrots, scraped
4 new potatoes, scraped
2 baby turnips, peeled and quartered
6 celery stalks, cut into 1-inch lengths
Freshly ground black pepper
Bouquet garni, consisting of 2 parsley
    sprigs, 1 thyme sprig, 1 small bay leaf
3 tablespoons dry vermouth
2 cups hot beef stock
⅓ cup button mushrooms
⅓ cup fresh green peas
3 tablespoons chopped parsley

If the artichokes are so young that they are still free of chokes, use them whole. Mature artichokes should be quartered lengthwise so that the chokes can be scooped out easily. Parboil the artichokes, whole or quartered, for 15 minutes in lightly salted, acidulated water. Drain them thoroughly in a colander.

In a heavy, heatproof casserole wide enough to take the artichokes in a single layer, melt 6 tablespoons of the butter. Add the onions and garlic, and cook gently, stirring, until they are soft but not colored.

Arrange the artichokes in the casserole together with the carrots, potatoes, turnips and celery, turning them to coat them with the buttery juices. Season to taste with salt and pepper, and bury the *bouquet garni* in the center. Cook gently for 10 minutes.

Add the vermouth and the stock and bring to the boil. Cover the pan, reduce the heat and simmer for 30 minutes, or until the vegetables are tender but still firm.

Meanwhile, in a small frying pan heat the remaining butter. Add the mushrooms and cook, stirring, until golden. About 10 minutes before the end of cooking time, add them to the casserole together with the peas. Finish cooking uncovered. Sprinkle with chopped parsley and serve.

Cut off the top third of the artichoke. Rub lemon juice over the cut edges or dip into acidulated water.

Using scissors, snip off the tops of the remaining leaves. Rub the cut edges with lemon juice.

Baked Stuffed Artichokes

The stuffing for this recipe can be made in seconds in an electric blender. First drop in the bread, cubed. Then add the onion, cut into chunks, two or three sprigs of parsley, the anchovy fillets, capers and olive oil. Whirl for a few seconds and the stuffing is ready.

SERVES SIX

6 artichokes, chokes removed
Lemon juice
Salt
1½ cups fresh white bread crumbs
1 medium-sized onion, finely chopped
6 anchovy fillets, finely chopped
3 tablespoons finely chopped parsley
2 tablespoons chopped capers
Olive oil
Freshly ground black pepper
2 cups chicken stock

Leave the artichokes to soak in acidulated water for 30 minutes. Parboil them in salted water for 10 minutes and drain thoroughly.

Preheat the oven to 375°F.

To make the stuffing, mix the bread crumbs, onion, anchovies, parsley and capers together. Add 2 tablespoons of olive oil. Season generously with pepper (no salt because of the anchovies) and mix lightly with a fork.

Fill the centers of the artichokes with the stuffing. If there is any filling left stuff it between the leaves, using a spoon.

Select a deep baking dish just large enough to hold the artichokes side by side. Brush it with oil. Brush each artichoke with oil and sprinkle a little of it over the stuffing in the center. Arrange the artichokes in the baking dish. Add the stock and bake for 1 hour, or until a leaf from near the base can easily be pulled out. Baste regularly with the stock, which should almost all have been absorbed by the end of the cooking time. Serve hot.

Pull out the prickly leaves surrounding the choke.

Artichokes with Herb Mayonnaise

Herb mayonnaise is a delicious sauce to serve with any hors d'oeuvre, especially those made with fish or hard-boiled eggs. And just as hollandaise may be served with hot artichokes, spooned into the cavity left by the chokes, so mayonnaise, plain or lightly herbed, is a classic accompaniment for cold asparagus. (See p. 149.)

SERVES SIX

6 artichokes, boiled
HERB MAYONNAISE
4 tablespoons fresh parsley
4 tablespoons watercress
Salt
2 egg yolks
Juice of ½ lemon
½ teaspoon mild French mustard
Freshly ground black pepper
1½ to 2 cups olive oil
2 tablespoons finely chopped fresh
    chervil
1 tablespoon finely chopped fresh
    tarragon

Leave the cooked artichokes to drain and cool upside down in a colander. Then chill in a refrigerator.

Take 2 sprigs each of parsley and watercress. Discard the stalks and chop the herbs finely. Set aside.

Bring a small pan of salted water to the boil. Drop in the remaining parsley and watercress and boil rapidly for 3 to 4 minutes. Drain in a strainer. Spray the herbs with cold water and press them as dry as possible between the folds of a clean cloth or paper toweling. Pound the cooked parsley and watercress in a mortar or purée them in an electric blender.

To make the mayonnaise use ingredients that are at room temperature. The oil should be clear. If it is cloudy, it is too cold.

Put the egg yolks, lemon juice and mustard in a bowl and mix gently with a generous pinch of salt and pepper. Pour the oil into a jug with a good pouring lip and start adding it to the egg yolks a drop at a time, beating vigorously with a spoon, a hand whisk or an electric mixer. As the mayonnaise thickens add the oil in a thin stream. Should it become too thick before all the oil has been incorporated, thin it down with a little more lemon juice or cold water, as the flavor demands.

When the mayonnaise is thick enough to hold its shape on a spoon, whisk in the puréed herbs, followed by all the chopped herbs. Correct the seasoning with more salt, pepper or mustard. Chill the herb mayonnaise until ready to serve.

Serve the artichokes cold with the mayonnaise in a separate bowl.

Scoop out the hairy choke, using a teaspoon. Sprinkle lemon juice over the exposed heart.

Press the artichoke leaves together again and give the cut edges a final rub with a piece of lemon.

Celery is an essential flavoring, a crisp addition to salads and a fine cooked vegetable. Tender young celery is best eaten uncooked; a larger head may be braised or stewed but never boiled. In France, celery is usually blanched in boiling water for 10 minutes and then braised (in a slow oven) on a bed of bacon rinds, onions and carrots in a light veal, chicken or vegetable stock. The braised head is then drained, sliced in half lengthwise and served with a sauce such as béchamel.

In England, a head of celery is traditionally offered with the cheese board in a tall, clear glass with an inch of cold water in the bottom, a nice touch even if there is no great practical justification for the water.

Celery sticks also make a good alternative (economic on calories) to bread or pastry as a base for hors d'oeuvres or snacks. Slice the stalks into short pieces and stuff the channels with a savory mixture—meat or fish pâté; a mixture of cream cheese, sour cream and red caviar; or a fine-flavored blue cheese, Roquefort, Danish blue or Gorgonzola, pounded with a little softened butter and cream and sharpened with a touch of cayenne or paprika.

An attractive celery garnish can be made by slitting short lengths of celery at one end in several places and dropping them into a bowl of iced water. In a short time the slit strands will curl up like little tassels.

Never throw away the green leaves trimmed from the top of a head of celery. They are invaluable for flavoring meatballs, meat loaves, stocks and salads which do not call for the crunchiness of the stalk. They may also be deep-fried until crisp and used to garnish meat or fish dishes, just like parsley sprigs. Alternatively, if you have no immediate use for the trimmed tops, either collect them in a bag in the freezer or spread them out on a baking sheet to dry—over the pilot light of a gas stove or on a radiator. Then crumble the leaves between your hands and store them in a screw-top jar.

Celery Amandine

A distinctive yet subtle combination of flavors, this dish is excellent with roast poultry or fried fish.

SERVES FOUR
1½ lb celery, trimmed
4 tablespoons butter
⅓ cup almonds, blanched and slivered
2 shallots, finely chopped
Salt
Freshly ground black pepper
⅔ cup light cream

Take the head of celery apart and cut the stalks into 1-inch pieces, splitting them lengthwise into two or three if they are very thick.

Heat the butter in a heavy pan. Add the almonds and sauté until crisp and a rich golden color, taking care not to let them burn. Lift out the almonds with a slotted spoon and set them aside.

Add the celery and shallots to the pan, mix well with the hot butter and season generously with salt and pepper. Cover the pan tightly and cook over low heat for 15 minutes, stirring frequently.

Stir in the cream. Replace the lid and continue to cook gently for a further 20 minutes, or until the celery is tender and the cream reduced and thickened.

Mix in the sautéed almonds. Correct the seasoning and cook gently over low heat for 5 minutes before serving to allow the flavors to blend.

Celery with Tomatoes

A vegetable accompaniment that goes well with roasts and other rich meat dishes.

SERVES FOUR
1 medium-sized celery, trimmed
2 tablespoons butter
1 small onion, finely chopped
1 medium-sized carrot, coarsely grated
1 small can peeled tomatoes
4 tablespoons stock
Salt
Freshly ground black pepper

Take the head of celery apart and cut the stalks into bite-size pieces.

Melt the butter in a large pan. Add the onion and carrot and cook, stirring, until softened. Add the celery and stir over moderate heat for 2 to 3 minutes.

Add the tomatoes and the stock and season to taste with salt and pepper. Cover the pan and cook for 30 minutes, stirring occasionally. Then remove the lid and let the mixture bubble, uncovered, for 15 minutes longer, or until the celery is tender and the sauce rich and reduced.

Celery, Date and Apple Salad

Raw fruit and vegetables have long been appreciated for their health-giving qualities. Celery, apple and dates combine well with a yogurt dressing to make a refreshing and attractive salad. It is best to use sour-sweet apples or add a little lemon juice to bring out the contrast of flavors of the main ingredients.

SERVES FOUR
1⅓ cups yogurt
2 tablespoons honey
1 tablespoon finely chopped fresh mint
1 medium-sized celery
12 dates, pitted
2 medium-sized apples
3 tablespoons walnut pieces

Blend the yogurt, honey and mint in an electric blender or, in a small bowl, whisk the yogurt, gradually add the honey and stir in the mint. Set aside.

Chop the celery into ½-inch pieces. Wash the dates in warm water. Dry thoroughly and cut into small pieces. Wash the apples, quarter them and remove the cores. Cut the apple into ½-inch cubes. Put the celery, dates and apple into a salad bowl. Pour in the yogurt dressing and toss gently to mix. Scatter the walnut pieces over the top. Serve immediately or chill until required.

Celery

Baked Celery with Parmesan

With the addition of a little more meat—ham or bacon—this will make a filling main dish on its own.

SERVES FOUR TO SIX
1 large celery, about 2 lb
1 tablespoon olive oil
6 slices streaky bacon, chopped
1 Spanish onion, finely chopped
2 garlic cloves, crushed
4 medium-sized tomatoes,
　peeled and chopped
4 tablespoons stock or water
Salt
Freshly ground black pepper
¾ cup Parmesan cheese, freshly grated

Take the head of celery apart. Trim off the leaves and cut the stalks into 1-inch pieces. Slit the stalks in two or three lengthwise if they are very thick.

Heat the olive oil in a large pan. Add the bacon and sauté until the fat runs. Add the onion and garlic and cook, stirring, over moderate heat until soft and golden. Mix in the celery, the chopped tomatoes, and the stock or water. Season to taste with salt and pepper. Cover the pan tightly and cook gently for 20 minutes, stirring occasionally.

Meanwhile, preheat the oven to 375°F. With a slotted spoon transfer the celery, the bits of bacon and onion to a baking dish. Reduce the juices in the pan by fast boiling before spooning them over the celery. Sprinkle the cheese evenly over the top.

Bake the celery for 30 minutes, or until it is quite tender and the crust on top bubbling and a rich golden brown.

Celery in Madeira Cream

A light and pleasant accompaniment for such dishes as roast chicken and sautéed chicken livers with rice.

SERVES THREE TO FOUR
1 lb trimmed celery stalks
2 tablespoons butter
1 tablespoon olive oil
2 shallots, finely chopped
1 garlic clove, crushed
4 tablespoons chicken stock
Salt
Freshly ground black pepper
Sugar
1 tablespoon flour
4 tablespoons Madeira
1 egg yolk, lightly beaten

Cut the celery stalks into 1-inch pieces, halving them lengthwise if they are thick.

Heat the butter and the oil in a wide pan. Add the shallots and garlic and cook, stirring, until a light golden color. Mix in the celery and moisten with chicken stock. Season generously with salt and pepper, and add a pinch of sugar. Cover the pan tightly and cook over very low heat for 15 to 20 minutes, or until the celery is soft but not mushy.

Mix the flour to a smooth paste with the Madeira and 4 tablespoons of water. Stir the paste into the pan and bring to the boil. Reduce the heat and simmer gently, stirring, for a minute or two. Then remove the pan from the heat and immediately mix in the egg yolk. When the sauce has thickened a little more, correct the seasoning and serve.

Cream of Celery Soup

Celery makes one of the best cream soups—delicately flavored and smooth. The carrots in this recipe add a touch of color to the creamy paleness.

SERVES FOUR TO SIX
1 large celery
2 carrots, thinly sliced
1 small parsnip, thinly sliced
3 tablespoons butter
4 cups chicken stock
About 1⅓ cups creamy milk
Salt
Freshly ground black pepper

Take the head of celery apart, washing each piece carefully, and put aside about 3 ounces of the delicate inner stalks. Slice the rest of the head into thin pieces. Put them in a pan together with the carrots, parsnip and 2 tablespoons of the butter. As soon as the vegetables start to sizzle, cover the pan tightly and cook gently for about 10 minutes, or until they have softened slightly without coloring.

Pour in the stock and bring it to the boil. Cover the pan, reduce the heat and simmer for 30 minutes, or until the vegetables are very soft.

Meanwhile, slice the reserved celery stalks thinly to make a garnish for the soup. Melt the remaining butter in a small pan. Mix in the sliced celery, cover the pan and cook gently for 7 to 8 minutes, or until they are just tender. Set aside.

Blend the cooked diced vegetables and their stock to a smooth cream in an electric blender, or rub them through the finest plate of a food mill. Dilute the soup to the desired consistency with creamy milk. Remember that reheating the soup will also make it thinner. Pour the soup back into the pan. Stir in the celery garnish. Season to taste with salt and pepper, and reheat gently before serving.

Stir-fried Celery with Sesame Sauce

Stir-frying is a quick way of cooking vegetables and one which preserves their color, taste and texture.

The Chinese ingredients in this recipe can be bought at most large supermarkets and at Chinese food shops. If sesame paste is not available substitute smooth peanut butter, either alone or mixed with sesame oil (2 tablespoons peanut butter, 1 tablespoon sesame oil).

SERVES FOUR
1 lb celery
3 tablespoons vegetable oil
1 small onion, finely chopped
2 garlic cloves, crushed
½-inch piece fresh root ginger, peeled
　and shredded
Salt
1 tablespoon dry sherry
1½ tablespoons soy sauce
1 teaspoon sugar
½ teaspoon monosodium glutamate
　(optional)
SESAME SAUCE
5 tablespoons sesame paste
3 tablespoons light stock
2 tablespoons soy sauce
2 tablespoons wine vinegar
2 teaspoons sugar
Chili sauce
5 garlic cloves, crushed

First prepare the sesame sauce. In a saucepan combine the sesame paste with the stock, soy sauce and vinegar. Add the sugar and chili sauce to taste. Cook over low heat, stirring constantly, for 3 minutes. Remove the pan from the heat and stir in the garlic. Set aside.

Cut the celery stalks diagonally in 2-inch pieces. Heat the oil in a large frying pan over high heat. Add the onion, garlic and ginger, and fry, stirring constantly, for 1 minute. Add the celery and salt to taste and reduce the heat to moderate. Turn the celery in the pan until it is well coated with the oil. Stir in the sherry, soy sauce, sugar and monosodium glutamate, if used. Continue to cook for 2 to 3 minutes.

Serve with the reheated sesame sauce in a separate bowl.

To make celery tassels, slice 2-inch-long pieces of celery into thin strips almost to the end. Place in a bowl of iced water. The ends will curl shortly.

Pods & Seeds

Peas, sweet corn and beans of various shapes and sizes—the long history of these pods and seeds embraces the world. Some of them, peas for example, have been in cultivation for so long that they cannot be found in a wild form. Others, such as the bush or runner bean and sweet corn were only introduced into Europe and to the rest of the world after the opening up of the New World.

Broad beans are the only beans that the Old World can claim as its own. Their origins, too, are lost in the mists of prehistory. These are the *ful nabed* of the Pharaohs and the early Copts. The dishes that were made in ancient times are still prepared today—purées, soups and the deep-fried spiced patties called *falafel*, now a national dish in Israel as well as in Egypt.

Dried seeds, such as broad beans and peas, were once a winter mainstay of the European peasants' diet. Some of the recipes have weathered the centuries well. Pease pudding, for example, which was served with the boiled salted meat that appeared so often on the medieval dining table, was much enjoyed by King Edward VII as an accompaniment to pickled pork and is still a popular dish in England today. The broad beans and peas of bygone days, however, were hard, wrinkled and fit only for heavy simple soups and puddings. It took hundreds of years of developing civilization and prosperity for these vegetables to be grown and eaten young, tender and fresh.

It was probably the French, encouraged by the Italians, who first discovered the delights of eating young fresh peas, *petits pois*, lightly cooked or straight from the pod. In one of her letters, dated 1696, Madame de Maintenon describes how the ladies at the French court, "having supped with the King, and supped well," would then retire to the privacy of their chambers to feast in secret on dishes of *petits pois*. "*C'est une mode*," she concluded, "*une fureur*"—it is all the rage.

There is another type of pea—the edible-podded pea. It is harvested when the peas are immature and the whole vegetable—the pea and the pod—is eaten. In France it is known as *mangetout*, literally "eat all"; in other parts of the world it is known variously as snow pea, Chinese pea or sugar pea.

The black-eyed pea, or cowpea, which is so closely associated with Southern cooking, is in reality a close relative of the bean. Okra is another characteristic Southern vegetable.

From China comes the most nutritious of all beans—the soybean. Although in the West soy sauce is taken for granted, and Oriental food enthusiasts have long appreciated the importance of bean curd in the cuisines of China and Japan, only recently have soybeans themselves begun to come to the attention of Western cooks. Hailed as the great miracle protein, soybeans are gradually acquiring a gastronomic, as opposed to a purely nutritional, reputation.

Although the mung bean is probably native to India, it is from China that the West learned how to eat the newly sprouted bean. Easy to germinate, bean sprouts are a crisp and delicately flavored vegetable and also provide a cheap and ready source of vitamins.

Of all the vegetables that came from the New World, the green bean and maize (the two major species are Indian corn and sweet corn) were the most important. The bean has a dual identity. When the pods are young and thin, they make a most delicate green vegetable. Left on the plant to swell to maturity, the beans are husked and dried for storage. Their culinary fortunes make curious reading—the dried beans were introduced to Europe and clever European cooks combined them with meat, turning them into rich casseroles. These dishes then traveled back to America to become adapted to such famous dishes as Boston baked beans.

Maize (Indian corn and sweet corn), too, has an interesting history. Although southern Europe in particular was quick to recognize the potential of Indian corn as a cereal—it is difficult to believe that Italian *polenta* and Romanian *mamaliga* did not exist before the explorers returned from the New World—there was no great enthusiasm for the fresh cobs of sweet corn. They were, and are still, widely grown as cattle fodder. It was America which taught the rest of the world how to prepare and appreciate fresh sweet corn.

Sweet Corn

According to a country saying, "You may walk to the garden to cut the corn, but you must run back to cook it." This may sound exaggerated, but the truth is that as soon as the cobs are cut, the natural sugar in the kernels begins to convert to starch. You can try to replace the lost sweetness by adding sugar to the cooking water, but leave out salt, which toughens the kernels.

Cook the cobs in a large saucepan. Strip off the husks and use some of them to line the bottom of the pan. Pull away the silks and lay the cobs on the husks. Pour over enough boiling water to cover the cobs and boil briskly, with the lid on, for 3 to 5 minutes, or until a kernel can be pried away from the cob easily. Serve with coarse salt and plenty of butter.

When a recipe calls for corn kernels, cook the cob first. Then scrape off the kernels with a sharp knife.

Corn Chowder

SERVES FOUR TO SIX
1 lb potatoes, peeled and diced
Salt
2 oz fat salt pork or unsmoked fat
    bacon in one piece, diced
1 Spanish onion, coarsely chopped
1 tablespoon flour
1⅓ cups milk
2 cups chicken stock
2 cups sweet corn kernels
1⅓ cups light cream
½ sweet green pepper, cored, seeded and
    finely chopped
Freshly ground black pepper
Paprika

Parboil the diced potatoes in salted water for 5 minutes. Drain them thoroughly in a colander and set aside.

In a large saucepan, fry the diced salt pork until the fat runs. Add the onion and continue to fry gently, stirring frequently, until it is soft and lightly colored. Sprinkle with the flour and stir over low heat for 1 minute. Gradually add the milk, stirring to prevent the flour forming lumps. Then add the stock, the corn kernels and the diced potatoes and bring to the boil, stirring. Reduce the heat, cover the pan and simmer gently for 7 to 10 minutes, or until the corn and the potatoes are tender.

Stir in the cream and the chopped pepper. Season to taste with salt, pepper and a pinch of paprika. Bring the soup back to boiling point and serve.

Pan-fried Corn

This dish is especially good served with fried pork chops, lamb chops or fried chicken.

SERVES FOUR
4 tablespoons butter
1 Spanish onion, sliced paper thin
1 sweet green or red pepper, quartered,
    cored, seeded and sliced paper thin
4 cups sweet corn kernels
Salt
Freshly ground black pepper

Melt the butter in a wide, heavy pan. Add the onion and pepper and cook gently, stirring, until the pepper is limp and the onion is a pale golden color. Add the corn. Season to taste with salt and pepper. Cook gently, stirring frequently, for 6 to 8 minutes.

If the dish is not to be served immediately, cover the pan and put it aside. Then reheat gently, stirring, just before serving. Serve hot.

Sweet Corn Fritters

Ideally served with maple syrup, these corn fritters make a delicious snack.

MAKES ABOUT TWELVE FRITTERS
3 cups cooked corn kernels
5 tablespoons heavy cream
4 tablespoons fine cornmeal
2 teaspoons sugar
½ teaspoon baking powder
Pinch of salt
2 eggs, separated
Butter, for frying

Drain the corn kernels thoroughly. Purée all the ingredients except the egg whites and butter in an electric blender. In a small bowl, whisk the egg whites until stiff but not dry. Fold them gently but thoroughly into the corn mixture.

Heat plenty of butter in a frying pan. Drop the batter into the pan in tablespoonfuls, well apart as they tend to spread, and fry the fritters until they are golden brown on both sides, turning them over once.

Serve straight from the frying pan.

Corn Soufflé

This substantial soufflé is a fine luncheon dish. Serve it with a green salad.

SERVES FOUR
2 tablespoons butter
2 tablespoons flour
1⅓ cups light cream
1 green pepper, cored, seeded and
    chopped
4 cups corn kernels
2 large eggs, separated
Salt
Freshly ground black pepper
¼ lb sliced bacon, grilled crisply and
    crumbled

Preheat the oven to 400°F. Grease a soufflé dish with butter and dust thoroughly with flour.

Melt the butter in a saucepan. Stir in the flour until it is well blended. Pour in the cream slowly, stirring constantly until the sauce is smooth. Stir in the green pepper and the corn and bring the mixture to the boil. Remove the pan from the heat.

In a small bowl beat the egg yolks lightly. Stir in some of the hot corn-and-cream mixture. Pour the egg mixture into the pan and return it to low heat. Cook gently, stirring constantly, for

5 minutes. Season to taste with the salt and pepper. Remove the pan from the heat and stir in the bacon. Cool the mixture slightly.

In a bowl, whip the egg whites until stiff but not dry and fold them carefully into the corn mixture. Pour the mixture into the soufflé dish and put it in the oven.

Reduce the heat to 350°F and bake for 30 minutes, or until the soufflé has risen and is golden brown on top and a knife or skewer plunged into the center comes out clean. Serve immediately.

Using a sharp knife, slice the stalk off the corn. Reserve the husks to cook with the cobs.

Peas

Pisum sativum—this name covers a variety of plants each of which, in the eyes of the cook if not the botanist, provides a very different vegetable, ranging from green garden peas to snow peas—specially cultivated for their pods —and dried and split peas.

Snow peas are so delicate that care must be taken in their preparation. If they are very young and delectably tender, just top and tail the pods and serve them raw in salads. More mature pods require stringing. The best way to cook snow peas is to steam them with a little butter for 5 minutes. They may also be boiled in salted water for about 2 minutes, or until they are just tender. Drain well, season and toss in hot melted butter before serving. Alternatively, stir-fry them for 5 minutes in the Chinese style.

The stage at which green peas are picked is a matter of taste. The French and Italians like them very small and sweet. Anglo-American taste seems to favor rather larger, more mature peas. If they are very large and floury, however, no amount of sugar in the cooking water will disguise the fact that they are overgrown, and it is best to make them into a fresh pea soup or purée.

Do not throw pea pods away. They may be simmered in the stock that will provide the foundation for a pea soup. Or they may be cooked, puréed and used to thicken the soup, for when the pods are put through a food mill their papery linings are left behind.

Fresh Pea Soup

Frozen peas or mature peas may be used for this soup. In summer, to serve the soup cold leave out the egg and instead dilute the soup with more cream. A few drops of lemon juice will also add a refreshing touch.

SERVES FOUR
1 lb green peas
1 medium-sized potato, peeled and thickly sliced
1 small, mild onion, thickly sliced
5⅓ cups well-flavored chicken stock
⅔ cup light cream
1 egg yolk
Salt
Sugar (optional)
Tiny croutons, to garnish

Boil the peas, potato and onion in the stock, covered, for 20 minutes, or until all the vegetables are very soft. Purée the contents of the pan in an electric blender or use a food mill.

Return the purée to the pan and bring it to the boil, stirring. Remove the pan from the heat.

Beat the cream and egg yolk together lightly and stir into the pan. Season with salt and a little sugar if necessary. Reheat the soup, but do not allow it to boil again as this will cause the egg yolk to curdle.

Garnish each portion with tiny croutons and serve immediately.

Chinese Snow Peas

Use a mild-flavored vegetable oil to stir-fry the peas, not olive oil, which has too strong a flavor of its own.

SERVES FOUR
1 lb snow peas
2 tablespoons vegetable oil
½ chicken stock cube
Salt
1 tablespoon lard

Wash the snow peas and drain in a colander. Top and tail them and string them as you would green beans, patting them dry with paper toweling if there is any moisture left on them.

Heat the oil in a wide, heavy pan. Add the pea pods and stir them over low heat for ½ minute. Crumble the stock cube and sprinkle a little salt over the pods. Add 4 tablespoons of hot water and stir-fry for ½ minute longer.

Remove the pan from the heat. Stir and turn the pea pods carefully for 1 minute. Return the pan to moderate heat and cook the pods, stirring, until most of the liquid has evaporated.

Add the lard in small pieces and stir over low heat until it has melted and the pods glisten. Serve immediately.

Petits Pois à la Française

Buttered peas with lettuce is a classic dish from France, the country that taught the world how to eat fresh green peas.

SERVES THREE TO FOUR
6 tablespoons butter
2 lb small green peas
2 shallots, finely chopped
1 medium-sized, crisp head lettuce heart, shredded
1 teaspoon sugar
Salt

In a pan with a tight-fitting lid melt the butter gently with 6 tablespoons of water. Mix in the peas, shallots and lettuce. Add the sugar and salt to taste. Cover tightly and cook gently, shaking the pan occasionally, for about 10 minutes, or until the peas are tender.

Remove the lid and cook for 1 or 2 minutes longer to evaporate any excess liquid.

Peas and Turnips

This delectable French dish, made with tender young vegetables, may be served either with cold meat or pâté, or alone after the main course.

SERVES FOUR
1 lb young turnips, peeled
1 cup water
4 tablespoons butter
2 savory sprigs
Salt
Freshly ground black pepper
Sugar
1½ lb shelled green peas
4 tablespoons lightly whipped cream

Cut the turnips into strips. Bring the water to the boil in a large saucepan. Add the turnips, half the butter, the savory and salt, pepper and sugar to taste.

Simmer the turnips, uncovered, for 5 minutes. Add the peas and the remaining butter and continue to cook, uncovered, until the vegetables are tender and almost all the liquid has evaporated.

Remove and discard the savory. Stir in the cream and adjust the seasoning.

"The peascod greene oft with no little toyle
Hee'd seeke for in the fattest, fertil'st soile,
And rend it from the stalks to bring it to her
And in her bosome for acceptance woo her."

Britannia's Pastorals *by William Browne of Tavistock*

Delicate mangetout *peas may be lightly steamed, boiled or stir-fried in a frying-pan or* wok—*the round-bottomed metal pan traditionally used in China.*

"I eat my peas with honey,
I've done it all my life.
It makes the peas taste funny
But it keeps 'em on the knife!"

Black-eyed Peas & Okra

Though unrelated botanically, black-eyed peas and okra are two of the vegetables that are most closely associated with the South. Both are natives of the Old World tropics. The black-eyed pea (*Vigna sinensis*) is known abroad as the China bean, and is more closely related to the bean than to the pea. Okra (*Hibiscus esculentus*) is actually a vegetable fruit, but its pod, or fruit, must be picked in the tender, unripe state to be edible.

Thomas Jefferson, who, among other talents, set one of the best tables ever enjoyed in America, mentioned black-eyed peas appreciatively in his 1774 *Garden Book*. In summer the peas were picked early in the morning, kept cool in spring water and savored, briefly cooked with bacon or salt pork, at supper. In winter they were dried and formed the basis of baked-bean-type casseroles seasoned with country ham, wild duck or sausages.

Okra, known as gumbo, along with filé powder made from dried sassafras leaves, is the distinctive ingredient that gives character and flavor to the soups and stews of Creole cooking. Such nineteenth-century travelers from Europe as Harriet Martineau and Fredrika Bremer generally found the French-and-Spanish-accented cuisine of New Orleans an oasis amid the rough frontier cooking of the time. But there are those who dislike the sticky quality of the okra pod. Combined with tomatoes, onions and sometimes peppers, okra forms the basis of soups, vegetable and seafood dishes, and chicken stews. Or the pods may be eaten as a salad, briefly simmered, dressed with a vinaigrette sauce and served with sliced fresh tomatoes.

Hoppin' John

Found in various versions throughout the Carolinas, Florida and as far away as Texas, this dish is served on New Year's Day with a dime hidden in its midst that brings luck to the finder. Legend has it named after a fast-moving waiter in Charleston.

SERVES SIX

2 cups dried black-eyed peas
2 ham hocks or a piece of salt pork weighing ½ lb
1 teaspoon salt
¼ teaspoon pepper
1 cup long-grain rice

Soak the peas overnight in cold water. In a large pot boil the ham hocks or pork for 1 hour. Add the peas, salt and pepper, and cook for 30 minutes more, or until the peas are nearly done. Then add the rice and cook 12 to 14 minutes, or until the rice is tender. Slice the pork or remove the meat from the ham hocks and shred. Keep the meat warm. Drain the rice and peas and fluff over steaming water. Serve with the meat on the side or on top.

Black-eyed Pea Casserole

This casserole resembles a French *cassoulet* and might be an idea that Jefferson borrowed on his trips to France.

SERVES SIX TO EIGHT

2 cups dried black-eyed peas
1 tablespoon salt
Freshly ground black pepper
½ cup diced salt pork
2 onions, sliced
1 stalk celery, chopped
1 cup diced country ham
1 lb pork sausages, cooked
½ cup dried bread crumbs
2 tablespoons butter

Soak the peas overnight. Drain the peas, put them in a large pot and cover with plenty of fresh cold water. Add salt and pepper and ¼ cup of salt pork and simmer for 1 hour, or until peas are tender. In a large saucepan heat remaining salt pork until it melts, then add the vegetables. When they are soft and golden, add the country ham and the cooked sausages and sauté till brown. Stir to prevent sticking.

Preheat the oven to 350°F.

Layer the beans and the meat mixture in a 3-quart casserole and barely cover with water in which the peas were cooked. Sprinkle top with the dried bread crumbs and dot with the butter. Bake for 1 hour, or until a crust forms.

Okra Soup

In this recipe for okra soup, beef stock is used instead of the more conventional chicken, making a heartier beginning for a winter meal.

SERVES FOUR

1 lb tender okra pods
1 large onion, finely chopped
½ green pepper, chopped
1 tablespoon olive or vegetable oil
Flour
1 tomato, peeled and chopped
Salt
Freshly ground black pepper
6 cups beef stock

To prepare the okra, slice off the stem ends, but leave the pods whole. In a large saucepan sauté the onion and pepper in the oil until soft and golden. Sprinkle with the flour and make a brown roux. Then add the okra and the tomato to the pan and simmer briefly. Season to taste with salt and pepper. Meanwhile, heat the beef stock, and when it starts to boil, add the okra mixture. Let it simmer, uncovered, for 30 minutes, or until it thickens.

Shrimp Gumbo

This is a version of the universal Creole gumbo that may contain any seafood or chicken.

SERVES FOUR

2 onions, chopped fine
1 green pepper, minced
2 tablespoons butter
1 tablespoon flour
1 lb tomatoes, canned or fresh, peeled and chopped
1 lb okra, sliced
1 clove garlic, minced
1 stalk celery, chopped
Salt
Freshly ground black pepper
Pinch of cayenne
1 lb medium shrimp, shelled

In a large saucepan sauté the onions and pepper in the butter until golden. Add the flour and make a light-brown roux. Then add the tomatoes, okra, garlic, celery and seasonings to taste and simmer until the mixture starts to thicken. Add the shrimp and cook 15 minutes, or until the shrimp are pink and firm.

Green Beans

When a recipe calls simply for "green beans" the cook is left to decide whether to use string beans (*haricots verts*) or runner beans. The choice is a matter of taste. When young, string beans are slender and stringless and have a more delicate flavor than the coarser, larger runner bean. The string bean is cooked and served whole, while the runner is either sliced diagonally or in long strips. The runner bean is more favored in Britain. In America and on the Continent, the string bean is preferred, although farther south, toward the eastern Mediterranean, the runner bean is considered superior.

Delicately flavored, young string beans need the minimum of cooking. Runner beans, which are less fragile, can be submitted to prolonged simmering, in a casserole for example, without loss of flavor or texture.

Both string and runner beans should be so fresh that they can be broken in half with a crisp snap. If they seem rather wilted, revitalize them by putting them in a plastic bag and chilling them in the vegetable compartment of the refrigerator.

Very young beans, in particular string beans, need only be topped and tailed before cooking.

More mature beans, especially the runners, can be stringy. Shave around the pods with a sharp knife or a vegetable peeler.

To avoid overcooking, string beans should be steamed, preferably, or boiled for about 5 minutes if very young, 12 to 15 minutes for older ones. Refresh the beans in a colander under running cold water, then reheat them gently in butter in a covered pan, shaking the pan frequently. They should remain *al dente*—slightly resistant to the bite.

The simplest, and many say the best, way of serving fresh beans is with salt, freshly ground black pepper, and plenty of butter or buttered bread crumbs spooned over the top. Another way to serve beans is with hot, crisp-fried bacon together with its fat in place of butter. Or toss the hot beans with sliced, white button mushrooms or a handful of blanched, slivered almonds which have been fried in butter to a rich golden color.

Cold cooked beans are delicious when dressed with a vinaigrette and sprinkled with fresh herbs. Leftover green beans dressed in this way frequently appear on French tables as part of a mixed hors d'oeuvre.

Bean Soup

String beans and dried flageolet beans make an interesting combination and produce a soup of a delicate green color. If flageolet beans are not available, dried white beans may be substituted.

SERVES FOUR TO SIX
2 oz flageolet beans, soaked
1 celery stalk, chopped
4 cups chicken stock
1 lb mature string beans
2 tablespoons butter
4 teaspoons flour
1⅓ cups milk
Salt
Freshly ground black pepper
Lemon juice
Light cream or half-and-half
Freshly chopped parsley or chervil,
  to garnish

Drain the soaked flageolet beans. Put them in a saucepan with the celery and 2⅔ cups of chicken stock. Place the pan over high heat and bring to the boil. Cover the pan tightly, reduce the heat and simmer for 45 minutes, or until the beans are soft. Add the string beans and the remaining stock. Replace the lid and cook gently for 15 minutes.

Meanwhile, melt the butter in another pan. Blend in the flour smoothly and stir over low heat for 1 minute to make a pale roux. Gradually add the milk, stirring vigorously to prevent lumps forming. Continue to stir until the sauce comes to the boil and thickens slightly.

Add some of the bean liquor to the sauce. Then pour all of the sauce over the beans and bring to the boil. Cover the pan, reduce the heat and continue to cook gently until all the beans are soft enough to purée.

Purée the contents of the pan in an electric blender or food mill. If the green beans are at all stringy, rub the purée through a fine sieve as well.

Return the purée to the pan. Season to taste with salt, pepper and lemon juice. Dilute the soup to the desired consistency with cream or half-and-half. Correct the seasoning and garnish with finely chopped parsley or chervil before serving.

Haricots Verts à la Paysanne

A rather elaborate dish, but substantial and one which is well worth the trouble.

SERVES FOUR
1½ lb young string beans
Salt
2 small potatoes, peeled and diced
¼ lb fat salt pork or unsmoked bacon,
  in one piece
4 tablespoons butter
2 medium-sized, mild onions, finely
  chopped
8 young carrots, thickly sliced
2 teaspoons sugar
1⅓ cups light chicken stock or water
Freshly ground black pepper
2 tablespoons finely chopped parsley

Top and tail the beans and cut them at a slant into 2-inch lengths. Boil them in salted water for 12 minutes, or until tender but still very firm. Drain thoroughly.

Parboil the potatoes in salted water for 5 minutes. Drain well.

Meanwhile, cut the fat salt pork or bacon into short, thick strips. Put them in a small pan. Cover with cold water. Bring to the boil and parboil for 5 minutes. Drain thoroughly and dry on paper toweling.

Melt the butter in a heavy pan. Add the pork or bacon strips and fry, stirring, until they are golden and the fat is transparent. Add the onions and carrots and fry gently until golden. Sprinkle

with the sugar. Add half of the stock or water and cook gently until the liquid has evaporated and the vegetables are slightly caramelized.

Add the potatoes and the beans to the onion-and-carrot mixture. Mix well and pour in the remaining stock or water. Season to taste with salt and pepper. Cover the pan and cook until all the vegetables are soft but not mushy. Serve very hot, sprinkled with the chopped parsley.

Use a sharp knife to top and tail green beans.

Green Beans

Green Beans en Salade

This is the simplest bean salad of all. Add a crushed clove of garlic or a tablespoon of chopped fresh basil to the dressing, and wedges of tomato, a few black olives, chopped anchovy fillets and hard-boiled egg quarters to the beans and serve the salad as a light main course for a summer lunch.

SERVES THREE TO FOUR
1 lb young string beans
Salt
6 tablespoons olive oil
2 tablespoons mild wine vinegar, cider vinegar or lemon juice
Sugar
Freshly ground black pepper
1 small, mild onion, finely chopped
2 tablespoons finely chopped parsley

Cook the beans in a large pan of rapidly boiling salted water for about 10 minutes, or until they are just tender and still on the crunchy side. Drain thoroughly and set aside in a bowl.

Meanwhile, make the dressing. Mix the oil, vinegar or lemon juice, and the sugar, salt and pepper to taste. Stir in the onion and parsley.

Pour the dressing over the hot cooked beans and let them cool completely. Toss lightly just before serving.

Italian Beans with Tomato Sauce

The Italian name of this dish, *Fagiolini rifatti*, means "twice-cooked beans." If ripe, flavorsome tomatoes are not available, use instead 2 cups of canned Italian peeled tomatoes, together with the liquid.

SERVES SIX
2 lb young string beans
Salt
2 garlic cloves, lightly bruised
6 tablespoons olive oil
1 lb ripe tomatoes, peeled and chopped
1 tablespoon chopped fresh basil
Freshly ground black pepper

Cook the beans in a large pan of rapidly boiling salted water for about 10 minutes.

Meanwhile, in a large saucepan, sauté the garlic in the oil until golden. Remove and discard the garlic. Add the tomatoes and basil to the oil and cook over high heat for 10 minutes. Season to taste with salt and pepper.

Drain the beans thoroughly. Add them to the tomatoes and simmer for 15 minutes, or until the sauce is rich and reduced. Correct the seasoning and serve.

String Beans with Peppers and Parmesan Cheese

Serve this dish as an accompaniment to a strongly flavored meat dish or a main-course quiche or tart.

SERVES FOUR
2 tablespoons vegetable oil
1 tablespoon butter
1 green pepper, cored, seeded and thinly sliced
1 shallot, finely chopped
1 garlic clove, crushed
1 lb young string beans

1 tablespoon chopped fresh basil or 2 teaspoons dried basil
Salt
Freshly ground black pepper
4 tablespoons freshly grated Parmesan cheese

Heat the oil and butter in a wide, heavy pan. Add the green pepper, shallot and garlic and fry until the pepper strips have wilted and the shallot is soft and golden.

Add the beans, turning them over to coat them with the buttery juices. Sprinkle with the basil and season to taste with salt and pepper. Pour in $\frac{2}{3}$ cup of boiling water. Cover the pan and cook over moderate heat for 10 minutes, or until the beans are tender but still firm. If at the end of the cooking time there is too much liquid left, raise the heat and cook briskly for a minute or two longer to evaporate the excess moisture. Remove the pan from the heat.

Gently mix in the cheese. Correct the seasoning and leave, covered, for a few minutes before serving.

Runner Beans à la Grecque

A Mediterranean appetizer or main course to enjoy at an informal lunch, this dish can be served in the Greek style—lukewarm with crusty bread to soak up the sauce.

SERVES FOUR TO SIX
2 lb runner beans
Salt
1 large, mild onion, finely chopped
4 large, ripe tomatoes, blanched, peeled and chopped

6 tablespoons finely chopped parsley
6 tablespoons olive oil
2 teaspoons sugar
Freshly ground black pepper

String the beans and slice them lengthwise into thin strips. Put the beans in a colander. Sprinkle them generously with salt and rub the salt gently into the beans. Set aside for 1 hour to allow the beans to wilt and soften.

Rinse the beans thoroughly under cold running water, then shake off as much moisture as possible.

In a heavy pan, combine the beans with the onion, tomatoes, parsley and olive oil. Sprinkle with the sugar and add a generous grinding of pepper. Add just enough boiling water to cover. Bring to simmering point, partially cover the pan and cook gently for 30 minutes, or until the beans are tender and the sauce is thick. Remove the pan from the heat and set aside to cool.

Correct the seasoning with salt, more pepper or sugar and serve lukewarm in the Greek style, or cold.

String Beans in Mushroom Cream Sauce

If the mushrooms are very small and white, trim their stems and halve or quarter them. Otherwise, they should be thickly sliced.

SERVES FOUR
1 lb young string beans
Salt
4 tablespoons butter
1 small, mild onion, finely chopped
¼ lb button mushrooms
Lemon juice
6 tablespoons light cream
Freshly ground black pepper

Drop the beans into a large pan of fast-boiling salted water and cook them briskly for 10 minutes, or until tender but still crisp.

Meanwhile, melt the butter in a large, wide pan and fry the onion gently until soft and golden. Add the mushrooms. Squeeze a little lemon juice over them to prevent them discoloring and cook gently for a further 3 to 5 minutes, or until they are golden and have softened slightly.

Drain the beans thoroughly and mix them with the onion and mushrooms. Add the cream and season to taste with salt and pepper. Cook over low heat, stirring gently, until the sauce comes to simmering point; then let it bubble for about 3 minutes until the sauce is reduced to a thick coating consistency. Serve immediately.

Broad Beans & Lima Beans

A pocketful of boiled broad beans, still warm from the pot, was the favorite snack of small boys in eastern Europe. More elegant is the Roman custom of nibbling raw baby broad beans with pieces of Pecorino cheese and a glass of white wine.

When broad beans are very young, before most people would consider gathering them for shelling, they are delicious boiled and eaten in the pod. When the beans are very large and mature, their tough outer skins must be peeled off after the beans have been cooked.

The lima bean, a native of Central America, migrated north and east, but never successfully crossed the ocean. This very American bean is eaten both young and mature, and is one of the most popular dried beans for winter consumption. However, it is at its most delicious as a baby lima, shelled, simmered and served with butter.

Buttered Broad Beans

This is a way to serve broad beans in the pod. They must be very young, the pods thin and not more than 4 or 5 inches (10 or 13 cm) long.

SERVES FOUR
1 lb baby broad beans
Salt
4 tablespoons butter, softened
1 tablespoon chopped fresh chervil or
*   2 teaspoons dried chervil*
1 tablespoon finely chopped parsley
Lemon juice
Coarse salt
Freshly ground black pepper

Top and tail the broad beans and cut each one diagonally into three or four pieces. Drop them into a bowl of cold water and leave them to soak until needed.

Bring a large pan of salted water to the boil. Drain the beans in a colander and drop them into the boiling water. When the water returns to the boil, cook the beans briskly for 10 minutes, or until tender.

Meanwhile, cream the butter with the chopped herbs and a few drops of lemon juice. Divide the herb butter into 4 equal pats.

Drain the cooked beans thoroughly. Return them to the pan and toss over high heat for 1 to 2 minutes to evaporate the excess moisture. Season to taste with the coarse salt and a grinding of pepper.

Serve the beans very hot, each portion topped with a pat of herb butter.

Broad Beans with Bacon

A simple, easy way to prepare broad beans.

SERVES FOUR TO SIX
2 tablespoons butter
4 slices unsmoked bacon, diced
1 medium-sized onion, finely chopped
1 lb shelled broad beans
⅔ cup stock or water
Salt
Freshly ground black pepper

Melt the butter in a heavy pan. Add the bacon and onion and fry until the onion is soft but not colored. Stir in the beans. Add the stock or water and bring to the boil. Cover the pan tightly and cook over moderate heat until the beans are soft but not mushy.

If there is too much liquid left by the time the beans are ready, boil them briskly, uncovered, for 1 to 2 minutes to evaporate the excess moisture. Correct the seasoning with salt and pepper. Serve immediately.

Succotash

This traditional dish is of Indian origin. Colonists, such as the Pennsylvania Dutch, added further refinements to the basic beans and corn, thus taking advantage of the rich summer profusion of vegetables from their gardens. This may be made with young or mature beans.

SERVES FOUR
2 lb lima beans, shelled
Salt
4 tablespoons butter
1 large onion, chopped
1 green pepper, chopped
2 cups cooked corn kernels
Freshly ground black pepper

Simmer the lima beans in a pot of salted water until easily pierced with a skewer. In a saucepan melt 2 tablespoons of the butter and fry the onion and pepper until brown. Add the cooked lima beans and the corn and stir until heated through. Add the remaining butter and season with salt and pepper to taste.

Barbecued Baked Lima Beans

This is the kind of Western dish that developed along the Texas border with Mexico and traveled north. The amount of chili powder depends on how authentic one wants the Tex-Mex flavor to be.

SERVES SIX TO EIGHT
2 cups dried lima beans
5 cups cold water
1 tablespoon salt
1 small onion, chopped
1 clove garlic, minced
1 green pepper, chopped
2 tablespoons butter or margarine
1 teaspoon prepared mustard
2 teaspoons Worcestershire sauce
1 teaspoon to 2 tablespoons chili powder
⅓ cup vinegar
1 cup tomato purée
¼ lb salt pork, diced, or bacon strips

Wash the lima beans and soak them overnight in 5 cups of cold water. In the morning, be sure there is enough water to cover the beans by 1 inch, add salt and put on to boil. Cook until the beans are tender, about 30 minutes. Drain, reserving 2 cups of the bean liquor.

In a saucepan brown the onion, garlic and green pepper in the butter. Add the bean liquid, seasonings and tomato purée. Add more salt to taste. Cook until the mixture starts to thicken, about 5 minutes.

Preheat oven to 350°F.

Put a layer of beans in the bottom of a greased 2-quart casserole, cover with the sauce, then add more beans and sauce. Top with the diced salt pork or the bacon strips and bake for 1 hour.

Dried White Beans

Ideally, white beans should be eaten when they are newly dried. They may be stored, of course, but they become tougher with keeping and the older the bean the longer it must be soaked before cooking. Young dried beans should be covered with cold water, brought to the boil, boiled for 1 minute, then left to soak in the covered pan for 1 hour. Drain the beans thoroughly; cover them with fresh unsalted water and boil them for about 30 to 40 minutes, or until the skin of a bean bursts when you lift it out and blow on it gently.

Serve cooked dried beans in the Mediterranean style as a cold appetizer, dressed with a well-flavored vinaigrette and plenty of chopped fresh parsley. Dried beans are used in many famous Tuscan dishes, such as *fagioli al tonno*, beans and tuna fish, and *ribollita*, a bean soup, or *fagioli nel fiasco*, beans cooked with garlic and olive oil in a Chianti bottle.

Fagioli al Tonno

One of the finest *antipasti* to come out of Italy, this is an earthy and deliciously satisfying dish. Its very simplicity makes it all the more important that its ingredients be of the best quality. Use good beans and Spanish or Italian tuna fish packed in olive oil.

SERVES FOUR TO SIX
1 cup dried beans, soaked
6 tablespoons olive oil
2 tablespoons mild wine vinegar
1 plump garlic clove, crushed
Salt
Freshly ground black pepper
7-oz can white tuna in olive oil
1 large, mild onion, thinly sliced
2 tablespoons finely chopped parsley

Drain the soaked beans. Cover them with fresh cold water and boil them until their skins burst when blown upon. Cooking time depends on the age of the beans. Begin testing the beans when they have cooked for 30 minutes.

Meanwhile, make a well-seasoned dressing. Beat the oil with the vinegar, garlic, salt and pepper. Empty the can of tuna into a bowl, together with its oil, and break it up roughly with a fork.

When the beans are tender, drain them thoroughly and put them in a serving dish. While the beans are still hot pour over the dressing, the tuna and its oil and the sliced onion. Mix gently but well.

Serve lukewarm or cold, garnished with parsley.

Baked Beans in White Wine

A variation on the familiar baked beans, with a French flavor.

SERVES FOUR
2 cups dried beans, soaked
2 Spanish onions
4 cloves
1 lb fat salt pork or
  unsmoked bacon, in one piece
2 tablespoons butter
4 tablespoons molasses
½ bottle medium dry white wine
3 tablespoons dark rum
2 teaspoons dry mustard
¼ to ½ teaspoon crushed, dried red
  peppers
Salt

Drain the soaked beans. Put them in a large saucepan and cover them with fresh cold water. Add the whole onions, each one stuck with 2 cloves. Put the pan over moderate heat and bring to the boil slowly. Boil gently for 30 minutes, or until the bean skins burst when blown upon.

Meanwhile, cut the pork or bacon in half. Slash the rind and fat on top in several places. Put the pieces of pork or bacon in a bowl. Cover them with boiling water and leave them to soak for 30 minutes.

Preheat the oven to 275°F.

Drain the beans, reserving their cooking liquor. Lift out the onions and as soon as they are cool enough to handle, discard the cloves and chop the onions coarsely.

Rinse and dry the pan. Melt the butter in it and fry the onions gently until they are lightly colored. Remove the pan from the heat. Stir in the molasses, wine, rum, mustard, red peppers and the cooked beans. Mix well and season lightly with salt. (Remember the saltiness of the pork or bacon with which they will cook.)

Drain the pork or bacon thoroughly. Lay one piece at the bottom of a heavy, ovenproof casserole with a tight-fitting lid. Pour the bean mixture over the top and bury the other piece of pork or bacon in the center so that only the top is visible.

Bake, covered, for 3½ hours. Remove the lid and continue baking for another 30 minutes. If the beans dry out too quickly during cooking, moisten them with some of the reserved bean liquor. At the end of the cooking time the sauce should be rich and reduced.

Correct the seasoning with more salt if necessary. Serve from the casserole.

Dried Beans with Roast Lamb

Try this dish when you are next roasting a leg or shoulder of lamb. It is extraordinarily good and a marvelous alternative to the usual dish of potatoes or rice. If you should find the lamb flavor too strong, increase the beans by ¼ to ⅜ cup rather than disturb the balance of the sauce.

SERVES FOUR
1 cup dried beans, soaked
2 tablespoons butter
2 tablespoons lamb fat, finely chopped
1 medium-sized Spanish onion, finely
  chopped
2 garlic cloves, crushed
2 cups canned Italian peeled tomatoes
6 tablespoons pan juices from the
  roasting lamb
Salt
Freshly ground black pepper
Finely chopped parsley, to garnish

Drain the soaked beans. Put them in a large pan, cover with plenty of fresh cold water and bring to the boil over high heat. Cover the pan, reduce the heat and simmer for 30 minutes or longer, depending on the age of the beans, or until they are barely tender and far from mushy.

Meanwhile, melt the butter in a heavy pan and fry the pieces of lamb fat (sliced from the roast before it was put into the oven) until the fat runs. Add the onion and garlic and fry until soft and golden. Add the tomatoes, with their juice, and cook gently, uncovered, for 15 minutes, or until they are reduced to a thick pulp. Cover the pan and set aside.

When the beans are soft, drain them thoroughly. Mix them gently into the tomato sauce, together with the juices from the roasting lamb. Season to taste with salt and pepper. Cover the pan and continue to simmer gently for 30 minutes, stirring occasionally.

Sprinkle with parsley and serve.

Soybeans

Although soybeans have been cultivated in Asia for more than three thousand years, in the West, until recently, they were considered suitable only for animal fodder. Today, however, the great nutritional value of soybeans is widely recognized and their flavor and versatility are appreciated.

Young soybeans may be cooked in the pod and eaten, pod and all, with melted butter. Any but the youngest soybeans must, however, be shelled. They are difficult to shell unless they are first blanched. Drop the pods into boiling water for 5 minutes, drain them, then break each pod in half and squeeze out the beans. To cook the beans, boil them for 15 to 20 minutes or until they are tender.

Dried beans must be soaked overnight as they take a long time to soften. Then either pressure-cook them for 45 minutes at high pressure (15 lb) or simmer them for about 4 hours.

Soybeans en Salade

By adding sliced or quartered hard-boiled eggs this salad can be turned into a satisfying and balanced main dish. Japanese soy sauce is best for the dressing, but if it is not available use good-quality Chinese soy sauce.

SERVES FOUR TO SIX
1 cup dried soybeans, soaked
   overnight and cooked, or about 3 cups
   fresh soybeans, cooked

3 shallots, finely chopped
2 celery stalks, finely diced
4 tablespoons finely chopped parsley
DRESSING
4 tablespoons oil
1 tablespoon lemon juice
1 tablespoon Japanese soy sauce
½ teaspoon monosodium glutamate
   (optional)
Sugar
Sea salt
Freshly ground black pepper

Make a well-seasoned dressing with the oil, lemon juice, soy sauce, monosodium glutamate, if it is used, a pinch of sugar, sea salt and pepper.

Drain the beans thoroughly and, while they are still hot, mix them gently with the dressing. Let the salad cool to lukewarm, then mix in the shallots, celery and parsley. Correct the seasoning. Let the salad cool completely to allow the flavors to develop before serving it.

Soybean Cutlets

Served with a salad or a green vegetable, these cutlets will make as pleasant and satisfying a main course as any steak or chop.

SERVES FOUR
1 tablespoon rendered bacon fat
4 slices fat bacon, finely chopped
1 cup dried soybeans, soaked overnight
   and cooked until soft, or 2½ cups
   fresh soybeans, cooked and drained
2 teaspoons chili powder
2 tablespoons finely chopped onion

4 tablespoons grated sharp Cheddar
   cheese
2 eggs
2 tablespoons finely chopped parsley
Salt
Fine dry bread crumbs
Lard or oil, for frying

Heat the bacon fat in a large frying pan. Add the bacon and fry until crisp. Add the beans and fry them steadily, stirring and crushing them with a potato masher or spoon. Remove the pan from the heat and stir in the chili powder, onion

and cheese. When the mixture has cooled slightly, add the eggs and parsley. Mix well. Season to taste with salt and let the mixture cool completely.

Divide the mixture into 8 balls. Roll them in fine dry bread crumbs and shape them into cutlets.

Fry the cutlets in hot lard or oil until they are hot and firm and the bread crumbs are crisp and golden on both sides. Serve hot.

Soybean Casserole

Serve this casserole as a main dish accompanied by vegetables or salad as you would a meat casserole.

SERVES FOUR
2 tablespoons butter
1 large, mild onion, finely chopped
1 garlic clove, crushed
3 celery stalks, coarsely chopped
2 cups soybeans, cooked
4 tablespoons finely chopped parsley
2 tablespoons Japanese soy sauce
Salt
Freshly ground black pepper

Melt the butter in a saucepan or casserole. Add the onion and garlic and simmer, stirring, until the onion is soft and golden. Add the celery and stir over low heat until it is golden. Moisten with 1 tablespoon of water, cover the pan and cook gently until the celery is tender but still firm.

Stir in the soybeans and parsley. Flavor with soy sauce (use 1½ tablespoons if Chinese soy sauce is being substituted and add a pinch of sugar) and season to taste with salt and pepper. Cover the pan and cook gently for 10 minutes longer, or until the beans are hot.

Curried Soybeans

This is a spicy curry. For a different flavor substitute two tablespoons of sweet mango or tomato chutney for the sugar.

SERVES FOUR TO SIX
2 tablespoons vegetable oil
1 medium-sized onion, finely chopped
2 garlic cloves, crushed
½-inch piece fresh root ginger, peeled
   and finely chopped
½ to 1 teaspoon cayenne pepper
2 teaspoons ground coriander
½ teaspoon turmeric
2 tablespoons brown sugar
2 cups dried or 3 cups fresh soybeans,
   cooked
2 cups canned peeled tomatoes
Salt
Freshly ground black pepper

Heat the oil in a large saucepan. Add the onion, garlic and ginger and fry, stirring frequently, over moderate heat until the onions are soft and golden brown.

Stir in the cayenne, coriander, turmeric and brown sugar and fry, stirring, for 5 minutes. Stir in the beans and the tomatoes with their liquid. Season to taste with the salt and pepper. Bring the mixture to the boil. Cover the pan, reduce the heat to low and simmer for 1 hour.

Serve hot.

Bean Sprouts

Bean sprouts, a favorite vegetable of the Chinese, are the young shoots of beans, of the mung bean in particular. Lightly cooked or raw, bean sprouts are a valuable food—they have a high protein and vitamin content.

Raw bean sprouts added to a conventional salad provide a welcome crunchiness and a delicate, elusive flavor. Stir bean sprouts into clear soup and simmer for a few minutes just before serving. Or try a bean-sprout salad dressed with a well-seasoned vinaigrette.

The Chinese stir-frying method is particularly suitable for cooking bean sprouts. They must be cooked quickly and eaten immediately or their precious crispness and delicate flavor will be destroyed.

There is no need to rinse home-grown bean sprouts, and resist the temptation to pick them over. Any stray little roots and hulls may look untidy, but they are full of vitamins and flavor.

Bean Sprouts with Green Peppers
An excellent dish to serve as part of a Chinese meal, or, American style, as a vegetable accompaniment to meat.

SERVES FOUR
4 tablespoons vegetable oil
1 lb bean sprouts
1 large green pepper, seeded, cored and
    finely chopped
2 tablespoons dry sherry
¼ teaspoon monosodium glutamate
    (optional)
Salt

Heat the oil in a large, heavy frying pan. Add the bean sprouts and pepper and fry over high heat, stirring constantly, for 5 minutes. Add the sherry. Sprinkle with the monosodium glutamate, if it is used, and season to taste with salt. Stir-fry for 1 minute more. Serve immediately.

Bean Sprouts with Fresh Ginger
A simple, quickly made dish suitable for serving in the Eastern or Western manner.

SERVES FOUR
4 tablespoons vegetable oil
2 teaspoons finely slivered fresh root
    ginger
4 plump scallions, thinly sliced
1 lb bean sprouts
1½ tablespoons Chinese soy sauce

Heat the oil in a large, heavy frying pan. Add the ginger and the scallions and fry over high heat, stirring, for 30 seconds. Add the bean sprouts and continue to stir-fry for 1 minute. Add the soy sauce. Lower the heat and continue to stir-fry for 4 minutes.

Bean Sprouts with Omelet Strips
A satisfying lunch dish easy and quick to prepare, the bean sprouts with their unusual delicate flavor and crunchy texture make an excellent contrast to the eggs.

SERVES TWO
4 eggs
2 teaspoons Chinese soy sauce
3 tablespoons vegetable oil
½ lb bean sprouts
1 tablespoon finely chopped parsley

Beat the eggs lightly with 1 teaspoon of soy sauce and 1 tablespoon of cold water. Heat 2 tablespoons of oil in a large frying pan. Pour the egg mixture into the pan to make a thin, flat, pancakelike omelet. There is no need to turn it. Just brown lightly on the underside.

When the omelet is firmly set, cut it into thin strips. Cut the strips into two or three pieces. Set aside.

In the same pan, heat the remaining oil and stir-fry the bean sprouts for 3 minutes. Sprinkle with the remaining soy sauce. Add the omelet strips and parsley and stir-fry for 1 minute longer. Serve at once.

Noodle-and-Bean-Sprout Soup
A light but delicious soup in the Chinese style. Vegetarians may use a strong, clear vegetable stock and substitute finely slivered bamboo shoots for the shredded chicken.

SERVES FOUR TO SIX
4 cups strong chicken stock
¼ lb fine egg noodles
Salt
¼ teaspoon monosodium glutamate
    (optional)
2 teaspoons cornstarch
½ cup shredded cooked chicken
6 tablespoons bean sprouts
6 watercress sprigs

In a large saucepan bring the stock to the boil. Drop in the noodles and boil for 2 minutes. Drain the noodles in a strainer over a bowl. Set the noodles aside.

Pour the stock back into the pan and return the pan to the heat. Add salt to taste and monosodium glutamate, if it is used.

In a cup, mix the cornstarch with 3 tablespoons of cold water and pour it into the soup. Cook over moderate heat, stirring constantly, until the soup thickens slightly and becomes clear.

Stir in the shredded chicken, the bean sprouts and the noodles. Bring the soup to the boil. Reduce the heat and simmer for 2 minutes.

Ladle the soup into individual soup bowls. Add a sprig of watercress to each bowl and serve immediately.

Bean Sprouts and Shrimp
This is a spicy dish. If a milder flavor is preferred, seed the chilies.

SERVES FOUR TO SIX
1 lb uncooked shrimp
3 tablespoons vegetable oil
1-inch piece fresh root ginger, peeled
    and slivered
1 garlic clove, crushed
1 to 2 green chilies, finely chopped
6 scallions, including the green part, sliced

1 tablespoon soy sauce
1 tablespoon dry sherry
1 teaspoon salt
1 teaspoon sugar
1 lb bean sprouts

Shell the shrimp and remove the black threadlike vein. Wash the shrimp and dry them well with paper toweling.

In a large frying pan heat the oil over high heat. When the oil is very hot, reduce the heat to moderate. Add the ginger, garlic, green chili and scallions and fry, stirring, for 30 seconds. Add the shrimp and fry, stirring, for 2 to 3 minutes, or until the shrimp turn pink. Stir in the soy sauce, sherry, salt and sugar. Add the bean sprouts and fry, stirring, for 3 minutes.

Serve immediately.

Onions

The onion, with its myriad layered skins, was regarded by the ancients as a symbol of eternity, a sacred object, almost a divinity, to be invoked when swearing a solemn oath. Onions have also been regarded as a food and as a flavoring probably longer than any other cultivated vegetable. Indeed, the very thought of cooking without them is almost as absurd as trying to get by without seasoning.

The onion family can be divided into two categories, white and green. The most delicate of all the white onions is the shallot. French *haute cuisine* recognizes no substitute for it in classic marinades, butters and such sauces as Béarnaise and Bordelaise. Because shallots are expensive and sometimes almost impossible to buy, they are a very satisfying onion to grow. With proper storage in a cool, dry place, shallots from the garden will last for almost the whole year until the next crop is ready.

The "ordinary" onion, strong, direct and uncomplicated, is added without a second thought to the stockpot or roasting pan, or fried for stews and casseroles. But there is a difference between strong onions and the magnificent, large, mild onions—Spanish, Italian red or Breton—which are so sweet that whole slices can be eaten raw on buttered fresh bread, sprinkled with coarse salt.

For those who find even the mildest onions strong in flavor or indigestible, the answer is to blanch them. Pour boiling water over the onions after they have been sliced or chopped, and either leave them to stand for a little while or parboil them for 3 minutes. Drain them, pat them as dry as possible with paper toweling and use them as you would raw onions.

Pickling onions, also called white onions, are the tiny, round bulblets, which should be picked before the onion has a chance to swell and grow. Besides being pickled they may be braised or sautéed. To peel pickling onions, first slice off the tops and tails. Put the onions in a bowl, pour over enough boiling water to cover and leave them to soak for 5 minutes. Then drain the onions and slip off the skins, which will come away very easily, particularly if the onions are still warm. After peeling, nick the root end with a small cross—this prevents the centers from popping out during cooking.

Garlic, a relative of the onion, is most often used as an herb, but it may also be used as a vegetable in its own right. It has a marvelously strange, Jekyll-and-Hyde character. Use one or two garlic cloves in a dish and the flavor is unmistakable. Take several heads of garlic, peel the cloves and pack them around a chicken or put them under a roast of lamb in a casserole, and somehow, after long, slow cooking, the pungency will have been transformed into a delicate sweetness.

The accepted procedure for crushing a garlic clove is to peel it, chop it into several pieces and then crush these to a paste with a sprinkling of salt, using the side of a broad-bladed knife. However, no matter how much the experts may demur, a garlic press is one of the most useful kitchen gadgets of all, not only for garlic but also for crushing small pieces of onion.

The green onions, which include chives, Welsh onions and scallions, are usually eaten raw in salads or mashed into flavored butters. Most delicate of all in appearance as well as in flavor are chives, those fine green spikes which, like a healthy lawn, grow all the better the more you cut them.

Chives are a summer herb, and in winter, scallions, although rather more oniony, make a perfectly good substitute. Shallot and garlic tops may be snipped off here and there as they grow, too. Chopped into a dish, they lend a faint yet unmistakable taste of the parent.

Undeniably, the most majestic of the green onions is the leek. Unlike the other onions, the leek does not seem to have had difficulty in establishing its identity as a vegetable in its own right. Yet its reputation has had to withstand derogatory allusions over the centuries—something very insignificant was once considered "not worth a leek." Yet few vegetables can have been honored like the leek, which was adopted by the Welsh as their national emblem. Apparently, the substitution of daffodils, although more picturesque, came about because it was thought that leeks and daffodils were one and the same—an error that the cook would certainly never make.

Welsh onions (true natives of Siberia, not Wales) are small, leeklike bulbs with a delicate flavor. Cook them as you would very young leeks or use them to flavor stews. They may also be eaten raw in salads.

Japanese bunching onions, so called because the bulbs grow in clusters, may be used as other onions in stews or casseroles. Their stalks and leaves make a tasty addition to salads.

Onions

Considering the extent to which onions are used in the kitchen, it is surprising how few people cook onions as a main dish or as a vegetable accompaniment. Yet, baked in their jackets, braised or steamed, stuffed or plain, glazed or frittered, onions make a most delicious dish.

When frying onions remember that only slow, careful cooking will bring out their flavor and sweetness. Raise the heat under the pan and, rather than speed up the process, you will only char the onions and make them bitter. The same is true of shallots and garlic.

A stew in which a large amount of onion is used will scarcely need any liquid. Use 1 pound of onions, raw or fried in butter or butter and oil, to 1 pound of meat. Provided the heat is kept very low, the onions will gradually dissolve into a purée, thick and rich enough to form the basis for the sauce.

To prevent streaming eyes when peeling and chopping onions, you can try paring them under running water—unless you are lucky enough to own one of the new food processors.

French Onion Soup

Once traditionally eaten in the early hours by the porters of the now defunct Paris vegetable market of Les Halles, this famous soup was also enjoyed by late-night revelers on their way home.

SERVES FOUR
3 tablespoons butter
1 lb mild, sweet onions, thinly sliced
1 teaspoon sugar
6⅔ cups well-flavored beef stock
2 tablespoons brandy
Salt
Freshly ground black pepper
4 rounds French bread, 1 inch thick
3 tablespoons freshly grated Parmesan cheese
3 tablespoons freshly grated Gruyère cheese

Melt the butter in a large saucepan. Add the onions and the sugar and cook slowly, stirring frequently, for 20 minutes, or until the onions turn a rich golden color.

Add the beef stock and bring it to the boil. Reduce the heat, partly cover the pan and simmer for 30 minutes. Add the brandy, season to taste with salt and pepper and simmer for 10 minutes longer.

Just before serving, preheat the oven to 450°F. Toast the round of French bread on both sides. Pour the boiling soup into an ovenproof casserole or tureen. Float the pieces of toast on the surface and sprinkle with the grated cheeses. Bake for 10 to 15 minutes, or until the cheese is golden brown and bubbling.

Tarte à l'Oignon

An excellent hors d'oeuvre, this tart also makes a good main-course lunch or supper dish, served with a fresh green salad or grilled tomatoes.

SERVES SIX TO EIGHT
6 tablespoons butter
1½ lb large, mild onions, thinly sliced
2 tablespoons finely chopped parsley
2 teaspoons dried basil
Dough to make a 10-inch pie shell
1⅓ cups light cream
3 large eggs
½ cup Gruyère cheese, freshly grated
Salt
Freshly ground black pepper

TOPPING
4 tablespoons Gruyère cheese, freshly grated
4 tablespoons fresh white bread crumbs

Melt the butter in a large saucepan. Add the onions and cook gently, tightly covered, for 15 minutes. Stir frequently. When the onions are limp, uncover the pan and continue to fry them gently, stirring frequently, for 15 to 20 minutes longer, or until they become very soft without coloring or losing their shape. Remove the pan from the heat and stir in the parsley and basil.

Preheat the oven to 425°F.

Roll the dough out and line a 10-inch pie pan with a removable base. Prick the pie shell with a fork and line it with greaseproof paper or foil. Fill the shell with dried beans and bake "blind" for 15 minutes. Remove the beans and paper and return the pie shell to the oven for 5 minutes longer to dry out the base. Remove the pie shell from the oven and set aside.

Reduce the oven temperature to 375°F. Heat a baking sheet in the oven.

Beat the cream lightly with the eggs and cheese and mix it into the onion mixture. Season with salt and pepper.

Put the pie shell on the hot baking sheet and pour in the filling. Mix the grated Gruyère with the bread crumbs and sprinkle over the top.

Bake the tart for 35 minutes, or until the filling is puffed and set and the crust is crisp and golden brown.

Pissaladière

The name of this onion pie from Provence, which is closely related to the pizzas of neighboring Italy, comes from *pissalat*, a highly flavored concoction of small sea fish.

SERVES SIX
4 tablespoons olive oil
1½ lb large, mild onions, finely chopped
1 large garlic clove, crushed
Thyme
Salt
Freshly ground black pepper
¾ lb once-risen bread dough
1 cup ripe tomatoes, peeled and sliced
2 oz canned anchovy fillets, drained and halved lengthwise
16 large black olives, halved and pitted

Heat the olive oil in a heavy frying pan. Add the onions, cover the pan tightly and fry them gently, stirring occasionally, for 15 minutes. Add the garlic and a pinch of thyme and cook, uncovered, for 15 minutes, or until the onions are reduced to a purée but are not colored. Season to taste with salt and pepper. Set aside to cool.

Preheat the oven to 400°F.

Roll the bread dough directly on the baking sheet into a circle about 10 inches in diameter. Spread the puréed onions evenly over the dough. Put the tomato slices on the onions and top with a decorative pattern of anchovy fillets and olives. Grind more pepper over the top.

Bake for 5 minutes. Reduce the oven temperature to 375°F and continue to bake for 30 minutes, or until the bread base is well risen and lightly browned underneath. Serve hot.

Glazed White Onions in White Wine

Glazed onions are a traditional garnish for many classic French dishes. They are just as delicious mixed with an equal quantity of glazed oval-shaped carrots or button mushrooms.

SERVES FOUR TO SIX
2 lb white onions
2 tablespoons olive oil
4 tablespoons butter
1⅓ cups chicken stock
1 bay leaf, torn in half
1⅓ cups dry white wine
4 teaspoons sugar
Salt

Put the unpeeled white onions in a large bowl. Cover them with plenty of boiling water and let them stand for 5 minutes. Drain them in a colander. Peel the onions while they are still warm.

Heat the oil and butter in a pan wide enough to take the onions in not more than two layers. Add the onions and roll them about to coat each one in the fat.

Pour in the stock and add the bay leaf.

Bring to the boil and cook briskly, shaking the pan frequently. When the stock has evaporated, add the wine. Sprinkle with the sugar and continue to cook until the wine has evaporated and the onions are soft and caramelized.

Discard the bay leaf and sprinkle the onions with salt. Serve immediately, or cover the pan and put it aside to be reheated when needed.

Mediterranean Onion-and-Pepper Appetizer

A summer appetizer, this dish may be served either lukewarm or cold with good crusty bread. For a more substantial dish, crisscross the top with anchovies and decorate with slices of hard-boiled egg. If any is left over it can be deep-frozen most successfully.

SERVES SIX
6 tablespoons olive oil
2 large, mild onions, thickly sliced
3 large green peppers
3 sprigs fresh basil, chopped, or
 2 teaspoons dried basil
Sugar
Salt
Freshly ground black pepper
2 cups canned Italian peeled tomatoes
4 tablespoons finely chopped parsley
1 tablespoon capers
Black olives, to garnish

Heat the olive oil in a large, heavy pan. Add the onions, cover the pan tightly and cook over low heat for 10 minutes.

Meanwhile, quarter the peppers. Discard the cores and seeds, and cut crosswise into thick slices. Add the peppers to the onions. Sprinkle with the basil, 1 teaspoon of sugar, and salt and pepper to taste. Continue cooking, stirring, for 2 minutes to wilt the peppers slightly. Stir in the tomatoes and the can juices and bring to the boil. Reduce the heat to low, cover the pan tightly and cook for 30 minutes. By this time the onions and peppers should be very soft but still keep their shape, and the tomatoes should be reduced to a thick sauce.

Remove the pan from the heat. Allow the mixture to cool to lukewarm and stir in the parsley and capers. Correct the seasoning, if necessary, with more salt, pepper and sugar. Serve garnished with black olives.

Onions in Madeira Cream

Marvelous with steak, liver or any grilled meat.

SERVES FOUR TO SIX
¼ lb (1 stick) butter
4 large, mild onions, thickly sliced
⅔ cup Madeira
Salt
Freshly ground black pepper
4 tablespoons heavy cream
4 tablespoons finely chopped parsley

Melt the butter in a wide, heavy pan. Add the onion slices and turn them thoroughly in the butter. Cover the pan and cook over very low heat for 10 minutes, shaking the pan occasionally.

Uncover the pan, increase the heat slightly and stir in the Madeira. Continue to cook, stirring frequently, until the Madeira has evaporated and the onions are soft and lightly caramelized.

Season to taste with salt and pepper. Stir in the cream and parsley and bring to the boil. Simmer for 1 minute.

Serve hot.

Onions Agrodolce

This delicious regional Italian dish can be served either hot or cold, as part of a mixed hors d'oeuvre or as an accompaniment to roast meat or chicken.

SERVES FOUR
3 tablespoons olive oil
1½ lb white onions, peeled
3 tablespoons white wine
3 tablespoons wine vinegar
2 tablespoons soft brown sugar
2 tablespoons pine nuts
2 tablespoons raisins
Salt
Freshly ground black pepper
Finely chopped parsley, to garnish

Heat the oil in a large, heavy frying pan. Add the onions and cook over a moderate heat, shaking the pan occasionally, until the onions begin to brown. Add the wine, wine vinegar, sugar, pine nuts and raisins. Season with salt and pepper. Reduce the heat, cover the pan and simmer until the sauce has become syrupy and the onions are tender. Correct the seasoning and serve garnished with the chopped parsley.

Onions

Onion Dolma

A Middle Eastern favorite, these stuffed onions have now become popular all over the world. This dish may be eaten cold, as an appetizer, or as part of a mixed hors d'oeuvre, or hot as a main dish, accompanied by mixed vegetables or a green salad.

SERVES FOUR TO SIX
6 large onions, unpeeled
1 lb minced lamb
2 tomatoes, peeled and chopped
⅓ cup long-grain rice
Juice and finely grated rind of 1 lemon
1 small onion, finely chopped
1 tablespoon sugar
1 teaspoon turmeric
½ teaspoon basil
½ teaspoon oregano
Salt
Freshly ground black pepper
3 tablespoons olive oil, for cooking

Put the unpeeled onions in a large saucepan. Pour in plenty of boiling water. Boil for about 20 minutes, or until the onions are tender. Remove the onions from the pan, drain them and allow them to cool slightly.

In a bowl, thoroughly mix the next 9 ingredients. Season to taste with salt and pepper. Set aside.

With a sharp knife, slit each onion down one side to the center. Separate the layers, which will slip off quite easily. Discard the outer papery skins and the cores of the onions.

Take a small handful of the filling and work it into a sausage shape; squeeze out some, but not all, of the liquid. Reserve the excess liquid for use later. Lay the stuffing in one of the onion layers and fold it tightly around the mixture. Fill the remaining layers in this way. Do not overfill the layers as the rice must have room to expand.

Heat the oil in a pan large enough to take the stuffed onions in one layer. Add the stuffed onions, packing them in close together. Pour in any liquid remaining in the bowl. Reduce the heat, cover the pan and simmer gently for about 1 hour.

Halfway through the cooking time turn the stuffed onions over.

Carefully remove the dolma from the pan with a spatula and serve immediately or set aside to cool.

Onion Pakoras

Pakoras—a variety of fritter—are among the commonest of Indian snacks. They can be made from almost any available vegetable, including spinach leaves, potatoes and eggplants. Usually fried in deep oil, they can also be shallow-fried with equally good results. Serve pakoras with a tomato or coconut chutney.

SERVES FOUR
1 cup gram (chickpea) flour
1 teaspoon salt
½ teaspoon chili powder
¼ teaspoon turmeric
½ teaspoon ground coriander
½-inch piece fresh root ginger, grated
Vegetable oil, for deep-frying
4 large onions, cut in rings or finely sliced

Sift the flour and salt into a bowl. Beat in sufficient water (about 2 cups) to make a thin, smooth batter. Mix in the chili powder, turmeric, coriander and ginger and leave the batter to stand for at least 30 minutes.

Heat the oil in a deep-frying pan until the temperature registers 375°F on a cooking thermometer. If you do not have a thermometer, drop a cube of stale bread in the oil; if it takes about 40 seconds to brown, the temperature is correct. Coat the onion rings in the batter and add them, a few at a time, to the oil. Fry until golden brown, drain on paper toweling and set aside in a warm serving dish. If you are using finely sliced onions, mix them in with the batter and then drop them by the spoonful into the hot oil. Repeat this process until all the onions are cooked. Serve immediately.

Stuffed Onions

For a more substantial main-course dish, stuff the onions with ½ lb of sausage meat mixed with 4 tablespoons of fresh, white bread crumbs, seasoned with salt and pepper. Sprinkle with more fresh, white bread crumbs, dot with butter and bake for 40 minutes.

SERVES EIGHT
4 large, mild onions, peeled
Salt
24 white onions
4 tablespoons butter
1 cup fresh white bread crumbs
4 tablespoons freshly grated Parmesan cheese
8 tablespoons heavy cream

Put the large onions into boiling salted water and simmer them, uncovered, for 15 minutes. Drain them and set them aside to cool.

Put the white onions in a bowl. Cover them with boiling water and leave them for 5 minutes. Drain them in a colander, then peel and trim them. Set aside.

Preheat the oven to 375°F.

Melt the butter in a small pan. Mix in the bread crumbs and stir over a low heat for 1 to 2 minutes, or until they are just golden. Set aside.

When the large onions are cool enough to handle, cut them in half horizontally. Scoop out and discard the centers. Arrange the onion "cups" side by side in a shallow baking dish and season lightly with salt.

Toss the white onions with the cheese and fill the onion halves with the mixture. Pour a tablespoon of cream over each half onion and spoon the buttered bread crumbs over the top. Bake the onions for 25 minutes, or until both the large and small onions are tender when pierced with a thin skewer and the topping is crisp and golden. Serve hot.

Garlic Bread

Garlic bread is delicious. Serve it straight from the oven with soups or main-course dishes. It will also add a wonderfully appetizing and welcoming aroma to a cold buffet.

SERVES FOUR
1 long French loaf
¼ lb (1 stick) butter, softened
2 plump garlic cloves, crushed
1 tablespoon finely chopped parsley
Sea salt
Freshly ground black pepper

Preheat the oven to 350°F.

Slice the loaf diagonally at 1½-inch intervals to within a ¼ inch of the base.

Pound the butter with the garlic and parsley. Mix in salt and pepper to taste.

Carefully easing the slices of bread apart, spread each one with the garlic butter. Wrap the loaf tightly in foil and bake it for about 20 minutes, or until the butter has melted and the bread is hot and crusty.

Leeks

In America the leek is little known except as an ingredient of the "soup bunch" sold in supermarkets. Yet in Europe, where they are both familiar and widely appreciated, leeks are the basis of many delicious recipes to enliven winter menus.

Leeks may be served hot or cold, steamed or poached whole, or sliced and simmered in butter until reduced to a purée. A *bouquet garni* of fresh herbs and spices may be sandwiched neatly in a split leek, the halves tied together with string—just as efficient and much quicker to make than the traditional cheesecloth bag.

Leeks require careful preparation, for every speck of grit must be washed out of them. To prepare leeks, first cut off the tops, leaving only about 2 inches of the green stem. The coarse green leaves are good only for the stock-pot. Trim the roots. Slip off the outer skin of the leek, removing more than one layer if they have been damaged by the spade.

Rinse the leeks thoroughly under cold running water. If there is any doubt that the leeks are not completely clean, slit them down one side with the point of a sharp knife and let the water run through the layers.

There are a number of simple but tasty ways to cook and serve leeks. They make a delightful salad, steamed, then chilled and served cold with a vinaigrette dressing garnished with chopped hard-boiled egg and parsley. Or serve them hot covered with a Mornay sauce. They may be parboiled for 8 minutes, drained and put in a baking dish with butter, sprinkled over with bread crumbs and baked in a moderate oven for 25 minutes. Cook leeks *à la paysanne*—trim, slice and cook them gently in butter with diced bacon for 30 to 40 minutes. Or bake them in a pie—slice the leeks and put them in a lined pie pan. Season well and pour in some heavy cream. Cover with rich piecrust and bake in a moderate oven for 50 to 60 minutes.

Flamiche

The traditional recipe for this leek pie, which is a specialty both in Belgium and in northern France, calls for leeks, butter, cream and eggs. This version is slightly different in that sausages are included in the filling as well.

SERVES SIX
6 tablespoons butter
1½ lb trimmed leeks, thinly sliced
8 link sausages
Lard or margarine for frying
3 eggs
⅔ cup heavy cream
Salt
Freshly ground black pepper
Dough for 2 10-inch crusts
1 egg yolk, lightly beaten

Melt the butter in a large pan. Stir in the leeks, cover the pan tightly and cook over low heat, stirring occasionally, for 30 minutes, or until they are almost reduced to a purée. Uncover the pan, increase the heat to moderate and cook, stirring, for a few minutes longer to evaporate excess moisture.

While the leeks are cooking, prick the sausages with a fork (to prevent them bursting) and fry them in lard or margarine until they are well browned on all sides. Drain thoroughly on paper toweling.

Preheat the oven to 425°F.

Beat the eggs and cream together with a generous seasoning of salt and pepper. Remove the pan of leeks from the heat, mix in the cream-and-egg mixture and stir until it has thickened slightly. Correct the seasoning. Set aside to cool to lukewarm.

Divide the dough in half and roll each piece into a circle 10 inches in diameter. Lay one piecrust on a lightly dampened baking sheet.

Pile the leek mixture onto the crust on the baking sheet, leaving a 1-inch border clear. Arrange the sausages in a star pattern on top of the leeks. Dampen the border of the crust with cold water. Lay the other crust in position on top and carefully but thoroughly seal the edges of the crust together. Flute or pinch the edges decoratively. Cut slits in the top to allow steam to escape and brush the whole pie with the beaten egg yolk.

Bake for 10 minutes. Then reduce the heat to 350°F and continue to bake for 30 to 35 minutes longer, or until the crust is puffed and golden brown. Serve hot.

Leek-and-Ham Rolls

A dish which requires no accompaniment except good crusty bread. These leek-and-ham rolls may be served as a first or main course.

SERVES FOUR AS A FIRST COURSE
8 thin leeks, trimmed
1⅓ cups boiling chicken stock
4 large slices cooked ham
Butter

2 tablespoons flour
⅔ cup heavy cream
4 tablespoons freshly grated Cheddar cheese
Salt
Freshly ground black pepper
3 tablespoons fresh white bread crumbs

Arrange the leeks side by side in a wide pan. Pour in the boiling stock and bring it back to the boil. Reduce the heat, cover the pan tightly and simmer for 8 to 10 minutes, or until the leeks are just tender. Drain them, reserving the cooking liquid.

Preheat the oven to 400°F.

Lay the ham slices flat on a board. Place 2 leeks in the middle of each slice and wrap the ham around the leeks. Put the rolls in a single layer in a buttered shallow baking dish.

Melt 2 tablespoons of butter in a saucepan. Blend in the flour and stir over low heat for 1 minute to make a pale roux. Gradually add ⅔ cup of the reserved leek liquid, stirring vigorously to prevent lumps forming. Stirring constantly, bring the sauce to the boil. Stir in the cream and, as soon as the sauce comes to the boil again, remove the pan from the heat. Beat in 2 tablespoons of the cheese and season to taste with salt and pepper.

Pour the sauce over the rolled leeks. Mix the bread crumbs and the remaining cheese together and sprinkle the mixture over the sauce. Dot with small pieces of butter.

Bake the leeks for 30 minutes, or until they are hot and the sauce is bubbling and golden brown on top. Allow the dish to rest and the sauce to stabilize for 10 minutes before serving.

Leeks

Creamed Leeks
A delicate vegetable accompaniment for broiled and sautéed meats and roasts.

SERVES FOUR
2 lb trimmed leeks
Salt
1⅓ cups heavy cream
2 tablespoons freshly grated Parmesan
  or sharp Cheddar cheese
Freshly ground black pepper
2 egg yolks, lightly beaten

Slice the leeks thickly. Put them in a saucepan. Sprinkle with salt and add just enough boiling water to cover. Bring the water back to the boil and cook the leeks, uncovered, for 6 to 8 minutes. Drain them thoroughly in a colander.

Pour the cream into the top of a double boiler and place it over lightly simmering water. Stir in the leeks. Cover the pan and continue to cook gently for 20 to 30 minutes, or until the leeks are very tender but have not quite disintegrated.

Remove the top part of the double boiler from the heat. Stir in the cheese and season to taste with salt and pepper. Stir in the egg yolks and put the pan back over simmering water. Stir gently until the sauce has thickened. Do not let it boil or it will curdle.

Vichyssoise
It is a culinary irony that chilled Vichyssoise, one of the best of summer soups, should be made with what are essentially winter vegetables—leeks and floury potatoes. Serve Vichyssoise with hot garlic bread.

SERVES FOUR TO SIX
4 tablespoons butter
6 large leeks, white part only, thickly
  sliced
1½ lb potatoes, peeled and thickly sliced
5⅓ cups chicken stock
Salt

Freshly ground black pepper
Freshly grated nutmeg
2 cups light cream
Chopped fresh chives, to garnish

Melt the butter in a large saucepan. Add the leeks, cover the pan and simmer for 15 minutes. Shake the pan or turn the leeks over to make sure they soften without changing color. Add the potatoes, pour in the stock and simmer gently, with the lid half on, for a further 15 to 20 minutes, or until the vegetables have begun to disintegrate.

Purée the soup in an electric blender or rub it through the finest plate of a food mill. Season with salt, pepper and a little nutmeg to taste.

If the soup is to be served cold, let it cool before diluting it with the cream. If it is to be served hot, add the cream and bring to boiling point. Garnish with chopped chives and serve.

To prepare leeks, cut away the coarse green leaves, leaving about 2 inches of green stem.

Leeks with Tomatoes and Olives
A traditional dish from Provence which may be served cold as an appetizer or salad, or hot as a vegetable accompaniment to meat or fish.

SERVES FOUR
2 lb trimmed leeks
3 tablespoons olive oil
4 large tomatoes, halved
½ cup black olives, pitted
Juice of 1 lemon
Rind of ½ lemon, in one piece
Salt
Freshly ground black pepper

Cut the leeks into 1-inch lengths. Heat the oil in a large, deep frying pan. Add the leeks, cover the pan and cook slowly for about 10 minutes, stirring occasionally.

Add the tomatoes, olives, half of the lemon juice, the lemon rind and salt and pepper to taste. Simmer, covered, for a further 10 minutes.

Remove and discard the lemon rind and add the remaining lemon juice. Adjust the seasoning. Serve hot or cold.

Trim the root and remove the outer skin of the leeks and any brown or damaged layers.

Leeks in Sour-Cream Sauce
A delightful dish to serve with hard-boiled eggs and cold meats. Homemade mayonnaise may be substituted for the sour cream.

SERVES FOUR
8 thin leeks
Salt
⅔ cup thick sour cream
3 scallions, finely chopped

2 tablespoons finely chopped parsley
1 small garlic clove, crushed
1 tablespoon horseradish sauce
1 tablespoon cider vinegar
Generous pinch sugar

Lay the leeks in a large saucepan. Pour in enough boiling water to cover and add salt. Cover the pan and cook over low heat for 8 to 10 minutes, or until the leeks are just tender.

Meanwhile, mix the remaining ingredients together and season generously with salt.

Drain the leeks in a colander. Let them cool to lukewarm; then arrange them side by side in a rectangular serving dish. Pour the dressing over and leave them to cool. Chill thoroughly before serving.

To ensure that the leeks are completely clean, slit them down one side with the point of a knife.

Leeks with Rice
This dish, originally from Greece, can be served as an accompaniment to sausages, hamburgers or broiled meat. As a variation, the leeks may be topped with grated cheese or accompanied by a rich tomato sauce.

SERVES FOUR
4 tablespoons olive oil
1 garlic clove, finely chopped
1 lb trimmed leeks, sliced
2 tablespoons tomato paste
1 teaspoon sugar
1 tablespoon lemon juice
1 teaspoon dried mixed herbs
Salt
Freshly ground black pepper
2 cups water or chicken stock
1 cup long-grain rice, washed,
  soaked in cold water for 30 minutes
  and drained.

Heat the olive oil in a large saucepan. Add the garlic and cook, stirring, over low heat for 1 minute. Add the leeks and cook, stirring, for 5 minutes. Stir in the tomato paste, sugar, lemon juice, herbs, and salt and pepper to taste.

Pour in the water or stock and bring to the boil. Reduce the heat. Cover the pan and simmer for 10 minutes, or until the leeks are slightly tender.

Pour in the rice. Increase the heat to high and bring the mixture to the boil. Allow the rice to boil rapidly for 1 minute. Cover the pan, reduce the heat to very low and simmer for 15 to 20 minutes, or until the rice is cooked and all the liquid has been absorbed.

Correct the seasoning and serve.

Wash the leeks under cold running water until all traces of dirt have been removed.

Roots

In the past, the great advantage of root vegetables was that, with few exceptions, they could be pulled and stored in a cellar to tide the household over the winter months. But even today, with so many imported vegetables bringing variety to winter diets, root vegetables provide a cheap and nourishing staple.

The most important root vegetable—because of its nutritious properties and its culinary uses —is the carrot. Once considered a "bad weed" —its family connection with hemlock probably did not help—it is now a popular year-round vegetable and an essential ingredient in stocks, sauces and garnishes.

Parsnips, sweet, floury and filling, are an excellent vegetable. They are delicious when scraped, parboiled and then cooked in sizzling butter, or simmered to tenderness and dressed with butter or served in a creamy white sauce.

If the sweetness of the parsnip is not to your taste, try the turnip-rooted chervil, also known as parsnip chervil. This vegetable deserves greater recognition. Chervil should be washed, never scraped. Steam or simmer the roots in salted water for about 30 minutes and serve them with butter or cream.

Everyone knows turnips, and their young, yellow-fleshed cousins, rutabagas, which the English call swedes. But not everyone appreciates that the smaller they are the more delicate they will be. Rutabagas may be used in any of the recipes suitable for turnips or kohlrabi. Kohlrabi, which like the turnips and rutabagas belongs to the brassica family, is difficult to classify in culinary terms. It is definitely not like cabbage. Its flavor is, if anything, closer to that of turnip. Kohlrabi can swell to a great size. Resist the temptation to let them do so. Ideally, pull kohlrabi when they are about 2 inches in diameter. Strip off the leaves, wash the bulbs and steam them whole for about 20 minutes. Or peel and slice or quarter the bulbs and steam-boil them in a tightly covered pan for about 15 minutes. They are excellent served with butter, cream sauce or a hollandaise. You can also hollow them out, stuff them with meat, replace the tops and simmer them in a little water or stock until they are soft. Serve the stuffed kohlrabi with a savory tomato or lemon sauce diluted with the cooking stock or water.

Beets are an ancient vegetable, originally cultivated solely for their vivid young leaves. It was the Romans who finally discovered that their roots were equally delicious. Today, we happily eat both. And it is accepted that although the beet came originally from the regions around the Mediterranean and the Caspian, it thrives best in cooler climates, hence its prominence in the cuisines of northern Europe and North America.

Celeriac, a relative of the carrot, tastes and looks like a greatly magnified celery root. Although it is justly prized throughout Europe, it unfortunately receives less attention in England and America. Another knobby root, Hamburg parsley, is also less well-known in the Anglo-Saxon world. On the Continent, it has been looked on with favor since ancient times, particularly in northern countries, where leaf parsley cannot survive the cold of winter in the open.

The strange, pale root, too long and thin and smooth to be mistaken for a parsnip, is salsify, also known as the vegetable oyster. How it got its nickname is a mystery, since it is impossible to find any resemblance to oysters either in its flavor or its texture. But it is very good indeed, and has a long and distinguished history. Scorzonera is similar to salsify, except for its rather dramatic black skin. Under this somber exterior, however, the root is white and tastes as delicious as its cousin. Its name, which comes from the Catalan word for viper, is a reminder that scorzonera was once grown as an antidote for snake bites. Today, it is cooked in the same way as salsify. The salsify/scorzonera tribe is grossly underrated, but as cooks become more inquisitive and gardeners more adventurous, its members will regain their place in our kitchen gardens.

Radishes and horseradishes stand apart from the rest of the roots, since both of them are considered condiments and "accessories" rather than vegetables in their own right. In the Orient, however, radishes occupy an important position in the cuisine. They may be red, white and even black, like the great Japanese *daikon*.

Although our gardens rarely provide more than a row of radishes at a time for the salad bowl or the drink tray, radishes make an appealing snack served chilled with fresh butter and coarse salt or hollowed out and stuffed with a creamy cheese mixture.

Parsnips

Parsnips look like ghostly carrots, but there the similarity ends. If anything, they taste more like sweet potatoes with a touch of turnip.

The natural sweetness of parsnips makes a perfect marriage with butter and cream. But the simplest and one of the best ways to cook parsnips is to parboil them for 5 minutes, skin them, thickly slice or quarter them—if the parsnips are old remove the hard core—and then roast them. They may be put in the roasting pan with a roast to soak up the meaty flavor or brushed with fat and roasted in a shallow pan, which makes them crisper.

Young parsnips may also be steamed for about 35 minutes and then served with a cream sauce. Or they may be steamed, peeled, sliced, dipped in a fritter batter and fried. They may also be mashed with milk, flour and egg and dropped in spoonfuls into hot fat. Parsnips combine well with other root vegetables in a purée.

Parsnips in Cheese Sauce

In this dish the sweetness of the parsnips is counterbalanced by the sharpness of the creamy sauce.

SERVES FOUR
1 lb parsnips
Salt
2 tablespoons butter
2 tablespoons flour
$\frac{2}{3}$ cup hot milk
$\frac{2}{3}$ cup light cream
$\frac{1}{2}$ cup Gruyère or sharp Cheddar
cheese, freshly grated
Lemon juice

Scrub the parsnips and boil them in salted water for 12 to 15 minutes, or until just tender.

Meanwhile, melt the butter in a heavy pan. Blend in the flour and stir over a low heat for 1 minute to make a pale roux. Gradually add the hot milk, stirring vigorously to prevent lumps forming. Blend in the cream and bring to the boil, stirring, and simmer very gently for 4 minutes. Then beat in the cheese. When the cheese has melted, season to taste with salt and sharpen the flavor with a good squeeze of lemon juice.

Drain the cooked parsnips in a colander. As soon as they are cool enough to handle, peel them and slice them thickly, leaving the thin ends in one or two pieces.

Fold the parsnips into the sauce and reheat gently. Correct seasoning. Serve the parsnips as they are, or put them into a *gratin* dish, sprinkle with a little more cheese mixed with coarse, dry bread crumbs, and brown the top under the broiler.

Glazed Parsnips

SERVES FOUR
8 parsnips
Salt
4 tablespoons butter
2 tablespoons light-brown sugar
Juice of 1 large orange
2 tablespoons lemon juice
Generous pinch nutmeg or mace
Freshly ground black pepper

Scrub the parsnips with a stiff brush. Trim them top and bottom, and boil in salted water until barely tender—about 12 minutes. Drain the parsnips thoroughly and allow them to cool. Peel them and slice off the thin root ends, leaving them in one or two pieces. Slice the thicker ends in half lengthwise.

Put the butter, sugar, orange juice and lemon juice into a wide, heavy pan. Stir over low heat. When the butter has melted and the sugar has dissolved, stir in the nutmeg or mace.

Put the pieces of parsnip in the pan, turning them to coat them with the buttery juices. Season with salt and a grinding of pepper. Cook over low heat, partially covered, until the parsnips are glazed on all sides and have absorbed the juices. Serve hot.

Parsnip-and-Cheese Roast

This dish makes a substantial main course served with a fresh green salad. The bacon may be left out if desired.

SERVES FOUR TO SIX
2 lb parsnips
Salt
2 tablespoons butter
4 slices smoked streaky bacon, chopped
1 medium-sized onion, finely chopped
1 cup Cheddar cheese, grated
8 tablespoons heavy cream
Freshly ground black pepper
TO FINISH DISH
6 slices smoked streaky bacon, halved
$\frac{1}{2}$ cup Cheddar cheese, grated
4 tablespoons quick-cooking oats or
coarse, fresh bread crumbs

Scrub the parsnips and boil them in salted water for 15 minutes, or until they are tender.

Meanwhile, melt the butter in a frying pan. Add the bacon and onion and fry until the onion is soft and transparent. Set aside.

Preheat the oven to 425°F.

Drain the cooked parsnips in a colander. Rinse them with cold water and, as soon as they are cool enough to handle, trim them and rub off their skins with your fingers. Chop the parsnips and add them to the pan with the bacon and onions. Using a fork, mash the mixture to a purée. Then beat in the cheese, cream, and salt and pepper to taste.

Turn the parsnip mixture into a buttered baking dish and with a spatula pat it into a smooth cake. Stick the halved slices of bacon around the sides of the cake and sprinkle the top thickly with a mixture of cheese and oats or bread crumbs.

Bake on the top shelf of the oven for 20 to 25 minutes, or until the topping is a bubbling golden crust. Serve hot.

Fried Parsnips and Potatoes with Eggs

An economical but unusual lunch or supper dish.

SERVES FOUR
1 lb parsnips, scraped
1 lb potatoes, peeled
Salt
6 slices fat bacon, chopped
2 tablespoons butter
4 eggs
Freshly ground black pepper

Cut the parsnips and potatoes into slices of the same thickness. Boil them in separate pans of salted water for 6 to 8 minutes, or until they are barely tender. Drain them in the same colander and leave to cool.

In a large, heavy frying pan that has a cover, sauté the chopped bacon in butter until the fat is transparent. Add the parsnip and potato slices, and fry them steadily until they are a rich golden color, turning them over and over with a spatula.

Spread the slices evenly in the pan. Make four hollows in the surface and carefully break the eggs into them. Season with salt and pepper. Cover the pan and continue to cook until the eggs are set to your taste. Serve straight from the frying pan.

To prepare parsnips, trim both ends and scrape off the skin with a sharp knife. Then slice off the narrow end. Cut the thick end into quarters.

Carrots

Sweet young carrots, not more than two or three inches long and topped with green, feathery fronds, are a delicacy from the kitchen garden that those who have to rely on the supermarket can never know. Such young carrots are best steamed briefly and served with plenty of butter, chopped fresh herbs—parsley, chervil, mint, marjoram or dill, for example—and perhaps a squeeze of lemon and a pinch of sugar.

Because most of the vitamins in vegetables are only skin deep, carrots should never be peeled, even when mature. A good scrub with a stiff brush under running water is usually all that is necessary. If you must peel old carrots, however, rub the skin off after cooking.

Only when carrots are mature and ready to go into winter storage should they be used to make such dishes as soups, purées and soufflés. And this is when you will discover how magnificently their flavor is partnered by orange, spices and herbs, including caraway and dill seed.

Traditional recipes for Christmas pudding often wisely include grated raw carrot. Just 1 ounce of grated carrot is enough to help keep a 2-pound pudding deliciously moist over a long period. Old cookery books included many recipes for sweet carrot puddings, pies and jams. Such imaginative use of carrots went out of culinary fashion until the Second World War, when housewives, rationed with sugar, turned to carrots to make a tart or cake for the rare family treat.

A little grated carrot mixed with the minced meat for hamburgers makes them lighter and juicier. And plain boiled rice looks unusually attractive if a little raw carrot is grated coarsely and forked into it shortly before serving.

Nothing could be simpler or more refreshing than a salad of coarsely grated carrots dressed with olive oil and lemon juice, salt and a pinch or two of sugar. Or try a carrot-and-red-currant salad. Grate $\frac{1}{2}$ pound of carrots coarsely into a bowl. Add $\frac{1}{2}$ cup of ripe red currants, stripped from their stalks and, only if necessary, washed and drained thoroughly on paper toweling. Toss lightly. Sweeten to taste with sugar, dress with lemon juice and toss again. Serve chilled on a bed of lettuce leaves.

Carrots and apples are natural partners. Coarsely grate 1 pound of carrots and $\frac{1}{2}$ cup of tart eating apples into a bowl containing $\frac{2}{3}$ cup of sour cream or heavy cream. Mix in about 1 tablespoon of horseradish sauce, a generous pinch of sugar and salt to taste. Toss the salad lightly but thoroughly and serve garnished with sprigs of parsley or fresh, crisp watercress.

Carrots Hollandaise

A luxurious but easy dish. The carrots may be cooked in advance, then reheated in the butter and mixed with the egg sauce just before serving.

If it is more convenient, put the sliced, cooked carrots with the butter and sugar in a shallow baking dish in a moderate oven to finish cooking. Then stir in the egg-and-cream mixture and return the dish to the oven for about 1 minute longer to allow the sauce to thicken without curdling.

SERVES FOUR
1 lb long, thin carrots
Salt
Chicken stock (optional)
4 tablespoons butter
2 teaspoons sugar
2 egg yolks
3 tablespoons heavy cream
2 tablespoons finely chopped parsley
Freshly ground black pepper

Scrub the carrots and steam them or simmer them in a very little salted water or stock for 10 to 12 minutes, or until they are barely tender. Put them in a colander and pour cold water over them until they are cool enough to handle. Trim the carrots and rub off the skins. Cut the carrots into 2-inch pieces and then slice them thinly lengthwise.

Melt the butter in a heavy pan. Carefully mix in the carrot slices, sprinkling them with the sugar as you do so. Cook over very low heat, shaking the pan occasionally, until the carrots are tender.

Before serving, beat the egg yolks with the cream. Mix in the parsley, salt and pepper to taste.

Remove the pan of carrots from the heat. Pour in the egg mixture and stir gently until it has thickened and amalgamated with the buttery juices to make a rich, creamy sauce. If necessary, return the pan to very low heat for 1 minute to allow the sauce to thicken without curdling. Alternatively, stand the pan in a larger one of barely simmering water to finish the sauce. Serve immediately.

Buttered Carrots and Mushrooms

A tasty accompaniment for poultry or roast lamb.

SERVES FOUR
1 lb carrots
Salt
3 tablespoons butter
1 tablespoon oil
1 small onion, finely chopped
1 garlic clove, crushed
1¼ cups button mushrooms, thickly sliced
1 whole cardamom pod, lightly crushed
Pinch of dried rosemary
Freshly ground black pepper

Scrub or scrape the carrots. Trim, and slice them at a slant. Steam the carrots or simmer in salted water for 5 minutes, or until the slices are barely tender. Drain well.

While the carrots are cooking, heat the butter and oil in another pan. Add the onion and garlic and fry, stirring constantly, until the onion is soft and lightly colored. Add the mushrooms and, stirring to coat them with the butter, fry for 2 to 3 minutes longer until they are golden.

Mix in the carrots. Add the cardamom pod (crushed in a garlic press), the rosemary, and salt and pepper to taste. Mix well. Cover the pan tightly and cook over very low heat for 15 minutes longer to develop and blend the flavors.

"*The Yellow Carrot has a large long Root, great or thick, and yellow, big above and small pointed below, without any Fangs or Twines, of a pleasant sweet Taste, and therefore generally spent for Food.*"

The English Herbal *by William Salmon, M.D., 1710*

Nothing could be simpler or more refreshing than a salad of coarsely grated carrots dressed with olive oil and lemon juice, salt and a pinch or two of sugar.

"Both seed and root are . . . good against the bitings of Venomous Beasts, Wind, and rising of the Mother."

The English Herbal *by William Salmon, M.D., 1710*

Carrots

Marinated Herbed Carrots

This salad is made with cooked carrots. Since the dressing provides a rich flavor, more mature carrots may be used if they are not woody.

SERVES FOUR
½ lb carrots
Sugar
Salt
1 tablespoon tarragon vinegar
¼ teaspoon Dijon mustard
4 tablespoons olive oil
1 small garlic clove, crushed
1 tablespoon finely chopped parsley

2 teaspoons finely chopped chives or
   scallion tops
1 teaspoon chopped fresh thyme
Freshly ground black pepper
Lemon juice

Trim and scrub or scrape the carrots and cut them into 1½-inch-long matchstick strips. Put them in a pan. Add 2 teaspoons of sugar, ½ teaspoon of salt and just enough water to cover. Bring to the boil and cook steadily, uncovered, for 5 minutes. The carrot strips should still retain their crispness. Set aside.

Prepare the dressing in a medium-sized bowl. Mix the vinegar and mustard together. Then beat in the olive oil, 1 tablespoon at a time, to make a creamy mixture. Stir in the garlic and herbs.

Drain the carrots thoroughly and while they are still hot mix them gently with the dressing. Season with salt and pepper, adding more sugar if wished. If necessary sharpen the flavor of the salad with about 1 tablespoon of lemon juice. Chill the salad for several hours before serving. The carrots will absorb most of the dressing.

Carrot Halva

This Indian sweet is traditionally decorated with edible silver leaf. Serve it at room temperature, accompanied by a pitcher of unsweetened heavy cream.

SERVES EIGHT
1 lb carrots, trimmed and scraped
2 quarts milk
1¾ cups sugar
2 tablespoons corn syrup

¾ cup unsalted butter
2 tablespoons blanched slivered almonds
Seeds of 12 cardamoms, coarsely
   crushed in a mortar

Grate the carrots into the milk in a heavy pan. Bring to the boil over moderate heat. Lower the heat and cook steadily, stirring frequently, for 1½ to 2 hours, or until the mixture is very thick. Be careful not to let it burn.

Add the sugar, corn syrup and butter, and cook over low heat, stirring frequently, for 20 to 30 minutes, or until the mixture is thick and starts coming away from the sides of the pan.

Spread the *halva* evenly in a buttered shallow dish. Sprinkle the top with the almonds and cardamoms.

Serve lukewarm.

Creamed Carrots with Peas

SERVES FOUR
1 lb young carrots
1 lb shelled peas
Pinch of sugar
1⅓ cups chicken stock
2 tablespoons butter
2 tablespoons flour
3 tablespoons heavy cream (optional)
Salt
Freshly ground black pepper
CROUTONS
1 egg beaten with 2 tablespoons milk
Salt
Freshly ground black pepper
4 slices day-old French bread, ¾ inch
   thick
Fine, dry bread crumbs
Butter and oil, for frying

Grate the carrots coarsely into a heavy pan. Add the peas and sprinkle with the sugar. Pour in the chicken stock and bring it to the boil. Reduce the heat, cover the pan tightly and simmer for 5 minutes.

Meanwhile, in another pan, melt the butter. Blend in the flour and stir over a low heat for 1 minute to make a pale roux.

Drain all the cooking liquid from the carrots and peas and add it gradually to the roux, stirring vigorously to prevent lumps forming. Gently mix the sauce with the carrots and peas. Cook over moderate heat, stirring constantly, until the sauce comes to the boil. Stir in the cream if used. Add salt and pepper to taste and more sugar if desired. Let the mixture bubble for 2 minutes longer.

Cover the pan and keep the vegetables hot while you prepare the croutons.

Lightly season the beaten egg and milk with salt and pepper. Dip each side of the slices of bread into the mixture. Then coat each slice with dry bread crumbs. Fry the bread slices in a mixture of butter and oil until they are crisp and a rich golden color on both sides.

To serve, divide the carrots and peas between 4 heated plates and garnish each portion with a crouton. Serve immediately.

Carrot Cake

This is an unusual and delicious cake. No one will guess that it is carrot which contributes both the rich color and the moistness. The cake is even better if left for a day or two before it is iced and eaten. A more luxurious Swiss carrot cake, made with ground almonds instead of flour, is traditionally decorated with tiny carrots made of marzipan. The cake may also be served without icing, in which case it should be baked in a loaf pan or an 8-inch cake pan for about 40 minutes.

MAKES ONE 8-INCH LAYER CAKE
2 cups all-purpose flour
2 teaspoons baking powder
1 teaspoon ground cinnamon
Mace
¼ teaspoon salt
1 cup grated carrots
Grated rind of ½ orange
2 tablespoons orange juice
¼ lb (1 stick) softened butter

⅔ cup sugar
2 eggs
½ cup hazelnuts, toasted, skinned and
   coarsely chopped (optional)
Lemon-, orange- or caramel-flavored
   icing, made with ¾ lb sugar

Butter two 8-inch layer-cake pans and line the bottoms with disks of buttered greaseproof paper. Preheat the oven to 350°F.

Sift the flour with the baking powder, cinnamon, a pinch of mace and salt. Mix the grated carrots with the orange rind and juice. Put aside until needed.

Cream the butter. Gradually beat in the sugar and continue beating until the mixture is white and fluffy. Beat in the eggs one at a time.

With a wooden spoon, beat in the carrot-and-orange mixture. Mix in the flour and spices, and the chopped hazelnuts if used.

Divide the mixture equally between the prepared cake pans, smoothing the batter evenly on top. Bake the layers for 30 minutes, or until they are well risen, firm to the touch and pulling away from the sides of the pans.

Cool the layers in the pans for at least 15 minutes. Turn them out onto wire racks and peel away the lining paper.

Sandwich the layers with half the icing. Then use the remainder to ice the top and sides of the cake.

There are few vegetables for which thick peeling is to be encouraged. The turnip is one of the exceptions. Even young turnips seem to have a tough and fibrous protective outer layer. Once this has been removed, however, the vegetable which is left is marvelously delicate and juicy. If the turnip is young, steam it for 20 to 30 minutes. If the turnip is old, boil it in salted water for about 20 minutes if sliced or quartered and for 30 to 40 minutes if whole. Turnips take kindly to butter or a rich cream sauce flavored with chives or scallion tops. Cut turnips into julienne strips, poach in light stock with an equal quantity of carrots, toss in melted butter and serve hot.

The flavor of turnip, light and subtle as it may seem, becomes surprisingly forceful when it is used in a bouquet of stock vegetables. Consequently it is best left out unless the turnips themselves are going to be served.

Spiced Turnips in Yogurt

This unusually flavored dish is a good partner for broiled and roasted meat.

SERVES SIX

2 lb young turnips, peeled
3 tablespoons butter
Seeds of 6 cardamom pods, crushed
1 teaspoon turmeric
½ teaspoon ground coriander
1 garlic clove, crushed
6 tablespoons chicken stock
⅔ cup yogurt
Salt
Freshly ground black pepper
Lemon juice (optional)
Parsley, to garnish

Cut the turnips into quarters or sixths, depending upon their size. In a large, heavy pan, melt the butter and toss the turnip pieces in it to coat them well. Cook over moderate heat for about 5 minutes, or until the turnips are lightly colored all over.

Stir in the spices and garlic. Add the chicken stock and all but 2 tablespoons of the yogurt. Sprinkle lightly with salt and pepper and mix well. Put a piece of greaseproof paper down directly over the turnips, tucking it against the sides of the pan. Reduce the heat and simmer gently for 20 minutes, or until the turnips feel tender when pierced with a sharp fork or skewer.

Remove the greaseproof paper. Increase the heat to moderate and boil the turnips for about 5 minutes. By this time the liquid should have evaporated, leaving just enough to coat the turnips with a rich, savory sauce.

Correct the seasoning. Stir in the remainder of the yogurt and sprinkle with a squeeze of lemon juice if desired. Serve garnished with parsley.

Turnips in Cream

This is a most elegant dish, which may be served with roast turkey, capon or any of the meats. It is particularly delicious if the turnips used are young, small and sweet.

Unless the turnips are very small, about the size of golf balls, they should be quartered or cut into sixths.

SERVES SIX

2 lb young turnips, peeled
⅔ cup heavy cream
5 tablespoons chicken stock
½ teaspoon dried basil
¼ teaspoon sugar
Salt
Freshly ground black pepper
1 teaspoon cornstarch
2 tablespoons finely chopped parsley

Put the turnips in a large, heavy pan. Blend the cream with the chicken stock and pour the mixture over the turnips. Add the basil, sugar, and salt and pepper to taste. Mix well and bring to simmering point over low heat. Cover the pan tightly and cook gently for 25 to 30 minutes, or until the turnips can be easily pierced with a sharp fork or skewer.

Remove the pan from the heat and, with a slotted spoon, transfer the turnips to a heated serving dish. Keep hot.

Blend the cornstarch to a smooth paste with 3 tablespoons of cold water and stir it into the liquid in the pan. Return the pan to the heat and cook, stirring, until the sauce comes to simmering point and thickens slightly. Taste and correct the seasoning if necessary.

Pour the sauce over the turnips. Sprinkle with parsley and serve.

Mustard-glazed Turnips

A fine accompaniment for such meats as lamb, pork or ham, mustard-glazed turnips may also be served with vegetable pies, custards or cutlets. If you are fond of strong flavors, increase the amount of mustard used, and always use French-type mustard.

SERVES SIX

4 tablespoons butter
2 lb young turnips, peeled
⅔ cup chicken stock
1 teaspoon brown sugar
Salt
Freshly ground black pepper
2 teaspoons Dijon mustard
2 tablespoons finely chopped parsley

In a large, heavy pan melt the butter over low heat until it is frothy. Add the turnips, turning them to coat them well. Cook over moderate heat for about 10 minutes, shaking the pan frequently so that the turnips turn an even, deep-golden color. Reduce the heat to low.

Pour in the stock and add the sugar, salt and pepper to taste. When the stock comes to simmering point, cover the pan tightly. Cook the turnips over low heat, shaking the pan occasionally, for 20 minutes, or until they feel tender when pierced with a sharp fork or skewer.

Using a slotted spoon, transfer the turnips to a plate. Stir the mustard into the pan juices and correct seasoning if necessary. Return the turnips to the pan and reheat them, swirling them around to coat them with the glaze. Sprinkle with parsley and serve.

Salsify, scorzonera and kohlrabi share a delicate, turnipy flavor. Salsify and scorzonera are best cooked as simply as possible—poached in salted water for about 15 minutes until barely tender, then well seasoned and finished in butter or folded into a well-flavored béchamel sauce. Some people maintain that because so much flavor lies just under the skin, the roots should not be scraped or cut into chunks until they have been cooked, but in some cases it is more convenient to scrape and cut them before cooking. If the roots are scraped before cooking they should be put in acidulated water to prevent discoloration.

Kohlrabi, when young and small, can be eaten raw, peeled and coarsely grated into a mixed vegetable salad. To cook kohlrabi, either peel it thinly and steam or simmer it in water, or cook it first and then peel it. In either case the cooking time will be approximately 30 minutes.

Salsify Fritters

There is more than one way to make salsify fritters. Short lengths of boiled salsify can be dipped in batter and deep-fried in oil until crisp and golden. The method given here is more complicated, but worth the effort.

SERVES FOUR
1½ lb salsify or scorzonera
Lemon juice
Salt
2 tablespoons butter
1 egg plus 1 egg yolk, lightly beaten
Freshly ground black pepper
Butter and oil, for frying

Quarter each salsify root crosswise. Scrape each piece, immediately dropping it into a bowl of water acidulated with lemon juice. Simmer the salsify in salted water for about 15 minutes, or until they are soft but not mushy when pierced with a fork.

Drain the salsify. Return the salsify pieces to the pan and shake it briefly over moderate heat to dry them out as much as possible. Then mash them to a purée, adding the butter. When the purée has cooled slightly, beat in the eggs. Season to taste with salt and pepper. Chill the mixture thoroughly; it will stiffen and become manageable.

Heat a mixture of butter and oil in a frying pan. Drop heaped tablespoonfuls of the salsify mixture into the hot fat, flattening them out into round little cakes. Fry them, turning them once, until they are crisp and golden on both sides.

Serve hot, sprinkled with lemon juice.

Stuffed Kohlrabi

When kohlrabi are out of season, young turnips may be substituted.

SERVES SIX
6 fist-sized kohlrabi
Salt
Butter
1 small onion, finely chopped
1 garlic clove, crushed
½ lb lean pork, minced
1 egg, lightly beaten
1 teaspoon tomato paste
2 slices trimmed brown bread,
    soaked in milk
Freshly ground black pepper
2 cups chicken stock
⅓ cup flour
Juice of ½ lemon
Finely chopped parsley, to garnish

Trim the kohlrabi, cutting off the stalks and shaving the bases so that each bulb will sit steadily. Peel the kohlrabi thinly. Cut a slice off the tops and scoop out the centers to make cups about ⅓ inch thick. Finely chop half of the scooped-out flesh and put it aside.

Place a steamer over a pan of simmering water. Arrange the kohlrabi cups upside down in the steamer. Sprinkle them with salt. Cover the pan and steam for 10 minutes.

Preheat the oven to 375°F.

Prepare the stuffing. In a medium-sized saucepan, heat 2 tablespoons of butter. Add the onion, garlic and chopped kohlrabi and fry, stirring occasionally, until they have softened and are lightly colored. Remove the pan from the heat. Mix in the pork, egg and tomato paste. Squeeze the bread dry. Crumble it into the pan and mix it in well. Season to taste with salt and pepper.

Arrange the steamed kohlrabi cups side by side in a buttered baking dish.

Put a flake of butter in the bottom of each cup and stuff them with the meat mixture. Pour 1½ cups of the stock around the kohlrabi. Cover the dish loosely with foil and bake on the top shelf of the oven for 20 minutes. Uncover the dish, baste with the cooking juices and bake for a further 15 minutes until the kohlrabi are tender and the stuffing is cooked through.

With a slotted spoon, transfer the kohlrabi to a hot serving dish. Keep hot.

Melt 2 tablespoons of butter in a small saucepan. Blend in the flour and stir over low heat for about 4 minutes to make a nutty brown roux. Gradually blend in the remaining stock, beating vigorously to prevent lumps forming. Add the juices left in the baking dish and a few drops of lemon juice to taste. Bring the sauce to the boil and simmer for 2 minutes. Correct the seasoning. Spoon the sauce over the kohlrabi, garnish with parsley and serve.

Salsify au Gratin

SERVES FOUR TO SIX
2½ lb salsify or scorzonera
Lemon juice
Salt
1 teaspoon sugar
3 tablespoons butter
⅓ cup flour
1⅓ cups hot milk
¼ chicken stock cube
2 egg yolks
4 tablespoons Gruyère or Swiss cheese,
    freshly grated

Scrape the salsify and cut them into 2-inch lengths, quickly dropping them into water acidulated with lemon juice to prevent them discoloring. Fill a saucepan with water, add salt and the sugar and bring to the boil. Drop in the salsify and simmer for 15 to 20 minutes, or until the chunks are tender when pierced with a skewer. Drain well.

Preheat the oven to 350°F.

Prepare the sauce. Melt the butter in a heavy saucepan. Blend in the flour and stir over low heat for 1 minute to make a pale roux. Gradually add the milk, beating vigorously to prevent lumps forming. Stir in the piece of stock cube. Bring the sauce to the boil and let it simmer gently, stirring occasionally, for

15 minutes. Remove the pan from the heat.

Beat the egg yolks lightly. Gradually beat a few tablespoons of the hot sauce into the yolks, then pour the mixture back into the pan. Flavor with a few drops of lemon juice and season to taste with salt.

Fold the salsify into the sauce. Pour the mixture into a gratin dish. Sprinkle with the cheese and bake for 15 minutes or until the salsify is heated through and the cheese on top has melted and begun to color slightly.

Beets

When beets are very young, both the tops and the beets make good eating. The tops may be used for soup or they may also be cooked in the same way as spinach.

To prepare beets, first cut off the tops, leaving about 1 inch of stem. Wash them in cold water, taking care not to pierce the skin, or the beets will "bleed" as they cook. Drop the beets into boiling salted water and cook for 45 minutes to 1½ hours if the beets are small to medium in size, longer if they are large. Test to see if they are ready—carefully lift out a beet and press it gently with your fingers. If the skin slips off easily, the beet is cooked. Alternatively, the beets may be baked. Put them in a baking dish and bake in the oven at 325°F. The timing is the same as for boiling. Cooked beets may be pickled in vinegar or sliced, flavored with orange and served in a sour-cream sauce.

Harvard Beets

This is a classic American recipe. Harvard Beets, according to some cookbooks, can be changed to Yale Beets by substituting fresh orange juice plus 1 tablespoon of lemon juice for the vinegar.

SERVES FOUR TO SIX
1½ lb beets, cooked
⅓ cup sugar
1 tablespoon cornstarch
6 tablespoons mild wine or cider vinegar
Salt
2 tablespoons butter

Trim the beets, rub off their skins and slice them thinly.

In the top of a double boiler, blend the sugar and cornstarch with the vinegar. Cook over low heat, stirring constantly, until the mixture comes to the boil and thickens.

Set the top part of the pan over simmering water. Carefully mix the prepared beets into the sauce. Season to taste with salt and cook gently, stirring occasionally, for 25 to 30 minutes, until the beets are hot and the sauce is a deep red.

Add the butter, stirring until it has melted. Serve immediately.

Christmas Beet Borscht

There are numerous versions of borscht, or borsht, most of them originating in eastern Europe. They range from light consommés, like this recipe, to thick vegetable soups reinforced with dried beans and chunks of meat. A Christmas borscht is traditionally served in Poland on Christmas Eve, when meat is not allowed. It is garnished with tiny "ears," or dumplings, stuffed with a mixture of chopped dried mushrooms, onions and bread crumbs. An Easter borscht is, however, based on a light ham stock. All clear beet soups taste better garnished with a spoonful of thick sour cream.

SERVES SIX
6 beets, scrubbed, peeled and
    thickly sliced
2 large carrots, cut into large pieces
2 leeks, cut into pieces
1 small onion, quartered
1 slice celeriac
8 black peppercorns
3 allspice berries
1 bay leaf
2 dried mushroom caps
Salt
TO FINISH BORSCHT
1 raw beet
Juice of ½ lemon
1 tablespoon sugar
2 teaspoons salt

Put all the vegetables, spices, bay leaf and mushroom caps in a large enameled saucepan. Cover with 2 quarts of cold water. Sprinkle generously with salt. Bring to simmering point over moderate heat. Reduce the heat to low, cover the pan and simmer for 1 hour.

Meanwhile, scrub, peel and grate the raw beet coarsely into a bowl. Stir in the lemon juice, sugar and salt.

Strain the borscht through a fine sieve. Pour a few ladlefuls of it over the grated-beet mixture. Then pour it all back into the pan, together with the rest of the strained stock. Reheat gently, but do not allow the borscht to come to the boil or its brilliant red color may be destroyed.

Strain the grated beet out of the soup. Correct the seasoning with sugar, salt or lemon juice, if necessary. Reheat gently before serving.

Creamed Beets

This dish is traditionally served with such strong game as venison or hare, and with pot-roasted beef.

SERVES FOUR
1 lb cooked beets
1 medium-sized, tart eating apple,
    peeled and cored (optional)
1 tablespoon butter
2 teaspoons flour
Light cream
Sugar
Salt
Wine vinegar or lemon juice

Trim the cooked beets, rub off the skins and grate coarsely into a bowl (or put through a meat grinder). Grate the apple, if used, into the same bowl.

Melt the butter in a heavy pan. Blend in the flour and stir over a low heat for 1 minute to make a pale roux. Remove the pan from the heat and gradually beat in 8 tablespoons of cream. Continue to beat until smoothly blended. Mix in the grated beets and apple. Add sugar and salt to taste and sharpen the flavor with vinegar or lemon juice.

Bring to simmering, stirring constantly. If the purée is too stiff, thin it with a little more cream. Simmer gently, uncovered, stirring occasionally, for a few minutes before serving.

Celeriac (Celery Root)

Rough and knobby as it may appear, celeriac is a marvelous vegetable for adding a fresh flavor to winter dishes. And it is very adaptable. Raw and coarsely grated, it may be added with advantage to many salads—for a more delicate flavor blanch the celeriac for 2 minutes in acidulated water. Cooked, it is not only a potent celery flavoring for stocks, sauces and stews, but it is also a fine vegetable in its own right.

Celeriac at its best should be the size of a large cooking apple, firm and unblemished. To prepare celeriac for cooking, trim and slice it, then peel it, dropping it immediately into acidulated water. If the celeriac is to be cooked whole, trim and scrub it and then cook it, peeling it later. Boil sliced or diced celeriac in salted, acidulated water for 25 to 30 minutes. Whole celeriac will take from 40 minutes to 1 hour to cook.

Celeriac may be served simply tossed in melted butter or dressed in a Mornay sauce.

Celeriac-and-Ham Salad

The classic French version of this salad, *Céleri-rave à la Rémoulade*, simply combines coarsely grated raw celeriac with a mustard mayonnaise. This recipe makes a more substantial but equally piquant and delicious dish.

SERVES FOUR
¾ lb celeriac root
Salt
1 egg yolk
2 teaspoons Dijon mustard
2 teaspoons tarragon vinegar
8 tablespoons olive oil
Freshly ground black pepper
½ cup lean cooked ham, cubed
2 medium-sized carrots, coarsely grated
2 tablespoons finely chopped parsley
Lettuce leaves, to garnish

Scrub the celeriac root thoroughly under cold running water. Drop it into a large pan of rapidly boiling salted water and boil for 30 minutes. The celeriac should still feel very firm when pierced with a skewer.

While the celeriac is cooking, put the egg yolk in a bowl. Blend in the mustard, vinegar and a pinch of salt. Beat in the olive oil, drop by drop at first, then in a thin stream as the mixture thickens. When all the oil has been incorporated, season to taste with salt and pepper. The mayonnaise should be highly flavored.

Drain the cooked celeriac. As soon as it is cool enough to handle, peel it and cut it into neat cubes the same size as the ham.

Fold the warm celeriac, the ham, the carrots and parsley into the mayonnaise. Correct the seasoning if necessary. Serve very cold in a bowl lined with lettuce leaves.

Celeriac and Brussels Sprouts au Gratin

Celeriac and Brussels sprouts make a most attractive combination.

SERVES SIX
¾ lb celeriac root
Salt
5 tablespoons butter
1 onion, finely chopped
⅓ cup flour
1⅓ cups milk
⅔ cup light cream
1 egg yolk
Freshly ground black pepper
Ground mace
1½ lb Brussels sprouts, trimmed, cooked and halved lengthwise (see page 143)
2 tablespoons fresh white bread crumbs

Scrub the celeriac under cold running water. Parboil it in salted water for 15 minutes. Drain it in a colander, then plunge it into cold water. As soon as the celeriac is cool enough to handle, peel it and cut it into ½-inch cubes.

Melt 4 tablespoons of the butter in a saucepan. Add the celeriac cubes and onion and stir to mix. Cover the pan and cook over low heat for 15 minutes, shaking the pan or stirring occasionally to prevent the vegetables sticking to the bottom.

Sprinkle the vegetables with the flour and stir over low heat for 2 minutes to blend it with the buttery juices. Gradually stir in the milk. Bring to the boil and simmer for 2 minutes. Remove the pan from the heat.

Beat the cream and egg yolk together lightly. Blend them into the sauce. Season to taste with salt, pepper and a pinch of mace.

Preheat the oven to 350°F.

Arrange half of the Brussels sprouts in a buttered baking dish. Pour over half of the celeriac and sauce. Cover with the remaining sprouts, followed by the remaining celeriac and sauce. Smooth the top with the back of a spoon. Sprinkle with the bread crumbs and dot with the remaining butter.

Bake the dish in the top half of the oven for 25 minutes, or until the surface is golden and the vegetables are piping hot.

Celeriac Cups Stuffed with Mushrooms

An unusual dish which makes a delicious appetizer or an accompaniment for a meat dish, especially pork.

SERVES SIX
3 celeriac roots
1 lemon, halved
Salt
Melted butter
4 tablespoons butter
1 cup button mushrooms, quartered or cut in eighths, depending on their size
3 scallions, chopped
Freshly ground black pepper
2 tablespoons finely chopped parsley
2 tablespoons freshly grated Parmesan cheese
⅔ cup thick sour cream
Paprika

Scrub, trim and peel the celeriac roots. Cut each root in half horizontally. Scoop out the flesh, reserving it, and leaving the cups ¼ inch thick. Rub the celeriac cups and the reserved flesh with a cut lemon half to prevent them discoloring.

Bring a large pan of salted water, acidulated with the juice of ½ lemon, to the boil. Put in the celeriac cups and simmer them gently, covered, for 10 minutes, or until they feel tender when tested with a skewer.

Drain them thoroughly. Brush them all over with melted butter and arrange them side by side in a baking dish.

Preheat the oven to 375°F. Finely chop the reserved celeriac flesh. Melt the butter in a medium-sized saucepan. Stir in the celeriac, mushrooms and scallions. Add the juice squeezed from the remaining half lemon. Mix well and season to taste with salt and pepper. Cover the pan and cook gently for 10 to 15 minutes, stirring occasionally. Remove the pan from the heat and stir in the parsley and cheese. Correct the seasoning.

Fill the celeriac cups with the mixture. Spoon sour cream over the top of each one and sprinkle with a pinch of paprika.

Bake the celeriac cups in the top half of the oven for 20 minutes. Serve hot.

Tubers

Tubers are a small but important group which includes the less well-known Jerusalem artichoke as well as the potato (white and sweet), a giant among vegetables and a staple food in many countries.

The Jerusalem artichoke, a native of North America, is a knobby, sweetish artichoke-flavored tuber which adds variety to the winter diet.

Surprisingly, the potato was not immediately accepted as a palatable vegetable. Although known in Europe by the sixteenth century, it was persistently treated as a curiosity.

The real hero of the potato saga is an eighteenth-century Frenchman, Antoine-Augustin Parmentier, who had a curious obsession for potatoes from early childhood. His missionary zeal was rewarded when Louis XVI appeared on the eve of the Feast of St. Louis with potato flowers in his buttonhole. From then on, potatoes had arrived, at least as far as Louis' courtiers were concerned.

By the middle of the nineteenth century, cookery writers were taking the potato seriously too, and today it is calculated that there are nearly 500 different ways of serving potatoes.

Unfortunately, familiarity has bred contempt for the poor potato, and the everyday ways of serving them are not always as good as they might be. To cook potatoes well, however, depends primarily on the variety of potato. By and large, the guiding principle is that waxy potatoes are good for frying and salads, and floury potatoes are best for boiling and baking.

Boiled potatoes, still called *pommes à l'anglaise* in menu French, rarely get the attention they deserve. To get the most flavor and nutrition from a potato, cook it in its jacket. If it must be peeled, then peel it very thinly, because most of the food value lies just under the skin. Boiling peeled potatoes in a large pot of water washes out even more goodness, so if possible steam them instead.

Once potatoes have been cooked and drained, dry them out by shaking them in a hot pan over low heat to steam off any remaining moisture.

The secret of really good mashed potatoes is freshness—they should be served as soon as they are ready. Cook, drain, dry out and peel the potatoes. Mash them smoothly, gradually beating in some nearly boiling milk and some butter —2 pounds of floury potatoes will take about ⅔ cup of milk and 4 tablespoons of butter. Beat the potatoes briskly over low heat until they are hot and fluffy. Season with salt, plenty of pepper and a light grating of nutmeg.

For baked potatoes, medium or large, floury white "old" potatoes are best. Scrub them clean, dry them and prick them with a fork in several places. Then rub them all over with a piece of buttered paper or, for an even crisper skin, use oil. Bake them at 350° to 375°F for at least an hour, or until they feel soft when pressed gently. Serve the baked potatoes immediately with plenty of butter and coarse salt—or with herb butter, or sour cream mixed with garlic or herbs.

Deep-fried potatoes come in a variety of forms, from French fries to *pommes allumettes* and *pommes pailles*, julienne potatoes, and potato chips, cut paper-thin on a mandoline.

Use a proper deep-frying pan fitted with a basket. For safety's sake, never have the fat higher than 2 inches from the top. Beef dripping, lard, vegetable and olive oil each has something different to offer to the flavor of the potato. As a rough guide, you will need 3 pints of oil or fat to fry about 2 pounds of potatoes. Finely cut potatoes (juliennes and chips) should be fried in handfuls to give them enough room to float free.

Temperature is probably the one most important factor in deep-frying of any kind. For perfect French fries, heat the fat to 350°F. The potatoes should be peeled, cut, rinsed and carefully dried. Put the potatoes into a frying basket, lower them into the fat carefully and deep-fry until they are soft and a pale golden color— about 5 minutes. Drain them on paper toweling and if they are not to be served immediately, wrap them in greaseproof paper. Then, shortly before serving, heat the fat to 425°F and fry the potatoes for another 2 to 3 minutes, or until they are crisp, golden brown and dry. Drain again, sprinkle with salt and serve at once.

Thin-cut julienne potatoes and chips are fried once only, for about 3 minutes at 425°F.

The native American sweet potato, of which the yam is one variety, developed in the tropics and migrated as far north as the Southern states, but never flourished in the temperate parts of Europe. It is, however, much appreciated in the warmer Pacific islands and eastern Asia. As integral to Southern cooking as greens, country ham or corn bread, the sweet potato appears on our tables in many forms from Maine to California and is considered essential to the Thanksgiving and Christmas feasts. Delicious when simply baked or mashed, it can double for squash or pumpkin in pies and puddings.

Potatoes

Pommes Soufflés

These are the puff potatoes of classic French cuisine. They are rather tricky to make—and like so many of the best dishes, they were discovered by accident. Apparently, the chef adding the final touches to a ceremonial dinner for the inauguration of the Paris–St. Germain railway line in 1837 was suddenly told that the guests of honor, Louis-Philippe and his queen, Marie-Amélie, would be late. The thinly sliced potato rectangles were already frying. He whipped them out, drained them and when the diners had assembled he plunged them back into even hotter fat. To the delight of all concerned, the shock of the contact with hot fat puffed the limp slices into crisp golden cushions.

If you wish to experiment with *pommes soufflés*, use good, old potatoes, preferably red-skinned ones. Cut them into paper-thin little oblongs, but do not rinse them. For the first frying, use oil at 275°F and fry the potatoes briefly until they are soft but not colored. For the second frying, heat the fat to 475°F. The potatoes should puff up and color almost as soon as they touch the fat. But if all the slices do not puff up they can be served as potato chips—even professional chefs admit to a high failure rate.

Potatoes Cooked with Yogurt

This unusual and tasty Indian dish is a mixture of sweetness, sourness and spiciness.

SERVES FOUR TO SIX
3 tablespoons clarified butter or
  vegetable oil
1 medium-sized onion, finely chopped
1-inch piece fresh root ginger, peeled
  and finely chopped
1 tablespoon ground coriander
1 teaspoon turmeric
2 green chilies, finely chopped
3 medium-sized tomatoes, blanched,
  peeled and chopped
1 teaspoon salt
1 teaspoon sugar
1⅓ cups yogurt
¼ teaspoon ground mace
4 tablespoons raisins
1½ lb small new potatoes, boiled
1 tablespoon chopped coriander leaves

Heat the butter or oil in a large frying pan. Add the onion and ginger and fry, stirring, until golden. Add the coriander and turmeric and fry, stirring constantly, for 30 seconds. Stir in the chilies, tomatoes, salt, sugar and yogurt. Simmer the sauce, uncovered, until it is thick.

Add the mace, raisins and potatoes and cook, stirring, for 5 minutes.

Turn the potatoes out onto a serving dish, sprinkle the coriander leaves on top and serve hot.

Buttered Potatoes and Mushrooms au Gratin

This is a very rich dish which goes particularly well with roast or grilled lamb or with scrambled eggs for supper.

SERVES FOUR TO SIX
2 lb potatoes
½ lb small white mushrooms
1 tablespoon olive oil
¼ lb (1 stick) butter
Salt
Freshly ground black pepper

Peel the potatoes and slice them very thinly. Spread the slices out on a cloth and pat them dry. Trim the mushroom stems. Wipe the mushrooms with a damp cloth and slice them thickly, stalks and all.

Preheat the oven to 375°F.

Heat the oil and half the butter in a wide, shallow, flameproof casserole. Add the mushrooms and toss them briefly over high heat so that they absorb most of the fat. Remove them to a bowl with a slotted spoon.

Melt 2 tablespoons of the remaining butter in the hot casserole, swirling it around to coat the sides. Arrange an overlapping layer of the larger potato slices over the bottom of the casserole and a row of medium-sized slices around the sides. Replace the casserole over moderately low heat. Then alternate two layers of mushrooms and their juices with layers of potato, ending with a neat, overlapping layer of potato. Sprinkle each layer with salt and pepper. Dot the top with the remaining butter.

Bake the casserole for 40 minutes, or until the potatoes feel soft when pierced right through with the point of a sharp knife or skewer, and are crisp and golden on top.

Potato-and-Mussel Salad

A specialty of Boulogne, this tasty fish salad makes an elegant start to any meal.

SERVES SIX
3½ quarts mussels, scraped, washed and
  bearded
½ cup dry white wine
4 shallots, chopped
1 thyme sprig
6 parsley sprigs
Freshly ground black pepper
2 lb potatoes, boiled, peeled and thickly
  sliced
½ cup vinaigrette dressing
GARNISH
Finely chopped parsley
Finely chopped chives

In a large saucepan cook the mussels, wine, shallots, thyme, parsley and a generous amount of pepper over high heat for 8 minutes, or until the mussels open. Discard those that remain shut.

Lift the mussels out with a slotted spoon as they open, and remove them from the shells. Discard the shells and set the mussels aside.

Put the potatoes into a large bowl. Strain the liquid the mussels were cooked in and pour it over the potatoes. Set aside to cool.

When the potatoes are cold, drain them and arrange them on a serving dish. Put the mussels on top of the potatoes and pour over the vinaigrette. Sprinkle with the chopped parsley and chives. Chill thoroughly before serving.

Potato-and-Carrot Soup

This is the ideal soup for a cold winter night. Serve garnished with crisp, tiny croutons fried in a mixture of butter and oil or in bacon fat.

SERVES SIX

3 large, floury potatoes
3 carrots
1 small parsnip (optional)
6 cups beef stock
2 tablespoons butter
1 large, mild onion, finely chopped
1 tablespoon flour
Marjoram
Milk or light cream
Salt
Freshly ground black pepper
Small croutons, to garnish

Peel and slice the potatoes. Scrape the carrots and parsnip, if used, and slice them thickly. Put the sliced vegetables into a large pan. Pour in the stock and bring to the boil. Reduce the heat, half cover the pan and cook gently for about 45 minutes or until the vegetables are very soft.

While the vegetables are cooking, melt the butter in another large pan. Add the onion and fry gently, stirring frequently, taking care not to let it burn, until it is a rich golden color. Sprinkle the flour over the onion and blend it smoothly into the fat. Stir over low heat for 2 minutes longer to make a golden roux. Stir in a pinch of marjoram.

Rub the vegetables and stock through a fine sieve or purée them in an electric blender. Add the puréed mixture, a little at a time, to the onion in the pan, stirring vigorously to prevent lumps forming. Bring the soup to the boil, stirring, and simmer for 5 minutes longer.

Thin the soup down as desired with milk or light cream and season with salt and pepper. Bring to the boil again and serve accompanied by a bowl of croutons to sprinkle over each portion.

Potato Salad au Vermouth

A summery salad, particularly good served with cold poached fish or shellfish mayonnaise, or with ham or hard-boiled eggs, sliced cucumbers and tomatoes dressed with vinaigrette.

The mayonnaise for this salad should be homemade, thick and richly flavored with good wine vinegar and French mustard.

SERVES SIX

2 lb small new potatoes
Salt
⅔ cup chicken stock
4 tablespoons dry white vermouth
8 tablespoons thick mayonnaise
3 tablespoons chopped chives, scallions or shallots
2 tablespoons finely chopped parsley
Freshly ground black pepper

Wash the potatoes and boil them in salted water or steam them. Mix the chicken stock and vermouth in a pitcher.

Peel the hot potatoes and slice them thickly. Put them into a bowl, moistening each layer with stock and vermouth. Set aside until the potatoes are quite cold and have absorbed most of the dressing.

Carefully drain off the excess liquid —it may be used to fortify a soup. Fold the mayonnaise and herbs in carefully to avoid breaking the potato slices, and season to taste with salt and pepper.

Chill until ready to serve.

Potato Soup with Barley

A thick, satisfying soup that makes a fine main course for a family supper.

SERVES SIX

2 tablespoons butter
1¼ cups small white mushrooms, sliced
1 large mild onion, finely chopped
½ cup pearl barley, soaked overnight
2 carrots, scraped and diced
6 cups beef stock
2 large potatoes, peeled and diced
1⅓ cups half-and-half
Salt
Freshly ground black pepper
Finely chopped fresh parsley or dill, to garnish

Melt the butter in the saucepan in which the soup will be cooked. Add the mushrooms and onion and fry gently, stirring occasionally, for 4 minutes, or until the onion is soft and golden, but not brown.

Drain the barley in a sieve and add it to the pan together with the diced carrots. Pour in the stock and bring to the boil. Reduce the heat and simmer for 20 minutes, or until the barley and carrots have softened.

Add the potatoes and continue to cook gently for 15 minutes longer until they, too, are soft but not mushy.

Add the half-and-half. The soup should be rather thick. Season to taste with salt and pepper. Bring the soup to the boil, sprinkle with parsley or dill, and serve.

New Potatoes Baked in Foil

These fragrant new potatoes baked in a package of aluminum foil are even more deliciously flavored than if the potatoes were simply boiled and tossed with herb butter.

SERVES FOUR TO SIX

1½ lb small new potatoes
4 tablespoons butter
2 sprigs fresh mint or dill
Coarse salt
Freshly ground black pepper

Wash the potatoes under cold running water, rubbing off the skins with your fingers. Alternatively, the skins may be left on. Dry the potatoes well.

Preheat the oven to 400°F.

Cut a double thickness of foil large enough to wrap the potatoes up in a package. Distribute a few small pieces of butter over the center of the foil. Put the potatoes on top, burying the sprigs of herbs among them. Sprinkle the potatoes generously with salt and pepper, and dot the rest of the butter over them. Wrap the potatoes up, tightly sealing the edges of the foil. Put the package on a baking sheet.

Bake for 1 hour, or until the potatoes feel soft when squeezed gently through the foil. Protect your hand with a cloth.

Undo the package carefully. Transfer the potatoes to a heated serving dish. Discard the herbs and pour the buttery juices in the foil over the top.

Potatoes

Sautéed Potatoes with Garlic

Quick and easy to prepare, this recipe makes a rather elegant accompaniment for poultry and lamb. It is important not to pierce the garlic cloves when you peel them, and vital that they do not burn, otherwise they will impart a bitter taste instead of the subtle garlic flavor that goes so well with potatoes.

SERVES FOUR TO SIX
2 lb potatoes
3 tablespoons olive oil or 2 tablespoons lard and 1 tablespoon cooking oil
3 plump garlic cloves, peeled
Coarse salt
Finely chopped parsley, to garnish

Peel the potatoes and cut them up into cubes of about 1 inch. Rinse the cubes in a colander and dry them thoroughly with paper toweling.

In a large, deep frying pan that has a lid and will take the potatoes in a single layer, heat the olive oil or the mixture of lard and oil. Fry the garlic cloves slowly until they are just golden. Add the potatoes and fry them, tossing them constantly, over moderate heat for 5 minutes, or until they have colored on all sides.

Sprinkle the potatoes with salt. Cover the pan and fry the potatoes very slowly, shaking the pan and turning them occasionally, for about 15 minutes, or until they are crisp and golden brown on all sides and feel soft inside when pierced with a fork or skewer.

Lift the potato cubes out of the pan with a slotted spoon. Discard the garlic cloves. Drain the potatoes thoroughly and serve immediately, sprinkled with more salt and garnished with parsley.

Gratin Dauphinois

Of the many fine French potato *gratins* this is without doubt the greatest and the best. It can partner any meat dish—roasts, broiled meats, steaks and chops of all kinds.

SERVES SIX
1 tablespoon butter
2 lb potatoes
1⅓ cups heavy cream
1⅓ cups milk
1 garlic clove, crushed
Salt
Freshly ground black pepper
½ cup Gruyère or Swiss cheese, freshly grated

Preheat the oven to 400°F. Grease a large, shallow baking dish about 9 inches square with the butter.

Peel the potatoes and slice them about ⅛ inch thick.

In a large saucepan, combine the potatoes with the cream, milk, garlic, and salt and pepper to taste. Bring to the boil over moderate heat.

Pour the potato mixture into the prepared dish, spreading the slices out in an even layer. Sprinkle grated cheese over the entire surface.

Bake the *gratin* for 45 minutes, or until the surface is bubbling and golden brown, and the potatoes feel soft when tested with a skewer or the point of a knife.

Let the *gratin* rest on top of the stove for about 15 minutes before serving.

To make French fries, peel the potatoes as thinly as possible, using a potato peeler.

Slice the potatoes, then cut each slice into strips about ⅓ to ½ inch thick.

Jansson's Temptation

Traditionally one of a selection of dishes in a smorgasbord, this famous Swedish potato-and-anchovy dish makes an excellent main dish for lunch or supper.

SERVES TWO AS A MAIN DISH, FOUR AS AN APPETIZER
4 medium-sized potatoes
Butter
1 large Spanish onion, shredded
⅔ cup light cream
⅔ cup milk
Salt
Freshly ground black pepper
2 oz flat anchovy fillets, drained
4 tablespoons coarse white bread crumbs

Peel the potatoes and cut them into matchstick-size strips.

Heat 3 tablespoons of butter in a deep frying pan. Add the onions and fry them gently until they are soft and transparent, but not colored. Mix in the potato sticks and fry them gently for 3 minutes, turning them to coat them with the butter. Stir in the cream and milk. Season to taste with salt and pepper (but bear in mind the saltiness of the anchovies to come) and simmer very gently for a few minutes longer so that the potatoes just begin to soften.

Preheat the oven to 400°F.

Spread half of the potato-and-onion mixture over the bottom of a shallow baking dish. Arrange the anchovy fillets evenly over the top and cover with the remaining potatoes, onions and cream. Sprinkle with the bread crumbs and dot with a few pieces of butter.

Bake the dish for 30 minutes, or until the potatoes feel tender when pierced with a skewer and the top is golden and bubbling.

Using a clean tea towel, dry the slices carefully.

Potato Salad with Bacon Dressing

This rather strongly flavored potato salad is an excellent accompaniment to cold meats, ham or poultry. Drain off any excess dressing before serving. It may be saved and used to dress a fresh green lettuce salad.

SERVES SIX TO EIGHT
2 lb new potatoes
Salt
6 slices bacon
1 large, mild onion, very finely chopped
8 tablespoons olive oil
4 tablespoons cider vinegar
2 teaspoons soft brown sugar
½ teaspoon coarse French mustard

Worcestershire sauce or Chinese soy sauce
Freshly ground black pepper
4 tablespoons finely chopped parsley

Wash the potatoes and rub the skins off under cold running water. Boil or steam the potatoes in salted water until they are tender but not mushy. Meanwhile, fry the bacon slices until crisp. Drain off excess fat and crumble the bacon.

When the potatoes are done, drain them and either slice them thickly or, if they are very small, quarter them or cut them into sixths. Put the potatoes into a bowl and lightly mix in the crumbled bacon.

In a small pan, mix the onion with the olive oil, vinegar, brown sugar, mustard, a few drops of Worcestershire sauce or Chinese soy sauce, a pinch of salt to taste and a grinding of black pepper. Over very low heat, bring this mixture very slowly to the boil, stirring constantly. When it comes to the boil, immediately pour the mixture over the potatoes and bacon. Add the parsley and mix gently but thoroughly. Taste for seasoning. Allow the salad to cool and serve slightly chilled.

In a deep-frying pan, heat the fat to 350°F. Put the slices in the frying basket, carefully lower it into the fat and fry for 5 minutes. Drain the French fries on paper toweling and serve them immediately.

Sweet Potatoes

America's gift to Asia, the sweet potato was once sold roasted on the streets of southern Chinese cities and was so cheap that it was known as "beggars' food." Because sweet potatoes do not propagate themselves from seed in warm temperate climates, they are not as commonplace in our Southern states as they are in tropical Asia, where they do flower and seed themselves. In American eyes, sweet potatoes often have an aura of "Sunday special" compared with the everyday white potato, but even the poorest field laborer or sharecropper in the South had access to a great repertoire of sweet-potato dishes, many of which appeared on holidays.

When baked, cut open and served piping hot with melted butter flowing into their hearts, sweet potatoes have a delicious, mellow flavor which many prefer to sweeter variations. They are equally delicious when prepared in the Southern way—boiled and mashed with just a touch of brown sugar and plenty of nutmeg or mace.

There are even those who finish off a dish of mashed sweet potatoes with a topping of marshmallows browned under the broiler. In response to this custom, one can only join the late Irma Rombauer, who marveled "at any cook who voluntarily dwarfs the possibility of a sweet potato with marshmallow."

The production of native sweet potatoes, which are mealy and somewhat dry when cooked, has dwindled in recent years in favor of the importation of the sweeter, moister yam from Central America and the Caribbean. They are interchangeable in recipes, except that the drier, paler sweet potato requires a little more liquid when used as the basis of recipes calling for puréed sweet potatoes.

Sweet Potato-Apple Casserole

For those who like to marry a tart flavor to the sunny, natural sweetness of this tuber, the combination with apples is particularly recommended.

SERVES SIX
6 medium-sized sweet potatoes, boiled
  and peeled
2 cups peeled and thinly sliced cooking
  or tart eating apples
6 tablespoons butter
Salt
½ cup brown sugar
Cinnamon or mace
¼ cup apple juice or water

Preheat the oven to 350°F.

Slice the potatoes about ¼ inch thick. Grease a 2-quart casserole and alternate layers of sweet potatoes and apples, topping each layer of apples with the butter, salt, brown sugar, and a sprinkling of cinnamon or mace. Pour the apple juice or water over the top layer and bake for 1 hour until the apples are tender and the top is lightly browned.

Sweet-Potato Pudding

There are many Southern variations on the theme of mashed sweet potatoes combined with various fruits, laced with rum or wine, and baked as a side dish with ham or turkey.

SERVES FOUR TO SIX
8 medium sweet potatoes
4 tablespoons butter

¾ cup crushed pineapple with juice
2 tablespoons brown sugar
2 tablespoons dark rum or sherry
1 teaspoon nutmeg

Boil the sweet potatoes in their jackets until tender when pierced with a skewer. When the potatoes are cool enough to handle, peel them and mash or purée them through a food mill with 3 tablespoons of the butter.

Preheat the oven to 400°F.

Stir in the pineapple, brown sugar, rum or sherry, and nutmeg, and mix thoroughly. Turn the mixture into a greased 2-quart casserole, dot with the remaining butter and bake about 20 minutes, or until the top is lightly browned.

Sweet-Potato Pie

Traditional recipes for sweet-potato pie are almost interchangeable with those for squash or pumpkin pie. This pie could be served as dessert with the Thanksgiving turkey, instead of as a side dish.

SERVES SIX
Dough to line a 9-inch pie pan
3 eggs, separated
⅓ cup brown sugar
2 cups mashed sweet potatoes made from
  6 medium potatoes boiled and mashed
  with 2 tablespoons of butter
1 teaspoon lemon juice
¼ cup milk
⅓ cup cider
½ teaspoon salt
2 tablespoons brandy
16 to 18 pecan halves
TOPPING
1 cup heavy cream
1 tablespoon powdered sugar
1 teaspoon vanilla

Preheat oven to 450°F.

Roll out dough to line a 9-inch pie pan. Beat the egg yolks with the brown sugar until light, and combine with the mashed potatoes, stirring until blended. Stir in the lemon juice, milk, cider, salt, and brandy. Whip the egg whites until stiff but not dry. Fold them into the potatoes and pour the mixture into the prepared pie shell. Top with the pecan halves arranged in a circle. Bake the pie in the hot oven for 10 minutes; reduce heat to 350°F and bake about 30 minutes more, or until a knife inserted in the center comes out clean.

To make the topping, whip the heavy cream until thick, then stir in the sugar and vanilla. Put a spoonful on each wedge before serving.

Jerusalem Artichokes

Jerusalem artichokes are only very distantly related to the globe artichoke—through the vast daisy family—and have certainly no historical connection with the ancient city of Jerusalem. The word is said to be a misinterpretation of the Italian name for the sunflower, *girasole*, a much closer relative.

Use Jerusalem artichokes as soon as possible after they have been dug up because they quickly lose their creamy color and begin to wrinkle and soften. Scrub them under cold running water. Scrape or peel away any discolored patches and any excessive knobs. Drop them into water acidulated with lemon juice (see page 233), since the cut surfaces will quickly discolor. Toward the end of the season, the skins will toughen and will have to be peeled away completely, a job easily done after cooking.

Jerusalem artichokes may be steamed, boiled or poached in milk for 15 to 20 minutes, or until just tender. Then they may be sliced and pan-fried in butter, or mashed with butter and a little cream or an egg yolk and garnished with crumbled bacon.

Artichoke Fritters

SERVES FOUR
1 lb Jerusalem artichokes
2⅔ cups chicken stock
2 eggs
Salt
Freshly ground black pepper
Fine dry bread crumbs
Oil for deep-frying

Parboil the artichokes in the chicken stock for 12 to 15 minutes, or until they are tender but still crisp. Drain them thoroughly. Beat the eggs with salt and pepper to taste in a wide, shallow bowl. When ready to serve, drop the artichokes into the beaten egg. Coat them well, then lift them out onto a flat dish on which you have scattered a thick layer of bread crumbs. Use two forks to separate the tubers and coat them individually if they are large, in bundles of twos or threes if they are small.

Heat the oil in a deep frying pan to 375°F. Put in the coated artichokes a batch at a time and fry for 3 to 4 minutes, or until they are crisp and golden. Drain them on paper toweling and serve immediately, sprinkled with more salt.

Jerusalem Artichokes au Gratin

A most elegant dish to accompany veal escallops, roast chicken or ham. Garnished with crisp bacon curls, it can also be served as an informal main course.

SERVES FOUR
2 lb Jerusalem artichokes
2 cups milk
⅔ cup chicken stock
Salt
3 tablespoons butter
2 tablespoons flour
½ cup Gruyère and ¼ cup Parmesan cheese, freshly grated and mixed
⅔ cup heavy cream, lightly whipped
Freshly ground black pepper

Scrub the artichokes and scrape them if necessary. Put them into a wide pan in one layer if possible. Pour over the milk and chicken stock. Season lightly with salt and bring to the boil. Reduce the heat, partially cover the pan and simmer for 15 to 20 minutes, or until the artichokes are just tender. Drain the artichokes in a colander over a bowl. Measure the liquid and if necessary return it to the pan and reduce it to a scant 2 cups by fast boiling.

Melt 2 tablespoons of the butter in another pan. Blend in the flour and stir over low heat for 1 minute to make a pale roux. Gradually add the hot artichoke liquid, beating vigorously to prevent lumps forming. Bring the sauce to simmering point and cook gently, stirring frequently, for 6 to 8 minutes, or until it has thickened and reduced slightly.

Meanwhile, cut the artichokes into thick slices. (If they need to be peeled completely, this is the point at which it should be done. It is probably easier to cut off any small knobs than try to peel them.)

Remove the sauce from the heat and beat in two-thirds of the cheese. Let the sauce cool slightly. Gently mix in the whipped cream. Season to taste with pepper and more salt, if necessary.

Preheat the oven to 400°F.

Fold the sliced artichokes gently into the sauce and pour into a shallow baking dish. Sprinkle with the remaining cheese. Dot the remaining butter over the top and bake on the top shelf of the oven for 20 minutes, or until the sauce is bubbling and the surface golden brown. Let the dish rest for a few minutes before serving.

Jerusalem artichoke tubers on the root stem.

Cream of Artichoke Soup

This soup is also called Palestine soup —a name which perpetuates the myth of the tuber's connection with Jerusalem.

SERVES SIX
2 lb Jerusalem artichokes
Lemon juice
2 medium-sized mild onions
4 tablespoons butter
5 cups chicken stock
1⅓ cups light cream
Salt
Freshly ground black pepper
1 tablespoon finely chopped parsley
Freshly grated Parmesan cheese

Scrub the artichokes thoroughly with a stiff brush. Scrape them or peel them if necessary, quickly dropping them into a bowl of water acidulated with lemon juice to prevent discoloration.

Peel the onions and slice them thickly. Melt the butter in a large, heavy saucepan over low heat without letting it color. Add the onions and fry gently, stirring with a wooden spoon to coat the slices thoroughly.

Lift the artichokes out of the water one at a time and slice them. Put the slices into the pan, turning them in the butter to coat them on all sides. Keep the heat low so that the vegetables do not color. Cover and simmer gently for 5 minutes, shaking the pan frequently to prevent the artichokes from sticking to the bottom and burning.

When the artichoke slices have soft-ened slightly, add the chicken stock. Increase the heat and bring the stock to the boil. Partly cover the pan, reduce the heat and simmer for 15 to 20 minutes, or until the artichokes are almost disintegrating.

Put the contents of the pan through the finest plate of a food mill, or purée in an electric blender. Return the purée to the saucepan. Stir in the cream and season to taste with salt and pepper. Bring the soup to just under boiling point, stirring. Garnish with parsley and serve with grated Parmesan to sprinkle over each portion.

To prepare Jerusalem artichokes, scrub them under cold running water, then peel or scrape away any discolored patches or excessive knobs.

To prevent the cut surfaces from discoloring, drop the peeled, sliced artichokes into acidulated water.

Vegetable Fruits

Tomatoes, cucumbers, pumpkins, all kinds of squashes, eggplants and peppers are all fruits which are almost always prepared and served as vegetables. They all originated in the Americas and Asia and were brought by travelers and explorers to Europe, where they became an integral part of many cuisines. Today it is almost impossible to imagine what Italian cooks would do without the tomato, and the dishes of southern France and Spain would be far less interesting and colorful if peppers had never traveled abroad.

The cucumber is an excellent example of a vegetable fruit that is used in different ways in different countries. It can evoke a scene of afternoon tea with paper-thin sandwiches (such as those immortalized by Oscar Wilde in *The Importance of Being Earnest*) or an old-fashioned crab feast along Chesapeake Bay with garden-fresh cucumbers and tomatoes. The scent and crunch of a cucumber can bring to mind any number of pictures, depending on your heritage —a garnish of crisp matchsticks in a creamy white casserole; a mixed, fresh salad chopped with Mediterranean abandon; in fact, anything from a fat dill pickle to the geometric poetry of a Japanese fish, its snow-white purity accented with lightly steamed cucumber lozenges.

Next to corn and beans, squash was one of the greatest gifts of our native Americans to those latecomers, the first English settlers. Among the Indians, the Cherokee and Seneca tribes were especially skilled farmers. The men cleared the fields, but it was the hardworking squaws who tended the crops.

All varieties of squash belong to the genus *Cucurbita* and are closely related, whatever the color or dimensions. Yellow summer squash and green zucchini, popular in Italy, may be cooked in similar ways. The yellow- and orange-fleshed winter varieties can be baked and mashed like sweet potatoes.

Botanically, the pumpkins that decorate our harvest fields and roadside stands are simply an oversized form of squash. In Europe, the pumpkin is usually limited to soups, although the resourceful cooks of southwestern France use pumpkin purée with maize flour to make many other dishes.

Most pumpkin dishes are made by mixing pumpkin purée with other ingredients. Pumpkin purée is, however, delicious on its own, served hot as a dessert, with butter, cream and a sprinkling of ginger. It can also be served as a vegetable. Heat the purée, add a lump of butter, season with salt and pepper, and garnish with parsley. When preparing pumpkin dishes, do not throw away the seeds. They are highly nutritious, and roasted and salted make a delicious snack.

Eggplants, peppers and tomatoes are the true exotics of the kitchen garden. With their rich coloring and sleek, generously rounded shapes, there is no mistaking their sun-soaked ancestry. The eggplant is native to Asia, while both the pepper and the tomato developed in tropical America. The voyage of the tomato across the Atlantic to the Mediterreaean shores of Italy and the Middle East and its return with a new generation of immigrants is one of the more colorful sagas of our melting-pot cuisine. Post-World-War-II foreign travel and the interest in vegetarianism have enhanced the popularity of the eggplant in recent years.

When cooking these vegetable fruits in the style of their countries of origin, strong flavors and fruity oils take the place of creams, butters and stocks. These smoky flavors can be recreated by turning tomatoes or peppers over charcoal until their skins have cracked and blistered off. The tomatoes and peppers are then bathed in a mixture of olive oil, wine vinegar, garlic, and such herbs as basil, oregano, rosemary, coriander and tarragon.

Wherever they grow in abundance, eggplants are made into tasty, filling dishes all remarkably similar, although they may originate in such dissimilar places as France and Egypt. One of the most popular dishes prepared throughout the Mediterranean and in the Middle East is "poor man's caviar," or, to give it its more sophisticated name, *caviar d'aubergines*. To make this delightful hors d'oeuvre for four, bake 2 large eggplants on the top shelf of a moderate oven for 20 to 30 minutes, or until they feel soft and pulpy. When they are cool, peel them and chop the flesh finely.

Meanwhile, fry 1 large finely chopped onion and 2 finely chopped garlic cloves in 6 tablespoons of olive oil until soft and golden. Stir in 1 pound of peeled, chopped tomatoes, 2 teaspoons of finely chopped parsley, a generous pinch of sugar, and salt and pepper to taste. Cook, stirring, until the tomatoes have disintegrated and the sauce is thick.

Add the eggplant pulp and continue cooking and stirring until the ingredients have blended into a thick purée. Cool and then chill the purée. Garnish with chopped parsley and black olives before serving with hot Greek *pita* bread.

The tomato is the most versatile of all the vegetable fruits. Superb served raw in a salad flavored with a handful of fresh basil leaves, it is also invaluable as a flavoring in dozens of cooked dishes. In addition, tomatoes can be made into juice, sauce and relish.

Tomatoes

Italy may have been the inspiration of modern Western gastronomy, but it is hard to imagine how the Italians earned their early culinary reputation without the tomato. For it was the tomato, more than any other vegetable except, perhaps, the potato, which changed the eating and cooking habits of the Old World.

The genius of the Mediterranean cooks lay in the ease with which they put this marvelous vegetable fruit to work. But for many years on both sides of the Atlantic, in northern Europe as well as in America, people were afraid to eat the tomato and little attention was paid to what the Italians were doing with it. Today, however, things are very different. The tomato is so popular in the West that, fresh or canned, it is an essential ingredient in hundreds of well-known dishes.

There are few dishes which cannot be enhanced by the flavor of the tomato. Our own cooks have even succeeded in using it to make a cake. This does seem a waste of effort, however, when a platter of sliced fresh tomatoes, seasoned with salt, freshly ground black pepper, a touch of sugar, and a thick dusting of basil or other chopped herbs, is so easy to prepare and so good to eat.

To peel tomatoes, either spear them on a fork and turn them slowly over a hot flame until the skin shrivels and chars and can be rubbed off or blanch them in a bowl of boiling water for one minute, dip them briefly in cold water and then peel off the skin.

Stuffed tomatoes, raw or cooked, served hot or cold, can be made with many different fillings. Leftover fish, meat, poultry or vegetables can be used, bound with cream or mayonnaise. Or there are the stuffings made with herbed or spiced meat and rice that are an outstanding feature of the Mediterranean kitchen.

To make stuffed tomatoes successfully, large, firm, fleshy tomatoes must be used. Drain the tomato by slicing off the stem end, give it a gentle squeeze to loosen the ball of seeds inside and leave it inverted, the cut surface rubbed with salt, on a rack or over a sheet of paper toweling to absorb the juice. After this preliminary salting and draining, the seeds and pulp can then be scooped out neatly and easily with a spoon without damaging the shell.

If the stuffed tomatoes are to be subjected to prolonged cooking, slice off the cap from the smooth end. The tomatoes then rest on the tougher stem ends as they cook.

Homemade concentrated tomato paste is superior to the commercial variety, which has a cruder flavor. Tomato concentrate is easy to make. Simply peel, seed and drain ripe tomatoes. Purée them in a blender or food mill. Simmer the purée in a heavy pan over moderate heat until it has reduced and is smooth and thick. Store in the freezer.

As summer draws to a close, there will inevitably be trusses of small, hard, green tomatoes that have missed their chance to ripen. They are ideal for making relishes, jams or pickles.

Surprise Broiled Tomatoes

This is a fine variation on plain broiled tomatoes. The herbs you use will depend on the rest of the menu. Basil, oregano, marjoram, dill or just parsley—all complement the tomato flavor.

SERVES FOUR
4 firm tomatoes
4 tablespoons fine, dry bread crumbs
1 small garlic clove, crushed (optional)
2 tablespoons finely chopped parsley
1 tablespoon chopped herbs
Olive oil or melted butter
Salt
Freshly ground black pepper
Sugar

Slice a cap from the stem end of each tomato and scoop out the centers. Leave the tomatoes to drain upside down until needed.

Dice the scooped-out pulp and mix it with the bread crumbs, garlic, if used, and herbs. Moisten with 1 tablespoon of oil or melted butter and season to taste with salt, pepper and a pinch of sugar.

Fill the tomatoes. Brush them lightly with more oil or butter and put them under a moderate broiler for about 10 minutes, or until they are heated through and have softened slightly.

Chilled Cream of Tomato Soup

With a basket of ripe tomatoes from the garden and an electric blender or an efficient food mill at your disposal, this excellent soup can be made in a matter of minutes, then left to chill in the refrigerator.

SERVES FOUR TO SIX
2½ lb ripe tomatoes
1 small shallot, roughly chopped
1 small garlic clove, finely chopped
⅔ cup thick sour cream
3 tablespoons lean ham, diced
2 tablespoons cucumber, peeled and diced
2 tablespoons diced green pepper
Salt
Freshly ground black pepper
Sugar
Lemon juice
Heavy cream, to garnish (optional)

Rinse the tomatoes and chop them roughly. Purée the tomatoes, shallot and garlic in an electric blender or put them through a food mill. If using the latter, first crush the pieces of shallot and garlic in a garlic press or pound them to a paste in a mortar.

Rub the purée through a fine sieve. Then beat in enough sour cream to make a smooth, thick soup.

Stir in the ham, cucumber and green pepper. Season the tomato cream with salt and pepper. Then taste again and, if necessary, add about 1 teaspoon of sugar and a few drops of lemon juice.

Chill until ready to serve. You may even find that it needs a few tablespoons of heavy cream to mellow the flavor.

Tomatoes

Tomato Rice

This spicy, well-flavored rice dish from India is the perfect accompaniment for vegetable cutlets or lamb kebabs.

SERVES FOUR TO SIX
4 tablespoons butter
1 lb ripe tomatoes, blanched, peeled and finely chopped
¼ teaspoon cayenne pepper
½ teaspoon sugar
Salt
1 large onion, sliced
½-inch piece fresh root ginger, peeled and finely chopped
1 garlic clove, crushed
1½ cups long-grain rice, washed, soaked in cold water for 30 minutes and drained

GARNISH
Chopped parsley
1 tablespoon chopped peanuts
2 hard-boiled eggs, quartered

Melt half the butter in a saucepan. Add the tomatoes, cayenne pepper, sugar and a little salt. Cook, stirring occasionally, for 10 minutes. Set aside.

Melt the remaining butter in a large saucepan. Add the onion, ginger and garlic and fry, stirring occasionally, over low heat until the onion is soft and golden.

Add the rice, increase the heat and fry, stirring, for 5 minutes. Pour in the tomatoes, season with more salt and add enough boiling water so that the liquid in the pan covers the rice by a

½ inch. When the liquid boils rapidly, cover the pan, reduce the heat to very low and simmer for 20 minutes, or until the rice is cooked and all the liquid has been absorbed.

Spoon the rice into a heated serving bowl. Sprinkle the parsley and nuts on top and arrange the eggs decoratively around the sides. Serve immediately.

Basic Tomato Sauce

This is a simple, fragrant and versatile tomato sauce, ideal to have on hand. It will keep in the refrigerator for well over a week in a sealed container, provided its surface is kept covered with a thin film of olive oil. It may also be quick-frozen. Use a few tablespoonfuls to finish a dish of meat, poultry or fish, to simmer meatballs or vegetables, or to reheat leftovers for a risotto.

It makes a good pasta sauce. Allow a generous 1⅓ cups per ½ pound of pasta.

MAKES 2 TO 2½ PINTS
3 lb ripe, fresh tomatoes, peeled, or 4 cups frozen tomato concentrate (see page 193)
5 tablespoons olive oil
2 medium-sized, mild onions, finely chopped
4 plump garlic cloves, peeled
½ large green pepper, cored, seeded and finely diced
1 large celery stalk, finely diced
1 bay leaf
2 teaspoons dried oregano or marjoram
1 teaspoon dried basil
Salt
Freshly ground black pepper
Sugar

If using fresh tomatoes, chop them up coarsely. Frozen tomato concentrate should be defrosted before use.

Heat the oil in a large pan. Add the onions and fry gently, until they are soft and golden. Add the whole garlic cloves, and as soon as they are lightly colored mix in the pepper and celery. Fry gently, stirring occasionally, until the vegetables have softened.

Add the tomatoes, herbs and a light seasoning of salt and pepper. Bring the sauce slowly to simmering point, cover the pan and cook gently, stirring occasionally and mashing the fresh tomatoes with the back of a spoon, for 45 minutes to 1 hour, or until the sauce is thick and richly flavored.

Adjust the seasoning, adding 1 teaspoon of sugar if necessary.

Remove and discard the garlic cloves before serving.

Ratatouille

Ratatouille is the classic summer vegetable casserole, one of the great dishes in the southern European tradition, varied and embellished by each local cuisine along the Mediterranean coast. Although ratatouille is not exclusively a tomato recipe, tomatoes are the one unvarying ingredient.

Ratatouille freezes well and is a useful stand-by either to serve on its own as a first course or as a vegetable accompaniment. With the addition of lamb, ratatouille makes a truly gourmet dish. To serve four, use half the ratatouille recipe and 1½ pounds of lamb. Cut the lamb into pieces, brown it in oil and then cook until tender. Stir in the ratatouille and serve immediately with rice or crusty bread.

To peel a tomato, spear it on a fork and turn it slowly over heat.

When the skin is shriveled and charred it can be removed easily.

SERVES SIX TO EIGHT
1 lb eggplants
Sea salt
2 large, mild onions
½ lb green peppers
1½ lb large, firm, ripe tomatoes
1 lb zucchini
8 tablespoons olive oil
3 large garlic cloves, peeled and halved lengthwise
2 teaspoons sugar
Freshly ground black pepper
GARNISH
Finely chopped parsley
Black olives

Trim off the stem ends of the eggplants and cut into 1-inch cubes. Toss them in salt and leave them in a colander to drain.

Peel and slice the onions thickly. Remove all the white pith and seeds from the peppers, and cut the flesh into 1-inch squares. Peel the tomatoes, cut into chunks and scoop out the pulp and seeds into a strainer set over a measuring cup. Trim the zucchini stems and cut into 1-inch slices. Finally, rinse the eggplants and gently squeeze them dry.

Heat the oil in a wide, heavy casserole. Add the onions and simmer, stirring frequently, for 10 minutes, or until they are a pale, transparent golden color.

Lift the onions out of the oil with a slotted spoon and set aside. In the same oil, soften the peppers over low heat for 5 minutes and put them with the onions. Raise the heat to moderate and fry the zucchini until golden. Put them with the other fried vegetables. Then fry the eggplants in the same way. Return all the vegetables to the casserole, together with the chopped tomatoes and the garlic.

Rub the drained tomato pulp through the strainer and make up to ⅔ cup with water or tomato juice if necessary. Stir in the sugar, 1 tablespoon of salt and a generous grinding of black pepper. Pour the mixture over the vegetables.

Carefully mix the contents of the casserole. Cover and cook over very low heat for 30 minutes. Turn the vegetables over from top to bottom and cook, covered, for a further 15 minutes, followed by a final 15 to 20 minutes uncovered to evaporate excess moisture. The vegetables should be soft but not disintegrating.

Allow the ratatouille to cool slightly before correcting the seasoning. Serve lukewarm or lightly chilled, garnished with finely chopped parsley and black olives.

Homemade Tomato Juice

When there is a glut of tomatoes count yourself lucky, for it gives you the perfect opportunity to lay up a supply of the most delicious, fresh, concentrated juice for the winter. Cocktails, clear consommés, soups and sauces can be made at a moment's notice. Just be sure to store the bottles in a dark cupboard, since strong light tends to fade the brilliant color of the juice.

Rinse the tomatoes. Chop them up if they are large and pack them into a heavy saucepan. Add a sprinkling of salt and sugar, but no water. Put the pan over the lowest possible heat and cook very slowly, uncovered, stirring and mashing occasionally with a wooden spoon or pestle. When the liquid comes to simmering point, continue to cook gently until the tomatoes are quite soft.

Continue simmering until some of the excess water has evaporated.

Purée the tomatoes and the juice through a food mill, discarding the seeds and skins. If the tomatoes are a very "seedy" variety, it is wise to push them through a coarse sieve first; too many seeds puréed into the juice can give it a bitter flavor. For the same reason, a blender should not be used without this preliminary sieving since it tends to do too efficient a job on skins and seeds.

Pour the juice back into the pan and let it simmer, uncovered, stirring occasionally, until it has thickened to a rich, creamy consistency.

Meanwhile, prepare screw-top bottles (Mason jars are best) for the juice. Wash them, rinse them out with boiling water and leave them to drain upside down on a rack.

Season the concentrated tomato juice to taste with more salt, sugar and freshly ground black pepper. A leaf or two of fresh basil pushed into some of the bottles will make a delightful variation.

Prepare a double thickness of corrugated cardboard, or use a thick cloth, to line the bottom of a pan large enough to take the bottles closely side by side. Funnel the hot juice into the bottles and put on the tops, but do not screw them down tightly. Arrange the bottles in the pan. Pour boiling water to come two-thirds of the way up the sides of the bottles. Then slowly let the water come back to the boil and simmer for 30 minutes to sterilize the juice.

As soon as the bottles can be handled, lift them out of the pan. Put the bottles aside to rest for 2 to 3 minutes before screwing down the tops as tightly as possible.

Tomato Tart

Fresh sun-ripened tomatoes put this delicate tart into a class of its own. It can be served as a first course or as a main course for lunch or supper. All that it needs as an accompaniment is a crisp green salad.

SERVES FOUR TO SIX

1½ lb ripe, firm tomatoes, peeled
Dough for a 9-inch piecrust
¾ cup Gruyère or mild Cheddar cheese, grated
2 tablespoons softened butter
4 tablespoons heavy cream
2 eggs, lightly beaten
Salt
Freshly ground black pepper

Preheat the oven to 450°F. Put a heavy baking sheet in the oven to heat.

Cut each tomato into quarters. Squeeze the quarters gently over a colander to rid them of excess moisture. Chop the tomatoes and leave them to drain in the colander.

Roll the crust out thinly and line a 9-inch fluted pie pan with a removable base. Sprinkle the crust evenly with ¼ cup of the grated cheese.

Work the remaining cheese to a fluffy paste with the butter and cream. Then beat in the eggs and season lightly with salt and pepper.

Season the chopped tomatoes and spread them evenly over the base of the pastry-lined pan. Spoon the egg-and-

cheese mixture over the tomatoes.

Put the tart on the hot baking sheet in the oven. After the first 5 minutes, reduce the temperature to 400°F; after another 5 minutes turn it down to 350°F. Continue to bake the tart for 30 minutes longer, or until the filling is puffed and richly colored and the crust crisp and cooked through. Should the crust brown too much around the sides before the tart is done, cover the top with a sheet of foil to protect it.

Stuffed Tomatoes à la Provençale

Serve these stuffed tomatoes as a first course or, using smaller tomatoes, as an accompaniment to broiled steak.

SERVES FOUR

4 large, firm tomatoes
4 tablespoons olive oil
1 small, mild onion, very finely chopped
1 garlic clove, crushed
4 anchovy fillets, chopped
8 tablespoons coarse fresh bread crumbs
2 tablespoons finely chopped parsley
Salt
Freshly ground black pepper

Slice the tomatoes in half horizontally. Scoop out the pulp and seeds and rub the pulp through a sieve. Set the purée aside. Turn the tomato cases upside down to drain until needed.

Heat the oil in a frying pan. Add the onion and garlic and fry, stirring occasionally, until the onion is soft and very lightly colored. Mix in the anchovy fillets and continue to cook very gently, stirring occasionally, until they have practically dissolved. Add the bread crumbs and fry gently, tossing with a fork, for 2 to 3 minutes longer to crisp them slightly.

Lightly mix in about 4 tablespoons of the puréed tomato pulp and the parsley. Season the stuffing with salt and pepper.

Preheat the oven to 375°F.

Arrange the tomato cases side by side in an oiled baking dish. Divide the stuffing among them. Brush the cases with oil and bake for 20 minutes, or until the stuffing has become slightly crisp on top and the tomato cases have softened but are not too mushy to lift out of the dish. Serve hot or cold.

Another way to peel a tomato is to dip it in a bowl of boiling water for 1 minute.

Baked Eggs in Herbed Tomato Cups

A festive dish, baked eggs in herbed tomato cups make a Sunday breakfast with a difference. You can vary the dish by putting a little finely chopped ham under each egg, by garnishing each case with a few thin slices of sautéed mushroom or by serving the tomato cups on crisp, round croutons.

SERVES FOUR

4 large, firm tomatoes
Salt
Freshly ground black pepper
Butter
2 tablespoons freshly grated Parmesan cheese
2 tablespoons light cream
Generous pinch of basil
4 eggs

Carefully slice a cap across the stem end of each tomato and scoop out the pulp. Season the cases with salt and pepper and pack them tightly side by side in a buttered baking dish.

Preheat the oven to 350°F.

Mix the cheese with the cream, basil and salt and pepper to taste.

Put the dish of tomato cups into the oven for 5 minutes to heat through. Carefully break one egg at a time into a bowl, then transfer it into a tomato cup and spoon some of the cream mixture evenly over the top.

Bake for 20 minutes, or until the eggs feel set, but not hard, to the touch.

Remove the tomato from the hot water, dip it in cold water and then peel off the skin.

Peppers

All the brilliant colors which the pepper adopts as it ripens are of no practical significance to the cook. Even the greenest pepper will be sweet enough for any dish, and for stuffing it will hold its shape better than one which is red and riper. Hot chilies may be red or green.

To prepare peppers, unless they are to be served whole, cut them in half, rinse out the seeds and with a sharp knife pare away all the white pith, which tends to be bitter.

To prepare a whole pepper for stuffing, cut around the stem with a sharp knife, ease out the stem and put it aside to plug up the hole later. Then, using a spoon, scrape away all the pith. Rinse out the seeds under cold running water and shake the pepper dry.

To peel a pepper, either hold it over an open gas flame or place it under a hot broiler until the skin chars and blisters. Then rub the skin off under cold running water.

Stir-fried Chicken with Peppers, Szechwan-style

In the last few years, devotees of the chili have been discovering the delights of a new variety of Chinese cooking, based on garlic and fiery hot peppers. Restaurants featuring Szechwan cooking and the equally spicy dishes of neighboring Hunan have been springing up overnight on city and suburban streets. Here is an old favorite as prepared in Szechwan.

SERVES FOUR
2 medium-sized dried black mushrooms
6 water chestnuts
1 whole uncooked chicken breast
2 or 3 red chilies
1 garlic clove
1 tablespoon soy sauce
½ teaspoon salt
½ teaspoon sugar
5 tablespoons vegetable oil
¾ cup stock
1 teaspoon cornstarch

Soak the mushrooms for 20 minutes in warm water, then drain them and pat dry. Slice the mushrooms and water chestnuts thinly. Skin and bone the chicken breast and cut it into thin strips. Slice the chilies thinly into crosswise slices. Mince the garlic and combine it with the soy sauce, salt and sugar. Heat 3 tablespoons of the oil in a large frying pan or a *wok*. Add the chilies and stir-fry until they start to color. With a slotted spoon, remove them to a warm plate.

Add the remaining oil to the pan and then add the chicken slices and stir-fry until they start to turn white. Return the chilies to the pan, add the water chestnuts and mushrooms and stir-fry for a minute or two. Then blend in the soy–garlic mixture. Set aside 2 tablespoons of the stock and add the remainder to the pan. Simmer, covered, for 3 or 4 minutes. Make a paste of the reserved stock and the cornstarch, stir it into the chicken mixture and heat until thickened.

Peppers en Salade

Superb as an appetizer, this delicious salad from Provence not only tastes good but looks good, too.

SERVES SIX
2 large green peppers
2 large red peppers
8 tablespoons olive oil
3 tablespoons tarragon vinegar
2 garlic cloves, finely chopped
Salt
Freshly ground black pepper
2 tablespoons finely chopped, mixed fresh herbs, such as parsley, thyme and chervil
6 tomatoes, peeled and thickly sliced
6 hard-boiled eggs, thickly sliced

GARNISH
24 black olives, pitted
24 anchovy fillets

Wipe the peppers with a damp cloth and dry them thoroughly. Put them under a hot broiler, turning frequently, until the skins blacken and blister. Rub off the skins under cold running water. Halve the peppers, remove the cores, wash out the seeds and cut each half lengthwise into 3 or 4 strips. Pat the pepper strips dry with paper toweling.

Prepare the dressing with the oil, vinegar, garlic, salt and pepper—take care not to add too much salt because the anchovies for the garnish are themselves very salty. Stir in the herbs.

Layer the peppers, tomatoes and eggs in a salad bowl, sprinkling each layer with the herb dressing. Arrange the anchovies and olives in an attractive latticework pattern on the top. Leave the salad to marinate for at least 30 minutes.

Serve chilled.

Biber Dolma

Every restaurant in Istanbul has a tray of these peppers waiting to tempt the lunchtime customers. The stuffing for this delicious appetizer is a classic one and is also traditionally used to stuff vine leaves.

SERVES SIX
1 cup short-grain rice
6 large green peppers
8 tablespoons olive oil
2 large, mild onions, finely chopped
6 tablespoons currants, washed
2 tablespoons pine nuts
Salt
Freshly ground black pepper
Sugar
6 tablespoons finely chopped parsley

Put the rice in a sieve and rinse it thoroughly under cold running water. Pour a kettleful of boiling water over the rice and leave it to drain in the sieve for 1 hour.

Carefully cut out the stems of the peppers with the point of a sharp knife. Put them aside. Scrape out the pith and cores, taking care not to pierce the skins. Rinse the peppers under cold running water and leave them to drain, upside down, while the filling is prepared.

Heat the oil in a large frying pan. Add the onions and fry, stirring, until they are transparent and a light golden color. Stir in the rice, currants and pine nuts. Season to taste with salt, pepper and sugar. Continue to fry over moderate heat, stirring constantly, until the rice is golden. Stir in the parsley.

Fill the peppers with the rice mixture, leaving room for the rice to expand. Place the reserved stems on top.

Put the upright peppers close together in a heavy saucepan large enough to take them in one layer. Carefully pour in enough boiling water to come halfway up the sides of the peppers. Put the pan on the heat and bring the water back to simmering point. Cover the pan, reduce the heat and cook the peppers very gently for 45 minutes to 1 hour, or until the rice is tender. If necessary add more water as the peppers are cooking.

Allow the peppers to cool in the pan before removing them to a serving dish. Serve chilled.

To prepare a whole pepper for stuffing, use a sharp knife to cut around the stem. Ease out the stem. Put it aside and use it later to plug the stuffed pepper.

"Cucumber . . . taken in meats, is good for the stomack and other parts troubled with heat. It yeeldeth not any nourishment that is good, insomuch as the unmeasurable use thereof filleth the veines with naughty cold humours."

John Gerard's Herball, *1633 edition*

"Cucumbers grow in gardens when the moon is full, and their growth is as visible as that of sea-urchins."

The Sophists at Dinner *by Athenaeus*

Eggplants

Eggplants are very juicy, but sometimes the juice can be bitter and will make a dish taste unpleasantly metallic. The solution is to drain off as much of the juice as possible. Slice the eggplants, rub all the cut surfaces with salt and leave the slices to drain in a colander for at least 30 minutes. To drain them more thoroughly, particularly before frying, cover the salted eggplants with a plate and put a heavy weight on top. Then rinse the eggplant slices, squeeze them gently and press them dry with paper toweling.

When frying eggplants, first dry the slices well and then seal them with a light dusting of flour.

Eggplant slices may also be broiled or baked. Brush them well with olive oil. Then either put them under a hot broiler or on a baking sheet on the top shelf of a hot oven. Turn the slices over when browned, and brush with more oil.

Parmigiana di Melanzane

On the menu in every little restaurant in southern Italy there is a dish of *parmigiana di melanzane*, baked eggplant with cheese, which is served as a first or a main course. It is equally delicious hot, warm or cold.

SERVES FOUR
3 lb round eggplants
Salt
Olive oil
1 medium-sized onion, finely chopped
2 lb ripe tomatoes, peeled, seeded and chopped
3 sprigs fresh basil, chopped, or 2 teaspoons dried basil
Freshly ground black pepper
Flour
1¼ cups Parmesan cheese, freshly grated
½ lb mozzarella cheese, thinly sliced
2 hard-boiled eggs, thinly sliced

Trim the stems from the eggplants. Cut the eggplants lengthwise into thick slices. Sprinkle each slice with salt. Put the slices in a colander and cover with a plate. Weight the plate down and leave the eggplant slices to drain for 30 minutes.

Heat 4 tablespoons of olive oil in a heavy pan. Add the onion and fry, stirring, until golden. Add the tomatoes and basil, mix well and simmer gently, uncovered, until the tomatoes are reduced to a thick sauce. Season to taste with salt and pepper.

Preheat the oven to 400°F. Oil a large, shallow, ovenproof dish.

Rinse the eggplant slices in cold water. Pat them dry and dust them with flour. Fry them in hot olive oil until soft and golden brown on both sides. Drain them on paper toweling.

Cover the bottom of the baking dish with a layer of eggplant slices. Sprinkle with Parmesan cheese and cover with slices of mozzarella cheese and a few slices of hard-boiled egg. Spoon some of the tomato sauce over the top. Repeat these layers until the ingredients are used up, ending with tomato sauce. Bake for 30 minutes.

Moussaka

Moussaka probably came from Turkey. It was adopted by the Greeks and is now the best known of all Greek dishes. A true *moussaka* is made with eggplants, but many variations have evolved, some using sliced or mashed potatoes instead of eggplants, others using zucchini as well as, or instead of, them. Whichever version is preferred, this rich and substantial dish needs no accompaniment except, perhaps, a green salad and a bowl of yogurt.

SERVES FOUR TO SIX
3 large eggplants
Salt
Olive oil
2 large, mild onions, thinly sliced
1½ lb lean lamb or beef, minced
1 teaspoon ground cinnamon
Freshly ground black pepper
1 large, ripe tomato, peeled and chopped
2 tablespoons tomato paste
2 tablespoons finely chopped parsley
2 tablespoons butter
Flour
1½ cups hot milk
1 egg yolk, beaten
1 cup freshly grated Kephalotiri cheese or a mixture of Gruyère and Parmesan cheese
Nutmeg

Wipe the eggplants and cut them crosswise into slices about ⅛ inch thick. Put them in a colander, sprinkling each layer with salt. Weight with a plate and leave to drain for at least 30 minutes.

Heat 2 tablespoons of oil in a large, deep frying pan. Add the onions and fry, stirring, until they are soft and golden. Add the minced meat and cinnamon and season to taste with salt and pepper. Fry steadily, stirring frequently, until the meat has browned. Mix in the tomato, tomato paste and parsley and continue to simmer for 20 minutes longer.

Meanwhile, prepare the sauce. Melt the butter in a saucepan. Blend in 2 tablespoons of flour and stir over a low heat for 1 minute to make a pale roux. Gradually add the milk, stirring vigorously to prevent lumps forming. Bring the sauce to the boil and simmer for about 5 minutes, stirring constantly, until the sauce is thick and smooth.

Remove the pan from the heat and allow the sauce to cool slightly. Beat in the egg yolk and the cheese and season to taste with salt, pepper and a pinch of nutmeg.

Preheat the oven to 375°F.

Wash the eggplant slices and dry them between the folds of a cloth or with paper toweling. Coat the eggplant slices with flour and fry them in oil until golden brown on both sides. Drain well.

Line the base and sides of a deep, round casserole or baking dish with eggplant slices. Layer the meat mixture and the remaining eggplant slices in the dish, ending with a layer of eggplants. Pour the sauce over the top.

Bake the *moussaka* for about 40 minutes, or until the top is bubbling with a rich, golden crust.

Squashes

When yellow squashes are young and tender, they may be enjoyed in the simplest ways, while recipes for zucchini tend to show its Mediterranean heritage. Both are at the peak of culinary perfection when no more than 6 inches long and still slender.

When they are this size they may be cooked whole. Simply top and tail them, and either steam them with a sprinkling of salt or poach them for no more than 5 minutes. They should remain crisp. Finish them in a tightly covered pan with butter, coarse salt, freshly ground pepper and a dusting of chopped, fresh herbs. Crisp, cooked zucchini, served cold with vinaigrette, make an excellent first or salad course.

Sliced, raw zucchini may be cooked entirely in butter or first salted to draw out some of their moisture, patted dry, dusted with flour or dipped in a light batter and deep-fried in olive oil to make crisp little fritters. These are delicious served with yogurt.

Stuffed zucchini are a classic Mediterranean dish. Scoop the pulp out from the stem end with a narrow corer or slim spoon, taking care not to damage the shells. Pack them with a savory concoction of rice, meat and tomatoes, with cheese, anchovies or herbs for seasoning. Do not waste the pulp. Use it to make a variation of poor man's caviar. Cook onion with the pulp and tomato in olive oil. Season, add chopped parsley and cook until the mixture is thick. Serve lukewarm or cold.

Winter squashes, which ripen on their trailing vines, as do pumpkins, include the pale-skinned butternut, the giant deep-blue Hubbard and the small, green acorn varieties. They may all be peeled, seeded and steamed or boiled until tender. Then they may be mashed with butter and simply baked in or out of their shells or combined with other ingredients to make a pudding or pie.

Small squashes, like the acorn types, are delicious when halved, the seeds and fibers scraped out with a spoon, dotted with butter, salt, paprika, and a dash of brown sugar, if you wish, then baked until tender and lightly browned. Acorn-squash cups are also useful as the starting point for an attractive luncheon dish because they may be stuffed and baked with a variety of meats and other vegetables.

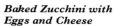

Baked Zucchini with Eggs and Cheese

This is a delightful dish to serve for brunch or supper. For hearty appetites, grilled sausage or bacon may be served as an accompaniment.

SERVES FOUR
6 tablespoons olive oil
2 garlic cloves, crushed
1½ lb zucchini, sliced
1 large, mild onion, thinly sliced
2 tablespoons fresh chopped parsley
1 teaspoon fresh chopped marjoram
1 teaspoon fresh chopped basil
Salt
Freshly ground black pepper
6 eggs
4 tablespoons light cream
¾ cup grated Gruyère cheese
¼ cup grated Parmesan cheese
1 tablespoon butter

Preheat the oven to 350°F.

Heat the oil in a large, deep frying pan. Add the garlic and fry, stirring gently, for 1 minute without letting it brown. Add the zucchini, increase the heat and fry, stirring frequently, until they are lightly browned. Stir in the onion and the herbs. Season to taste with salt and pepper. Reduce the heat and continue to cook, stirring occasionally, until the onions are soft. Turn the contents of the pan into a baking dish.

In a bowl, beat the eggs lightly with the cream, mix in the cheeses and pour it over the zucchini. Dot with the butter and bake for 20 to 30 minutes, or until the eggs have set and the top is golden.

To prepare zucchini for stuffing, carefully scoop out the pulp, using a narrow corer or slim spoon.

Zucchini look particularly attractive if, before cooking, thin strips of the skin are removed with a peeler to give a striped effect.

Deep-fried Zucchini

This dish makes an excellent accompaniment for lamb. If frying large quantities, keep the fried zucchini hot in the oven, set at 225°F, on a baking sheet lined with paper toweling.

SERVES FOUR TO SIX
1⅛ cups all-purpose flour
¼ teaspoon salt
1 tablespoon olive oil
⅔ cup lukewarm water
1½ lb zucchini
Oil for deep-frying
1 egg white

Sift the flour and salt into a bowl. Make a well in the center and add the oil and a little water. Using a wooden spoon, begin stirring the liquid, slowly incorporating the flour. Add the remaining water a little at a time. When the batter is smooth and it is thick enough to coat the back of the spoon, cover the bowl and set it aside for 30 minutes.

Meanwhile, trim the zucchini and slice them thickly.

Heat the oil in a deep-frying pan to 375°F or until a cube of stale bread dropped into the oil turns brown in 60 seconds.

Just before frying, whip the egg white until it is stiff and fold it into the batter.

Put the zucchini slices into the batter. Remove them with a skewer and drop them into the hot oil. Turn them once. Using a slotted spoon, lift out the zucchini slices when they are golden brown. Drain well on paper toweling and keep hot until all the zucchini slices have been fried. Serve hot.

Squashes

Squash-and-Tomato Casserole

For a more substantial dish add a thick, creamy cheese sauce before baking.

SERVES FOUR
1 lb young summer squashes
1 lb tomatoes
½ lb onions
4 tablespoons butter
Salt
Fresh basil, chopped
Freshly ground black pepper

Cut the squashes into ½-inch slices. Peel them and remove the seeds and stringy fibers if necessary. If old put the slices in a colander, sprinkle them with salt and leave them to stand for 30 minutes. Rinse the slices.

Preheat the oven to 400°F. Butter a deep casserole.

Slice the tomatoes and onions thickly. Put a layer of squash in the bottom of the casserole. Cover this with a layer of tomato followed by a layer of onion.

Dot each layer with a small amount of butter and sprinkle with a little salt, basil and a grinding of pepper. Continue in this way until all the vegetables are used up, finishing with a layer of squash.

Flake any remaining butter over the top of the casserole. Cover and bake for 1 hour.

Stuffed Summer Squash

This is a spicy variation of a traditional dish. If desired, mashed, cooked eggplant may be substituted for the meat.

SERVES FOUR TO SIX
3 lb medium-sized summer squashes
Salt
½ cup short-grain rice
1 tablespoon olive oil
5 tablespoons butter
1 large onion, finely chopped
2 garlic cloves, crushed
¼-inch piece of fresh root ginger, peeled and finely chopped
1 green chili, seeded and finely chopped
1 teaspoon turmeric
1 teaspoon ground coriander
¼ teaspoon cayenne pepper
1 lb lean lamb, minced

2 large, ripe tomatoes, peeled and chopped
1 tablespoon tomato paste
2 tablespoons chopped fresh coriander leaves or parsley
3 tablespoons raisins

Halve the squashes horizontally. Scoop out the seeds and stringy fibers. Rub the squashes, inside and out, with salt and leave them to drain, upside down, for about 1 hour.

Parboil the rice in salted water for 3 minutes. Drain thoroughly. Heat the oil and 1 tablespoon of the butter in a saucepan. Add the onion and fry, stirring occasionally, until it is tender and golden. Add the garlic, ginger and chili and fry, stirring, for 2 minutes. Add the turmeric, coriander and cayenne pepper and fry, stirring, over low heat for 5 minutes. If the mixture gets dry and begins to stick to the pan, stir in 1 tablespoonful of water.

Add the meat, increase the heat slightly and fry, stirring and mashing the meat down with a wooden spoon, until it is well browned. Stir in the rice, tomatoes, tomato paste, the chopped coriander leaves or parsley and the raisins. Season to taste with salt. Mix the ingredients well together. Remove the pan from the heat.

Rinse the squash shells in cold water and wipe them dry with paper toweling. Stuff the squashes with the mixture. Melt the remaining butter in a wide, flameproof dish. Arrange the stuffed squash shells in the dish and cook for 2 minutes. Cover the pan, reduce the heat and simmer gently for 1 hour.

Serve hot.

Acorn Squash Stuffed with Ham and Spinach

This makes a splendid and good-looking luncheon dish. The sweetness of the squash is an excellent foil for the tangier flavors of the ham and spinach.

SERVES FOUR
2 medium acorn squashes
7 tablespoons butter
1½ teaspoons salt
Freshly ground black pepper
2 lb fresh spinach
1 cup diced Virginia ham
1 tablespoon chopped onion

1 tablespoon flour
1 cup milk or stock

Preheat the oven to 375°F.

Cut the acorn squashes in half and scoop out the seeds. Using 1 tablespoon for each half, grease the outside shell of the squashes and dot the inside with butter. Sprinkle ½ teaspoon salt and some pepper over the halves and bake them on a cookie sheet until tender when pierced with a skewer, about 45 minutes.

Meanwhile, wash the spinach in several waters until the grit is removed.

Drain the spinach in a colander. Using only the water that has clung to the leaves, cook the spinach until it is just wilted; then drain it and chop it finely. Heat the remaining butter in a skillet and brown the ham and onion; blend in the flour. Add the milk or stock and whisk until smooth and thickened. Then add the spinach, the remaining salt, pepper to taste, and simmer for 5 minutes.

Remove the squash halves from the oven, fill them with the spinach–ham mixture and brown them under the broiler. Serve piping hot.

Squash-Nut Bread

In Grandma's kitchen, squash and pumpkin purées were used interchangeably to make quick breads and muffins. Fragrant with cinnamon and nutmeg, this bread gives an aroma of holiday feasting to breakfast and brunch.

MAKES TWO LOAVES
4 cups sifted flour
4 teaspoons baking powder
1 teaspoon baking soda
1 teaspoon salt
½ teaspoon nutmeg
1 teaspoon cinnamon
4 eggs
2 cups squash purée
2 cups brown sugar
½ cup (1 stick) butter
1 cup chopped pecans or walnuts

Preheat the oven to 350°F.

Sift together the first six ingredients. Beat the eggs until light. In a large mixing bowl combine the squash, sugar, butter and eggs. Add the dry ingredients to the squash mixture and stir until thoroughly blended. Stir in the nuts.

Pour the batter into two 8½ × 4¼ inch loaf pans and spread it evenly with a spoon or spatula. Bake in the preheated oven 50 minutes to 1 hour, or until a skewer inserted in the center comes out clean. Let cool for 10 minutes before turning out on racks. Wrap the loaves in foil. They will keep up to two weeks in the pantry and they freeze well.

Pumpkins

Our native pumpkins are associated more with Halloween and Cinderella than with the kitchen. Most popular cookbooks contain only a handful of pumpkin recipes—apart from pumpkin pie.

Surprisingly, it was the cooks of eastern Europe who devised one of the most satisfying culinary solutions for this beautiful vegetable fruit—a spiced preserve.

Pumpkins also make delicious vegetable dishes, fine soups and good puddings. Most pumpkin recipes require pumpkin purée. To prepare the purée, cut the pumpkin in half horizontally and remove the seeds and strings. Peel the pumpkin and cut it into pieces. Cook the pumpkin in simmering water for 20 to 30 minutes. Drain and purée. Pumpkin may also be baked in a moderate oven and then puréed; cut it in half and scrape out the seeds and strings, but do not peel or cut it into pieces.

Pumpkin Soup

This warming winter soup can be made richer by adding ⅔ cup of heavy cream just before serving.

SERVES FOUR
1½ lb pumpkin (2 cups puréed)
4 cups milk
1 tablespoon butter
1 teaspoon basil
Salt
Freshly ground black pepper
Sugar
2 tablespoons beurre manié
  (1 tablespoon flour and 1 tablespoon butter mashed together)

Remove the seeds and pith and peel the pumpkin. Cut the flesh into cubes. Cook the pumpkin in simmering water for 20 minutes, or until it is tender. Drain well. Purée the pumpkin in a food mill.

Return the purée to the pan. Stir in the milk and butter. Add the basil and season to taste with salt, pepper and sugar.

Bring the soup to the boil. If it is not thick enough, add the *beurre manié* a little at a time, stirring constantly, until the soup is the right consistency.

Adjust the seasoning and serve.

Spiced Pumpkin Preserve

Use a good wine vinegar for this preserve. A French vinegar marked at 6° or 7° is best, if available—mild, mature but strong enough to pickle the pumpkin well.

MAKES ABOUT THREE POUNDS
2½ lb firm, ripe pumpkin
Salt
1¼ cups sugar
2⅔ cups wine vinegar
6 cloves
2 small sticks cinnamon

Peel the pumpkin, scrape it clean of seeds and pith and cut it into 1-inch cubes. Drop the pumpkin cubes into an enameled saucepan of lightly salted boiling water. Parboil them for 1 minute and drain thoroughly.

In the same pan, over low heat, slowly dissolve the sugar in 4 tablespoons of water. Stir in the vinegar, cloves and cinnamon, raise the heat and bring to the boil. Return the pumpkin cubes to the pan and bring to boiling point. Remove the pan from the heat, cover it and put it in a cool place for 24 hours.

The next day, drain off the syrup into another enameled pan and bring it to the boil. Pour the boiling syrup back over the pumpkin. Cover the pan and set it aside once again for 24 hours.

On the third day, slowly bring the pumpkin to simmering point in the vinegary syrup. Test the cubes with a skewer and if they have not softened sufficiently, continue to cook them gently for a few minutes longer. Set aside until quite cold, then seal the preserve in clean, dry glass jars. Store in a cool, dry, dark place.

Sour-Cream Pumpkin Pie

A variation on the traditional Thanksgiving dessert, this pumpkin pie should be served with whipped cream.

SERVES SIX
Dough for a 9-inch pie shell
1½ cups pumpkin purée
1⅓ cups sour cream
3 eggs, separated
¼ teaspoon salt
1 teaspoon ground cinnamon
½ teaspoon ground ginger
¼ teaspoon grated nutmeg
1 cup sugar

Preheat the oven to 425°F.

Roll out the pastry and line a 9-inch pie pan. Prick the crust all over with a fork. Line the crust with greaseproof paper and fill with dried beans. Bake the pie shell for 10 minutes. Remove the paper and beans and reset the oven to 350°F. Return the pie shell to the oven for 10 to 15 minutes to dry out the base.

In the top of a double boiler, combine the pumpkin with the sour cream and the lightly beaten egg yolks. Mix in the salt, spices and half the sugar. Place the saucepan over gently simmering water.

Cook the pumpkin mixture, stirring constantly, until it thickens.

Whip the egg whites in a bowl until they form soft peaks. Gradually beat in the remaining sugar. Fold the meringue into the pumpkin mixture.

Spoon the pumpkin mixture into the pastry shell. Bake the pie for 45 minutes, or until the top is lightly browned.

Savory Pumpkin Mold

This attractive and unusual vegetable dish can be baked in a ring mold, turned out onto a plate and served with the center filled with buttered peas or creamed mushrooms.

SERVES SIX
3 eggs
3 tablespoons milk
2½ cups pumpkin purée
3 tablespoons butter, melted
½ cup fresh bread crumbs
1 small onion, coarsely grated
1 garlic clove, crushed
½ teaspoon chopped fresh parsley
½ teaspoon chopped fresh thyme
Salt
Freshly ground black pepper

Preheat the oven to 350°F.

In a large bowl, beat the eggs with the milk. Mix in the pumpkin purée, butter, bread crumbs, onion and garlic. Add the herbs and mix thoroughly. Season to taste with salt and pepper.

Pour the mixture into a buttered ovenproof dish and bake for 45 minutes, or until the mixture has set.

Cucumbers

Cucumbers are usually served raw and sliced in salads. To prevent the juice from emerging and diluting other flavors, the cucumber slices may be salted, drained in a sieve or colander for 30 minutes, then rinsed and pressed dry between the palms of your hands. Never salt cucumber slices when they are being used as decoration.

Cooked cucumbers make a delicious vegetable and lose none of their vitality by being steamed or poached. Peel them, cut them in half length-wise and remove the seeds. Then cook the cucumbers for a few minutes. Serve dressed with melted butter, lemon juice and herbs.

Sautéed cucumbers are excellent with fish. Cut them into thick slices. Do not peel them unless the skins are tough. Soak the slices in ice water for 1 hour, then dry them, dust them with flour and sauté in butter and oil until golden. Dress them with butter, lemon and herbs or serve with a hollandaise sauce.

Cucumber Soup

A good soup to serve on a hot summer's day, this cucumber soup should be well chilled and liberally garnished with chopped chives and sour cream.

SERVES SIX
3 cucumbers, peeled
5 cups good chicken stock
2 tablespoons butter
1 medium-sized, mild onion, finely chopped
1 garlic clove, crushed
1⅓ cups light cream
1¼ cups mushrooms, sliced
Salt
Freshly ground black pepper
GARNISH
Chopped chives
Sour cream

Reserving half of one cucumber, put the remaining cucumbers through the finest plate of a food mill.

In a large saucepan, bring the chicken stock to the boil. Add the puréed cucumber and simmer for 10 minutes. Heat half the butter in a frying pan. Add the onion and garlic and fry, stirring occasionally, until they are soft and translucent. Add the onion and garlic to the soup and stir in the cream.

Heat the remaining butter in the same frying pan. Add the mushrooms and fry, stirring, for 1 minute. Add the mushrooms to the soup and season to taste with salt and pepper. Simmer gently for 10 minutes.

Dice the remaining half cucumber and stir it into the soup. Remove the pan from the heat and set aside to cool.

Chill the soup thoroughly and garnish each serving with the chopped chives and sour cream.

Cucumbers in Sour-Cream Dressing

The cucumbers should be sliced paper-thin for this delicious summer salad. Fresh heavy cream mixed with lemon juice may be used as a substitute for commercial sour cream. Leave the skin on the cucumber.

SERVES FOUR
1 large cucumber
Salt
⅔ cup sour cream
3 tablespoons chopped fresh chives or dill
1 tablespoon chopped fresh parsley
Freshly ground black pepper
Sugar

Cut the cucumber, unpeeled, into very thin slices. Put them in a large colander, sprinkling each layer with salt. Leave the slices to drain for at least 30 minutes, then rinse them and squeeze out the excess moisture firmly but gently.

In a bowl, mix the sour cream with the chives or dill and the parsley. Gently stir in the cucumber slices and season to taste with salt, pepper and sugar. Serve immediately.

Tuna-stuffed Cucumber

This dish may be served alone as an appetizer or as part of a selection of mixed hors d'oeuvre. The herbs should be used according to taste and availability—a good mixture is thyme, oregano, tarragon and chives.

SERVES FOUR
1 large cucumber
Salt
7 oz canned tuna fish, drained (1 small can)
2 tablespoons butter
2 tablespoons cream cheese
1 tablespoon chopped parsley
1 tablespoon chopped mixed fresh herbs
Freshly ground black pepper
1 lemon, thinly sliced, to garnish

Peel the cucumber and cut it crosswise into 2-inch pieces. Drop the pieces into boiling salted water and cook gently for 8 minutes. Drain and refresh the cucumber pieces in cold water until they are firm again and cold. Scoop out and discard the seeds and pulp from the center of each piece. Dry the pieces on paper toweling. Mash the tuna fish with the butter and cream cheese to make a smooth paste. Blend in the herbs and season to taste with salt and pepper.

Stuff the cucumber pieces with this mixture and chill until firm. Cut each piece across into ½-inch slices and serve immediately garnished with lemon slices.

Mushrooms

Mushrooms are essential to fine cooking—their flavor is incomparably subtle and their texture both crisp and fleshy.

The commonest mushroom, and one of the best, is the field mushroom. It grows wild in open pastures free for the picking. It is the same type of mushroom as the kind grown commercially and those grown by amateur gardeners in their tool sheds and cellars.

When the mushroom first pushes its delicate white cap through the soil it is known as a button mushroom. As it grows, opening out like a parasol, it displays pinkish-beige gills beneath the cap. It can grow, if it is permitted, to almost 5 inches in diameter.

The button mushroom is delightful eaten raw, especially when it is perfectly fresh. To make a marinated mushroom salad, slice the mushrooms thinly, toss them thoroughly with light olive oil and lemon juice, using 2 tablespoons of oil and the juice of 1 lemon for $\frac{1}{2}$ lb of mushrooms, season and chill in the refrigerator for at least 2 hours. Before serving, garnish the mushrooms with chopped parsley, a little dill or a sprinkling of chives.

When cooking mushrooms, the golden rule is never to wash or peel them unless it is absolutely necessary. Clean mushrooms will at most need to be wiped with a damp cloth, or rinsed quickly in a sieve. Much of the flavor is in the peel and in the stalks, so just trim the stalks, do not discard them. If a recipe calls for only mushroom caps, keep the stalks in the refrigerator and use them to flavor a soup or sauce, or to make *duxelles*.

Having gone to the trouble of growing snow-white mushrooms, it is not difficult to preserve their perfection right up to the moment they arrive on the table, whether it be in the form of a garnish or as a dish in their own right.

The simplest way to prepare mushrooms for a garnish is to poach them in barely enough lightly salted water to cover, with a squeeze of lemon juice to keep them white. If the pan is tightly covered they will in effect steam, rather than poach, in a matter of minutes. The mushrooms can then be put aside until needed without loss of color or texture.

Sautéed mushrooms—the kind that add a final touch to all sorts of dishes, from creamy *blanquettes* of poultry or veal to such rich casseroles as *boeuf bourguignon* and *coq au vin*—are cooked in fat rather than in water, but the general principles remain the same. Protect the color with lemon juice and do not overcook them. Use butter, melted in a little oil to ensure that the butter does not brown. When the butter is foaming, add the mushrooms. Squeeze some lemon juice over the mushrooms and sauté them over moderate heat, keeping the mushrooms constantly on the move so that they color evenly. Initially, they will release an alarming amount of water, but this will rapidly evaporate. As soon as the butter is clear again, the mushrooms are ready to use.

There are many ways to use mushrooms, both buttons and the full-blown open caps, which are the ones to use for stuffing and for broiling and which some people prefer for their undeniably stronger taste.

The French have a marvelously practical and versatile way of using cultivated mushrooms—this is the *duxelles*, a concentrated paste or mince, often made from second-grade mushrooms. It is used for flavoring stuffings, soups, stews and sauces. To make a *duxelles*, first chop a couple of shallots or a small, mild onion as finely as possible. Melt 4 tablespoons of butter in a wide, heavy pan and simmer the onion very gently until it has practically dissolved. Finely chop 1 pound of mushrooms—plus any stalks you have been saving in the refrigerator—and add them to the pan, together with another 6 tablespoons of butter. Cook very gently, stirring frequently, for at least 1 hour, or until the mixture is thick and richly flavored. Season at the very end.

Store the *duxelles* in a tightly covered jar in the refrigerator, ready to be dipped into whenever a sauce, a soup, a casserole—or even a plain omelet—calls for a boost. It will keep in the refrigerator for several weeks, but any surplus can be quick-frozen in convenient-sized cubes for future use.

Dried mushrooms retain such potency that just a few slivers will make their mark on a dish. If you are growing your own mushrooms and have some to spare, this is an excellent way to use them. Invest (and they *are* expensive) in 2 ounces of best-quality dried mushrooms and put them away in an airtight container. These will be wild mushrooms, which have a stronger flavor and which you will later mix with your own dried mushrooms. Put your mushrooms out on a baking sheet lined with several thicknesses of paper toweling. Cut the mushrooms in half vertically, stems and all, or leave them whole —they will shrink dramatically as they dry. Over the next few days, have the baking sheet ready to take advantage of any mild, *dry* heat —a switched-off oven, a cooling radiator or just a warm, well-ventilated kitchen. When the mushrooms have given up all their moisture and are as dry as leather, mix them with the bought mushrooms. Leave them for several weeks to allow the flavors to mix, and then you will have created a precious new flavoring ingredient to store and use when needed.

Mushroom Pie

An ideal lunch dish, mushroom pie can be served with a mixed salad or with green vegetables. If desired, 2 ounces of bacon may be fried with the onions.

SERVES FOUR TO SIX
3 tablespoons butter
¼ lb white onions, peeled
1 lb button mushrooms, cleaned
1 tablespoon finely chopped parsley
Salt
Freshly ground black pepper
2 tablespoons sherry or Madeira
1 cup heavy cream
2 egg yolks, lightly beaten
¼ teaspoon freshly grated nutmeg
¼ teaspoon paprika
Dough to make a 9-inch pie crust
Egg white, for glazing

Preheat the oven to 400°F.
Melt the butter in a large frying pan. Add the onions and fry, shaking the pan occasionally, over low heat for 5 minutes.
Add the mushrooms, turning them gently in the pan so that they are well coated with the butter. Stir in the parsley, season with salt and pepper to taste and cook for 2 minutes.
Using a slotted spoon, transfer the onions and mushrooms to a deep pie pan.
Increase the heat, pour the sherry or Madeira into the pan and stir well to mix. Remove the pan from the heat and pour the contents over the mushrooms and onions.
In a small bowl, combine the cream and egg yolks. Season with nutmeg, paprika and a little salt. Pour the mixture into the pie pan.
Roll out the dough and cover the pie pan with it. Brush the crust with egg white and bake for 30 minutes, or until it has risen and is golden brown. Serve immediately.

Mushroom Soup

A delicious and easy-to-make soup. Use a strong, well-flavored stock.

SERVES SIX
6 tablespoons butter
4 shallots, finely chopped
1 lb button mushrooms, thinly sliced
Juice of ½ small lemon
2 tablespoons flour
4 cups chicken or vegetable stock
6 tablespoons dry sherry
1⅓ cups light cream
Salt
Freshly ground black pepper
2 tablespoons finely chopped parsley,
    to garnish
Paprika or cayenne pepper

Heat the butter in a large saucepan. Add the shallots and fry, stirring, until they are golden but not brown. Stir in the mushrooms. Squeeze the lemon juice over them (this helps to preserve the color of the mushrooms) and cook over moderate heat for 2 to 3 minutes until the mushrooms have softened slightly.
Sprinkle the flour over the mushrooms and blend it into the butter. Stir for 1 minute longer over low heat. Stir in the stock and bring it to the boil. Reduce the heat and simmer the soup for 15 minutes. Stir in the sherry and the cream. Season to taste with salt and pepper and bring the soup to just below boiling point.
Stir in the parsley. Sprinkle each portion with a dash of paprika or cayenne before serving.

Mushrooms en Brioche

The addition of Madeira to the classic cream-and-egg sauce makes this a rich and delicious dish. It is an ideal first course for a dinner party. *Vol-au-vent* cases or soft round rolls may be substituted for the *brioches*.

SERVES SIX
6 day-old brioches
4 tablespoons butter
2 tablespoons olive oil
1 lb tiny button mushrooms, trimmed
1 shallot, finely chopped
Salt
Freshly ground black pepper
4 tablespoons Madeira
3 egg yolks, lightly beaten
1⅓ cups heavy cream
1 garlic clove, halved
Melted butter

Cut off the tops of the *brioches* and scoop out the insides, making sure the shells remain undamaged.
Preheat the oven to 375°F.
Heat the butter and oil in a large, wide pan. Add the mushrooms and shallot and fry gently, stirring, for 2 minutes. Season to taste with salt and pepper. Add the Madeira, mix it well in and cook gently for a minute or so longer. Remove the pan from the heat.
Mix the egg yolks and the cream together and stir them into the mushrooms. Return the pan to very low heat and stir for 10 to 15 minutes or until the sauce has thickened. The sauce must not boil or the egg yolks will curdle.
Alternatively, cook the sauce and mushrooms in the top of a double boiler over simmering water, stirring occasionally, for 15 to 20 minutes.
Meanwhile, rub the insides of the *brioches* with the garlic and brush them with melted butter. Place them on a baking sheet in the oven for 15 to 20 minutes.
Divide the mushrooms and sauce between the hot, crisp *brioche* cases and serve immediately.

Mushroom-and-Barley Casserole

This may be served either as an accompaniment for lamb, beef or such game as venison, or as a substantial vegetarian main course.

SERVES THREE TO FOUR
3 tablespoons butter
½ cup pearl barley, well rinsed
1 medium-sized onion, finely chopped
½ lb button mushrooms, sliced
⅔ cup light cream
Freshly ground black pepper
Milk
1 egg
2 tablespoons grated Cheddar cheese

In a saucepan, bring 1¼ cups salted water to the boil with 1 tablespoon of the butter. Stir in the barley. Cover the pan tightly and simmer for 30 minutes, or until the barley is soft and has absorbed all the water.
Meanwhile, melt the remaining butter in another pan. Add the onion and fry, stirring, until it is soft and lightly colored. Add the mushrooms and stir to coat them with the buttery juices. Fry gently for 2 to 3 minutes longer. Moisten with 4 tablespoons of the cream and season to taste with salt and pepper. Cover the pan and simmer very gently for 10 to 15 minutes longer.
Meanwhile, preheat the oven to 375°F. Make up the cream to ⅔ cup with milk and beat it lightly with the egg.
Spread half of the cooked barley over the bottom of a baking dish. Cover with the mushrooms and cream and top with the remaining barley, smoothing it out with the back of a spoon. Pour the cream-and-egg mixture over the top and sprinkle the surface with the grated cheese.
Bake the casserole for 20 to 30 minutes, or until it is set and golden on top, but still slightly creamy inside.

Fruits

It is curious how fruits seem to be endowed with the character of their season. The season of most berries is as short as a Northern summer, while the season of the orchard fruits is longer, without the urgency to make the most of only a few weeks' bounty. In the same way, berries will take very little of the cook's time, while the apples and pears of autumn give the opportunity to make pies and puddings and all sorts of tarts, which are certainly not quick to prepare.

The typical fruits of the kitchen garden are various kinds of berries and, possibly, one or two apple and pear trees. The outsider is the vine, included for the sheer joy of growing grapes.

The most modest suburban kitchen garden is capable of supplying the kitchen with fruit throughout the year, even without the help of a freezer. And when you run out of one fruit for a favorite recipe there always seems to be another ready to take its place. A summer pudding becomes an early autumn pudding as the blackberries ripen. Then, later, you can make a winter pudding. Line a bowl with ladyfingers and fill it with an apple or pear mousse lightly set with gelatin. And when the first rhubarb comes in, you can make a spring pudding. Simply cut the rhubarb into short lengths, cook it slowly, until it has nearly disintegrated, with sugar and a little lemon juice in a tightly covered pan over low heat. Stir in a little butter, let it cool and pour it into a bread-lined bowl. Cover with more bread and leave overnight in the refrigerator until it is firm. Serve with cream or *crème anglaise*, the real egg custard sauce, for a refreshing dessert suitable for any occasion.

There are recipes galore for berries. Blackberries are frequently cooked with apples in pies, but they may also be made into pancakes. To make blackberry pancakes, mix $1\frac{1}{2}$ cups of blackberries into a batter made from 2 cups of flour, 1 large egg, $1\frac{1}{3}$ cups of milk, 1 tablespoon of butter and a little sugar.

Loganberries, a dull red, acid fruit, may be cooked in much the same way as blackberries, but require more sweetening. They also make excellent jam.

Fresh summer fruits offer the opportunity to make magnificent fruit ice creams, fresh creams and yogurts based on uncooked purées and crushed fruits.

Red currants are the best of the currants to eat raw with a little sugar. They also make the best jelly. No oversweetened commercial preserve can compare with fine-flavored, soursweet, homemade jelly. And it is so easy to make because the red currant is endowed with more than its fair share of pectin.

Nothing so evokes the memory of a lost America as the native blueberry and the almost-black huckleberry. The easiest of all berries to pick, they could fill up a country child's pail in an hour. Though belonging to different families, the blueberry and the huckleberry are cousins and may be treated the same in the kitchen. Since the bushes are easy to grow and decorative, no suburban gardener need be without a fresh supply of berries, far superior to the bland supermarket type.

Visitors to New England resorts in Maine or Cape Cod know that at the height of blueberry season the tangy berries appear in muffins, pies, quick breads, puddings, cobblers and just plain to sprinkle on the morning cereal—all superb recipes for the cook to reproduce if she has her own blueberry patch. Try cooking blueberries briefly with a little sugar as a sauce to pour over ice cream. They also combine especially well in fruit salad.

Gooseberries are related to currants and they have in common fine, translucent skins and acid, juicy flesh. The gooseberry leads a double life in the kitchen. The small, green gooseberries, picked when they are hard and unripe, are ideal for making compotes, pies, tarts and fools. Green gooseberries may also be made into green-gooseberry sauce, which is served with fried or broiled mackerel to counteract its oiliness.

Dessert varieties of gooseberries are left on the bushes to ripen and are delicious eaten raw, plain or with whipped *sabayon*-style sauces and wafer-thin biscuits.

Cooking and dessert gooseberries are both rich in pectin and acid and make good jam and jelly.

With autumn fruits the challenge is not what to do with them, but how, for example, to make an apple pie or crisp that does justice to the quality of the fruit that your garden has produced.

Grapes are not really a kitchen fruit. They are rarely cooked, but make excellent additions to both vegetable and fruit salads. And young, tender vine leaves are used in making *dolmas*, stuffed vine leaves, which are served as an hors d'oeuvre or main course, either hot or cold.

Many fruits have an affinity with cheese: berries with lightly sweetened cream cheese, apples with Cheddar and pears with any cheese from a well-matured, creamy Brie to a vintage Parmesan.

Fruits should never be considered simply as potential desserts. Roast duck, partridge or even chicken surrounded by a garnish of lightly poached apples stuffed with both fresh and frozen raspberries sums up not only the principles of cooking with fruit, but also the whole philosophy of cooking—simplicity, elegance and sophistication without pretentiousness and with, above all, respect for the natural qualities of the ingredients.

Apples

"Comfort me with apples"—the cry echoes down through the centuries. The sighs of Solomon mingle with proverbs, maxims and nursery rhymes to make the apple the most written and talked about of fruit. It is so much a part of Western man's myths and legends that it has come to symbolize perfection in shape, color and taste.

Although it caused the fall of man—and woman—the apple has managed to retain its premier position, in spite of the modern market gardener. Unfortunately, too often the most expert and well-meaning research into yield and disease resistance has resulted in apples which are totally without scent or flavor.

In no country have the demands on the large-scale fruit grower for apples that "ship and keep" produced a more dreary uniformity than in the United States, where generally insipid and mealy apples are often the only ones available in the stores. Fortunately, one may grow much more interesting apples at home.

The best thing about growing your own apples is that you can choose the variety of apple you like and grow it for its taste and texture —sweet or sharp, juicy-crisp or mealy, good for eating, cooking with or storing.

Apples eaten raw are perhaps the best, but stewed, puréed, baked or cooked in pies, charlottes, puddings and tarts they make some of the most universally popular desserts. To savory dishes they add a refreshing tartness that no other ingredient can match.

When using apples in cooking there are a few points worth noting. Peeled apples left for any length of time will discolor if not treated with a brushing of lemon juice or acidulated water. Poached apples are less likely to disintegrate if they are simmered for two to three minutes in the prepared syrup, then tightly covered, the heat turned off and the cooking finished in the syrup as it cools. To prevent a baked apple bursting, score a very fine equatorial line around the skin before putting it into the oven.

To make applesauce, purée apples in their own juice in a covered pan. A lump of butter at the bottom of the pan is usually enough to keep the apples moist for the few minutes it takes them to release their own juice. Even when cooking a very large pot of apples filled to the brim, keep the water to just a bare ripple at the bottom of the pan.

Experiment with eating apples as well as cooking apples. "Start" them with a finely chopped onion or shallot and bacon softened in butter. In fact, applesauce can be flavored with anything that seems complementary to the dish it is intended to accompany, from the usual cinnamon-orange-lemon variations, fortified wine or a drop of fruit liqueur, right through to horseradish. There is no reason for applesauce to always be smooth, either. Vary the texture by frying apple cubes lightly in butter and finishing them with a little dry vermouth and cream, or by adding another texture altogether—nuts or a crisp vegetable such as celery.

Apple Charlotte à la Polonaise

There are dozens of versions of charlotte, some simple, some very complicated. This one is easy to make and suitable for any occasion. If possible use vanilla sugar in preference to sugar and vanilla extract. It does make a difference.

SERVES SIX

FILLING
3 lb cooking or well-flavored, firm eating apples, at room temperature
Vanilla sugar, to taste
2 teaspoons ground cinamon
Finely grated rind of 1 orange (optional)
1 cup white raisins
Lemon juice
1 tablespoon butter
PASTRY
4½ cups self-rising flour
1 teaspoon baking powder
⅔ cup butter, chilled
4 tablespoons pure lard or white vegetable fat, chilled
2 eggs
½ cup sugar
TO SERVE
Sifted powdered sugar
Unsweetened lightly whipped cream

Peel, quarter and core the apples and cut them into small pieces. Toss them with vanilla sugar, cinnamon, orange rind, if used, and the white raisins. Sharpen the flavor if necessary with a few drops of lemon juice.

To make the pastry, sift the flour and baking powder into a bowl. Cut the butter and lard or vegetable fat into small pieces. Rub the fat into the flour until the mixture resembles bread crumbs. Make a well in the center.

Beat the eggs and sugar together until fluffy and lemon colored. Work them into the flour mixture by hand until they blend into a dough. Knead briefly, roll into a ball and seal in plastic wrap or foil. Chill for at least 1 hour, until very firm.

Preheat the oven to 400°F.

To assemble the charlotte, use a baking pan 2 to 3 inches deep and measuring roughly 10 by 12 inches. Line the base and at least 2 inches up the sides with two-thirds of the pastry, returning the remainder to the refrigerator.

Bake the pastry shell for 30 minutes, or until it is golden. Remove the pastry

from the oven and let it settle for a few minutes. Fill the pastry shell evenly with the apple mixture. Dot the surface with the butter. Take the remaining dough, which should be chilled very hard, and grate it coarsely and evenly over the entire surface.

Return the charlotte to the oven. Bake for 45 minutes to 1 hour, or until the charlotte is a rich golden color, the apples are soft and a piece of topping picked off with a fork tastes cooked.

Serve warm or cold, cut into rectangles, dusted with sifted powdered sugar and accompanied with whipped cream.

Apfelstrudel

Follow this recipe step by step and you will have a strudel to be proud of. Use a good-quality, high-gluten bread flour. It will markedly improve the elasticity of the dough. Filo pastry, available at Greek food shops, may be used by those nervous about making the dough.

SERVES TEN TO TWELVE
DOUGH
3¼ *cups all-purpose flour*
½ *teaspoon salt*
1 *egg, well beaten*
3 *tablespoons flavorless oil*
½ *teaspoon white wine vinegar*
FILLING
⅜ *cup fine toasted bread crumbs*
2 *teaspoons ground cinnamon*
1 *tablespoon grated lemon rind*
Juice of ½ lemon
¾ *cup sugar*
½ *cup blanched, toasted almonds,*
  coarsely chopped
½ *cup ground almonds*
¾ *cup white raisins*
3 *lb well-flavored eating apples, peeled,*
  cored and finely chopped
TO SHAPE
Oil
Flour
About ½ lb (2 sticks) melted butter
TO SERVE
Sifted powdered sugar
Lightly whipped cream

First make the dough. Sift the flour and salt into a large bowl. Make a well in the center. Pour in the egg, oil and vinegar, and work the mixture lightly with your fingertips until it is crumbly. Gradually incorporate ⅔ cup lukewarm water, working it in evenly, until the dough is soft and very sticky. Slightly more or less water may be needed, depending on the absorbency of the flour.

Continue to work and knead the dough until it is smooth. Stretch and throw the dough onto a pastry board until it becomes satin smooth and shiny, leaving the board and fingers absolutely clean.

Shape the dough into a smooth brick. Brush it all over with a generous coating of oil and leave it to rest on the pastry board, covered with a warm bowl, for at least 2 hours.

To make the filling, assemble all the ingredients together in a large bowl, adding them in the order given, and tossing with a large fork so that the ingredients retain a crumbly texture.

To shape the strudel, cover a large table, about 6 feet by 4 feet, with a cloth —a clean cotton bed sheet is ideal. Dust cloth lightly with flour.

Place the dough in the center of the cloth and press it out as uniformly as possible with the palm of your hand, keeping it to its rectangular shape as far as you can. Do not use a rolling pin.

Work your hands, palms downward, under one side of the dough and gradually but firmly stretch it out by lifting the backs of your hands and easing the dough gently toward you, working your way steadily around the table so that the dough stays uniformly thin all over.

Continue until it is paper-thin. (The Viennese say you should be able to read a love letter through it.) The dough should measure about 5 feet long by 3 feet wide. Take care not to tear the dough—it is very difficult to patch at this stage. In warm, dry weather, you will have to work quickly as the dough soon starts to dry out and become brittle.

Trim the edges of the dough with a pair of scissors. Shake melted butter generously over the entire surface with a pastry brush.

Preheat the oven to 425°F. Butter a large baking sheet.

Starting at one of the shorter ends, spoon the filling in a long strip onto the dough, leaving a clear border of about 2 inches on the three sides. Fold the two longer sides of the dough over the filling and brush the folds with melted butter.

Lift up the cloth at the end covered with filling and flop the dough over the filling. Continue flopping the dough loosely until it is rolled up to the end and ending with the seam underneath.

Transfer the strudel to the baking sheet, carefully bending it into a horseshoe. Brush generously with melted butter and put it in the oven. Turn the heat down to 350°F and bake for about 45 minutes, or until the strudel is crisp and golden brown.

Serve the strudel warm or cold, dusted with powdered sugar and accompanied by a bowl of lightly whipped cream.

Special Apple Fritters

These fritters taste special, even if the liqueur is left out. If it is included, use apricot brandy with the apricot jam syrup, and Grand Marnier, Curaçao or Cointreau with either apricot jam or good-quality, rich, dark-orange marmalade.

SERVES SIX
FRITTER BATTER
1½ *cups plain flour*
Salt
1 *tablespoon liqueur (optional)*
2 *tablespoons oil*
2 *whites from large eggs*
APPLES
4 *small cooking apples or crisp, tart*
  eating apples
½ *teaspoon finely grated lemon rind*
1 *tablespoon lemon juice*
1 *tablespoon liqueur (optional)*
4 *tablespoons powdered sugar*
COATING SYRUP
1 *tablespoon sugar*
6 *tablespoons sieved apricot jam or thick,*
  dark orange marmalade
TO FINISH
¼ *lb ladyfingers, very finely crushed*
Oil for deep-frying
Sifted powdered sugar
Chilled, lightly whipped cream, to serve

Start by making the fritter batter so that it has a chance to rest for at least 30 minutes, longer if possible, before it is used. Sift the flour into a bowl with a pinch of salt. Make a well in the center and gradually blend in ⅔ cup of lukewarm water, and the liqueur, if used, followed by the oil. Beat vigorously to a thick, glossy cream. Cover and set aside.

Peel and core the apples, and slice them into ¼-inch-thick rings. Sprinkle with lemon rind, the lemon juice mixed with liqueur, if used, and sifted powdered sugar. Turn the slices to coat them evenly.

In a heavy pan, dissolve the sugar and the jam over low heat, diluting the mixture with enough water to make a syrup of coating consistency. Simmer the syrup for 1 minute and keep it warm. Coat each apple ring with the syrup, allowing the excess to drain off. Put the ladyfinger crumbs on a large plate. As each apple ring is coated with the syrup dip it into the crumbs. Pat them on lightly but firmly on both sides. The apple rings may be left to dry out until they are coated with batter and fried.

Beat the egg whites with a pinch of salt until soft peaks form. Mix them into the batter with a broad-bladed knife.

Heat the oil for deep-frying to 375°F. Use two long skewers, one for coating the apple rings with batter, the other for taking them in and out of the oil. Deep-fry the apple rings until they are crisp and puffed, flipping them over once or twice. Drain on absorbent paper. Dust with sifted powdered sugar and serve immediately, with a bowl of lightly whipped, chilled cream.

Apples

French Cream and Apple Tart

Vary this delicious apple tart by using apricot or orange liqueur instead of the brandy, and brushing the base of the pastry shell with warmed, sieved apricot jam or puréed orange marmalade before filling it.

Serve the tart lukewarm, cold or chilled, on the day it is made.

SERVES SIX TO EIGHT
One 10-inch rich tart shell, prebaked
CUSTARD CREAM
6 tablespoons sugar
Pinch of salt
3 tablespoons cornstarch
⅔ cup milk
⅔ cup light cream
3 egg yolks, lightly beaten
1 tablespoon brandy or 1 teaspoon good-quality vanilla extract
⅔ cup heavy or whipping cream
APPLES
1 tablespoon brandy
1 teaspoon lemon juice
4 large, fragrant eating apples
2 tablespoons melted butter
2 tablespoons sugar, sifted

In a heavy pan, mix the sugar, salt and cornstarch together and blend in the milk and cream. Bring the mixture to the boil, stirring, and continue to simmer for 3 to 4 minutes. Remove the pan from the heat and cool the mixture slightly, stirring. Then gradually beat in the egg yolks.

Return the pan to a very low heat and cook, stirring constantly, for 3 to 4 minutes or until the custard is very thick and smooth. Do not let the custard bubble. Stir in the brandy or vanilla. Cool, beating occasionally to prevent a skin forming on top. Set the custard aside in a covered bowl until you are ready to use it.

Prepare the apples. Mix the brandy and lemon juice with 2 tablespoons of cold water in a large bowl. Peel, quarter, core and slice the apples very thinly into the bowl, turning them in the brandy mixture to coat them.

Whisk the heavy or whipping cream stiffly and fold it into the custard. Spread the custard cream over the base of the pastry shell. Arrange the apple slices in overlapping concentric circles over the top, shaking them free of excess moisture as you lift them out of the bowl. Brush the apples with melted butter and dust with sugar.

Place the tart under a moderate broiler and broil steadily for 15 to 20 minutes, or until the surface is golden and lightly caramelized. Regulate the heat of the broiler so that the sides of the shell do not get too brown before the top is caramelized, or shield the pastry with a little crumpled foil.

German Apple Pancakes

The flavor of these pancakes depends entirely on the apples. Use well-flavored eating or cooking apples, using additional sugar if they are tart. Otherwise they need nothing at all. It is an excellent dish for supper or Sunday brunch.

SERVES FOUR
4 large apples
1⅓ cups all-purpose flour
1 teaspoon baking powder
Powdered sugar
Salt
4 eggs, separated
1⅓ cups milk
1⅓ cups heavy cream
1 teaspoon vanilla extract
Butter

Peel, core and slice the apples into thin rings.

Sift the flour, baking powder, 1 tablespoon of powdered sugar and salt into a bowl. Make a well in the center and work in the egg yolks, followed by the milk, cream and vanilla, beating vigorously to make a smooth batter.

Make the pancakes in an 8- or 9-inch frying pan. Melt enough butter to swirl around the bottom of the pan. Pour in a thin layer of batter to coat the entire surface. As the underside starts to set, gently push a few slices of apple into the surface. Let the pancake brown on the underside and begin to turn firm on top. Then invert it onto a large, lightly buttered plate. Slide the pancake back into the pan to brown the other side. Serve apple-side up, dusted with powdered sugar.

Chinese Caramelized Apples

These apples are a favorite dessert in Chinese restaurants in the West. Any other firm fruit can be used instead of apples.

SERVES FOUR
4 tart, firm cooking or eating apples
Lemon juice (optional)
Peanut oil for frying
Ice cubes
1⅓ cups sugar
Sesame seeds
BATTER
4 tablespoons cornstarch
3 tablespoons all-purpose flour
4 egg whites

Quarter, core and peel the apples, and cut each quarter in half. If they are not to be used immediately, toss them (and any other fruit that might discolor) with a little lemon juice.

With a wire whisk, mix the batter ingredients together thoroughly to make a smooth, coating paste. Fold in the prepared fruit, making sure each piece is individually coated.

Pour enough peanut oil into a wide, deep pan so that the cubes will float comfortably free of the bottom. Deep-fry the fritters in batches to a light-golden color, making sure the oil does not get too hot. Remove the fritters with a slotted spoon and drain them on paper toweling. Do not worry if they go limp at this stage.

Just before serving, pour 8 tablespoons of the peanut oil into another pan that will take a large batch of the fried fruit at one time. Have ready a large bowl of iced water.

Add the sugar to the oil and swirl the pan gently over a low heat until the sugar has melted and turned a light-golden color—the syrup and the oil will not amalgamate.

As soon as the caramel is ready, drop in a batch of fritters, turn them around with two forks so that they are all individually coated and sticking together in clusters. Still using the forks, lift the clusters from the hot caramel. Shake sesame seeds all over them and drop them into the bowl of iced water.

The syrup will instantly turn into a glassy caramel. Shake the chunks free of water and serve immediately.

Most pears make good desserts, but the best and juiciest should be eaten uncooked. The rest may be poached, stuffed and baked, cooked in a tart or cooked in spiced and sweetened vinegar and served with meat. To poach pears, first dissolve $\frac{2}{3}$ to $\frac{3}{4}$ cup of sugar in $3\frac{1}{3}$ cups of water. Add a vanilla pod, a twist of lemon peel or a cinnamon stick to the liquid and simmer it down to $2\frac{2}{3}$ cups. Peel, halve and core the pears, immediately brushing the exposed surfaces with lemon juice to prevent them turning brown. Drop them into the simmering syrup—$2\frac{2}{3}$ cups will usually be enough for 6 medium-sized pears. Push a sheet of greaseproof paper right down over the surface and cook gently until the pears are tender. Cool in the syrup.

The simple, classic ways of serving poached pears are still among the best—such as Cardinale (coated with a Kirsch-flavored raspberry purée and sprinkled with flaked almonds) or Belle Hélène (two pear halves sandwiched together with vanilla ice cream and served with hot chocolate sauce).

Pears in Red Wine

Any firm pears can be used for this dish, even those hard, thin pears which obstinately refuse to surrender to any other method of cooking.

There are many delicious variations on this basic recipe: having reduced the syrup to coating consistency, stir in 4 to 6 tablespoons of Cassis, black currant liqueur. For a luxury touch, poach the pears in port or sherry instead of red wine, adjusting the amount of sugar to take into account the sweetness of the wine.

SERVES SIX
6 *firm pears*
Lemon juice
1¼ *cups sugar*
2-inch cinnamon stick
2 cloves
2 strips orange peel
2 strips lemon peel
½ *bottle red wine*
Red food coloring (optional)
Heavy cream, lightly whipped

Peel the pears, leaving their stalks on. Drop them into acidulated water as you prepare them.

Dissolve the sugar in $\frac{2}{3}$ cup of water. Add the cinnamon, cloves, orange and lemon peel. Pour in the wine and bring to the boil. Reduce the heat and simmer for 10 minutes.

Arrange the pears side by side, upright, in a wide pan or ovenproof casserole large enough to hold them comfortably without letting them tip over. Pour in the boiling wine syrup. Cover the pan tightly and either cook over the lowest possible heat or bake the pears in a 325°F oven, basting occasionally with the syrup. It will take from about 30 minutes to 1½ hours for the pears to soften.

With a slotted spoon, transfer the pears to a wide, shallow serving dish. Boil the syrup down to a medium-light coating consistency. Test it by cooling the syrup a little and spooning it over the side of a pear. It should have a definite gleam. If the color is not bright enough, intensify it with a few drops of red food coloring.

Spoon the hot syrup over the pears and continue to baste them regularly until they are quite cold. Serve with lightly whipped, chilled, unsweetened cream.

Poires en Chemise

Solid, well-rounded, fragrant pears should be used for this dish. Serve hot, lukewarm or cold—the pastry will even hold well until the following day—with lightly sweetened whipped cream or a fluffy sauce such as a *sabayon*.

SERVES FOUR
4 pears, about 1½ lb
Lemon juice
Sugar
1 egg white, lightly beaten
PASTRY
1⅞ *cups all-purpose flour*
2 tablespoons powdered sugar
Pinch of salt
7 tablespoons chilled butter
1 egg, lightly mixed
ALMOND FILLING
½ *cup ground almonds*
2 tablespoons powdered sugar
1 tablespoon softened butter
1 egg yolk, lightly mixed
1 teaspoon lemon juice
Pure almond extract (optional)

First make the pastry. Sift the flour, sugar and salt into a bowl. Cut in the chilled butter with a knife, then rub it in lightly with your fingertips until the mixture resembles coarse bread crumbs. Stir in the egg with a knife. Gently press the crumbs together with cupped hands until they hold together in a ball. Knead lightly until no buttery streaks remain. Divide the pastry in half, seal each ball in plastic wrap or foil and chill for 1 hour.

To make the almond filling, work the ground almonds, sugar and butter together with enough egg yolk to make a smooth, malleable paste. Flavor with lemon juice and 1 or 2 drops of almond extract, if it is being used.

Peel the pears thinly, leaving the stalks on, and carefully core them from the base. Drop each pear into a bowl of acidulated water as soon as it is prepared.

Preheat the oven to 375°F.

Drain and dry the pears thoroughly with paper toweling inside and out and stuff them with the almond filling.

Take one ball of pastry from the refrigerator at a time and divide it in two. Roll each piece out into a 6- or 7-inch circle and cut out a wedge of about one-third. Bring the cut edges together to make a "cup" for a pear. With a 2-inch pastry cutter, cut out 2 rounds from the leftover wedge of pastry—rolling out a little if necessary. Press one round gently into the base of the "cup" to reinforce it.

Put a pear in the cup and gently mold the pastry shell around it, working it right up toward the stem with cupped hands, and making sure there is no air trapped between the pastry and the pear. Push the other little round of pastry over the stalk and press it down gently over the top of the pear. Dust the pastry very lightly with sifted sugar. Use the remaining scraps of pastry to decorate the pears, fixing the decorations on with a little egg white.

Arrange the pears on a lightly buttered baking sheet and bake for 30 minutes, or until the pastry is golden and the pears inside feel tender when pierced with a thin skewer. Brush the pears with lightly mixed egg white after the first 15 minutes.

Blueberries

The only problem with home-grown blueberries is to get to them before the birds do. That problem solved, the cook can go on to enjoy the summer bounty, reproducing traditional recipes and trying new ones. A more practical consideration from the cook's point of view is the extreme juiciness of blueberries. Even though they may seem quite firm when picked, they will give off incredible amounts of juice as soon as they start to bubble in a pie. The result can be soggy crust.

There are several ways to deal with this characteristic of the blueberry, but don't adopt the solution of the commercial baker of using so much cornstarch that it turns the filling of the usual restaurant or supermarket pie into a kind of blue mucilage containing tiny unidentifiable blue beads. Because of this, Grandma often baked a deep-dish pie or cobbler, eliminating the bottom crust, thus producing a dessert with all its natural juices unthickened. If one wishes to make a traditional blueberry pie, 3 tablespoons of quick-cooking tapioca is usually the best solution, yielding a thickening that does not camouflage the basic flavor of the fruit.

Blueberry Muffins

For blueberry muffins, you should use the smallest, tartest berries available to give the proper New England flavor. The muffins are easy to make and do wonders to perk up what is all too often the dullest meal of the day—breakfast.

MAKES 18 MUFFINS
3 cups sifted flour
4 teaspoons baking powder
1 teaspoon salt
½ cup (1 stick) butter
½ cup sugar
2 eggs
1 cup milk
1 cup blueberries

Preheat the oven to 425°F.

Sift together the flour, baking powder and salt. Cream the butter, gradually add the sugar to it and beat until light and fluffy. Beat the eggs into the butter. Then stir the dry ingredients and milk alternately into the dough, being careful not to overmix, which will make the muffins heavy. Fold in the blueberries. Fill greased muffin cups about two-thirds full. Bake for 20 to 25 minutes, or until muffins are golden and pulling away from the sides of the cups.

Fresh Blueberry Cake with Lemon Sauce

A light and slightly tart, fluffy lemon sauce is particularly good to set off the summer sweetness of this old-time favorite.

SERVES SIX
CAKE
½ cup (1 stick) butter
1 cup sugar
1 egg
½ teaspoon vanilla
1½ cups flour
1 teaspoon baking powder
½ teaspoon salt
⅓ cup milk
2 cups fresh blueberries
½ teaspoon cinnamon
SAUCE
4 eggs, separated
1 cup sugar
⅓ cup lemon juice
1 teaspoon grated lemon rind

Preheat the oven to 375°F.

Cream together half the butter and half the sugar until light; beat in the egg and vanilla. Sift together 1 cup of the flour and the baking powder and salt. Add the flour alternately with the milk to the creamed butter–sugar mixture. Blend briefly. Pour the batter into a greased 9-inch baking dish or pie pan. Pour the blueberries over the batter. Sprinkle with the cinnamon. Combine the remaining sugar and flour; with a pastry blender or two knives cut in the remaining butter until the mixture is reduced to coarse crumbs. Sprinkle the crumbs over the blueberries and bake 40 to 45 minutes. After taking the cake out of the oven, allow it to cool slightly. Meanwhile, make the sauce.

Beat the egg yolks until very light and thick. Add half the sugar and beat until well blended. Add the lemon juice and rind. Cook in a double boiler over boiling water until thick and smooth, stirring constantly; remove from heat. Beat the egg whites until stiff but not dry; then add the remaining sugar gradually to the egg whites, beating after each addition. Fold into the hot sauce. Cut the cake into squares. Serve the sauce warm over the cake squares.

Blueberry Kuchen

Immigrants to America from Germany and Austria brought with them a tradition of fine cake making which greatly benefited both commercial and home baking. They created most of the kinds of coffeecake we now eat, except Danish pastry (which the Danes call Vienna bread). Simpler to prepare than the cakes made with yeast are the fruit kuchens (based on the German word for cake) using a dough called *Mürbeteig*, which resembles French tart pastry but is less rich.

SERVES SIX
DOUGH (*Mürbeteig*)
2 cups flour
½ cup sugar
½ teaspoon salt
¼ lb (1 stick) butter at room temperature
1 egg beaten
Grated rind and juice of 1 lemon

FILLING
1 quart blueberries
½ cup ground almonds
1 teaspoon cinnamon
¼ cup sugar
2 eggs, beaten
MERINGUE
2 egg whites
½ cup powdered sugar
Pinch of cream of tartar

For the dough, sift the flour, sugar and salt into a bowl. Make a well in the center and put in the softened butter, cut in half, the beaten egg, and lemon rind and juice. Work the egg, butter and lemon into a ball, gradually incorporating the dry ingredients. Wrap the dough in wax paper and put it in the refrigerator for at least 1 hour.
Preheat the oven to 375°F.

Take the dough out of the refrigerator and roll it out into a circle to fill a 9- or 10-inch pie pan or spring form. Cover the bottom and sides of the pie pan with dough. Pour the berries onto the dough. Sprinkle with almonds, cinnamon and sugar. Pour the beaten eggs over the berries. Bake for 30 to 40 minutes, or until hot and bubbly. Remove from oven.

Meanwhile, beat the egg whites until they form soft peaks, then gradually beat in the powdered sugar, a tablespoon at a time, and the cream of tartar. Raise oven heat to 425°F. Pile the meringue on top of the berries and bake for 5 minutes, or until lightly browned.

Strawberries

If one had to choose just a single fruit to symbolize perfection in a summer garden, it could only be the strawberry, jewel-red against its bright-green cap. It should be treated with the care it deserves.

Unless strawberries are very dirty avoid washing them. If it is necessary, however, put them in a colander, one layer at a time, spray them with water and shake them dry. If they are not very dirty, dampen a clean kitchen towel and roll the strawberries up in it carefully to avoid bruising them. Any grit will adhere to the cloth.

If strawberries have to be stored for any length of time, put them at the bottom of the refrigerator, then let them come back to room temperature before serving.

When serving strawberries, do not be inhibited by the purists, for whom it is cream or nothing. Eat them with orange juice or lemon juice, covered in raspberry purée, dipped in sour cream and brown sugar, or in sweet white wine, in red wine—even in champagne.

Strawberry Babas

This dessert takes something from two very different strawberry classics—the French *coeur à la crème* and the American strawberry shortcake. If French *Petit Suisse* is not available, cottage cheese can be substituted. If using the cottage cheese, squeeze it dry in a piece of muslin. Cottage cheese can be blander than *Petit Suisse*, so add a tiny pinch of salt and a drop or two of lemon juice to flavor it if necessary.

SERVES SIX
2 cups medium-sized ripe strawberries, hulled
½ cup sugar
4 tablespoons orange liqueur or Kirsch
6 oz Petit Suisse cheese or about ½ lb cottage cheese
1 cup powdered sugar, sifted
Lemon juice (optional)
⅔ cup whipping cream
6 individual babas
Orange juice

Toss the strawberries with the sugar and the liqueur and set aside for at least 1 hour to draw out the juices.

Beat the cheese and powdered sugar together until fluffy, adding a few drops of lemon juice if you are using cottage cheese. Whisk the cream until soft peaks form and mix it lightly but thoroughly into the cheese mixture. Chill until required.

Carefully scoop out the insides of the babas to leave firm shells about ⅓ inch thick.

Drain the strawberries thoroughly. Measure the juice and if necessary make it up to 1¼ cups with fresh orange juice.

Shortly before serving, saturate the soft interiors of the baba shells with the juice. Reserve some of the cheese mixture for decoration and use the remainder to coat the insides of the shells. Divide the strawberries between them, piling them up attractively. Sprinkle any remaining juice over the strawberries.

Finish each baba with a swirl of the reserved cheese cream and either serve immediately or chill briefly—but no longer than it would take to reach the dessert from the start of the meal.

Strawberry Shortcake

A traditional dessert and a delicious way to serve strawberries and cream.

MAKES ONE 8-INCH CAKE
2¼ cups all-purpose flour
3 teaspoons baking powder
1 tablespoon sugar
½ teaspoon salt
4 tablespoons butter, cut into small pieces
¾ cup milk
FILLING
2 cups strawberries, hulled
2 tablespoons sugar
1¼ cups heavy cream

Preheat the oven to 450°F. Lightly butter two 8-inch cake pans.

Sift the flour, baking powder, sugar and salt into a mixing bowl. Add the butter and mix it in, using your fingers, until the mixture resembles coarse bread crumbs.

Make a well in the center and pour in the milk. Using your fingers, incorporate the dry ingredients into the milk until the mixture forms a dough. Knead the dough lightly on a floured board.

Divide the dough in half. Pat each half into the buttered cake pans and bake for 10 minutes, or until golden.

Turn out the shortcakes onto a rack and set aside to cool.

Slice half the strawberries into a bowl and sprinkle them with half the sugar. Whip the cream until it is very thick but not stiff.

To assemble the cake, spread half the cream on one of the shortcakes and arrange the sliced strawberries on top. Cover with the other shortcake. Swirl the remaining cream on top and decorate with the remaining whole strawberries. Sprinkle the remaining sugar on top.

Strawberry Meringue

A glorious concoction of strawberries, cream and crushed meringues. It can be flavored with an orange liqueur, Kirsch, Framboise or brandy, or simply use powdered sugar.

SERVES SIX TO EIGHT
4 cups strawberries, hulled
8 tablespoons powdered sugar
6 tablespoons liqueur—see above
1¼ cups heavy cream, chilled
⅔ cup light cream, chilled
Meringues, made with 2 egg whites

Chop the strawberries up roughly or leave small ones whole. Put a dozen of the most perfect aside for decoration.

Sift the powdered sugar over the strawberries and sprinkle them with the liqueur. Mix lightly and chill for 1 hour.

Whisk the creams together until they hold their shape in firm peaks. Gently fold in the strawberries and their juices. Crush the meringues into pieces and fold into the cream-and-strawberry mixture. Taste and add more sugar if necessary. Pile into a serving bowl. Dot with reserved whole strawberries and serve immediately.

Raspberries

After strawberries, raspberries are the most popular of the berries. For the cook, however, raspberries are more versatile and useful. Furthermore, raspberries freeze well, which is important when there is an abundance of berries in the summer.

Raspberries are comparative newcomers in the kitchen. Few early nineteenth-century cookery books mention them except occasionally in recipes for vinegars, cordials and sometimes for jams and tarts.

Washing is disastrous for fresh raspberries. Just be sure they do not have the stray little worm or bad spot, and serve them as they are with a little sugar and cream. If you are tempted to flavor the cream with anything but sugar, do be discreet—a drop of lemon or lime juice, a little sherry, sweet port or Kirsch, or the raspberries' own liqueur, Framboise.

Raspberries can also be made into compotes, jam and ice cream—raspberry sherbet is particularly delectable and refreshing.

Raspberry Sherbet

The flavor of this sherbet can be changed by mixing three tablespoons of such liqueurs as Framboise or Kirsch into the purée, or by substituting a handful of red currants for some of the raspberries before puréeing. For either of these variations the lemon juice should be left out.

If the sherbet is to be frozen in a refrigerator, reduce the temperature to its lowest setting.

SERVES FOUR
1⅓ cups raspberry purée made with
  about 1½ cups raspberries
8 tablespoons sugar
Juice of 1 small lemon
2 egg whites
Salt
⅔ cup whipping cream, chilled

Put the raspberry purée into a bowl. Add 5 tablespoons of the sugar and the lemon juice and stir until the sugar has completely dissolved.

Whisk the egg whites with a pinch of salt, and, as soft peaks begin to form, gradually whisk in the remaining sugar, a tablespoon at a time. Continue whisking vigorously until the mixture is stiff and glossy.

Whisk the cream to a soft peak stage. With a large metal spoon or spatula, fold the cream into the meringue, then gently fold in the raspberry purée.

Freeze the mixture in a shallow dish until hard, folding the mixture over from sides to center after the first hour, or when the edges have begun to harden. Then remove to a refrigerator at normal setting for at least 1 hour before serving.

Raspberry Mousse

Use fresh or frozen raspberries for this delightful dessert. Serve the mousse decorated with whole raspberries and whipped cream.

SERVES SIX
½ oz gelatin (½ env.)
2 cups fresh raspberries or 2 packages
  frozen raspberries
1⅓ cups heavy cream
4 tablespoons sugar
4 eggs, separated
¼ lb macaroons

Dissolve the gelatin in 2 tablespoons of water in a cup placed in a pan of hot water.

Put the raspberries in a blender and purée at high speed. Line a strainer with cheesecloth or muslin and strain the purée through it into a bowl. Set aside.

In the top of a double boiler, whisk the cream, sugar and egg yolks together. Put the pan over barely simmering water and cook, whisking, until the custard is thick and smooth. Stir in the dissolved gelatin and the raspberry purée and set aside to cool, stirring occasionally.

Whip the egg whites until they are stiff and fold them gently but thoroughly into the raspberry cream mixture. Put the mixture into a serving bowl. Cover it and put it in the refrigerator until the mousse is nearly set.

Meanwhile, crush the macaroons into coarse crumbs with a rolling pin.

Remove the mousse from the refrigerator and fold in the macaroon crumbs. Cover the bowl and return it to the refrigerator and chill for 4 hours, or until the mousse is completely set.

Raspberry Bavarian Cream

A Bavarian cream should be creamy in texture, yet firm enough to turn out of a decorative mold. Raspberries picked from the garden on a dry day will purée to a slightly thicker consistency than those which have been frozen. If frozen raspberries are being used, either drain off the juice as they defrost—in which case it will take about ½ cup more to make up the 2 cups of purée—or blend 2 teaspoons of cornstarch with the sugar before beating it with the egg yolks to make the custard.

SERVES SIX TO EIGHT
About 2 cups raspberries—see above
½ oz powdered gelatin (½ env.)
2 cups milk
5 egg yolks
⅔ cup sugar
5 egg whites
Salt
¼ cup sugar
⅔ cup whipping cream, chilled
Lemon juice (optional)

Prepare the raspberry purée and chill it in the refrigerator until required. Sprinkle the gelatin over 3 tablespoons of cold water in a cup and leave it to soften.

Prepare an egg custard. Scald the milk in a saucepan by heating it gently until the surface just begins to tremble slightly. Meanwhile, in the top of a double boiler or a bowl, beat the egg yolks with the sugar until fluffy. Gradually beat in the scalded milk.

Fit the pan over the base of simmering water. The bottom of the top container should not be in contact with the water. Stir the custard steadily over simmering water until it is so thick that when you draw a finger down the back of the spoon you leave a distinct trail. Do not let the custard boil or it will curdle.

Put the cup of softened gelatin in a pan of hot water and stir until it is clear. Pour the custard into a bowl. Stir in the dissolved gelatin and set aside until cool, but not yet beginning to set.

Whisk the egg whites with a pinch of salt. As peaks start to form, gradually whisk in 2 tablespoons of sugar. Continue to whisk until the whites form soft peaks. Whisk the cream to the same consistency in another bowl. Stir the remaining sugar into the chilled raspberry purée. Taste it—it should be very sharp and may need a tablespoon of lemon juice.

With a large metal spoon, fold the egg whites into the cream. Stir about two-thirds of the raspberry purée into the bowl of custard. Fold the rest of the raspberry purée into the cream mixture, then combine the two, folding the custard into the cream mixture.

Pour the mixture into a 1-quart mold rinsed out with cold water. Refrigerate for 6 hours, or until completely set.

To unmold, dip the mold in and out of a bowl of very hot water. Run a knife around the edge. Place a serving dish on top and reverse the mold onto it, shaking gently to ease it out. Refrigerate the Bavarian cream until it is served.

A sharp knife and a flexible wrist is all you need for chopping herbs. For a large quantity of herbs, however, a mezzaluna *is quicker and more efficient.*

Used imaginatively and with finesse, herbs add an exciting new dimension to cooking. The culinary role of herbs, from the simplest parsley sauce to the most sophisticated *pâté aux fines herbes*, is essentially that of giving a dish character. Stuff a chicken with tarragon, for example, roast it and you have a classic French *poulet à l'estragon*. Substitute dill for the tarragon and the dish is unmistakably central European. Stuff the chicken with sage and onion and you have a British dish that crossed the Atlantic with the Pilgrims.

Some herbs taste best fresh; others contribute more flavor when they are dried. Some should be added in the early stages of cooking a dish. Others are so volatile that their flavor would be destroyed by prolonged cooking. And there are herbs—sorrel, chervil and parsley, for example—which can be the dominating ingredient in a dish.

Herb sugars, made like vanilla sugar, are as delightful as herb-flavored honey and as interesting as herb salts. Herb sugars can be used to flavor cakes, sweet breads and drinks.

Herbs may also be drunk in *tisanes*. A sage infusion was a popular drink in England until it was ousted by tea, and mint tea is still Morocco's national beverage.

Preserving Herbs

Herbs which are to be preserved should be picked at the height of their season, just before they flower. They should be cut in the morning on a fine day. Cut long stems and tie them loosely in slim bunches. Then leave them in a cool, dark place to dry naturally—avoid artificial heat if possible. An airy closet or shed or the attic may be used. Keep different herbs separate or the flavors will blend.

If you are drying for seed, cut the stems with the seed heads as soon as they are ripe. Dry the whole stalks, then thresh them out over a sheet of clean paper. Give the seeds a few hours further drying in the sun or in a warm, dry place. The attic is ideal.

Hang dried herbs in bunches in a dry place or rub the brittle leaves off the stalks between your palms and store them in tightly stoppered, dark glass jars. (A faded appearance is one of the sure signs of staleness.)

The flavor of dried herbs is much stronger than that of fresh herbs. One teaspoon of dried herbs equals approximately three teaspoons of chopped fresh herbs.

Freezing Herbs

Freezing is the most successful method of preserving the natural flavor of herbs. To prepare herbs for freezing, cut them with their stems. Dip them carefully in boiling water to set the color, pat them dry and deep-freeze, spread out loosely in well-sealed plastic envelopes. Another method is to chop the herbs finely, pack them tightly into individual ice-cube trays, cover with water and freeze. Put the frozen cubes in a plastic bag for storage in the freezer.

The herbs may also be chopped, mixed with butter to make a paste and deep-frozen in small, sealed boxes. Use herb butter to flavor and enrich delicate cream or buttery dishes. If the preparation of the dish involves frying, add the butter after this has been done.

Herbed Oils and Vinegars

A small bunch of fresh herbs—three or four sprigs—put into a bottle of olive oil or wine vinegar, will give it an exquisite fragrance. Add a pinch of sea salt and, if it is a strong herb like rosemary, a peppercorn or two. Give the oil or vinegar a few weeks to absorb the flavor of the herb (or herbs—you can make an oil or vinegar *aux fines herbes*) before using it.

Salted Herbs

Chop the herbs finely. Make $\frac{1}{4}$-inch layers, sprinkled generously in between with salt, in a glass jar. Use a dark jar or cover an ordinary jar with foil to exclude the light. Salted herbs will keep for several months.

Basil

With its sunny-sweet, light yet spicy fragrance, basil is the ideal partner for vegetable fruits, above all the tomato. Try slices of tomato covered with a thick layer of chopped basil, parsley and shallot and dressed with oil and vinegar.

The Genoese use basil to make *pesto*, their superb classic sauce. A large bunch of basil leaves is pounded to a paste with 1 or 2 garlic cloves and 1 tablespoon of toasted pine nuts. $\frac{1}{2}$ to $\frac{3}{4}$ cup of Parmesan cheese or a mixture of Parmesan and Pecorino cheese are gradually incorporated, and the paste is diluted with olive oil to make a thick sauce. *Pesto* is used to dress Italian noodles, or as a last-minute flavoring for minestrone.

Bay

This is one of the few herbs which is better dried than fresh. The flavor of a dried bay leaf is not only more concentrated, but somehow richer, particularly if it is torn or crushed.

Bay, automatically included in the standard *bouquet garni*, improves the flavor of many different meat and fish dishes, including *carbonnades à la Flamande*, the famous Belgian beef stew made with beer, chicken fricassée and fish chowder. Use bay, too, when you are making soups, marinades and stock. It may even be added to rice pudding.

Remember, however, that you can spoil a dish if you use too much of this herb; an excess of bay is definitely unpleasant.

Chervil

Chervil and parsley are practically interchangeable—to the extent that chervil is often referred to as "flat-leaf parsley." The flavor of chervil, although stronger, is sweeter and more subtle than that of parsley.

Chervil plays a vital part in the classic *fines herbes*, and it may be added to *bouquets garnis* together with, or instead of, parsley. Sprinkle chervil over raw or cooked salads and delicate-flavored soups.

Use chervil with other herbs, too. For example, a little chervil complements tarragon beautifully in chicken dishes, and it does the same for thyme.

The flavor of chervil is best preserved by freezing or salting.

Herbs

Dill
Although a southern European herb by origin, dill is a northerner by adoption. Even its name is Norse. Dill is used extensively in Scandinavian and central European cooking and is commonly used to flavor pickled cucumbers.

Dill is at its best uncooked. Chop it into sour cream for a central European-style dressing for green salads or sliced cucumbers. Use it with mayonnaise for a Scandinavian fish salad, or with butter for young vegetables, in particular new potatoes, and sprinkle it over fresh vegetable soups.

Dill seed is less pungent than caraway. If you prefer the milder flavor, use dill seed instead of caraway to sprinkle over bread rolls and to flavor coleslaw.

Dill seeds dry well. Home-dried dill leaves are not usually a great success; the commercial manufacturers do it better. Dill leaves are, however, ideal for salting. Dill vinegar will be very useful, the oil less so.

Fennel
Fennel has the sweet, forceful flavor of anise. Its great role in cooking is for flavoring fish, particularly fish which is oily.

Otherwise, use fennel leaves and seeds as you would dill. A pinch of fennel seeds adds an unusual but pleasant flavor to a traditional apple pie.

Be sure that fennel seeds are perfectly dry before storing them in a jar, as they are prone to black mold.

Fennel oil and vinegar are invaluable for brushing over baked fish of all kinds and may also be used to make salad dressings and mayonnaise.

Horseradish
Grating the roots of fresh horseradish is more trying on the eyes than peeling the strongest onion. If possible, use a blender—a hand grater should be used only as a last resort.

Grated horseradish may be folded into whipped cream to serve with roast beef, or mixed into a mayonnaise.

Boiled beef is superb with a rich cream sauce based on the cooking stock and flavored with grated horseradish.

To preserve horseradish, grate it and cover with vinegar in a screw-top jar. Use it either just as it is, or mixed with grated cooked beets.

Marjoram
Sweet marjoram, cousin to the wild oregano, is almost as versatile as parsley. Its sweet, lightly spicy flavor will give a lift to soups. Rub marjoram into roasts, add it to casseroles and sprinkle it over such vegetables as baby carrots and turnips. And do not forget it when you are preparing a stuffing for chicken or lamb. Fish also benefits from a touch of marjoram.

Marjoram should be dried carefully and slowly. Use sprigs collected when the plant is flowering and store it either in bunches or crumbled.

Marjoram vinegar and oil are useful.

Mints
Probably the most useful varieties of mint are spearmint and the strongish Bowles mint. Both are good for making mint sauce. Use peppermint and apple mint for sweet dishes.

The flavor of mint enhances young vegetables and salads, and fruit salads benefit from just a touch of its flavor. Use a mint leaf to garnish raspberry ice cream or half a grapefruit.

Preserve and store mint in the usual way or make a mint sugar using 1 sprig of mint to flavor ⅓ cup of sugar, to sprinkle over buns and cakes.

Parsley
Parsley, the most commonly used of all the herbs, boasts a staggering list of vitamins, headed by vitamin C.

Parsley is the most versatile of culinary herbs. It may be used simply as a garnish or made into parsley sauce or soup. The French use parsley as one of the main ingredients of *persillade de jambon*, in which pink chunks of ham are set in a jelly colored bright green with finely chopped parsley.

Parsley need not be dried, it survives the winter quite happily. Freeze leftover parsley in cubes for economy rather than convenience—there is no point in letting it go to waste.

Rosemary
Mediterranean cuisines use a great deal of rosemary in all kinds of dishes. Its pungent fragrance, slightly reminiscent of a pine forest, flavors such delicate meats as veal, spring lamb and poultry, as well as beef casseroles enriched with wine. It is also used with vegetables and in summer fruit salads and drinks.

Although rosemary is an evergreen, it will not survive extreme cold, so bring it indoors in a pot. It is a wonderful flavoring for oil and vinegar as well as for sugar—use a large sprig of rosemary and the dried grated rind of a small orange to ⅔ cup of sugar.

Sage
If any herb, apart from parsley, could be said to characterize Anglo-American cooking, it would be sage, as represented in the traditional sage-and-onion stuffing. But its warm, slightly camphorlike fragrance is familiar in many cuisines.

Sage complements the fatty flavor of rich meats, which is why it has been used traditionally to flavor stuffings for pork, duck and goose—remember the Cratchit family's dinner in *A Christmas Carol*?

Sage is also good for flavoring bland, soft cheeses and delicate meat dishes. Fresh sage leaves are used in the famous Roman dish *saltimbocca* (literally "jump in the mouth").

Dried, rubbed sage is easier to use than fresh sage. Dry it very slowly to preserve the maximum flavor and color. Crumble the leaves and store in an airtight jar.

Sage vinegar and oil are worth making. A few mustard seeds added with the sage gives the oil a pleasant flavor.

Savory
Strong, spicy, bordering on the peppery, savory is such a natural flavoring for beans that the Germans call it *Bohnenkraut*, the bean herb.

Summer savory is milder than winter savory, but both should be used sparingly with all peas and beans, with cucumber and in salads. Cook heavy meats, like pork, with a touch of savory. Savory is also a classic fish herb, traditionally used to flavor trout.

Sorrel
It is difficult to deal with sorrel without mentioning spinach—the two are treated so similarly in the kitchen. Sorrel soup, for example, is made in the same way as the spinach soup on page 145, except that the dill is left out. For a more muted flavor, use a mixture of sorrel and fresh spinach.

Sorrel is also good in green salads, and it may be chopped into omelets or puréed to a sauce for fish.

Sorrel can be dried, but it is better fresh.

Tarragon (French)
Tarragon, one of the greatest herbs of all, transforms any ingredient with which it comes in contact. Try wrapping a fresh egg in tarragon leaves. Seal the egg in foil or plastic wrap, leave it in the refrigerator for at least 24 hours, then soft-boil it. It will be an egg such as you have never tasted, for the flavor of the herb will have penetrated the porous shell.

Use tarragon with respect, however mild it may taste when picked, for no herb is more deceptive. A chicken stuffed with a few sprigs of tarragon and a lump of seasoned butter will come out of the oven vibrating with flavor. When making dishes which need long cooking, tarragon should be added toward the end, not at the beginning.

Tarragon comes into its own in sauce Béarnaise, the herbed version of hollandaise. This sauce makes a wonderful accompaniment for steaks, grilled chicken, fish, shellfish and various vegetables, including artichokes.

French tarragon will not survive the winter in the North. You may dry or freeze the leaves but do not salt them. Flavor oil and vinegar with the herb: use the oil to make dressings and to brush over roasts, barbecued and broiled meat, and the vinegar for dressings and sauces.

Thyme
Thyme has been valued for centuries, not only for its wonderful, pungent aroma, which enhances meats, soups, poultry stuffings, herb vinegars and such vegetable fruits as eggplants and zucchini, but also for its antiseptic and disinfectant thymol content.

The refreshing flavor of lemon thyme is used in herb butters, custards and in fruit salads. Thyme is best when fresh but is sometimes useful dried.

To dry garden thyme, pick the branches before flowering, then hang them in a cool, dry place for a few weeks. Rub the leaves off the stems and store in a tightly stoppered jar.

Parsley, bay leaves and thyme are the herbs most commonly used together to make a traditional bouquet garni.

Tie a bouquet of herbs in a split leek to make a convenient flavoring for stocks and stews.

A bouquet of dried herbs and flavorings can be tied in a small piece of muslin or cheesecloth.

Freezing

For the cook with a kitchen garden the freezer is a great ally. It safely stores all those vegetables and fruits that would otherwise go to waste, for there are few gardens that do not have a glut at one time or another.

Freezing preserves the texture, flavor and nutritional value of garden produce better than any other method of preserving. It is simple and efficient and, if the rules are observed and the food used intelligently, it is difficult to distinguish the frozen from the fresh.

Quality should be of prime importance. Only the youngest, freshest and best vegetables and fruit should be frozen. Once picked they should go into the freezer as quickly as possible. Delay should not extend beyond a few hours, and during that time the vegetables and fruit should be kept cool to prevent deterioration and wilting. Correct processing and, later, thawing (when necessary) and cooking will all help to keep flavor and food value intact.

The techniques of preparing and packing food for freezing are easy to master and the equipment required is minimal and inexpensive. The storage life of most vegetables and fruit in the freezer will usually extend from one growing season to the next.

However large your freezer, every inch of space is precious and it is wise to work out a plan for how best to utilize it. Decide how much of the total freezer space you can devote to the vegetables and fruit you expect to come from the garden. Then divide it in three to take into account dishes that have been precooked, vegetables or fruit that are being frozen in portions (to serve a given number) and the produce that you intend to freeze in large bags, for drawing on as necessary.

Any precooked dish of fruit or vegetables will freeze admirably, except for those containing large amounts of such emulsified sauces or dressings as mayonnaise, hollandaise and Béarnaise, which tend to separate when defrosted.

Blanching

According to many experts, almost every vegetable should be blanched before it is frozen. There are others, however, who think differently. They suggest that in some cases, provided the produce is garden-fresh and processed on the day it has been picked, blanching is quite unnecessary. If you have reservations, try both methods and compare the results. (See individual entries, which follow.)

When blanching is necessary, it should be done systematically, particularly for a large crop. Have ready a large, deep, wide pot of boiling water (at least 3 quarts of water is needed for 1 pound of vegetables) and a blanching basket. A blanching basket is the only specialized piece of equipment you will need and you can substitute a large, wide sieve or a salad shaker, provided the mesh is fine enough not to let through small pieces of vegetables. Next, put one colander in the sink under the cold tap and have another close at hand on the draining board.

Put a layer of vegetables, no more than 1 pound at a time, in the blanching basket. Submerge it in the pot of boiling water. The water must return to the boil over high heat before you start to time the blanching. As soon as the specified time is up, transfer the contents of the basket to the colander under the cold tap. Let cold water spray over the vegetables for the same length of time as the blanching took. (The water must be very cold. If necessary use ice to chill the water in a large pan or bowl and submerge the basket in it.) Finally, pour the vegetables into the other colander and let them drain while you blanch the next batch.

Packing

To avoid the danger of all the vegetables sticking together, unless you can be sure that the blanched or unblanched vegetables are quite dry, it is best to freeze them in a single layer on a tray before packing them in boxes or plastic bags.

It is also important to remember that liquids will expand as they freeze. Therefore space must be left to allow for this—$\frac{1}{2}$ inch will usually be sufficient. Boxes and bags should be tightly sealed so that air cannot circulate around the food itself while it is in the freezer. In the case of boxes, special self-sealing ones are available. Unless the food is particularly fragile and vulnerable—like asparagus spears, which have to stay in a rigid box to avoid the danger of snapping into pieces—the most economical way to use boxes is to freeze the vegetables or fruit in boxes and then to transfer the frozen blocks to plastic bags. Square or rectangular boxes are best since they will stack well. Round containers are difficult to fit in among the square ones and result in a great waste of freezer space.

If you are freezing directly in plastic bags, you must extract as much air as possible before sealing the bag. Fill the bag with the vegetables or fruit, gather the top together in one hand and insert a straw in the opening with the other. Then, holding the sides of the bag as tightly as possible around the straw, suck out the air inside until the plastic clings to the food inside like a second skin.

Always label and date the contents of bags and boxes. Be sure that any labels stuck onto the containers will not come adrift in the freezer. Tie-on tags or those that come already attached to a coated wire are the best for bags, and there are labels and sticker tapes treated with special adhesive available from stores specializing in freezer accessories. Use a ball-point pen or special freezer pen for writing the labels. Ordinary felt pen or ink will smudge and become illegible.

To blanch vegetables, put them in a blanching basket and lower it into boiling water. When the water returns to the boil begin timing the blanching.

Transfer the blanching basket with the vegetables to a bowl filled with iced water and cool for the same length of time as for blanching.

	Vegetable preparation and blanching chart	
Vegetable	*Preparation*	*Blanching time after water reboils, in minutes*
Asparagus	Wash. Trim tough stems and buds. Grade the stalks. Cut into even lengths to fit rigid containers. Or freeze cooked.	2 (thin) 3 (medium) 4 (thick)
Beans, broad (unblanched) Beans, bush Beans, lima Beans, runner	Shell and freeze in bags, or peel off outer skin, freeze in trays, then put in bags. Wash, string if necessary, top and tail. Keep whole or slice, freeze in bags or boxes. Shell, freeze in bags. Wash, string, if necessary, top and tail. Slice diagonally in ½-inch slices. Freeze in bags.	2 (young) 3 (old) 3 (whole) 2 (sliced) 2 to 4 2
Broccoli	Trim off woody stems and stray leaves. Wash in salted water. Freeze on trays before packing in bags or boxes.	3
Brussels sprouts	Trim off outer leaves. Cut stems. Grade by size. Freeze in boxes or bags.	3 (small) 4 (medium)
Carrots (young) Carrots (old)	Wipe clean. Leave whole. Freeze in bags. Scrape, slice or dice. Freeze in bags.	2 3
Cauliflower	Separate into large flowerets. Wash in acidulated water. Freeze on trays before packing in bags or boxes.	2
Chicory	Trim and wash. Blanch in acidulated water. Squeeze out moisture. Freeze on trays before packing in bags or boxes.	2
Globe artichokes Globe artichoke hearts	Slice leaves low and scoop out chokes. Cool in iced water. Freeze in boxes. Prepare and blanch. Cool in iced water. Pat dry and freeze on trays before packing in bags or boxes.	6 (small) 7 (medium) 8 (large) 4 (small) 5 (medium)
Leeks	Trim, wash and blanch. Freeze whole or sliced. Or freeze cooked.	1 to 2
Mushrooms	Whole or sliced. Cook in butter, flavored with a squeeze of lemon juice. Freeze in bags or boxes.	
Parsnips (young)	Trim and brush clean, or peel thinly. Quarter or dice. Freeze in bags.	2
Peas (unblanched) Peas *Petits pois* (unblanched)	Pod and freeze in bags or boxes. Pod and freeze in bags or boxes. Pod and freeze.	1
Peppers	Seed and core. Halve or cut in strips or rings. Freeze in boxes or bags.	1½
Potatoes (new) Potatoes (French fries)	Clean with damp cloth. Freeze in a large bag. Peel and slice. Deep-fry for 5 minutes. Drain on paper toweling. When cold, freeze in a large bag. Or blanch and freeze. Potatoes for roasting may be treated in the same way.	3 (small) 4 (medium) 3
Salsify and Scorzonera	Trim. Scrape the scorzonera. Blanch whole or sliced. Freeze in bags.	2
Spinach	Wash carefully, leaf by leaf. Only blanch a little at a time. Squeeze out moisture. Leave whole or chop and freeze in boxes or bags.	2
Sweet corn Corn on the cob (unblanched) Corn on the cob Corn kernels	Strip off husks and silks. Do not wash. Freeze on trays. Wrap individually in freezer paper or self-sealing plastic wrap before packing in bags. Prepare as above but blanch before freezing. Blanch the cobs first as above. Scrape off the kernels. Dry on a cloth. Freeze in bags.	3 (small) 5 to 6 (medium) 7 to 8 (large)
Tomatoes	Freeze only as pulp, juice or in cooked dishes.	
Zucchini	Wash, trim and dry. Cut into thick slices. Blanch in salted water. Freeze in bags or boxes. Or freeze cooked.	2 to 3

Prepare a fruit pie in a foil pie pan as for baking, but brush the pastry shell and top with vegetable fat. Add 1½ times the usual amount of cornstarch to the fruit. Place the pie in a plastic bag. Remove air and seal before freezing.

Pack asparagus head to tail in rigid containers to protect the fragile spears.

Freezing vegetables

Most vegetables freeze reasonably well, but there are some which, because of their high water content, are not suitable for freezing except in cooked dishes. These include most green salad plants, cabbage, celery, Jerusalem artichokes, cucumbers, tomatoes (except as pulp), eggplants, squashes, pumpkins and mushrooms. Some vegetables, including soybeans, onions, mushrooms, cucumbers, beets and many other roots, are better stored or preserved in some other way.

Thawing vegetables

Vegetables, with the exception of corn on the cob, should not be thawed before cooking. Put the unthawed vegetables in a very little salted, boiling water. When the water has returned to the boil, cover the pan and simmer until the vegetables are tender. If the vegetables were blanched before freezing, they will take about one-third to one-half the time it takes to cook fresh vegetables, a little longer if they were not blanched.

Asparagus

Speed is essential when freezing asparagus. Ideally it should go straight from the asparagus bed via the kitchen into the freezer. Trim off woody stems and stray buds and divide into bundles of stalks of equal thickness. Blanch for 2, 3 or 4 minutes, depending on thickness, and cool. Either pack the asparagus head to tail in rigid containers, or cook until tender, cool, arrange in boxes and cover with melted butter, lightly seasoned and flavored with lemon juice. To use, put the frozen asparagus into the top pan of a double boiler and heat over simmering water.

Beans, broad and lima

There is no need to blanch broad beans. Shell them and either freeze them in bags or peel off the outer skins and freeze the beans on trays. (Once skinned, the surfaces tend to be moist, with the result that freezing them packed tends to make them stick together.)

To freeze broad and lima beans in the conventional way, the shelled beans may be blanched for 1½ to 4 minutes, cooled, packed and frozen.

Beans, bush

Top and tail. Blanch the whole beans for 3 minutes, sliced beans for 2 minutes. Cool and pack in bags or boxes.

Beans, runner

If the beans are very young and have not yet developed strings, treat them like bush beans. But if you prefer to let them grow to maturity, string them and slice them rather more thickly than usual. Blanch for 2 minutes, cool and pack in bags. Runner beans are also excellent in made-up, deep-frozen dishes, particularly Greek-style bean and lamb casseroles.

Broccoli, green/purple

Trim off woody stems and stray leaves and wash the sprigs carefully in salted water. Blanch the sprigs for 3 to 4 minutes, depending on the thickness of the stalks. Cool and drain thoroughly. Freeze on trays before packing in bags or boxes.

Brussels sprouts

Prepare the sprouts as for immediate use. Blanch for 3 to 5 minutes, depending on size. Cool and freeze, graded by size, in boxes or bags.

Carrots

Perfect, sweet young carrots should be frozen as soon as possible after they are pulled. Cut off the feathery tops. Wipe the carrots clean with a damp cloth. Blanch them for 2 minutes. Cool and pat dry; pack and freeze.

Mature carrots should be scraped, sliced or cut into cubes and blanched for 3 minutes before freezing.

Cauliflower

Separate the heads into large flowerets; trim them and wash them in acidulated water. Blanch the flowerets for 2 minutes. Drain very thoroughly and freeze on trays before packing in bags or boxes.

Chicory

Trim and prepare as if you were cooking the chicory immediately. Blanch for 2 minutes in acidulated water. Cool and drain thoroughly, squeezing out as much moisture as possible, taking care not to spoil their shape. Freeze on trays before storing in boxes or bags.

Globe artichokes

Prepare the artichokes as you would for immediate use, slicing the leaves low and scooping out the chokes. Blanch two or three artichokes at a time for 6 to 8 minutes, depending on their size. Cool by plunging into a large bowl of iced water. You can also freeze artichoke hearts. Blanch them for 4 to 5 minutes, according to size. Cool as above; pat dry and freeze on trays. Store whole artichokes in boxes and hearts in boxes or bags.

Leeks

Wash leeks carefully and trim them. Blanch them for 1 to 2 minutes, depending on thickness. Cool and drain thoroughly. Freeze them whole, cut into chunks or shredded. However, you may prefer to precook the leeks, pack them in boxes, cover them either in seasoned butter flavored with lemon juice or in a white sauce. To use, heat through in the top pan of a double boiler over simmering water.

Parsnips

Scrub if very young or peel thinly. Quarter or slice, blanch for 2 to 3 minutes before freezing in bags.

Peas

Young, perfect peas should be shelled and frozen without blanching. If you prefer the conventional method, however, they need only 1 minute's blanching.

Even if you have decided to blanch everything else, on no account blanch *petits pois*. Blanching added to the inevitable cooking they will undergo before serving will destroy their flavor.

Floury mature peas that you would hesitate to serve as a fresh vegetable should be frozen, unblanched, in large bags for use in soups and casseroles of meat or poultry.

Potatoes

Potatoes can be frozen very successfully. New potatoes should be rubbed clean of soil with a damp cloth and blanched unpeeled for 3 to 4 minutes, depending on size. Cool, drain and pat dry. Freeze them in a large plastic bag.

Older potatoes should be peeled, imperfections cut out and the potatoes cut to a standard size for frying and/or roasting. They may also be kept whole, blanched for 5 minutes, cooled, drained, dried and frozen. Or—and this is the ideal solution for potatoes which are going to be roasted—dry the prepared potatoes thoroughly and deep-fry them for 5 minutes. Drain on paper toweling. When they are quite cold, freeze them in a large plastic bag. When you need roast potatoes, take them straight from the freezer and put them around the roast—they will be ready in half the time it takes to roast raw or parboiled potatoes. French fries may be fried and frozen in the same way.

Salsify and scorzonera

Trim and wipe salsify clean with a damp cloth. Scrape scorzonera. Blanch for 2 minutes. Cool and pat dry. Pack and freeze.

Spinach

Spinach and other leaf vegetables are all dealt with in the same way. Wash carefully leaf by leaf under cold running water. Blanch for 2 minutes, a small portion at a time, shaking the basket gently so that the leaves do not stick together in a clump. Cool. Squeeze out excess moisture gently but firmly with the back of a wooden spoon. Then either leave the spinach whole or chop it finely before packing it in boxes or bags.

Sweet corn

Corn on the cob will freeze beautifully if it is handled properly. The speed at which the cobs travel from the garden to the freezer is important. Strip off husks and silks, but do not wash or blanch the cobs. They must be perfectly dry when they go into the freezer, since any drops of moisture, which would be left trapped between the kernels, would expand as they turned into ice, causing damage.

If you prefer the conventional method, blanch small cobs for 3 minutes, medium-sized ones for 5 to 6 minutes, large ones for 7 to 8 minutes. Freeze the cobs individually, either on trays or individually wrapped in freezer paper or self-sealing plastic wrap. When the cobs are frozen transfer them to a large plastic bag so that you can take as many as you need when you need them.

For frozen corn kernels, use up all the misshapen cobs first. Blanch the kernels on the cob before scraping them off. Dry them by spreading them out on a clean cloth. Transfer to bags and freeze.

Use a straw to suck out as much air as possible from a plastic bag before sealing it.

Zucchini

The only way whole zucchini can be frozen is to cook them through, cool, arrange in boxes and cover with melted butter, lightly seasoned and flavored with lemon juice. To use, put the frozen zucchini into the top pan of a double boiler and heat through over simmering water. To freeze sliced, uncooked zucchini, first cut them thickly, then blanch them in salted water for 2 to 3 minutes. Drain, pat dry and freeze in boxes or bags.

Varieties for freezing

Asparagus: Mary Washington.
Beans, broad: Broad Windsor Long Pod; Express.
Beans, bush: Greensleeves; Green Crop; Royalty; Masterpiece; Tender Green.
Beans, lima: Fordhook 242; Henderson's Bush.
Beans, runner: Prize-winner; Streamline; Kelvedon Marvel.
Broccoli: Premium Crop; Green Comet (F₁); Italian Sprouting.
Brussels sprouts: Peer Gynt; Early Dwarf Danish.
Carrots: Coreless Amsterdam; Tiny Sweet.
Cauliflowers: All the Year Round; Snowball; Burpeeana.
Peas: Wrinkled Little Marvel; Wando; Burpee's Blue Bantam.
Spinach: Melody; New Zealand Spinach.
Sweet corn: Golden Sweet EH; Polar Vee; Golden Midget; Bantam Evergreen.
Swiss chard: Lucullus.

Freezing fruit

With the exception of strawberries, which present problems if you wish to serve them straight from the freezer (see below), and pears, some of which are not only too juicy but are also too delicately flavored to withstand the freezer, the fruits of the kitchen garden are ideal for freezing, either in their natural, raw state (with or without sugar), transformed into purées, sauces and juices—or made into such dishes as tarts, pies, puddings and homemade, fresh-fruit ice creams and sherbets.

If you have been too busy to make all the jam you will need until the following season, simply freeze the raw fruit in a large bag, and use it when you have time, in midwinter if necessary. However, a certain amount of pectin is lost when fruit is frozen, so it may be necessary to make the jam—particularly strawberry jam—with commercial pectin or with another pectin-rich fruit.

The fruit should be of the best quality and frozen as soon after picking as possible. If the fruit requires washing, wash it in ice-cold water and dry thoroughly but gently with paper toweling.

Fruit—particularly berries—is often frozen with sugar. Place the hulled fruit on a tray, sift fine granulated sugar over the fruit and mix it very gently. As soon as the fruit is well coated in the sugar, pack it in boxes, leaving room for expansion—½ inch for every 1 pound box or pack. The amount of sugar needed varies according to the fruit. The berries require ⅔ cup of sugar to 1 pound of fruit. Strawberries must first be pricked with a fork to release excess air before combining with the sugar. For 1 pound of currants use ¾ cup of sugar; green gooseberries require 1 cup; and rhubarb ⅔ to 1 cup.

Thawing frozen fruit

Proper thawing lessens the tendency to mushiness in most frozen fruit. They must be thawed slowly in unopened containers. For the best results, thaw fruit for 6 to 8 hours in the refrigerator. If you are in a hurry, thaw at room temperature, which will take half the time. Dessert fruits (particularly berries) should be served just before they have completely thawed. Fruit which is to be baked in a pie or tart must be completely thawed first or the pastry will get soggy. Unsweetened fruit which is to be stewed may be added unthawed to the hot syrup.

To prevent any deterioration of quality and loss of nutritional value in the fruit, it must be used or served as soon as possible after thawing is completed.

Apples

Apples do well in the freezer, and you should never be without a supply of purées for sauces, charlottes and pies. If you have several varieties in your garden, start with the surplus of those that will not winter well in storage. For a supply of frozen apple rings, or quarters, prepare them as though you were doing to use them fresh; dip them in water acidulated with lemon juice, then pat them dry and store them in large plastic bags—perfectionists might like to take the precaution of freezing them on trays, but this is not really necessary—or toss them quickly in butter over a low heat as though making a chunky applesauce, cool and freeze in bags or boxes.

Blueberries and currants

Strip the berries from their stems, rinse, dry and pack them in boxes or bags and freeze. Or put them in boxes, cover with sugar, mix gently to coat well, cover and freeze.

Gooseberries

There are two stages at which gooseberries may be frozen—when they are ripe or when they are hard and green for use in pies and fools. Top and tail them, wash them if necessary, dry them and pack in bags. The only disadvantage—and it does not affect their flavor—is that even hard, green gooseberries become soft when they are defrosted.

Raspberries, loganberries, blackberries

No fruits come out of the freezer as little affected as these berries, except perhaps currants. On a dry day, the best way to pick them is to take a large basket filled with freezer cartons; transfer the fruit to them straight from the canes, then put the boxes in the freezer. If, however, the fruit is not quite perfect, freeze on trays so that any juice which escapes will not make them stick together when frozen. If you intend to make ice creams and cream molds out of season, you will find it more economical of space to store the fruit in blocks of sieved purée, sweetened or not as you prefer, frozen in boxes, and the frozen blocks then turned out into plastic bags. But make a point of measuring the purée and labeling it before freezing.

Rhubarb

Rhubarb is delicate and blanching often results in its disintegration when it is thawed and cooked. The early pink rhubarb should be washed, cut into short lengths, dried on a clean cloth, then packed in boxes or plastic bags as it is or coated in sugar. Mature rhubarb may be cooked to a purée, then frozen in blocks.

Strawberries

Whether or not you like defrosted strawberries is a matter of taste. Unless they are served chilled to the point of being frosty (and not everyone likes this), strawberries alter in color and become limp when completely thawed. There is no way around this, but it is better to use small, rather than large, berries for freezing. Then instead of freezing them as they are, mix them into a very thick raspberry purée, which will not only provide an interesting and delicate summer-in-winter dessert but has a practical advantage in that the juice released by the strawberries automatically blends with the raspberry purée.

To freeze finely chopped herbs, pack them tightly into individual ice-cube trays.

Pour enough water to fill the trays and freeze. Transfer the frozen cubes to a plastic bag and store in the freezer.

To use, thaw the frozen cube in a strainer. The water runs off, leaving the chopped herbs ready for use.

Canning

Canning is a convenient way of preserving fruit in sterilized conditions so that it can be stored for about one year. (The maximum storage period should be two to three years.)

Canning vegetables, other than such vegetable fruits as tomatoes, is not recommended. It is more difficult and requires more elaborate sterilizing equipment.

It is important to follow the times and temperatures given in the chart.

Equipment Needed for Canning Fruit
Jars. Canning jars vary in capacity from 1 pint to 4 quarts. The timings given on the chart are for 1 pint and 1 quart jars. Beneath the chart, timings are given for large jars.

There are two types of jar available—screw-band jars and clip-top jars.

Screw bands. Metal screw bands are put over metal lids fitted with rubber gaskets, or glass lids fitted with separate rubber rings. Screwed on loosely during processing, the bands allow air and steam to escape. Immediately afterward they must be tightened so that a vacuum is created and air cannot enter the bottles.

Clip-tops. Flexible clips fit over metal rings, which are separated from the top of the bottle by a rubber ring. When the contents of the bottle become hot, the clip expands to let air and steam escape. During cooling, the clips hold the lid firmly in place.

Thermometer. If fruit is canned by the slow-heating method a thermometer is essential.

Canning pots. Use a special canning pot or, if you are preserving only a small amount of fruit, use a fish kettle or a large, deep saucepan. The pan must be fitted with a false bottom to prevent the jars from touching its base. Use a rack, or make a false bottom out of pieces of wood, a cloth or folded newspaper.

Canning may also be done in a pressure cooker, provided it is deep enough to hold the jars when the lid is in place. It must also be able to maintain 5 pounds of pressure (low setting).

Testing the equipment. Before canning, examine each jar and lid for chips or cracks which will prevent the seal from being airtight.

Rubber rings which have been exposed to heat or light may have lost their elasticity. After being stretched they should return to their original shape. Never use the rings more than once.

Preparing the equipment. Wash, rinse and drain the jars, but do not dry them, as fruit slips more easily into wet jars.

Soak the rubber rings for about 10 minutes in cold water. Dip them in boiling water just before you fit them onto the bottles.

Preparation of fruit. Wash and, if necessary, hull the fruit, which should be perfect, then follow the instructions on the chart.

Syrup. Fruit bottled in syrup has a better flavor than fruit bottled in water. Make syrup by dissolving granulated or lump sugar in water.

(See chart for quantities.) Bring the syrup to the boil and boil for 1 minute. If the syrup is to be used cold, make it with half the amount of water, then dilute it to the correct strength by adding the remaining amount of water, chilled. If the syrup is to be kept hot for a time, cover it to prevent evaporation.

Packing the jars. Pack the fruit into the jars tightly. Add the liquid, then tap the jars on a thickly folded cloth to dislodge any air bubbles. Put on the lids, the rubber rings, if separate, and the screw bands or clips.

Canning tomatoes. Whole, small tomatoes, peeled if desired, are bottled in a brine of 2 teaspoons of salt to 5 cups of water. Larger tomatoes should be peeled, halved or quartered and packed into jars so tightly that no liquid is needed. Season with 1 teaspoon of salt and $\frac{1}{2}$ teaspoon of sugar for each 1 pound of tomatoes.

Three Methods of Canning Fruit
There are three methods of canning fruit. Slow heating in water and quick heating in water are recommended both for economy of fuel and the appearance of the fruit. Canning in a pressure cooker is quick and economical, but the fruit may not look as good.

Slow heating in water. Fill the jars with fruit, then pour cold syrup almost to the top of each jar to cover the fruit. Put on the lids, rubber rings, screw bands or clips. Screw bands should be put on loosely.

Stand the jars in a large, deep pot which has been fitted with a false bottom. Use newspaper to prevent them touching one another or the sides of the pot. Cover the jars with cold water. Put a lid on the pot or cover with a board.

Heat the water very slowly, using a thermometer to keep a check on the temperature—after 1 hour it should be 130°F. After a further 30 minutes the water should reach the temperature on the chart. Maintain the temperature for the time specified, then remove the jars from the pot. Use wooden bottle tongs or ladle out the water until the jars can be gripped with oven gloves. Lift the jars out, one at a time, and put them on a wooden surface. Tighten the screw bands immediately.

After 24 hours, remove the screw bands or clips. Test the seal by lifting each jar by the lid. If the lid remains firm, a vacuum has been created. Label the jars with the name of the fruit, the type of liquid used (syrup or water) and the date. Store in a cool, dry place.

If the lid comes off when tested, the fruit must be reprocessed or served as stewed fruit within one or two days. Re-examine the jars, the lids and rubber rings for flaws.

Quick heating in water. Although the temperatures are given, this method can be used even if a thermometer is not available. It differs from the slow-heating method in several ways. First, the bottles should be warmed before they are filled. Instead of using cold syrup, use hot syrup or water (140°F). Put the filled and

To can small tomatoes, peel them, if desired, leave them whole and pack them tightly into jars.

Pour hot or cold brine over the tomatoes and cover them completely.

After processing, remove the screw bands or clips from the jars. Lift each jar by the lid to test the seal.

covered jars into the pot, which should be fitted with a rack or false bottom. Fill the pot with warm water (100°F) and heat to simmering (190°F) in 25 to 30 minutes. Keep simmering for the time given on the chart. Finish as for the slow-heating method.

Using a pressure cooker. Pour water into the pressure cooker to a depth of 1 inch. Put in the rack and bring the water to the boil. Pack the fruit into warm jars, fill with boiling syrup or water, put on the lids, rubber rings, screw bands or clips and place on the rack. Loosen the screw bands by a quarter of a turn. Put on the lid of the pressure cooker, with the vent open, and heat until steam escapes. Close the vent, bring the pressure to 5 pounds and maintain the pressure for the time specified on the chart. Then remove the pressure cooker from the heat and leave for 10 minutes before opening. Leave for 24 hours. Test and label.

There are two types of canning jars: screw-band jars (above) and clip-top jars (below).

Fruit Preparation and Processing Chart

FRUIT	SUGAR to 2⅔ cups of water	PREPARATION	METHOD 1		METHOD 2		METHOD 3
			Temp °F	*Time maintained in min.	Temp °F	*Time maintained in min.	Time maintained at 5-lb (low) pressure in min.
Raspberries	1 lb	Discard stalks. Inspect for maggots.	165	10	190	2	1
Loganberries	1 lb	Same as raspberries.	165	10	190	2	1
Blackberries	½ lb	Discard stalks and damaged fruit.	165	10	190	2	1
Strawberries	1 lb	Hull and rinse in cold water. Strawberries lose color when canned and are better made into jam.	165	10	190	2	Not recommended
Currants and blueberries		Discard stems and calyx.	180	15	190	10	1
Gooseberries (for pies) (for dessert)	½ lb ½ lb	Top and tail. If they are being bottled in syrup, prick the skins to prevent shriveling.	165 180	10 15	190 190	2 10	1 1
Apples (in syrup)	⅔ to 1 cup	Peel, core and slice. Immerse in salted water—½ oz salt to 1 quart of water. Rinse before bottling.	165	10	190	2	1
Apples (solid pack)	1⅓ to 2 cups	After preparing, as above, blanch in boiling water for a few minutes or steam until just tender.	180	15	190	20	3–4
Pears	⅔ to 1 cup	Peel, halve and core. Immerse in salted water, as for apples. Stew cooking pears until tender.	190	30	190	40	5
Rhubarb (for pies) (for dessert)	½ lb	Remove leaves and trim base. Wipe stalks and cut into even lengths.	165 180	10 15	190 190	2 10	1 1
Tomatoes (whole)		Remove calyx. Peel if desired.	190	30	190	40	5
Tomatoes (solid pack)		Peel, halve or quarter. Pack into jars. Add 1 teaspoon of salt and ½ teaspoon of sugar to each jar.	190	40	190	50	15

*Increase processing time for large jars (methods 1 and 2):
1½ and 2 quart size by 5 min. all packs except tomatoes solid pack 10 min.
2½ and 3 quart size by 10 min. all packs except tomatoes solid pack 20 min.
3½ and 4 quart size by 15 min. all packs except tomatoes solid pack 30 min.

Jams & Jellies

Homemade jams and jellies should have a good, bright color, a fresh, fruity flavor, and should set well and keep well. Basically all jams and jellies are made by boiling fruit or fruit juice with sugar until the mixture sets lightly when cold.

The fruit. Use dry, slightly underripe fruit as soon as possible after picking. Remove the stalks and leaves, and stones if desired. Wash the fruit just before using.

Pectin is a substance present in most fruit—without it jams and jellies will not set. Acid, too, is important as it helps to release the pectin. Fruits rich in pectin and acid include cooking apples, crab apples, currants and gooseberries. Blackberries, loganberries and raspberries contain a little less pectin, while pears and some varieties of strawberries have so little that they are difficult to make into preserves with a good set. When using fruits which contain little pectin, commercially made pectin or the juice of a pectin-rich fruit may be added. Acid deficiency may be corrected with 2 tablespoons of lemon juice to 4 pounds of fruit.

Pans. Pans should be large and heavy, made preferably of stainless steel or aluminum. If enamel pans are used they must not be chipped, because the exposed iron will spoil the color of the preserve. To help prevent the preserves from burning and to reduce scum, rub the bottom of the pan with butter or glycerine.

Sugar. Use preserving, lump or granulated sugar. To help the sugar dissolve more rapidly, warm it in a slow oven before adding it to the fruit. For fruit rich in pectin and acid, you will require $1\frac{1}{4}$ to $1\frac{1}{2}$ pounds of sugar to each pound of fruit. For fruit that has a moderate amount of pectin and acid, 1 pound of sugar will be sufficient for 1 pound of fruit.

Testing for pectin. Test for pectin just before you add the sugar. Put 1 teaspoon of the juice of the simmered fruit into a warm glass. When the juice is cool, add 3 teaspoons of grain alcohol. Shake gently and leave for 1 minute. The pectin will concentrate into a jellylike clot. If there is one fair-sized clot it indicates that there is adequate pectin. If the clot is broken into 2 or 3 pieces, the pectin is present in moderate quantity, but if it appears in many small pieces the pectin is inadequate.

Water. Usually only enough water to prevent the fruit from burning is required. Raspberries and other such berries require no water. They are heated gently until their juices flow.

Testing for a set. Put a little of the liquid from the cooking jam or jelly onto a saucer and let it cool. If it wrinkles when pushed with a finger it is ready. While testing, take the pan off the heat.

A quicker and more reliable method is to use a thermometer. Keep the thermometer in hot water in between testing. Stir the jam and insert the thermometer into the center without touching the bottom of the pan. The temperature needed is 220°F, but sometimes 221° or 222°F may give better results.

Jam. Prepare and wash the fruit and put it in a large pan. Add water, if necessary, and simmer gently to soften the skins and release the pectin in the fruit. If extra acid is required add it at this stage. Test for pectin.

When the fruit is soft, and not before, add the warmed sugar—the pan should not be more than half full after the sugar has been added—and stir until it is completely dissolved. Then increase the heat and boil rapidly, stirring occasionally. Cook the jam for as short a time as possible after the sugar is added. Cooking time varies from 5 to 35 minutes depending on the fruit. Test for setting.

When the jam is ready, remove the scum. Pour the jam into clean, dry, warm jars. Whole-fruit jams should first be allowed to cool until a skin forms, then stirred and poured. This gives the jam time to thicken and to suspend the fruit evenly.

Wipe the neck of the jars. Pour $\frac{1}{8}$ inch of melted paraffin on top of the hot jam and cover with metal lids or foil. Label, date and store in a cool, dark, ventilated cupboard.

Whole-fruit jam. Using 1 pound of sugar to each pound of fruit, layer the fruit and sugar in a bowl. Cover the bowl and leave in a cool place for 24 hours.

Pour the fruit and sugar into a pan, add acid, if necessary, and stir well. Bring slowly to the boil, stirring carefully to keep the fruit whole. Then boil rapidly—testing for setting—until the jam sets. Remove the scum. Let the jam cool until a skin forms and bottle.

Low-sugar jam. Jam can be made with only $\frac{3}{4}$ pound of sugar to 1 pound of a good setting fruit. Test for setting by the saucer test only. The jam will not have a firm set and will keep for only a few weeks. It will, however, have a very fine fruity flavor.

Jelly making. Because the fruit pulp is discarded, you will get less jelly than jam from the same amount of fruit. Fruits with a rich flavor are best for jelly. Cooking apples can be added to improve the set. It is not possible to give exact yields in jelly recipes, but on average you can expect 10 pounds of jelly for every 6 pounds of sugar used.

Wash the fruit and discard any unsound parts. Cut large fruit into pieces. Put the fruit into a pan with water—$\frac{2}{3}$ to 2 cups to 1 pound of fruit. Hard or firm fruit requires the larger amount of water. Simmer slowly until the fruit is soft. Test for pectin.

Meanwhile, scald a jelly or muslin bag and hang it over a large bowl. Pour the softened fruit into the bag. Leave it, without stirring or squeezing, until the dripping ceases.

Measure the juice and pour it into a large pan. Bring to the boil and stir in $\frac{3}{4}$ to $1\frac{1}{4}$ pounds of sugar to $2\frac{2}{3}$ cups of juice. Use the larger amount of sugar for fruit which gives one firm pectin clot when tested. Finish making the jelly as you would jam.

Apple Jelly

Although cooking apples and crab apples do not have much flavor, they have good setting properties. Other fruits and flavorings can be added to make really excellent jellies.

To make an herb jelly, replace the spices in this recipe with a few sprigs of any one of the following herbs: chervil, mint, sage, marjoram, thyme, basil or tarragon. Ten minutes before the sugar is added, stir in 2 tablespoons of red or white wine vinegar. Remove the herb sprigs before bottling.

If you are preparing large quantities of apples for relish, canning or freezing, the skins and cores can be used to make apple jelly.

4 lb cooking, crab or windfall apples
6 cups water
2 teaspoons ground ginger, cloves or
    cinnamon—or bruised root ginger or
    lemon rind in a muslin bag
Sugar

Wash the apples and cut them up roughly, discarding any bad portions. Put them in a large pan with the water. Add the spices and simmer for about 1 hour, or until the fruit is soft. Follow the instructions for making jelly adding 1 pound of sugar to each $2\frac{2}{3}$ cups of juice.

If you do not have a jelly bag improvise by tying a cloth to the legs of an inverted stool.

Blackberry Jam

Blackberries contain a moderate amount of pectin and apple is often added to improve the set and to stretch the fruit. If desired, the fruit may be sieved to remove the seeds and then the pulp weighed and 1 pound of sugar added for each 1 pound of pulp.

MAKES ABOUT SEVEN POUNDS
4 lb blackberries
$\frac{2}{3}$ cup water
2 tablespoons lemon juice
4 lb sugar

Pick over the blackberries and wash them. Put them into a pan with the water and lemon juice. Simmer gently until the fruit is soft. Test for pectin. Add the sugar and stir to dissolve. Increase the heat and boil rapidly until setting point is reached. Remove the scum, pour into jars, cover and label.

Raspberry-and-Currant Jelly

The best of all jellies for those who prize the fragrance of ripe raspberries, this classic jelly combines them with pectin-rich red currants.

2 quarts currants
1 quart raspberries
Sugar

Crush the fruits and cook together until the currants are soft and colorless. Strain. Add $\frac{3}{4}$ to 1 cup of sugar for each cup of juice and follow jelly-making procedure.

Mint Gooseberry Jelly

Gooseberries are rich in pectin and acid and both the cooking and dessert varieties can be used to make jams and jellies. If the mixture is cooked for any length of time after the sugar is added the jam will turn red.

A delicate muscatel flavor can be given to gooseberry jam if 12 elderflower heads, in a muslin bag, are boiled with the fruit for 30 minutes.

Dessert gooseberries make a red jam and the color and flavor can be improved by adding $\frac{1}{2}$ pound of raspberries to every 3 pounds of red gooseberries.

The following jelly recipe uses fresh mint as a flavoring.

3 lb gooseberries
Water to cover
1 tablespoon white wine vinegar
Sugar
Fresh mint

Wash the gooseberries and put them in a pan. Add the water and vinegar and simmer until the fruit is very soft. Strain the fruit and test for pectin. Add 1 pound of sugar to each $2\frac{2}{3}$ cups of juice, and suspend a bunch of washed mint in the pan. Stir until the sugar has dissolved. Increase the heat and boil until setting point is reached, tasting from time to time and removing the mint when the flavor is strong enough.

Uncooked Raspberry Jam

For a traditional raspberry jam, follow the general directions for jam making. The fruit may be sieved before the sugar is added, to remove the pips. Uncooked raspberry jam is not traditional, but is much more delicious.

Put equal weights of fruit and sugar in separate bowls in a 350°F oven for 20 to 25 minutes, or until they are really hot. Add the sugar to the raspberries and beat them together until the sugar is dissolved. Pour the jam into jars and cover.

Make small quantities of this jam as it does not store well.

Strawberry Jam

Usually, small strawberries are used in jam making so that they can be left whole. This means they are not cooked to the stage when the pectin is completely extracted from the pulp and so commercial pectin or red currant or gooseberry juice is usually added. If red currant or gooseberry juice is used, add 2 cups of juice to 6 pounds of strawberries.

Put equal quantities of hulled strawberries and sugar in a large saucepan and heat slowly, stirring carefully, until the sugar is dissolved. Add pectin (following the directions on the bottle) and boil rapidly to setting point. Remove the pan from the heat and cool until a skin forms on top of the jam. Stir the jam and pour it into jars.

Rhubarb Jam

This is a fine jam to make in the spring. To vary the flavor, replace the lemon rind and ginger with any one of the following: $1\frac{1}{2}$ pounds of chopped, pitted dates, 1 pound of chopped, dried figs, the grated rind and juice of 2 medium-sized oranges, 1 pound of dried apricots, soaked for 24 hours and chopped, or chopped crystallized ginger.

MAKES ABOUT FIVE POUNDS
3 lb rhubarb
3 lb sugar
Rind and juice of 1 lemon
About 2 oz root ginger, bruised

Cut the rhubarb into chunks. Put it into a bowl with alternate layers of sugar and leave it for 24 hours.

Put the fruit and sugar into a pan with the lemon juice and lemon rind. Put the ginger in a muslin bag and add it to the pan. Follow the directions for whole-fruit jam, removing the ginger before pouring into jars.

Pickles & Relishes

The making of pickles and relishes and, indeed, of jams and jellies, satisfies one of the most primitive human instincts—to store food for future use. Although the need to do so no longer exists, the pleasure of making one's own preserves remains.

Pickles are vegetables or fruits, or both, preserved in vinegar or salt. Sugar, spices and herbs are sometimes added for additional flavor and can be adjusted to suit individual tastes. Try adding an extra bay leaf, a sprig of mint or peppercorns. Dried or fresh chilies, cayenne pepper and fresh root ginger will add extra pungency.

Vinegars. Distilled white vinegar, malt, cider and wine vinegars are all suitable for making pickles.

Spiced vinegar is used for some pickles and relishes and is easy to make. Use whole spices as ground spices make the vinegar cloudy. To make spiced vinegar, tie 2 ounces of mixed pickling spice or $\frac{1}{2}$ ounce each of stick cinnamon, cloves, mace and allspice and a few peppercorns in a muslin bag. Put the bag in a large pan with $2\frac{1}{2}$ quarts of vinegar and 1 tablespoon of kitchen salt and bring to the boil. Cover the pan and boil for 5 minutes. Strain and use the spiced vinegar immediately or pour it into a jug to get cold before removing the spices. The cooled vinegar can now be used or bottled and stored. Use cold vinegar to make crisp pickles or hot for such soft pickles as plums and walnut.

Salt. Salt is used to draw out water from vegetables and to toughen them a little. If this is not done the vinegar will be diluted by the water in the vegetables and its preserving properties will be reduced.

Brine—a solution of salt and water—is sometimes used instead of salt; its action is more gentle. But for vegetables with a high water content salt is preferable. When vegetables are immersed in brine, weigh them down with a plate so that they remain below the surface. To make brine, dissolve $\frac{1}{2}$ pound of kitchen salt in $2\frac{1}{2}$ quarts of water.

Pans. Use aluminum, stainless steel or unchipped enamel pans. Iron, brass and copper must *never* be used as the reaction of vinegar to the metal gives the pickles an unpleasant taste.

Jars. Any type of jar is suitable, providing it can be fitted with a suitable lid or cover. A vacuum-sealed lid is best as this prevents the vinegar evaporating. Metal lids must not be used unless they have a coating of plastic. Paper and cellulose covers are not recommended as they allow evaporation, which exposes the vegetables, causing them to discolor.

Making Pickles

Always use fresh, young vegetables. Trim the vegetables and, if necessary, peel and cut them into even-sized pieces. At this stage some vegetables are blanched. The vegetables are first put into boiling water for 1 to 5 minutes, depending on their size, and then in cold water for the same length of time.

Immerse the vegetables in brine or put them on a flat dish and sprinkle liberally with kitchen salt. Leave for 12 to 48 hours, depending on the vegetable, then rinse in cold water and drain.

Pack the vegetables into clean jars to within 1 inch of the top. Fill the jars with vinegar, covering the vegetables by at least $\frac{1}{2}$ inch. Fix the covers and store the jars in a cool, dry place.

Making Sweet Pickles

Sweet pickles are made from fruits and such vegetable fruits as tomatoes and cucumbers. They are stewed in sweetened, spiced vinegar to which thinly peeled lemon rind and bay leaves are added—use the rind of 1 lemon and 2 bay leaves to every $2\frac{1}{2}$ quarts of spiced vinegar. If whole fruit is used, prick them with a needle or a fine skewer to keep the fruit from shriveling.

To make a sweet pickle, dissolve the sugar in the spiced vinegar. Add the fruit and simmer in a covered pan until it is just tender—be careful not to overcook the fruit. Lift out the fruit and pack into jars. Boil the vinegar rapidly until it forms a thin syrup and there is enough to cover the fruit. Pour the vinegar syrup into the jars. Cover the jars and leave the pickle for at least 4 to 6 weeks before eating it.

Making Relishes

Relish can be made from a variety of fruits and vegetables combined with vinegar, spices and sugar. The ingredients are usually chopped or minced. Long, slow cooking helps to blend the flavors, which improve if the relish is left to mature and mellow after bottling. Relishes should not be opened for two to three months and will keep for about three years. Uncooked relishes, however, should be eaten within two to three weeks. If kept longer they discolor.

For a light-colored relish, add the sugar toward the end of the cooking time. For a dark relish, add the sugar at the beginning. Brown sugar also gives relish a rich, dark color.

Use ground spices when making relish. If whole spices are used, double the quantity specified in the recipe. Bruise the spices and tie them in a muslin bag. Remove the bag before bottling.

Dried fruit is often an ingredient in the highly spiced relish called chutney. If it is omitted, slightly increase the amount of sugar used.

Pans and jars used for relishes are the same as for pickles.

Pickles & Relishes

Pickled Beets
Boil whole beets until tender. When cool, peel and cut the beets into $\frac{1}{4}$-inch slices or cubes and pack them into jars. Cover with cold spiced vinegar or, if the pickle is to be stored for some time, use boiling spiced vinegar.

Pickled Cauliflower
Separate the cauliflowers into small flowerets and soak them in brine for 24 hours. Remove the flowerets, rinse, drain and pack them into jars. Cover with cold spiced vinegar.

Pickled Gooseberries
1$\frac{1}{2}$ lb white sugar
2$\frac{2}{3}$ cups spiced vinegar
2$\frac{1}{2}$ lb gooseberries

Follow the instructions for making sweet pickles, taking care that the gooseberries are very slightly undercooked.

Dill Pickles
This pickle is made in a slightly different way and will not keep as well as the other pickles.

4 lb small garden cucumbers
Brine
Fresh dill sprigs
Peppercorns
Dill seeds
3$\frac{1}{3}$ cups white vinegar
3$\frac{1}{3}$ cups water
4 tablespoons coarse salt

Wash the cucumbers, prick them all over with a fork and soak them in brine for 24 hours. Rinse the cucumbers, drain them well and pack them into jars. To each jar add a sprig of dill, 4 peppercorns and 1 tablespoon of dill seed.

Put the vinegar, water and salt into a pan and bring to the boil. Boil for 1 minute and pour into the jars to within $\frac{1}{2}$ inch of the top. Seal the jars. Leave for 4 days before eating.

Pickled Pears
2 lb cooking pears
1 lb white or brown sugar
2$\frac{2}{3}$ cups spiced vinegar

Peel the pears. Cut the larger ones into halves or quarters and remove the cores. Leave small pears whole.

Follow the instructions for making sweet pickles.

Mustard Pickles
This is a little different from the other pickles as the vegetables are cooked in a sauce. It is a flexible recipe and the balance of flavours can be altered to suit personal taste. For a less pungent flavor omit the chilies and cloves and increase the turmeric and mustard. For a thicker sauce mix a little flour with the mustard. The vegetables may include cauliflowers, zucchini, cucumbers, onions, bush beans, green tomatoes; hard, sour apples may also be used.

6 lb mixed vegetables
$\frac{3}{4}$ lb coarse salt

SAUCE
8 cups white vinegar
6 dried chilies
6 cloves
1$\frac{1}{2}$ oz root ginger, bruised
$\frac{1}{2}$ lb granulated or lump sugar
6 tablespoons dry mustard
1$\frac{1}{2}$ tablespoons turmeric

Prepare the vegetables and cut them into even-sized pieces. Put them in a large dish, sprinkle with salt and leave for 24 hours. Rinse and drain.

To make the sauce, pour all but 2 cupfuls of the vinegar into a large saucepan. Tie the chilies, cloves and ginger in a muslin bag and add them to the pan. Bring the vinegar to the boil and simmer for 20 minutes.

Add the sugar and stir until it has dissolved. Add the vegetables and simmer for a further 20 minutes.

Meanwhile, mix the mustard and turmeric with the remaining vinegar. Stir the mixture into the simmering vegetables and continue cooking for 10 minutes. Bottle, seal and store in a cool, dry cupboard.

Salted Beans
You will need 1 pound of coarse salt (never use table salt) to every 3 pounds of beans. These proportions are important. Use too little salt and the beans will not keep, use too much and the flavor will be spoiled. Wash tender, fresh young beans and string them, if necessary. Slice runner beans; leave bush beans whole. In a glass jar or earthenware crock, layer the salt and beans, beginning and ending with the salt. Press the beans down well. This is important for if they are not pressed down hard enough the beans will not keep. Cover the jars with wax paper or plastic sheeting and leave for four days. As the beans shrink, the jars should be filled with more beans and salt. Repeat this until there is finally no more room in the jar. As the moisture is drawn from the beans a strong brine is formed which preserves them.

Cover the jar with plastic sheeting or wax paper tightly tied. The beans can be stored in this way for a year or more.

To cook the beans: remove as many as are required and wash them several times in cold water. Soak the beans in warm water for no longer than 2 hours. Drain, rinse and simmer in unsalted water until tender.

Green Tomato Chutney
3 lb green tomatoes
$\frac{1}{2}$ lb cooking apples
$\frac{1}{2}$ lb onions
$\frac{1}{2}$ lb raisins
$\frac{1}{4}$ lb crystallized ginger, chopped
2$\frac{2}{3}$ cups vinegar
$\frac{1}{2}$ lb brown sugar
2 teaspoons salt

Peel the tomatoes. Chop them finely with the apples and onions and put them into a large pan. Add the raisins, ginger and half the vinegar and bring to the boil. Reduce the heat and simmer, uncovered, until the mixture thickens.

Meanwhile, dissolve the sugar in the remaining vinegar and add it with the salt to the chutney. Continue cooking until the chutney is thick. Pour the chutney into jars and cover.

Uncooked Fruit Chutney
This chutney cannot be stored. Use it within two to three weeks.

1 lb cooking apples
$\frac{1}{2}$ lb onions
6 oz red or green pepper
2 oz pitted dates
$\frac{1}{4}$ lb white raisins
1 oz crystallized ginger
2 tablespoons white wine vinegar
1 teaspoon salt
1 teaspoon granulated sugar

Mince the apples, onions, pepper, dates, white raisins and crystallized ginger together. Stir the vinegar, salt and sugar together until the sugar dissolves and mix it into the minced fruit. Spoon the chutney into jars and cover.

Wine Making

Wine is basically easy to make, but it requires care, patience and time to produce good, consistent results. And it is not exclusively a country craft—virtually every early cookery book included a section on wine making. However, to quote from P. P. Carnell's *Treatise on Family Winemaking*, published in 1814, "The causes that produce the effects of vinous fermentation are imperfectly known." Today we know exactly how fermentation works and, consequently, the home wine maker can produce wines that are made to suit his or her own particular palate.

Quite simply, wine is made by adding yeast to a liquid that contains sugar. The yeast converts the sugar into carbon dioxide and alcohol, in roughly equal proportions. If the sugar content is high to begin with, the amount of alcohol produced will kill the yeast before all the sugar is converted and the result will be a sweet wine. If the sugar content is low, the yeast will convert all the sugar and a dry wine will result.

Equipment and Ingredients

The illustration opposite shows all the equipment required. If you use full-length wine corks, you should buy a corking tool. But you could use flanged corks, which can be inserted by hand.

Most serious wine makers use a hydrometer to assess the amount of sugar in the wine; but you can use your sense of taste instead—at least at first.

You will also require certain essential ingredients in addition to the main fruit or vegetable to help produce your wine.

Yeast. Wine yeast is best. There are many types. Start with an "all purpose" yeast. Bakers' yeast will do if necessary, but never use brewers' yeast, except for making beer. If you use wine yeast the amount needed will be given on the label. If you use bakers' yeast, 1 level teaspoon will be enough for the recipes in this book.

Citric acid. Not always essential, but necessary to produce a "balanced" wine when the main ingredient is deficient in acid.

Sugar. Ordinary white sugar. Brown sugar has too much flavor for most wines.

Yeast nutrient. This helps the yeast to work better. Half a level teaspoon will be the amount needed for the recipes in this book. Yeast nutrient is sold at wine-making shops.

Campden tablets. Used for sterilizing the "must," or ingredients.

Pectic enzyme. Ingredients containing pectin will create a "pectin haze" if this enzyme is not added at an early stage.

Tannin. To introduce "bite" when the main ingredient is lacking in tannin.

Making Wine

There are several different methods of making wine, but they are all variations on a basic procedure.

First, pour the main ingredients, and the sugar, into a plastic pail. Bring the water to the boil and pour it over the ingredients. You now have what is called the "must." Cover with a close-weave cloth or plastic sheet.

When the must has cooled, add the Campden tablet or pectic enzyme if required. If either ingredient is added, wait 24 hours before the next stage.

Add yeast, yeast nutrient and acid. In a few days, when fermentation starts, everything will rise to the surface, forming a "cap."

Stir every day, breaking the cap thoroughly. Keep the must covered except when stirring. Continue this procedure for the length of time specified in the recipe.

Strain the must into a fermentation jar through a nylon strainer and funnel. Fit the fermentation lock and pour a little water into the S-bend of the lock. The bubbles popping around the S-bend tell you that fermentation is in progress. At first the bubbles will pass through every few seconds, but after a few days they will slow down considerably.

The completion time for fermentation is variable and depends on many things, the most important being temperature. In a warm place, fermentation might be complete in several weeks, in a colder place it might take several months. If the temperature rises above 90°F the yeast will die. If the temperature drops below 50°F fermentation will slow down or stop, but it will resume when the temperature is increased.

When there has been no movement in the fermentation lock for two days, taste the wine. If it is too dry, add some sugar and ferment on.

If the wine is ready, wait until all trace of cloudiness has gone and rack the wine off the sediment. To do this, place the full jar on a table and an empty jar on the floor. Dip one end of a siphon into the wine in the top jar, until it is 2 inches clear of the sediment. Drop the other end to a point lower than the sediment and place it in your mouth. Suck gently and the wine will flow smoothly down the tube. As soon as the wine trickles through, place this end of the tube into the neck of the lower, empty jar. Hold the tube in position while the wine transfers to the lower jar, but ensure that no sediment is dragged through. If this happens repeat the procedure when the wine has settled again.

It might take several rackings to clear the wine thoroughly. If it has not cleared after this, seriously consider buying one of the filter devices on the market. These ensure bright, clear wine every time.

Bottling

If your wine now tastes just right, there is no problem—just drink it. However, it is usually at least three to six months before the wine will be drinkable. So you will have to bottle it.

Fill the thoroughly clean bottles by racking. While you are doing this, place the corks in a saucepan of boiling water, taking each cork out of the water as required.

1 Plastic pail
2 Glass fermentation jar
3 Bottles
4 Large pot
5 Nylon sieve
6 Funnel
7 Corking tool
8 Siphon tube
9 Full-length wine corks
   and flanged corks
10 Fermentation lock and bung

Wine Making

Apple Wine

Apples produce a superb medium wine, provided enough fruit is used. At least 10 pounds are required if the wine is to have sufficient body. Cooking apples are ideal and require no additional acid, but if you have to use eating apples, add ¼ ounce of citric acid.

MAKES ABOUT SIX BOTTLES
11 lb cooking apples
5 qts water
Yeast and nutrient
½ teaspoon tannin
3½ lb sugar

Chop the apples very finely and put them in a plastic pail. Bring the water to the boil and pour it over the apples. When cool, add the yeast, nutrient and tannin. Stir in the sugar. When fermentation starts, allow it to continue for 5 days. Strain the must into a fermentation jar, fit the fermentation lock and ferment on.

Fermentation lock. The water in the fermentation lock will look like this while the wine is fermenting because the pressure of the gas given off by fermentation will be constantly pushing the water toward the opening.

Artichoke Wine

This wine is made from Jerusalem, not globe, artichokes. It makes an excellent dry wine. The recipe includes raisins, which give the wine extra body. If you would like to try a pure artichoke wine, add 1½ pounds of artichokes and ¼ pound of sugar to the recipe and omit the raisins.

Scrub the tubers well before slicing them. This is a time-consuming job because of the number of folds in the tubers, but if any soil is present it will spoil the taste of the wine.

MAKES ABOUR SIX BOTTLES
5 lb Jerusalem artichokes, finely
   chopped
2 lb sugar
5 qts water
Yeast and nutrient
½ lb raisins, minced
½ teaspoon tannin
1 tablespoon citric acid

Place the tubers and sugar in a large saucepan, add the water and bring to the boil. Remove the pan from the heat. When cool pour into a plastic pail and add the yeast, nutrient, raisins, tannin and acid. Allow the mixture to ferment for 4 days. Strain into a fermentation jar, fit the fermentation lock and ferment on.

When fermentation has ceased, the water in the fermentation trap will level off at both sides, as shown. Ensure that the level has remained like this for at least two or three days before you start racking.

Broad Bean Wine

One of the hardiest of vegetables, the broad bean often produces a glut of seed. When it does the kitchen gardener can utilize them to make an excellent dry white wine. It can be made as a sweet wine, but this produces a particular flavor that can only be described as an acquired taste.

MAKES ABOUT SIX BOTTLES
4 lb shelled broad beans
5 qts water
2 lb sugar
¾ lb white raisins, minced
Yeast and nutrient
1 tablespoon citric acid
¼ teaspoon tannin

Ensure that there are no beans that have been broken or split. Throughout the procedure do not stir or disturb the beans; if the skins break the wine will become cloudy and almost impossible to clear.

Put the beans in the water and bring to the boil. Turn the heat off as soon as the water boils. Leave to cool, then carefully strain off the liquid and add to it the sugar, white raisins, yeast, nutrient, acid and tannin. Pour into a fermentation jar, fit the fermentation lock and ferment on.

Carrot Wine

Carrots are one of the best vegetables for making excellent dry or sweet wine. Carrot wine has plenty of body and a good flavor. It is essential to scrub the carrots clean, because any soil left on will spoil the wine. If you want a dry wine, omit the currants and reduce the sugar to 2½ pounds.

MAKES ABOUT SIX BOTTLES
9 lb carrots
5 qts water
4 lb sugar
½ lb currants, minced
1 tablespoon citric acid
Yeast and nutrient
Pinch of tannin

Scrub (never peel) and grate the carrots. Put them in the water and bring to the boil, stirring the sugar in at the same time. Remove the pan from the heat and when the mixture is cool, pour into a plastic pail. Add the currants, acid, yeast, nutrient and tannin. When fermentation starts, allow it to continue for 2 days. Strain the must into a fermentation jar, fit the fermentation lock and ferment on.

Gooseberry Wine

Gooseberries are one of the best fruits for making a fine medium wine. With care, they can be made into a wine that your friends will not be able to distinguish from hock, Moselle or Chablis. But to do this you must use the wine yeast for those particular wines. Many home wine makers add raisins or other ingredients, but before you do that, try gooseberry wine just as it is.

MAKES ABOUT SIX BOTTLES
6 lb ripe gooseberries, crushed
3½ lb sugar
5 qts water
1 tablespoon pectic enzyme
Yeast and nutrient
½ teaspoon tannin

Put the gooseberries and sugar in a plastic pail. Bring the water to the boil and pour it over the fruit and sugar, stirring. Allow the mixture to cool. Add the pectic enzyme and set aside for 24 hours. Add the yeast, nutrient and tannin. After fermentation has started, leave it to continue for 4 days, stirring daily. Strain the must into a fermentation jar. Fit the fermentation lock and ferment on.

Grape Wine

To make true grape wine you will require the juice from about 15 pounds of grapes for only a few bottles of wine. This recipe, however, is more economical. It uses dessert grapes to make a medium wine. Because dessert grapes are deficient in acid, this has been added. A true wine grape is much more sour and does not require the addition of acid.

MAKES ABOUT SIX BOTTLES
9 lb dessert grapes, crushed
1 lb sugar
1½ teaspoons citric acid
3½ qts water
1 Campden tablet
Yeast and nutrient

Put the grapes, sugar, acid and cold water in a pail. Crush and stir in the Campden tablet and set aside for 24 hours. Add the yeast and nutrient. After fermentation has started, allow it to continue for 6 days. Strain the must into a fermentation jar, fit the fermentation lock and ferment on.

Wine Making

Lemon Thyme Wine

This is one of the better herbs for wine making. It makes a medium wine that is delicately scented with lemon. To measure the amount of thyme leaves required for this recipe fill a 1-pint mug to the brim with leaves (no stalks), pressing down lightly.

MAKES ABOUT SIX BOTTLES
2⅔ cups lemon thyme leaves
2½ lb sugar
5 qts water
1 lb white raisins
1½ teaspoons citric acid
Pinch of tannin
Yeast and nutrient

Put the thyme leaves and sugar in a plastic pail, add the cold water and stir well. When the sugar is completely dissolved, add the white raisins, acid, tannin, yeast and nutrient. When fermentation starts, allow it to continue for 3 days, stirring daily, then strain the must into a fermentation jar. Fit the fermentation lock and ferment on.

Squash Wine

Plain squash wine is rather insipid, but if raisins are added and brown sugar is used, it can be made into an excellent rich, sweet wine. If you really want to put some zip into the wine, add 1 ounce of root ginger powder 24 hours before you strain the must into the fermentation jar.

MAKES ABOUT SIX BOTTLES
6 lb finely chopped squash
¾ lb raisins, minced
3½ lb brown sugar
5 qts water
1 tablespoon pectic enzyme
Yeast and nutrient
1 tablespoon citric acid

Make sure that the squash is ripe—unripe squash makes the wine taste woody. Place the squash, raisins and sugar in a pail. Bring the water to the boil and pour it over the ingredients. When cool, add the pectic enzyme and set aside.

Leave for 24 hours. Add the yeast, nutrient and acid. When fermentation starts, leave it for 3 days, stirring daily. Strain the must into a fermentation jar, fit the fermentation lock and ferment on.

Parsnip Wine

Parsnip is one of the most popular vegetable wines, but it is rather insipid and requires the addition of other ingredients —in this case white raisins—to make a really pleasant, medium wine. On the credit side, its lack of strong flavor makes parsnip wine a good mixer, and it can be used safely with most other ingredients.

MAKES ABOUT SIX BOTTLES
4 lb parsnips, scrubbed and grated
2½ lb sugar
5 qts water
Yeast and nutrient
1 lb white raisins, minced
1½ teaspoons citric acid

Put the parsnips, sugar and water in a large saucepan and bring to the boil. Remove the pan from the heat. When the mixture is cool, pour into a plastic pail and add yeast, nutrient, white raisins and acid. When fermentation has started, allow it to continue for 3 days. Strain the must into a fermentation jar, fit the fermentation lock and ferment on.

Pea-Pod Wine

If peas are grown, the gardening cook will have plenty of pods left over after shelling. These are usually put on the compost heap, but save some and try pea-pod wine. This recipe is for a dry wine, but if you have a sweet tooth, replace the raisins with currants and add 1½ pounds of sugar.

MAKES ABOUT SIX BOTTLES
6 lb pea pods, finely chopped
2 lb sugar
5 qts water
½ lb raisins, minced
1½ teaspoons citric acid
½ teaspoon tannin
Yeast and nutrient

Put the pea pods, sugar and water in a large saucepan and bring to the boil. Remove the pan from the heat. When the mixture is cool, pour it into a plastic pail and add the raisins, acid, tannin, yeast and nutrient. When fermentation has started, allow it to continue for 4 days then strain the must into a fermentation jar, fit the fermentation lock and ferment on.

Racking. This is how to rack wine off the sediment and into another jar. Make sure that the top end of the siphon tube stays well clear of the sediment, otherwise it will drag some up. If this does happen, the wine can be reracked after it has settled.

Pear Wine

Pears produce a wine that is too light for most people, so it is more usual to find pears in combination with other ingredients. White raisins are added to the pears in this recipe to make a medium wine. If you want to try something a little different omit the white raisins and add the flesh of three ripe bananas. The wine can be made sweet or dry by adding or subtracting 1 pound of sugar.

MAKES ABOUT SIX BOTTLES
5 qts water
3 lb sugar
9 lb pears, minced
½ lb white raisins, minced
1½ teaspoons citric acid
Yeast and nutrient

Bring the water to the boil and stir in the sugar. Remove the pan from the heat and set aside to cool. Put the pears, white raisins, acid, yeast and nutrient in a plastic pail and pour in the sugared water. When fermentation starts, allow it to continue for 4 days, then strain the must into a fermentation jar, fit the fermentation lock and ferment on.

Strawberry Wine

One characteristic of wine is that the final flavor rarely resembles the parent ingredient—orange wine does not taste of oranges and grape wine does not taste of grapes. One of the exceptions is strawberry wine, which has the aroma and the taste of the fruit. The most popular type of strawberry wine is sweet, and that is the recipe given here, but dry strawberry wine is superb also. To make the dry wine just reduce the sugar to 2½ pounds.

MAKES ABOUT SIX BOTTLES
4 lb strawberries, crushed
5 qts water
1 tablespoon pectic enzyme
4 lb sugar
Yeast and nutrient

If possible, use a Sauternes yeast. Put the strawberries and cold water in a plastic pail. Add the pectic enzyme and leave for 4 days, stirring daily. Then add the sugar, yeast and nutrient, and stir well. Strain into a fermentation jar, fit the fermentation lock and wait for fermentation to start. Leave to ferment on.

When the wine in the top jar drops down near the end of the tube, tilt the jar very gently and move the end of the tube into the corner of the jar, as shown. This will enable you to transfer as much wine as possible without waste.

Acid soil. Soil lacking in lime.

Aggregate. A material—coarse sand, gravel, small pebbles or vermiculite—which is used to grow plants hydroponically.

Alkaline soil. Soil in which there is enough lime to counteract all acidity.

Aphis, aphids. Plant lice (greenfly, blackfly).

Blanching. The process of excluding light to whiten such stalks and leaves as celery and chicory, and make them less bitter.

Bolting. The premature flowering of a plant, which makes it "run to seed."

Brassicas. Wide range of vegetables, including cabbages, cauliflowers, Brussels sprouts and kales, which belong to the Cruciferae family.

Catch crop. Quick-maturing crop grown in ground in which another crop is to be raised later.

Chard. The young stems of salsify, Swiss chard and globe artichokes.

Cloche. Small portable glass or plastic structure under which plants are grown to protect them from the weather.

Compost. Confusingly, compost is both manure made largely from vegetable matter by bacterial action and a growing medium for seeds and plants, based on soil, peat and sand, or peat and sand, with added fertilizers.

Cordon. A type of espalier training applied to fruit trees, usually to form a single stem with horizontal branches (cordons) in one, two or three tiers.

Crown. That part of the plant where root and stem meet.

Cultivar. The word is a contraction of "cultivated variety." It is the subdivision of a species which has acquired, in cultivation, certain characteristics distinguishing it from other forms of the species.

Diploid. Most plants have cells which contain two sets of matching chromosomes (the diploid number).

Drill. Shallow trench in the soil in which seeds are sown. It is usually made with a garden hoe, and is therefore V-shaped.

Dutch light. A light, wooden frame grooved to hold a single pane of glass measuring $56 \times 28\frac{3}{4}$ inches.

Earthing up. Drawing soil around the stems of plants for the purpose of blanching them, for example, celery, or to prevent the tubers of potatoes from being exposed to the light and turning green and poisonous.

F₁ hybrid. The result of crossing two true parent strains of plants—a vigorous hybrid with such characteristics as hardiness, early maturity, disease resistance and flavor. Because F_1 seed is pollinated by hand, it is more expensive than seed of ordinary varieties. Seed saved from F_1 hybrids does not breed true.

Foliar spray. A solution of plant nutrients sprayed on the leaves and quickly absorbed by the plant.

Force. To hasten growth by providing warmth. Some vegetables, for example rhubarb and chicory, are forced in the dark.

Frame. A low structure of brick, wood, or metal and glass, in which plants can be given protection from the weather. Often called a cold frame.

Fungicide. Fungi-killing chemical.

Germination. Sprouting of seeds.

Green manuring. Digging a growing crop, such as mustard or lupins, into the soil to enrich it.

Hardening-off. Gradual process of acclimatizing plants grown under glass to colder conditions outside. It is usually done in a frame to which more air is admitted each day.

Heel. The base of a cutting taken from a plant that includes a little of the harder growth of the stem from which the cutting was taken. The heel aids propagation.

Herbicide. Weed-killing chemical.

Humus. Black, amorphous substance in fertile soil, derived from organic matter through the action of bacteria.

Hybrid. A plant produced as a result of crossing different species.

Hydroponics. Method of growing plants without the use of soil. The plants are fed with mineral nutrients in solution.

Inorganic fertilizers. Chemical compounds, which, when added to the soil, provide the plants with vital elements.

Insecticide. Insect-killing chemical.

Intercrop. A crop grown between rows of another crop.

Lateral. Side shoot growing from the leading shoot of a plant.

Leader. The leading shoot of a plant.

Legumes. Members of the Leguminosae family, such as peas and beans.

Loam. Well-balanced soil composed of sand and clay particles and humus.

Maiden. Fruit tree—usually one straight stem—in its first year after being grafted.

Main crop. The vegetable crop which is allowed to develop to maturity. The term is usually applied to winter roots which are to be stored.

Mulch. A covering, usually made of compost, peat or straw, which is spread over the surface of the soil to suppress weeds and conserve moisture.

Neutral soil. Soil with a pH rating between 6.5 and 7.5, which is neither too acid nor too alkaline. (See pH factor.)

Nymph. An immature insect resembling the adult, but without fully developed wings and reproductive organs.

Offsets. Bulbs growing from the parent bulb as one way of reproduction (for example, shallots).

Organic fertilizers. Matter such as farmyard manure, compost and fish meal which, when added to the soil, feeds it and improves its texture.

pH factor. Indicates the degree of acidity or alkalinity in the soil. Below pH 7 the soil is increasingly acid; above pH 7 the soil is increasingly alkaline.

Peat bags. Plastic bags filled with peat compost in which such vegetables as tomatoes and cucumbers can be grown.

Peat-lite. A sowing and potting mix composed of peat moss with vermiculite and/or perlite, such as Jiffy-Mix and Terralite planting soils. Modern commercial peat-lite formulas often contain a slow-release fertilizer.

Pelleted seeds. Small seeds coated with soil-clay to make them larger and therefore easier to handle.

Perennial. A plant that lives for more than two years.

Perlite. White volcanic rock in ground form. Used in peat-lite mixes and to lighten heavy soils.

Planting-out. Transplanting a plant from a box or pot to the open ground.

Potting-off. Transplanting a young plant from a box to a pot.

Potting-on. Transplanting a plant from one pot to a larger one.

Pricking-out. Transplanting a seedling from the seed tray to another tray or pot soon after germination.

Propagator. Basically a heated box in which seeds are germinated and cuttings are rooted.

Ring culture. Method of growing plants, especially tomatoes, in bottomless pots called rings. The roots absorb nutrients via the compost in the ring and take up water from the aggregate (for example coarse sand, gravel or pebbles) on which the ring stands.

Rootstock. Plant onto which a scion, or young shoot, of a fruit tree is grafted.

Runners. Long shoots sent out by strawberries by which they propagate themselves. The runners root when they come into contact with moist soil and a new plant begins to grow.

Scion. Young shoot of a fruit tree grafted onto a different rootstock.

Seed leaves. The first two leaves that appear after germination. Some plants have only one seed leaf.

Seedling. Very young plant raised from seed.

Setting. The start of growth of fruits or seeds after pollination.

Sphagnum moss. Natural bog moss useful in dried milled form for sowing vegetable seed.

Spit. The depth of a spade when it is dug into the ground.

Spur. On most varieties of apple trees, the short branch growing close to the branches which carry the fruit.

Station. The position at which seeds are sown in ones, twos or threes, at intervals along a row.

Succession crop. Crop which follows another crop.

Thinning. Pulling up some growing seedlings to allow the rest adequate space to grow.

Thongs. Cuttings from the roots of seakale, from which the next year's crop is grown.

Tilth. Soil broken down into fine crumbs.

Transplanting. Removing a plant from one place and planting it somewhere else.

Triploid. Plants which have three sets of chromosomes in the cell nucleus.

True leaves. Leaves typical of the plant. They grow after the seed leaves have appeared.

Truss. Collective name for a group of flowers, which will develop into fruit.

Tuber. Natural swelling of an underground stem. This is the edible part of a potato or Jerusalem artichoke plant.

Variety. The widely used term for a cultivar.

Vermiculite. Golden-colored exploded mica. Useful to lighten soils, hold additional moisture, and an important part of the peat-lite formulas.

Virus. Invisible organism living in the soil and in plants. Viruses cause some of the worst and, so far, incurable vegetable diseases.

Acidulated water. Water to which lemon juice or vinegar has been added. Cut fruit and vegetables are dipped in acidulated water to prevent them discoloring. Add 2 teaspoons to 1 tablespoon of lemon juice or vinegar to 1 pint of water.

Al dente. An Italian culinary term used to describe food which is cooked but remains resistant to the bite.

Antipasti. The Italian name for hors d'oeuvres.

Bagna cauda. Hot oil-and-butter sauce flavored with garlic and anchovies and served with raw vegetables. It is a specialty of the Piedmont region of Italy.

Bean curd. A cream-colored, custardlike, slightly spongy substance prepared from soybeans and used extensively in Chinese and Japanese cooking.

Béarnaise. Rich, delicate, classic sauce composed of butter and eggs, acidulated with reduced, herb-flavored, white wine vinegar.

Béchamel. Basic white sauce made with a roux and milk flavored with onions, carrots, herbs and seasoning.

Beurre manié. A paste made from equal quantities of flour and butter kneaded together. It is used to thicken soups, sauces and stews.

Blanch. Culinary term meaning to plunge fruits, vegetables or nuts briefly into boiling water to loosen skin prior to peeling; to reduce strong flavors or bitterness; or to set the color and prepare food for freezing.

Bleed. A culinary term used to describe the loss of color from some vegetables when their skin is broken during cooking or the loss of nutrients from sliced vegetables.

Boeuf Bourguignon. Beef cooked in the Burgundian style, that is with red wine, usually burgundy.

Bordelaise. Basic, rich sauce made with red wine, beef marrow, shallots and various herbs. It is usually served with roast beef, steak and game.

Bouquet garni. A bunch of various herbs, including parsley, bay and thyme, sometimes contained in a cheesecloth bag. It is used to flavor many dishes, including soups, sauces and stews.

Bread crumbs, dry brown. These may be made from bread crusts dried in an oven and crushed with a rolling pin or in a blender.

Bread crumbs, dry white. Fresh bread crumbs dried slowly in a very low oven or warm, dry place.

Bread crumbs, fresh. Bread crumbs made from day-old bread. The crust is cut off, then the bread is rubbed through a sieve or grated by hand or in a blender.

Brioche. Sweet bread made from a rich yeast dough.

Caramelized. Culinary term used to describe sugar which has been cooked until it is a rich brown color, and a process by which food is cooked with a little sugar and butter until it is coated with a rich golden syrup.

Cassoulet. French stew made with haricot beans, pieces of goose or mutton (or both) and various other ingredients.

Chili powder. Commercially prepared ground spice mixture.

Clarified butter. Melted, purified butter. The butter is melted and then cooked very gently without being allowed to color. The scum is skimmed off and the butter poured through a strainer. It is then left to stand, and when the sediment has settled the clarified butter is poured carefully into another container.

Coating consistency. Sauce has reached a coating consistency when you can draw your finger down the back of the wooden spoon you have been using, and the edges of the trail this makes stay perfectly sharp and clear.

Compote. Fresh or dried fruit cooked in syrup and served cold.

Daikon. Large Japanese radish, which can be eaten raw or cooked.

Duxelles. Primarily the name given to a paste made from minced mushrooms and/or mushroom stalks. It is used to flavor soups, stews and various other dishes.

Emincé de veau. Traditional Swiss dish of thinly sliced strips of veal served in a rich, creamy sauce.

Fool. Traditional English sweet dish of puréed fruit, which is stewed and usually mixed with whipped cream and served cold.

Glaze. Culinary term denoting a glassy finish given to food by coating it with egg, water, syrup or puréed jam after cooking.

Gnocchi. Small dumplings made of semolina, *choux* paste or potatoes. They are poached, drained and often mixed with butter, covered with cheese and baked or grilled.

Gram flour. Flour made from dried chickpeas.

Gratin. Culinary term used to describe a dish which has been covered with a sauce, sprinkled with bread crumbs and/or grated cheese and baked or broiled.

Herb butter. Butter which has been blended with various finely chopped herbs. It is used as a garnish or added to soups and sauces.

Herb salt and herb sugar. Salt or sugar which has been mixed with herbs and stored until matured. They are used to flavor savory or sweet dishes.

Hollandaise. Rich egg-and-butter sauce acidulated with vinegar and sometimes with lemon juice. It is served with fish, eggs and vegetables.

Julienne. The name given to vegetables cut into small, narrow strips. It is also used to describe a clear soup to which narrow strips of various cooked vegetables have been added.

Mamaliga. In most East European countries *mamaliga* is the name for a type of corn-meal porridge. It is a staple food in Romania.

Mandoline. Utensil used to slice vegetables. It is a blade set in a piece of wood. The blade, wavy or flat, can be adjusted to cut in various thicknesses.

Monosodium glutamate. The chemical name for a salty white powder that is used extensively in Chinese cooking to bring out the flavor of many foods. Also called gourmet powder, monosodium glutamate is sold under the name of Ac'cent.

Mornay. Béchamel sauce to which grated cheese, usually Gruyère or Parmesan, has been added. It is served with fish, egg and vegetable dishes.

Mouli (French food mill). A vegetable mill which has plates, with perforations of varying sizes, which fit into a metal base. A disc with a handle is rotated to push the food through the perforations to make a purée.

Pan-fry. Culinary term used to describe the process of cooking food with a small amount of fat in a shallow pan.

Pecorino. Hard Italian cheese, similar to Parmesan, made from ewe's milk.

Pissalat. The Provençal name of a highly flavored dish of small sea fish.

Polenta. Finely ground corn meal used in Italy to make a type of cereal.

Render. Culinary term used to describe the process of melting down fat into dripping.

Roux. A base for sauces composed of flour gently cooked in fat. According to the length of time it is cooked, the roux will be white (*blanc*), pale golden (*blond*) or a deep biscuit color (*brun*).

Sauce Maltaise. Hollandaise sauce flavored with the juice of oranges.

Sauce Mousseline. Hollandaise sauce with whipped cream folded into it. It is served with asparagus, seakale, broiled sole and other dishes.

Sauté. Method of cooking ingredients in very hot fat, shaking the pan to make them "jump."

Tomato concentrate. A concentrated paste made from tomatoes.

Vinaigrette. French dressing, made with oil, vinegar and various seasonings.

Metric Conversions
The following are the basic metric equivalents for our standard weights and measures.

Weight: 1 ounce = 28.35 grams. For convenience, it may be rounded out to 30 grams.

Volume: $\frac{1}{4}$ cup = 56 milliliters, $\frac{1}{3}$ cup = 75 milliliters, $\frac{1}{2}$ cup = 113 milliliters and 1 cup = 227 milliliters.

Temperature: 32°F = 0°C. To convert Fahrenheit into centigrade: subtract 32, multiply by 5, divide by 9.

Length: 1 inch = 2.54 centimeters.

Index/recipes

Acknowledgments

A. E. Bicknell
Ray Desmond, The Garden
History Society
Mike Janulewicz
The National Society of
Leisure Gardeners
Limited
Royal Botanic Gardens,
Kew
The Royal Horticultural
Society
Carol Todd

Artists :
Norman Barber
Helen Cowcher
Ian Garrard
Peter Morter
Jim Robins
Rodney Shackell
Kathleen Smith
Michael Woods
Sidney Woods

Indexer :
Brenda Hall, M.A.,
Registered indexer of the
Society of Indexers

Photographers :
Rex Bamber
Chris Barker
Michael Boys
David Meldrum
Roger Phillips

Picture libraries :
Mansell Collection, pages 6,
13
Marshall Cavendish Picture
Library (Rex Bamber,
David Meldrum and
Roger Phillips), cover
Radio Times Hulton,
pages 13, 14, 15
Ronan Picture Library,
page 12

Studio services :
A. C. Cooper
Face Photosetting
Roy Flooks
Mitchell Beazley Studio
Summit Art